Closing the Books

This book offers an analysis of transitional justice – retribution and reparation after a change of political regime – from Athens in the fifth century B.C. to the present. Part I, "The Universe of Transitional Justice," describes more than thirty transitions, some of them in considerable detail, others more succinctly. Part II, "Analytics of Transitional Justice," proposes a framework for explaining the variations among the cases: why after some transitions wrongdoers from the previous regime are punished severely and in other cases mildly or not at all, and why victims are sometimes compensated generously and sometimes poorly or not at all. After surveying a broad range of justifications and excuses for wrongdoings and criteria for selecting and indemnifying victims, the book concludes with a discussion of three general explanatory factors: economic and political constraints, the retributive emotions, and the play of party politics.

Professor Jon Elster is the Robert Merton Professor of Social Science at Columbia University. He received his Ph.D. from the University of Paris in 1972, and before coming to Columbia University, he taught in Paris, Oslo, and Chicago. His publications include *Ulysses and the Sirens* (1979), *Sour Grapes* (1983), *Making Sense of Marx* (1985), *The Cement of Society* (1989), *Solomonic Judgments* (1989), *Nuts and Bolts for the Social Sciences* (1989), *Local Justice* (1992), *Political Psychology* (1993), *Strong Feelings* (1999), *Alchemies of the Mind* (1999), and *Ulysses Unbound* (2000). His research interests include the theory of rational choice, the theory of distributive justice, and the history of social thought (Marx and Tocqueville).

Closing the Books

Transitional Justice in Historical Perspective

JON ELSTER
Columbia University

PUBLISHED BY THE PRESS SYNDICATE OF THE UNIVERSITY OF CAMBRIDGE
The Pitt Building, Trumpington Street, Cambridge, United Kingdom

CAMBRIDGE UNIVERSITY PRESS
The Edinburgh Building, Cambridge CB2 2RU, UK
40 West 20th Street, New York, NY 10011-4211, USA
477 Williamstown Road, Port Melbourne, VIC 3207, Australia
Ruiz de Alarcón 13, 28014 Madrid, Spain
Dock House, The Waterfront, Cape Town 8001, South Africa

http://www.cambridge.org

First published 2004

Printed in the United States of America

Typeface Sabon 10/13 pt. *System* LaTeX 2ε [TB]

A catalog record for this book is available from the British Library.

Library of Congress Cataloging in Publication Data

Elster, Jon, 1940–
Closing the books : transitional justice in historical perspective / Jon Elster.
p. cm.
Includes bibliographical references.
ISBN 0-521-83969-6 – ISBN 0-521-54854-3 (pb.)
1. Political crimes and offenses. 2. Justice and politics. 3. Ex post facto laws.
4. Revolutions. 5. Restorative justice I. Title.
K5250.E44 2004
303.6′6–dc22 2004043581

ISBN 0 521 83969 6 hardback
ISBN 0 521 54854 3 paperback

For Torolf and Henrik

Contents

Preface and Acknowledgments

The topic of transitional justice has been with me, one way or another, for a long time. Let me illustrate with three episodes, beginning with the most recent.

On April 10, 2003, the day after the fall of Baghdad, I got an e-mail from a Canadian journalist who wanted to ask me some questions about "de-Baathification" in Iraq. (I told him that the main policy options were purges, trials, and exposure by truth commissions, each of these having several subvarieties.) By the beginning of the twenty-first century, one of the first questions that comes to mind when an autocratic regime falls is indeed how to hold the leadership to account and to block its influence in the future. Another, of course, is how to build a new and better regime. A third question is how to deal with the victims of the regime. The present book is mainly concerned with the two backward-looking issues: how societies respond to wrongdoings and sufferings. I also consider forward-looking issues such as economic reconstruction and constitution making, but only to the extent that they interact with the backward-looking ones. I mainly try to *describe and explain variations* in how societies close their open accounts from the past after regime transitions. Normative considerations enter indirectly, however, through the conceptions of justice and fairness that may animate the actors of transition and enter in the explanation of their behavior. Although my own normative views may sometimes shine through, they are not a main or even secondary concern of the book.

My attempts to think about these topics in a systematic way go back to June 1990, when I participated in a conference in Pécs (Hungary) on how to build new institutions and constitutions in Eastern Europe. Inevitably, questions of retribution and reparation also came up. In the notes that I wrote up for myself afterward I summarized the debates as follows:

> Several politicians present at the conference agreed that retribution should not be carried out, except against those who had committed clear criminal acts (such as torture). The "Spanish solution" of complete amnesty was the only workable one. The injustice inherent in amnesty was the price one had to pay for democracy.
>
> The former Minister of Justice in Hungary was especially insistent on this point. He observed that since the mid–nineteenth century 14 Hungarian prime ministers had been executed or forced into exile; it was time to break with this tradition of a highly politicized judiciary. In Hungary a commission had started looking into the sources of the wealth of high officials. About 4,500 dossiers were opened, but after a while the investigations died out. In his opinion, they were strongly anticonstitutional. Although not himself a participant in the roundtables, he did not believe that retribution was ever a topic of discussion, or that any promises of amnesty were made.
>
> In GDR [German Democratic Republic] the old leaders tend to invoke the very principles they had violated. Although they constantly had violated the principle of legality (*nulla crimen sine lege*), they now invoke it against attempts to bring them to court.
>
> The President of the Polish Senate observed that the Polish example had been very important for the transition in GDR, by showing that it is possible to "live quietly in the new society." (He had heard this from the East German ambassador.) He reported that the Sejm recently had voted to transform pensions for party officials into normal pensions without special privileges. A Polish law professor argued that former party members could be demoted – e.g., from school principal to teacher.
>
> Later, the issue of rectification – giving back property to those from whom it had been confiscated – was raised. Again, the general tendency was to argue against this form of backward-looking justice.

I do not know whether these ideas were as consensual at the time as I reported them, but – except to some extent in Hungary – they were certainly not confirmed by subsequent developments. The Spanish solution was not adopted. Some countries carried out extensive purges in the public administration. In several countries, restitution of property was carried out on a large scale. Few were put on trial, however.

From an earlier transition, I can recount an experience that illustrates the often extraordinary climate in these times. On May 9, 1945, the day after the German capitulation, my father returned from Stockholm where he had spent the last years of the war. When he dropped by his prewar haunt in central Oslo, Theatercaféen, the maître d'hôtel called him aside to say, "Mr. Elster, there is a dead German officer in the men's toilet. Could you please help me." My father somehow got rid of the officer. Being five years old at the time, I was unaware of this particular event. As I grew up after the war, however, I could not fail to notice how individuals in public and sometimes in private life were assessed, chosen, or rejected according to what they had done or failed to do, and at what times, during the German occupation. Someone who panicked in April 1940 would never again be seen as totally reliable, whatever his behavior at later stages in the war. The memory of the many shades of defeatism or opportunism was not allowed to fade away. Children of collaborators, too, suffered in numerous ways. In one case known to me, a mother told her two daughters that it was unpatriotic to play with the children of a convicted Nazi collaborator. In one sense, the legal and administrative proceedings that form the core of this book are only the most visible part of a larger complex.

These early memories may have been important in shaping the approach I take in the book. Although I consider a fairly large set of cases, from Classical Antiquity to the present, the episodes of transitional justice that occurred in the wake of World War II receive more than their proportionate share of attention. There is also another and less personal reason for this bias, if that is what it is. By far the most prominent historical instance of regime wrongdoings assessed in courts of justice is provided by the fate of perpetrators and victims of the Holocaust. The wrongdoings of the Stalinist regime may have been of a comparable magnitude, but there the only way in which wrongdoers were made to pay was by becoming victims themselves. Those who were merely victims, without having first been part of the circle of wrongdoers, received little reparation. By contrast, the prosecution of the Nazi regimes and the compensation of their victims occurred on a scale that, although inadequate in numerous ways, was utterly unprecedented and remains unequaled. It does not seem unreasonable, therefore, to dwell, as I do especially in Chapters 5 and 6, more extensively on these processes than on others.

The lack of an Introduction to the book is matched by the absence of a Conclusion. If I had had a theory of transitional justice, I might have begun the book by stating it and finished by evaluating it. Since I do not have one, this conventional parsing seemed pointless. My hope is that readers with the patience to sift through the material I present will find discussions that match their interests. Moral philosophers may find some hard dilemmas that had escaped their attention, and ponder the relevance of counterfactuals for ethics. Legal theorists may discover new difficulties in the idea of letting the punishment fit the crime. Political scientists may find that transitional justice is a fertile area for the study of the role of emotions in politics. Historians may be surprised to discover that the problem of "dual ownership" of property after a transition was resolved in the same way in Athens in 403 B.C., in the Second French Restoration, and in Germany after reunification. I write, then, for those whose intellectual excitement is triggered by the fine grain of societies, rather than for those seeking the large picture. Implicitly, I suppose, I do not think there is a large picture to be found, since if I had thought there was one, I would have been searching for it, too.

My first education in these matters came about through my participation in the Center for the Study of Constitutionalism in Eastern Europe, which was established in 1990 at the University of Chicago Law School, under the guidance of Gerhard Casper (who also attended the Pécs conference). Later, Geoffrey Stone provided unfailing support for the activities of the Center. My codirectors there, Stephen Holmes, Wiktor Osiatynski, and Cass Sunstein, helped me understand what I was observing during my subsequent travels in Eastern Europe. Later, the insights of Vojtech Cepl, Rumyana Kolarova, Claus Offe, and Andras Sajo into the East European transitions were invaluable. I thank them all.

This experience led me to think about transitional justice more generally. In 1998–99, with the generous funding of the Mellon Foundation, I organized a yearlong seminar series at Columbia University on "Retroactive justice." (The now-standard term "transitional justice" had not yet taken hold.) The papers presented at the seminar will be published, together with some additional contributions, as a companion volume to the present book, under the title *Retribution and Reparation in the Transition to Democracy*. Around the same time, Hans Fredrik Dahl, Stein Ugelvik Larsen, Øystein Sørensen, and I initiated a project, funded by the Research Council of Norway, on Norwegian transitional justice in 1945. I thank my codirectors of this project for discussions and comments. Other valuable support has been provided by the Wissenschaftskolleg zu Berlin and the Norwegian Academy of Science. I am very grateful to Monika Nalepa for invaluable research assistance and for many useful discussions, to Avi Tucker for comments on an earlier draft of the manuscript, and to two anonymous reviewers for valuable comments.

Unless otherwise indicated, translations from Danish, French, German, and Norwegian are mine.

PART I

THE UNIVERSE OF TRANSITIONAL JUSTICE

Transitional justice is made up of the processes of trials, purges, and reparations that take place after the transition from one political regime to another. A fuller characterization is provided in Chapter 4. The task of the present book is, first, to describe the variety of cases of transitional justice and, second, to propose an analytical framework that can help us explain the variations among the cases. Part I is devoted to presentation of the cases. In the first two chapters I describe several historical examples in some detail. Chapter 1 describes the processes of transitional justice that occurred in the wake of the restorations of Athenian democracy in 411 and then again in 403 B.C. In Chapter 2, I discuss the measures of retribution and reparation that took place in France after the two Restorations of the Bourbon monarchy in 1814 and 1815. Chapter 3 is a more compact survey of transitional justice in other cases, mainly transitions to democracy in the twentieth century.

There are several reasons that I single out the Athenian and French episodes for a fuller discussion than what I provide for other cases. First, they will be less known to most readers than the more recent cases. Second, they show that transitional justice is not limited to modern regimes nor to democratic regimes. Third, both cases show exceptionally clearly that in transitional justice, nations can *learn from experience*. The measures taken after the second restoration of Athenian democracy were shaped by what was perceived as excessive severity in the first. Conversely, transitional justice after the Second French Restoration was shaped by the perceived failure to strike hard enough in the First. In our century, too, transitional justice can be shaped by the memory of earlier transitions, the most striking instance being the three German transitions of the twentieth century: after World War I, after World War II, and after reunification in 1990. On each of the last two occasions, many of those who wanted to hold the outgoing regime to account were adamant that they would not repeat the mistakes that had been made the previous time.[1] In Belgium, the desire to hold speedy trials of collaborators after World War II was shaped in part by the memory of the failure to prosecute those who had collaborated with the Germans during World War I (see Chapter 8).

[1] On the back cover of a book documenting the lack of denazification of the West German judiciary (Friedrich 1998), a high judge and a law professor both draw the lesson that the same error must not be repeated in dealing with the East German judiciary. For a criticism of this argument, see Rottleuthner (1994). For the relation between 1918 and 1945, see Chapter 7.

I

Athens in 411 and 403 B.C.

1. INTRODUCTION

Democratic transitional justice is almost as old as democracy itself. In 411 B.C. and then again in 404–403 B.C., the Athenians saw the overthrow of democracy by an oligarchy, followed by defeat of the oligarchs and restoration of democracy.[1] In each case, the return to democracy went together with retributive measures against the oligarchs. In 403, the Athenians also took steps toward restitution of property that had been confiscated by the oligarchic regime. The next episode of transitional justice occurred more than two thousand years later, in the English Restoration.

The Athenians had *two* episodes of transitional justice that followed closely upon each other. It seems likely that after the first episode some learning took place, shaping the next occurrence. After the collapse of the first oligarchy in 411, the Athenians restored the pre-oligarchic democracy, carried out harsh retribution, and enacted new laws to deter future oligarchs from trying to take power. What they did not do was to attack the root causes of the oligarchic coup. In 403, the returning democrats reacted differently. On the one hand, they enacted constitutional changes to eliminate features that had brought democracy into disrepute. On the other hand, they pulled their punches in dealing with the oligarchs,

[1] In the following I rely heavily on Ostwald (1986). My indebtedness to Hansen (1991) will also be obvious. The most recent monograph on the transition in 403 is Loening (1987). Although many of the stark statements in the text ignore important controversies in the scholarly literature, I do not think this affects the substance of the argument, as summarized toward the end.

preferring the forward-looking goal of social reconciliation over the backward-looking goal of retribution.

II. ATHENIAN DEMOCRACY

To understand the two transitions and the decisions taken in their aftermath, we have to go back to the beginning of Athenian democracy almost two hundred years earlier. In 594, Solon was given carte blanche by two opposing factions to reform the laws.[2] Three of his reforms are directly relevant for transitional justice. He enacted an amnesty law that restored civil rights to those who had been disenfranchised, except exiles condemned on charges of homicide or massacre, or for seeking to establish a tyranny.[3] This law was the model for the amnesty legislation of 405 B.C. that, in the wake of the defeat of Athens by the Spartan fleet, canceled some of the harsh sentences passed after the overthrow of the oligarchs in 411.[4] (The purpose of the amnesty was to reunite the city, but it came too late.) Also, Solon enacted a "peculiar and surprising law, which ordains that he shall be disfranchised who, in time of faction, takes neither side," the citizen being expected to "espouse promptly the better and more righteous cause, share its perils and give it his aid, instead of waiting in safety to see which cause prevails."[5] Finally, he introduced an important change in the Athenian legal system. Then and later, there was no public prosecutor. All suits had to be brought by private individuals. Solon's reform was to allow any citizen to start a prosecution, either on behalf of the injured person or simply in the public interest. One effect of the law was to create an incentive for frivolous suits by "sycophants," or professional denunciators, who would bring a suit against a wealthy man in order to blackmail him by offering to drop the case. They were widely resented by the upper classes, and vigorously prosecuted under the second oligarchy.

Other pieces of Solon's legislation are indirectly relevant, qua impetus to a process of democratization that eventually led to untrammeled popular rule triggering an oligarchic backlash. He abolished debt slavery, thereby creating an important condition for effective democracy. Before

[2] The basic sources are Plutarch's *Life of Solon* and Aristotle's *Constitution of Athens*. The latter is usefully interpreted and corrected by Moore (1975).

[3] Plutarch, *Solon* xix.3–4.

[4] Andocides, "On the Mysteries," 73–79.

[5] Plutarch, *Solon* xx.1.

he enacted his reforms, all citizens could vote in the assembly and serve on the popular courts, but eligibility for some offices was reserved for the nobles ("wellborn"). After the reforms, all criteria of eligibility were defined in purely economic terms, so that birth no longer was decisive. Among the four property classes, members of the lowest were excluded from all state offices. For the most important offices, only members of the top class or the two top classes could be chosen. In 457, members of the third-ranked class became eligible for some of these high offices. Yet even though members of the lowest class remained ineligible, they exercised great influence as members of the Assembly, of the popular courts, and (after the reforms of Cleisthenes in 507) of the Council of the Five Hundred, which controlled the agenda of the Assembly.

The rights to vote and to hold office may be spurious if their exercise is costly. As Aristotle notes in the *Politics* (1308b–1309a), "If office bought no profit, then and only then could democracy and aristocracy be combined; for both notables and people might have their wishes gratified. All would be able to hold office, which is the aim of democracy, and the notables would be magistrates, which is the aim of aristocracy." A decisive step to a more effective democracy was taken by Pericles in the mid–fifth century, when he instituted daily pay for jurors, for members of the Council of the Five Hundred, and for magistrates.[6]

The class structure could also influence politics by its link to military functions. By and large, the navy was manned by the lowest property class (*thetes*) and the infantry (*hoplites*) by the second lowest. As Athens in the period that concerns us was more or less constantly at war, the presence or absence of these groups in the Assembly could sway the outcome:

> Radical democracy was introduced by Ephialtes' reforms in 462 which were passed by the Assembly when 4000 hoplites of the middle class were away fighting in Messina. Fifty-one years later the radical democracy was replaced by the oligarchic rule of the Four Hundred, and that constitutional change was passed by an Assembly in which the *thetes* were probably under-represented, because the meeting was held outside the walls and because the entire Athenian navy was stationed off Samos.[7]

[6] Payment for going to the Assembly was established only in the following century. By contrast, at that later time payment for magistrates seems to have been abolished, arguably "a retreat from radical-democratic principles and another sign that the Athenians from 403/2 had opted for a more 'moderate' form of democracy" (Hansen 1991, p. 241). Other aspects of this retreat from radical democracy are discussed in Section IV.

[7] Ibid., p. 126.

Not surprisingly, the impetus for the restoration of democracy came from that very same navy at Samos. The second-highest group, the cavalry (*hippeis*), was seen as closely associated with both oligarchies.

As members of the Assembly, the Athenians could vote laws and decrees, but it remained to implement them. Perhaps the most remarkable feature of the full-fledged Athenian democracy is the degree of control the citizens exercised over those who were to carry out their decisions. Although most officeholders were chosen by lot, the important offices were elective. Whether chosen by lot or elected, all magistrates had to undergo a mandatory scrutiny before and after taking office. Whereas the ex ante scrutiny was usually a formality (but see Section V for exceptions), the ex post examination could be a serious business. Moreover, magistrates were also subject to prosecution for "crimes against the state." These control functions had originally been lodged in the Areopagus, an elite body consisting of former high officials belonging to the highest property group, but after the reforms of Ephialtes, they devolved on the Council and finally on the popular courts.

By the mid–fifth century, a succession of reforms had created the potential for abuses of unrestrained popular power.[8] As reflected in the title of Martin Ostwald's work, the Athenians had popular sovereignty but not yet the rule of law. For a while, as he also writes, "Pericles' intelligence and psychological and political insight prevented unreason from dominating policy."[9] One cannot, however, judge the robustness of institutions by looking at the outcomes they generate under good leadership: Enlightened statesmen will not always be at the helm. The next generation of leaders, of lesser stature or lesser prudence, showed the vulnerability of the

[8] We may wonder how this came about. There was certainly no democratic revolution. Although the masses may have used their voting rights to expand their power, this does not seem to have been the main mechanism. Rather, the elites found it in their interest to sponsor popular measures. Ober (1989), p. 85, notes that "by the time of Cleisthenes, the elites recognized mass ambitions as a new weapon to use against each other. As a result, politically ambitious elites actively sponsored democratizing reforms.... Ironically, as the elites gained victories over their enemies by sponsoring democratic reforms, there were fewer and fewer institutions that they could control directly." Similarly, Ostwald (1986), pp. 179–80, writes that "Ephialtes' reforms had the effect of establishing the sovereignty of the people in political affairs, but that does not mean this was their intent. His primary purpose may well have been to outflank those who had been most effective in supporting Cimon's now-discredited policy of 'giving a higher priority to the interests of Sparta than to the expansion of his own country.'" Ober's comment is especially interesting, in that it suggests that the elites were engaged in something like a prisoner's dilemma, in which they all lost power by trying to outdo one another in appealing to the people.

[9] Ibid., p. 200.

institutions. Although the system contained some safeguards,[10] these were least effective in the supremely important realm of military decisions.

III. THE FIRST OLIGARCHY AND ITS DEMISE

Athens had strong expansionist and imperialist traditions. At its height around 460, the Athens-led Delian League comprised nearly two hundred member states in the Eastern Mediterranean. The idea of empire appealed both to the Athenians' desire for glory and to their desire for tribute. Yet when decisions to go to war were taken by the popular assembly, they were not always wise. In particular, the disastrous Sicilian expedition of 415 was undertaken on a wave of popular enthusiasm, against the more realistic assessment of Nicias. Summarizing Thucydides, Ostwald writes that

> Nicias himself recognizes that the sobriety and circumspection of his seasoned military expertise have little chance of stemming the irrational enthusiasm of the Assembly (6.9.3). Even before Alcibiades had opened his mouth, lust for adventure had made the commons deaf to Nicias' warnings: a Sicilian expedition would only swell the number of already existing enemies (6.10); even if the expedition succeeded, it would be difficult to control a large population from a great distance, and if it failed in any way, the Sicilians would join the Spartans, eager to recoup their lost prestige, in attacking Athens itself (6.11), and what strength had been recovered after the recent plague should not be dissipated on alien ventures (6.12).[11]

The effect of the disaster was "the rise of oligarchic opposition, putting all the blame on the leaders who had persuaded the people and on the people themselves for being cozened by them."[12] In the summer of 411, the oligarchs staged a coup and terrorized the assembly into abdicating its powers to them. Organized as the Council of the Four Hundred, they stayed in power for four months only, as the alliance with Persia on which they had counted fell through and the naval troops at Samos turned against them.

The restoration of democracy, including transitional justice, took place in two steps. The first (or "intermediate") successor regime, which lasted

[10] These safeguards included notably the use of *delegation* of decision making to smaller bodies and *delays* (Ostwald 1986, pp. 78–79; Hansen 1991, p. 307). See, however, Ruzé (1997, Chap. 22) for important reservations to the idea that the role of the Council in preparing proposals for the Assembly served as a delaying device.

[11] Ostwald (1986), p. 318.

[12] Hansen (1991), p. 40.

for about eight months, was a truncated democracy, limiting franchise to the Five Thousand, "of which body all who furnished a suit of armor were to be members."[13] The regime immediately engaged in what Ostwald calls "a relentless prosecution of extremist oligarchs."[14] Three of them were tried and two executed for treason, because they went on an embassy to Sparta after news of the revolt of the troops at Samos had reached Athens. Some avoided trial by going into exile, only to return in 403 to become members of the Thirty Tyrants. After the restoration of the full democracy, "vindictive measures against those who had been associated with the Four Hundred widened in scope."[15] Soldiers who had stayed in the city during the regime of the Four Hundred suffered partial loss of their political rights.[16] Three democrats are cited as having exploited the retributive apparatus for private gain.[17] An oligarch who had already been tried and convicted under the intermediary regime was retried under a more serious charge.

Yet three indicators show that the measures were not simply victors' justice. First, as Ostwald adds, "it was a prosecution not a persecution: we hear of no lynchings or terrorism but only of orderly legal proceedings initiated soon after the new regime had been established." Second, many who served on the Council of the Four Hundred to the very end were tried *and acquitted*. Third, the restored democracy resisted the temptation of retroactive legislation. Because there was no law against attempts to overthrow the democracy, the three oligarchs had to be prosecuted for treason; others presumably were not prosecuted at all. Although the new regime enacted a law against such attempts, the legislation was prospective, not retroactive. It was intended to deter "oligarchic recidivism," not to punish members of the oligarchy that had just been overthrown.[18]

[13] Thucydides, *The Peloponnesian War*, 8.97.1. This measure, and the abolition of pay for public office, were voted by the people as a whole.

[14] Ostwald (1986), p. 401.

[15] Ibid., p. 420.

[16] Andocides, "On the Mysteries," 75–76.

[17] Lysias, "Defence against a charge of subverting the democracy," 26.

[18] Ostwald (1986), p. 418. In his account of why the "intermediary regime" tried three oligarchs for treason but not for their "revolutionary activities," Ostwald (1986), p. 402, cites the fact that "their accusers had themselves been active in establishing the Four Hundred and had been members of the Council but had turned against the extremists and were now leaders of the new regime." After the restoration of the full democracy, this self-serving reason was presumably less important in the explanation of democratic self-restraint.

IV. THE SECOND OLIGARCHY AND ITS DEMISE

The next oligarchic regime owes its origin to an event that both discredited the democracy internally and made it vulnerable to external threats. After a great victory in a sea battle against the Spartan fleet off the Arginusae Islands in 406, the Athenians tried eight of their generals for failure to rescue the surviving sailors (or perhaps for a failure to recover the bodies of the dead). The proceedings, which may have involved breaches of legality,[19] led to the condemnation of all the generals and the immediate execution of the six who were present in Athens. The charged emotional atmosphere that made this outcome possible is captured in Xenophon's description of what happened when a member of the Council, Callixenus, proposed to vote over the guilt of the generals without a proper trial:

> Euryptolemus . . . and some others served a summons upon Callixenus, alleging that he had made an unconstitutional proposal. And some of the people applauded this act, but the greater number cried out that *it was monstrous if the people were to be prevented from doing whatever they wished*. Indeed, when Lyciscus thereupon moved that these men should also be judged by the very same vote as the generals, unless they withdrew the summons, the mob broke out again with shouts of approval, and they were compelled to withdraw the summonses. Furthermore, when some of the Prytanes [the executive committee of the Council] refused to put the question to the vote in violation of the law, Callixenus again mounted the platform and urged the same charge against them; and the crowd cried out to summon to court those who refused. Then the Prytanes, stricken with fear, agreed to put the question – all of them, except Socrates, [who] said that in no case would he act except in accordance with the law.[20]

The phrase that I have italicized is commonly taken as the most extreme expression of unconstrained popular sovereignty in Athens. There is a special irony in that one of the executed generals, Thrasyllus, had been a key actor in restoring the democracy in 411. Although later "the Athenians regretted their action and voted that charges be brought against those who had deceived the people, Callixenus among them,"[21] this could not undo the twofold harm that had been done. First, the episode rekindled divisions among the citizens and strengthened those who distrusted the democrats. Second, in choosing new generals to replace those who had been executed, the Athenians favored loyalty to the democracy over military competence. In itself, this would not have mattered had the

[19] For opposing views on this important point, see Ostwald (1986), pp. 439–41, and MacDowell (1978), pp. 178–79.

[20] Xenophon, *Hellenica*, I.vii.

[21] Ibid.

Athenians accepted a peace offer from Sparta after the defeat at Arginusae. According to Aristotle, the Assembly rejected the offer because it was deceived by Cleophon, whom he depicts as a notorious demagogue.[22] Whether the Assembly acted emotionally or took a calculated gamble based on distrust of Sparta,[23] the outcome was disastrous. Led by less-than-outstanding generals, the Athenians suffered a devastating defeat in the battle of Aegospotami in 405, which marked the end of the Athenian empire. In the wake of the defeat, a second oligarchy was installed in 404 under Spartan auspices. The reasons why the Spartans preferred to install a relatively autonomous oligarchic "Vichy" regime, rather than a puppet "Quisling" government, remain conjectural.[24]

The peace treaty included provisions for the return of the oligarchs who had gone into exile after the collapse of the previous oligarchy, and a vague clause allowing Athens to retain its "ancestral constitution," a phrase susceptible of several interpretations. In practice, the regime installed by the Thirty Tyrants, as the new oligarchic leaders came to be called, was one of terror. Among other things, they required each of their members to prove his mettle by killing one metic (alien resident). Also, more than fifteen hundred citizens were killed. One motive for the atrocities may have been revenge: The leading oligarch Critias "showed himself eager to put many to death because . . . he had been banished by the democracy"[25] after the demise of the previous oligarchy. For some oligarchs, the ultimate goal may have been to remake Athens on the austere model of Sparta.[26] Economic gain may also have been a motive. To consolidate their rule, the Thirty created a privileged body of Three Thousand, as they came to be called, and expelled the rest of the citizens from the city.

The expelled took up residence in Piraeus, the main port of Athens. Ultimately, with the assistance of an exile democratic army, they routed the oligarchs in battle and killed two of their main leaders. The Spartan leaders once more pulled their punches and supervised a treaty of reconciliation between "the men in the city" and "the men in Piraeus." According to Aristotle, the terms of the reconciliation were as follows:

> Those of the Athenians who had remained in the city and wished to leave should live in Eleusis, where they should retain full citizen rights, have complete

[22] *The Constitution of Athens* xxxv.1; see also xxviii.3.
[23] For the latter view, see Kagan (1987), pp. 378–79.
[24] Ibid., pp. 405–10.
[25] Xenophon, *Hellenica,* II.iii.
[26] Ostwald (1986), pp. 485–87.

self-government and enjoy their incomes. The temple was to be common to both sides.... Those living at Eleusis were not allowed to visit the city of Athens, nor were those living in Athens allowed to visit Eleusis, with the exception for both sides at the celebration of the Mysteries. The people at Eleusis were to contribute to a defence fund from their revenues like the other Athenians. If any of those leaving the city took over a house at Eleusis, they were to do it with the agreement of the owner; if agreement proved impossible, each was to select three assessors, and the owner was to accept the price they fixed. Any inhabitants of Eleusis acceptable to the new settlers were to live with them there. Those wishing to move out to Eleusis had to register within ten days of the swearing of the reconciliation oaths if they were in the city at the time, and move out within twenty; those abroad had the same periods from the moments when they returned to Athens. Nobody living at Eleusis could hold any office in the city of Athens until he had been registered as having moved his residence back to the city. Homicide trials in cases where someone had killed or wounded a person with his own hands were to be conducted in accordance with traditional practice. There was to be a total amnesty covering everyone except the Thirty, the Ten, the Eleven and the governors of the Piraeus; even they were to be immune from prosecution once they had rendered their accounts.... Those who had held office in the city were to appear before citizens with taxable property. On this basis those who wished to leave could leave the city. Each side was to repay separately the money which it had borrowed for the war.[27]

The terms of the agreement need some comments. Both sides had to swear an oath to the effect that they would "harbor no grievance" against anyone except for one specific act and four specific groups. Prosecution for murder was possible when the accused had killed "with his own hands" (*autocheiria*). "The means which the Thirty had employed to eliminate their opposition made it difficult, however, for potential plaintiffs to demonstrate *autocheiria* in its strictest sense. Few victims of the oligarchy were murdered outright; more often they were deposed by an informer on a spurious charge, arrested, convicted before the oligarchic Council (unless a trial were dispensed with altogether) and compelled to drink hemlock."[28] The four groups excluded from the amnesty were the Thirty Tyrants, the Ten who succeeded them in a brief transitional stage before the restoration of democracy, the Eleven who were responsible for executing the orders of the Thirty, and the governors of Piraeus who administered the port on behalf of the oligarchy. The reference to "rendering accounts" is to the ex post scrutiny to which all officials were subject.

[27] *The Constitution of Athens* xxxix.

[28] Loening (1987), p. 83. The example of Polemarchos discussed in Section V indicates that the demand for each member of the Thirty to kill one metic did not imply that they had to do it by their own hands.

Normally, the scrutiny was carried out by a popular jury chosen by lot among all citizens or even by the assembly as a whole. In this exceptional case, the requirement of scrutiny by citizens with taxable property ensured that nobody from the lowest property group (*thetes*) would sit in judgment of the oligarchs, so that former members of the Three Thousand would be overrepresented on the juries.[29]

It is relevant to mention here that the normal ex post scrutiny was widely seen as a manifestation of untrammeled democracy, capable of leading to "excesses, injustice and plain inefficiency,"[30] as when generals were punished for defeats that might be due simply to bad luck.[31] Hence, stacking the juries in favor of the oligarchs may have been proposed or accepted by the democrats to signal their intention to retreat from extreme forms of popular rule. The clause may of course also have been proposed or imposed by the Spartans to protect their former allies.[32] Other evidence that I shall cite shortly suggests, however, that the returning democrats were willing to limit retribution for the sake of civil peace.

Although Aristotle does not mention the fate of property confiscated by the oligarchs, other texts show that this issue was also covered by the treaty. In the summary of Thomas Loening:

> Individuals who had purchased confiscated goods will retain possession of them, and any property which had not been auctioned off will revert to the original owner.... This provision only involves movable property. Presumably, the original owner would have to establish undisputed title to these unsold goods before regaining possession of them. Acceptance of the reconciliation agreement meant a renunciation of all legal claims to movables confiscated and sold by the oligarchy. There may have been a provision whereby the exiles could repurchase their goods for the amount of money paid by the buyer, provided that he were willing to sell. Such a clause would prevent profiteering on the part of persons who had bought confiscated property cheaply and who then later attempted to sell it back to the original owner at an inflated price. There would be no obligation to resell, unless the buyer wanted to do so.... Not all confiscated property remained in the hands of the purchasers. The reconciliation treaty ordains that immovable property, such as land and houses, will be returned to their former owners... on the condition that they paid.[33]

[29] Ostwald (1986), p. 499.

[30] Ibid., p. 78.

[31] See, for instance, Kagan (1981), pp. 318–20.

[32] I disagree, therefore, with Loening (1987), p. 49, when he argues for a different reading of Aristotle's text, on the grounds that "[i]n all likelihood the exiles would not concede such an important advantage which would probably result in the exoneration of many of the oligarchs."

[33] Loening (1987), pp. 51–52. The last clause ("on the condition that they paid") is conjectural.

The most significant provision is the distinction between the confiscated goods that had been sold to private citizens and those that remained in the hands of the state. With regard to the former, which might legitimately be claimed by both the old and the new owners, the treaty settled in favor of the new owners. While the new owners were not necessarily oligarchs, they had certainly profited from the oligarchy, yet their gains were not canceled. Here, too, we can see evidence of a willingness to compromise on the part of the returning democrats.

The main architects in restoring the democracy were Thrasybulus and Archinos. Thrasybulus, who had led the democrats in exile, was concerned with rewarding those who had struggled on their side. Consequently, he proposed "to give citizenship to all who had had a part in the return from Piraeus although some were manifestly slaves."[34] Archinos was worried, however, that this might change the balance of power in the city too much in favor of the democrats. When the proposal was passed by the Assembly, he had it annulled through a *graphe paranomon*, a device by which the Athenians could reconsider their own past decisions. Aristotle, who praises this move by Archinos, also cites approvingly two other actions, both of questionable legality, that he undertook to cement the reconciliation. First, he arbitrarily abridged the deadline for registration for emigration to Eleusis, thus compelling oligarchs to stay in the city "against their will."[35] Aristotle refers to this as a "sound move," perhaps because he thought the balance of forces would be as upset by oligarchs leaving the city as it would be by giving voting rights to returning slaves.[36] Second,

> [w]hen one of the returned exiles began to violate the amnesty, Archinus haled him to the Council and persuaded them to execute him without a trial, telling them now they would have to show whether they wished to preserve the democracy and abide by the oaths they had taken; for if they let this man escape they would encourage others to imitate him, while if they executed him they would make an example for all to learn by. And this was exactly what happened; for after this man was put to death no one ever again broke the amnesty.[37]

An editor of the text comments that Archinos's "action in attacking someone for violating the amnesty was indeed right, for the only way of

[34] Aristotle, *The Constitution of Athens* XXXX.2.

[35] Ibid., XXXX.1.

[36] After a few years, however, "the atmosphere in Athens had changed sufficiently to enable Thrasybulus to try again, this time with more discrimination and success, to fulfill his promise to those who had fought on his side" (Ostwald 1986, p. 509).

[37] Aristotle, *The Constitution of Athens* XXXX.2.

reestablishing the state after such a traumatic period was for the Athenians to turn their backs on the past, but it is legitimate to ask whether an illegal execution was the best way of reestablishing the rule of law."[38] In turning their backs on the past, the Athenians resorted to the methods of the past – but they only had to do it once. Although the amnesty did not altogether eliminate lawsuits related to behavior during the oligarchy,[39] these were isolated events.

A final restraining measure initiated by Archinos, not mentioned by Aristotle, was the enactment of the procedure of *paragraphe*, perhaps best translated as "counteraccusation." It is described in a passage from Isocrates that is worth citing at some length:

> Now after your return to the city from Piraeus, you saw that some of the citizens were bent upon bringing malicious prosecutions and were attempting to violate the Amnesty; so, wishing to restrain these persons and to show to others that you had not made these agreements under compulsion, but because you thought them of advantage to the city, you enacted a law, on the motion of Archinos, to the effect that, if any person should commence a lawsuit in violation of the oaths, the defendant should have the power to bring a *paragraphe*; the magistrates should first submit this question to the tribunal, and that the defendant who had entered the plea should speak first; and further, that the loser should pay a penalty of one-sixth of the sum at stake. The purpose of the penalty was this – that persons who had the effrontery to rake up old grudges should not only be convicted of perjury but also, not awaiting the vengeance of the gods, should suffer immediate punishment.[40]

The new procedure thus had a double purpose. The immediate aim was to deter attempts to bring suit in violation of the amnesty. The broader end was to show that the reconciliation agreement treaty had not been imposed by the oligarchs or their Spartan allies, but freely chosen by the democrats in order to promote the good of the city.

The moderation displayed by the victorious democrats was quite remarkable.[41] In Thucydides, for instance, we find numerous accounts of the horrors of civil war that might have led us to expect a far worse outcome.

[38] Moore (1975), p. 272.

[39] Loening (1987), Chap. III, has a full account of the cases that arose.

[40] Isocrates, *Against Kallimachos* 2–3.

[41] In his catalogue raisonné of violent episodes in classical Greece, Bernard (1999) does not note the lack of vindictiveness following the demise of the oligarchy in 403. The contrast he draws (pp. 423–24) between the vindictiveness of pre-Christian societies and the charitableness of Christianity leaves no room for simple prudence. One can abstain from revenge merely because one perceives that it will be counterproductive, which arguably is what the Athenians did in 403.

The willingness to show clemency went hand in hand with constitutional reform intended to remove the root causes of oligarchic discontent. A key provision stated that "[t]he magistrates shall under no circumstances whatever employ a law that is not part of the written code. No decree of either Council or Assembly shall have higher authority than a law. No law shall be directed against an individual without applying to all citizens alike, unless an Assembly of six thousand so resolve by secret ballot."[42] Also, legislation was removed from the Assembly and delegated to a smaller group of *nomothetai*. In Ostwald's words, "The procedures are democratic, since they mandate repeated discussions in the Assembly before a new law can be validated, but they represent a restriction on popular sovereignty because the validation does not come from the Assembly but from a broadly based group of *nomothetai*."[43] Even that smaller group was subject to constraints. If the Assembly, in its annual review of all legislation, found that a set of laws was unsatisfactory, it had to elect five men to speak in the defense of those laws before the matter could go forward to the nomothetai. These long-term measures, which impose procedural constraints on popular rule,[44] complement the short-term measures that were taken to alleviate the enmity between oligarchs and democrats.

The reconciliation treaty brought about amnesty, but neither oblivion nor silence. Although there are examples of "gag rules" that take certain matters off the table to protect social peace,[45] the amnesty decree of 403 is not among them. The clause stating that the Athenians should abstain from harboring grievances did not, as is sometimes asserted,[46] impose a total ban on referring to past strifes. It provided immunity for prosecution but did not exclude that a person's behavior under the oligarchy could be relevant for his suitability to hold public office. Membership of the Council in this period seems to have been viewed as more aggravating than simply belonging to the Three Thousand, although less serious than being one of the Thirty. Nor was the amnesty violated by the decrease in pay for the cavalry, who had largely supported the oligarchy, or by an increase

[42] Andocides, "On the Mysteries," 87.

[43] Ostwald (1986), p. 522.

[44] MacDowell (1975), p. 74, states that "after the turmoil of 403 the Athenians . . . wanted to make it difficult for themselves to introduce changes in the laws." Ostwald (1986) similarly writes that the reforms "show that law was to be supreme in the new democracy and that the *demos* could no longer regard whatever it pleased as valid and binding."

[45] Holmes (1989).

[46] E.g., by Loraux (1997).

in pay for the mounted archers, who were more likely to have opposed it.[47] The cavalry could also be punished by other means. When asked to send troops to Persia, "the Athenians sent some of those who had served as cavalrymen in the time of the Thirty, thinking it would be a gain to the democracy if they should live in foreign lands and perish there."[48]

V. LYSIAS

To explore some of these issues, and to view other aspects of the amnesty through the eyes of a contemporary, I shall consider some speeches of Lysias (ca. 458–380). As a resident alien in Athens, he belonged to a group targeted for persecution by the Thirty Tyrants. His brother Polemarchos was put to death by the tyrants, and Lysias himself had a narrow escape. In three speeches delivered between 403 and 399, Lysias discusses moral issues concerning the oligarchs, their supporters, the resisters, and the beneficiaries of their rule, as well as those who chose to remain neutral. In one speech, he personally accuses one of those responsible for the murder of his brother. In another, he writes as a hired pen for a citizen defending himself against the accusation that his passive behavior during the oligarchy makes him ineligible for public office. In the third, Lysias is himself penning such accusations.

The speech "Against Eratosthenes," one of the Thirty, was probably given at the scrutiny of the latter after the fall of the oligarchy. As noted earlier, the jury is likely to have been stacked in his favor, whence certain constraints on the rhetorical strategies Lysias can deploy. Lysias begins by stating that the Thirty moved against resident aliens, alleging that they were hostile to the administration:

> Therefore they had an excellent pretext for appearing to punish while in reality making money; in any case, the State was impoverished and the government needed funds. They had no difficulty in persuading their hearers, for those men thought nothing of putting people to death, but a great deal of getting money. So they resolved to seize ten, of whom two should be poor men, that they might face the rest with the excuse that the thing had not been done for the sake of money (6–7).[49]

[47] Loening (1987), p. 119; Ostwald (1986), p. 506.

[48] Xenophon, *Hellenica*, III.1.4.

[49] The passage raises an intriguing question: Exactly whom were the Thirty trying to fool? In including two poor individuals, the Thirty showed that they were subject to what I have called the "imperfection constraint" in the process of misrepresenting one's preferences (Elster 1999, pp. 375–80). If the stated aim of an action (persecuting resident aliens for their political views) coincides *too well* with the agent's self-interest (confiscating their

Lysias then states that Eratosthenes had arrested Polemarchos in the street and taken him to prison, where he received the order to drink hemlock: "[M]y brother, as I said before, was put to death by Eratosthenes, who was neither suffering under any private wrong himself, nor found him offending against the State, but eagerly sought to gratify his own lawless passions" (23–24).[50] Against a possible defense by Eratosthenes that he was acting out of fear and just following orders (25), Lysias responds by asking "whom, in fact, will you ever punish, if the Thirty are to be allowed to state that they merely carried out the orders of the Thirty?" (29–30).

Toward the end of his speech, Lysias joins together the "men of the city" and the "men of the Piraeus" as victims (92), saying that he wants to recall the events of that period so that both groups will remember their grievances against the Thirty and their common desire for revenge. He says to the men of the city, "You were so oppressed by the rule of these men that you were compelled to wage war against your brothers, your sons, and your fellow citizens" (92). The purpose of the argument is clearly to make the men of the city, who were overrepresented in the jury, think of themselves as co-victims with the exiled democrats, rather than as co-perpetrators with the Thirty.[51] Whereas it would be absurd for Eratosthenes, a member of the Thirty, to claim to have acted under coercion by the Thirty, that excuse *is* available to their supporters. Yet with the end of the oligarchy, the excuse is no longer valid: "[I]f you condemn this man, you will declare your indignation at the things that have been done; but if you acquit him, you will be recognized as aspirants to the same conduct as [the Thirty], since today nobody is compelling you to vote against your judgment" (90–91).

wealth), the claim of being politically motivated lacks credibility. To create an appearance of political motivation, the Thirty would either have to abstain from prosecuting some wealthy individuals or to prosecute some poor ones; the latter strategy is the one Lysias mentions. Yet at the time when the Thirty published a list with the names of the Three Thousand, they decreed "that none of the Three Thousand could be put to death without a verdict of the Council but that the Thirty had the right to put to death anyone not on that list" (Ostwald 1986, p. 486). Since that decree was probably given *before* the measures against the resident aliens (ibid., p. 487), it is hard to see whom they needed to "persuade."

50 Note that Lysias here suggests an alternative way in which Eratosthenes could have sought to misrepresent his motives, by claiming to act for personal revenge rather than for gain. In Elster (1999), p. 213, I argue that for the Athenians, acting for revenge, although an inferior motivation to acting for the good of the state, was superior to that of acting out of self-interest.

51 D. Cohen (2001) emphasizes this aspect of much of the post-403 rhetoric.

In an earlier passage, presumably addressed to the exiled democrats in the jury, Lysias had told the jury that

> anyone who was ill-disposed towards your people lost nothing by holding his peace; for there were other men to speak and do things of the utmost possible detriment to the city. As for the men who say they are well-disposed, how is it that they did not show it at the moment, by speaking themselves to the most salutary purpose and deterring those who were bent on mischief? (49)

In the first part of this passage, Lysias argues that inaction or passivity is consistent with malignant motives; in the second, that benign motives are inconsistent with passivity. This resonates with Solon's ban on neutrality during civic strife, but contrasts oddly with another speech by Lysias from about 399, "Defense against a charge of subverting the democracy," written for an (anonymous or hypothetical) candidate for public office. The main thrust of the speech is to show that since this speaker was not an active supporter of the Thirty, but "behaved as the best citizen in the Piraeus would have done, if he had remained in the city" (2), there can be no objection to his holding office.

The speaker begins by stating a theory of political motivation: "[N]o human being is naturally either an oligarch or a democrat: Whatever constitution a man finds advantageous to himself, he is eager to see that one established" (8). He goes on to claim that some leaders of the Four Hundred were later found among the men in Piraeus, while some who had helped in the expulsion of the Four Hundred appeared among the Thirty: "There is thus no difficulty concluding that the questions dividing men are concerned not with politics but with their personal advantage" (9–10).[52] He then, inconsistently, claims that because he chose not to hold office under the Four Hundred or under the Thirty, he deserves to be honored by the jurors. As a next line of defense, he argues that "if everyone had been of one mind with me, not one of you would have experience of a single misfortune" (15).[53]

[52] The speaker applies the theory to himself: After citing his many largesses to the city, he adds that "my purpose in spending more than was enjoined upon me by the city was to raise myself the higher in your opinion, so that if any misfortune should chance to befall me I might defend myself on better terms" (12–13).

[53] This use of (something like) the categorical imperative to justify passivity in the face of violence might seem perverse, unless "everyone" is taken in the most inclusive sense. An analogy may be found in a novel by Astrid Lindgren (1985, p. 165), *The Brothers Lionheart*, which takes place in a mythical country governed by a cruel tyrant, to whom an underground opposition emerges. The leader of the opposition – one of the brothers of the title – refuses to use violent means to overthrow the tyrant. A frustrated follower

In a remarkable series of arguments, the speaker then goes on to develop three important *topoi*. The first, like the argument just mentioned, is a *defense of the passive bystander:*

You would not be justified in hating those who have suffered nothing under the oligarchy, when you can indulge your wrath against those who have done your people mischief; or in regarding as enemies those who did not go into exile instead of those who expelled you, or those who were anxious to save their own property instead of those who stripped others of theirs, or those who stayed in the city with a view to their own safety instead of those who took part in the government for the purpose of destroying others. If you think it your duty to destroy the men whom they passed over, not one of the citizens will be left to us (18).

The second is an objection to *indiscriminate persecution of indiscriminate persecutors:*

If the Thirty had kept their punishments for [those who had committed crimes under the previous democracy], you would have held them yourselves to be honest men: but when in fact you found them deliberately oppressing the people because of the offences of those persons, you were indignant; for you considered it monstrous that the crimes of the few should be spread over the whole city. It is not right therefore that you should resort to those offences which you saw them committing, or regard those deeds, which you deemed unjust when done to you, as just when you do them to others (19–20).

The third is a claim of a *negative correlation between resistance and vindictiveness*. The speaker claims that "in the Piraeus party, those who are in highest repute, who have run the highest risk, and who have rendered you the most services had often before exhorted your people to abide by their oaths and covenants, since they held this to be the bulwark of democracy" (28). By contrast, "the men who give us good cause to wonder what they would have done if they had been allowed to join the Thirty are the men who now, in a democracy, imitate those rulers" (30) by their indiscriminate persecution. Those who took greater risks in fighting the oligarchs when they had power are less prone to persecute them when they have lost it.

In the last speech I shall consider, "Against Philon, on his scrutiny," Lysias states that he will "demonstrate that Philon ... has set his private safety above the public danger of the city, and has held it preferable to pass his life without danger to himself than to save the city by sharing her dangers with the rest of the citizens" (6–7). This behavior, which is

tells him: "If everyone were like you, then evil would reign forever," to which the other brother replies, "If everyone were like [him], there wouldn't be any evil," thus implicitly extending "everyone" from opponents of the regime to include its supporters as well.

presented as blamable in this speech as well as in "Against Eratosthenes," is presented as blameless in the "Defense against a charge of subverting the democracy." The discrepancy may be due to the fact that in the latter speech, he is coming up with self-serving arguments for a client, rather than expressing his own convictions.[54] Alternatively, the speech may have been on behalf of a purely hypothetical client and thus more in the nature of a stylistic exercise.[55]

Philon's case was unlike that of the citizen whom Lysias defended against a charge of subverting the democracy. Whereas the latter remained in the city for the duration of the oligarchy, Philon was exiled and went abroad. Lysias reproaches him not only for his unpatriotic neutrality, when he preferred to stay at Oropus north of Athens for private gain rather than join the democrats at Piraeus, but also for "making a profit out of the disaster" (18) of the city. While not himself a wrongdoer, he was the beneficiary of wrongdoing when, traveling in the Athenian countryside from his base in Oropus,

> he met with the most elderly citizens ... – men who were attached to the democracy but unable owing to their age to give it their support – he stripped them of their resources, thinking it more important to make his own petty gains than to spare them injury. It is not possible for all these to prosecute him today, from the very same cause that disabled them from supporting the city: yet this man ought not to benefit twice from their disability (18–19).

Lysias goes on to anticipate and rebut a defense he expects Philon to offer:

> He argues, so I am told, that, if it was a crime to absent himself at that crisis, we should have had a law expressly dealing with it, as in the case of all other crimes. He does not expect you to perceive that the gravity of the crime was the reason why no law was proposed to deal with it. For what orator would ever have conceived, or lawgiver have anticipated, that any of the citizens would have been guilty of so grave an offence? (27)

54 This seems to be the view of Nouhaud (1982), pp. 370–76, who offers a detailed comparison between "Against Erastothenes" and "Defense against a charge of subverting the democracy."

55 This view is suggested by Dover (1968), pp. 188–89, who argues that the lack of specific details in "Defense against a charge of subverting the democracy" suggests that it is "a hypothetical defence of a man against whom the charge is made at a *dokimasia* [ex ante scrutiny] that he remained in the city during the rule of the Thirty Tyrants." To Dover's argument one might perhaps add that the cynically blatant appeal to self-interest in that speech would render it ineffective in an actual trial.

Although Solon had enacted a law exactly to that effect two centurie earlier, it seems to have fallen into oblivion. In the absence of a known law, Lysias then appeals to suprapositive or natural law: Some actions are so intrinsically and self-evidently wrong that one cannot imagine that anyone would commit them. He then concludes by drawing attention to the contrast between the resident aliens who "supported the democracy beyond the requirements of their duty" and Philon who "betrayed the city in violation of his duty." Having bestowed honors on the former, how could the Athenians fail to impose "if not some heavier punishment of another kind [excluded by the amnesty], at least the dishonor which you hold over him today" (29–30)? Lysias makes it clear that the allocation of honor and dishonor is justified on strictly consequentialist grounds: "In either case the distinction has been made not so much for the sake of those who have come into the world, as of those who are yet to come, in order that they may strive to become worthy" (30).

VI. SUMMARY

The Athenians faced problems and proposed solutions that are strikingly similar to those of recent transitions. They also encountered situations and offered solutions for which there are no contemporary parallels. To bring out the general features of the process, I shall recast the narrative in a more conceptual form.

The transition in 411 took place by a combination of regime implosion and insurrection. In 403, there was a negotiated transition under the supervision of Sparta. The fact that there were two oligarchic episodes, each of them succeeded by the restoration of democracy, enabled the democrats to learn from experience and to focus on eliminating the root causes of the oligarchic temptation.

In 411, the dominant aim of transitional justice was retribution. With regard to the executed oligarchs, incapacitation may also have been a motive since (Athens having no jails) they could not be rendered harmless by being imprisoned.

In 403, the dominant aim was reconciliation, although retribution and deterrence may also have played a role. By offering an extensive amnesty from prosecution and the option of exile for those not covered by the amnesty, the reconciliation treaty embodied a very moderate form of transitional justice. The Athenians may have concluded from the previous episode that severity might work against its purposes, angering its victims rather than deterring them.

The moderate procedures may have been (i) imposed by Sparta, (ii) a condition stipulated by the oligarchs in exchange for giving up power, or (iii) freely chosen by the Athenian democrats. For all we know, moderation may have been the first preference of all three parties.

The main cast of characters in transitional justice emerges clearly: wrongdoers, victims, resisters, neutrals, and beneficiaries from wrongdoing. The first two categories are the most important. Wrongdoers were to be sanctioned and victims to be compensated. After 403, a law was enacted to give citizenship to slaves who had fought the oligarchs, but later canceled. Other resisters may have received a pay increase as a reward for their efforts.

What constituted wrongdoing is not clear. After 411, oligarchs were charged with treason and soldiers with having remained in Athens during the rule of the Four Hundred. After 403, the amnesty covered instigation to murder but not murder "with one's own hands." Membership of the cavalry or of the Council during the rule of the Thirty Tyrants might be held against a candidate for public office.

The sanctions on wrongdoing (and on benefiting from wrongdoing) included execution, the imposition of fines, ineligibility for a given public office, and loss of civil and political rights. The reconciliation treaty of 403 allowed the oligarchs the option of exile, which, even if chosen voluntarily, must be viewed as a sanction. Bypassing the amnesty, the Athenians also penalized military supporters of the oligarchy by reducing their pay and sending them on perilous expeditions.

Transitional justice occurred through the actions of private individuals. These included prosecution, objections to a candidate before he took up a public office for which he had been chosen, and accusation of an official after the expiration of his term. Verdicts were usually given by large juries, who voted by secret ballot after hearing speeches for the accusation and the defense. Although jurors were normally chosen at random among the citizens, after 403 the composition of the juries that conducted the ex post scrutiny was biased in favor of the oligarchs. We might call this "losers' justice."

After 403, the victorious democrats also restrained themselves when they struck down the law that would have given Athenian citizenship to slaves and others who had fought on their side. By canceling the law, they prevented a shift in the balance of power in the city away from the defeated oligarchs. Measures were also taken to reduce the outflow of oligarchs from the city. A further measure of moderation was the establishment of a procedure that made it more risky to bring suits that might violate the amnesty.

Transitional justice seems to have been carried out in legal forms, at least in the sense that retroactive legislation was not used. Some abuses may have occurred after 411.

Transitional justice was supplemented by legal and (as we would say today) constitutional reforms. After 411, the main aim was to provide negative incentives for would-be oligarchic coupmakers. After 403, the aim shifted to eliminating their positive incentives, by imposing constraints on the previously all-powerful citizen assembly.

After 403, provisions were made for exiled democrats to recover confiscated property. Movable property (including slaves) that had been sold to private individuals remained in the hands of the latter.

One aspect of the Athenian solution that merits attention is that retributive emotions were attenuated by allowing their targets to remove themselves from the city. The democrats probably understood that a situation in which killers and relatives of their victims intermingled freely would be highly unstable, especially in a face-to-face community such as Athens. When the oligarchs returned from exile a few years later, emotions had had time to cool down.

The speeches of Lysias offer important but not always consistent arguments about the conduct of transitional justice. (i) A member of the Thirty could not claim to have acted under coercion. (ii) Supporters of the Thirty may claim to have acted under coercion. (iii) Neutrality is not a ground for punishment. (iv) Neutrality is a ground for punishment. (v) Benefiting from wrongdoing is a ground for punishment. (vi) Those who engage in relentless persecution of the oligarchs are guilty of imitating their methods. (vii) Those who were least vigorous in opposing the oligarchs during their reign are most likely to persecute them relentlessly afterward. (viii) In the absence of a written law, one can appeal to unwritten suprapositive law.

2

The French Restorations in 1814 and 1815

I. INTRODUCTION

Transitional justice in the restoration of monarchy has occurred several times in history. In the next chapter, I briefly summarize some salient features of the English Restoration in 1660. In this chapter, I consider in more detail transitional justice after each of the two Restorations of the French monarchy, in 1814 and in 1815, separated by the Hundred Days in which Napoleon returned to power.[1] During the First Restoration, the Bourbons undertook limited measures of reparation, but otherwise did nothing. During the Second, they carried out vast punitive and reparative measures. To explain the dynamics of these events, I begin in Section II by considering the political constraints on transitional justice, which followed from the fact that these were *negotiated* transitions. In Section III I consider public and private retribution, before turning in Section IV to the issues of restitution and compensation. Section V offers a brief summary.

II. CONSTRAINTS ON TRANSITIONAL JUSTICE IN THE FRENCH RESTORATIONS

Transitional justice in the return of the Bourbons took place twice within a short interval of time. In this section, I explain the constraints on transitional justice that followed from the fact that in both cases, the post-Napoleonic regimes were established under the auspices of the Allied forces with some of Napoleon's leading officials serving as go-betweens.

[1] The best modern exposition is Sauvigny (1999). An exhaustive, even if occasionally dated, treatment is Nettement (1860).

In 1814, Talleyrand, Napoleon's former Foreign Minister and at the time de facto leader of his senate, was the main mediator. In 1815, he was supplemented by Fouché, Napoleon's Chief of Police. Because these officials had the support of the Allies – Tsar Alexander in 1814 and Wellington in 1815 – they could to some extent impose constraints on what might otherwise have been strongly vindictive transitional justice.

When Napoleon was about to capitulate before the Allied (English, Austrian, Russian, and Prussian) forces in March 1814, the nature of the successor regime was initially wide open. Tsar Alexander was strongly opposed to the return of the Bourbons. Wellington was discreetly in favor of this option, but did not press it. Other options included the regency of the Empress Marie-Louise and conferring the throne on Bernadotte or the Duc d'Orléans. In the end, Talleyrand served as a kingmaker when on March 31, he persuaded Alexander that only a restoration of the monarchy would have the focal-point quality necessary for a stable regime.[2] He further persuaded Napoleon's senate to express a wish for the return of the Bourbons, since the Allies would not accept any solution that could not be presented as desired by the French nation. The senate used the bargaining power conferred on them by this situation to offer, on April 6, a constitutional draft that, among other things, stipulated strong political powers and extravagant economic privileges for the existing senators.[3]

[2] Talleyrand (1967), vol. 2, p. 165. Gorce (1926), p. 9, comments ironically that "Talleyrand praised the principle of legitimacy as if he himself had never varied in his views." The idea of monarchy as a focal point goes back to Pascal (*Pensée* 786, ed. Sellier).

[3] The draft is reproduced in Rosanvallon (1994), pp. 193–96. A key article deserves to be cited in full: "There are at last one hundred and fifty senators and at most two hundred. Their dignity is inamovable and hereditary in the male line, by primogeniture. They are named by the king. The existing senators, except for those who might give up their French citizenship, are maintained in their office and are included in this number. The existing endowment of the senate and the 'sénatoreries' belong to them. The revenues derived therefrom are divided equally among them, and are passed on to their successors. If a senator should die without leaving a male descendant, his share returns to the Treasury. Senators to be named in the future will not share in this endowment." Rosanvallon does not mention, however, that the first project (elaborated by a senatorial subcommittee supplemented with other members, among them the Russian Foreign Minister) that was presented to the Senate for discussion had an even stronger pro-senatorial bias. In this project, "the Senate was the true successor to Napoleon. It would be made up exclusively of its existing members, one hundred in all; this number could not be exceeded. The Constitution would make the office hereditary. The senators would recruit themselves, since in case of the extinction of a family line the king had to choose from a list of three candidates . . . presented by the Senate" (Nettement 1860, vol. 1, p. 229).

The senators had overreached themselves. Their self-serving draft created so much public indignation that Louis XVIII was able to defeat their political ambitions. In other respects one might agree with Chateaubriand when he wrote, inverting a phrase of François Ier, that they lost nothing except their honor.[4] The constitutional Charter that was adopted on June 4 did, in fact, serve their interests in several ways. Article 9 says that "All properties are inviolable, no exception being made for the so-called *national* properties, the law making no distinction between them." These national properties, or *biens nationaux,* had been confiscated from the Church or émigré nobles during the Revolution. Although some of them, mainly forests, remained in the hands of the state, most had been sold, usually at artificially low prices, to private individuals, and sometimes resold. The senators, as part of the economic elite that was the main beneficiary of the sale, had an obvious interest in blocking restitution of the confiscated properties. A similar provision was already included in the document of April 1 in which the senate laid down the guidelines for the provisional government.[5]

Louis XVIII's personal inclination was to return all confiscated properties. In a declaration from exile in 1796, he asserted that on his return, "*biens nationaux* were to be returned to their original owners."[6] In a statement from 1799, he added that the purchasers whose acquired properties were to be returned might receive an indemnification.[7] In a declaration from 1805, which otherwise showed great moderation, he still "could not bring himself to sanction their sale openly."[8] He seems to have thought that his return "would provoke such a panic among the purchasers that the émigrés would get their properties back at low prices."[9] Yet after his brother, the Comte d'Artois, had been forced by Alexander, on April 14, to accept the sale of the biens nationaux as irrevocable,[10] Louis XVIII's hands were tied. According to his collaborator Villèle, "among all the concessions extracted from the King, the confirmation

4 Chateaubriand (1814), p. 106.

5 Rosanvallon (1994), p. 190.

6 Mansel (1999), p. 115.

7 Gain (1928), vol. 1, p. 25. In this book I draw extensively on Gain's fundamental study. One may note, as a minor irony, that after Liberation in 1944, Gain was discharged from his position as Rector of his university for unpatriotic conduct (Singer 1997, pp. 254–55; see also Baruch 1997, p. 512).

8 Gain (1928), vol. 1, p. 119.

9 Ibid., p. 92.

10 Nettement (1860), vol. 1, pp. 276–80.

of the sales was the only one whose injustice he deplored in his conscience."[11]

Article 11 of the Charter states that "[a]ll investigations into opinions and votes expressed before the Restoration are forbidden. The same oblivion is commanded for the courts and for the citizens." On this point, there is a curious discrepancy between the Charter and all drafts or statements issued after April 6, on the one hand, and the April 1 statement, on the other hand. Whereas all the former give an amnesty for "opinions and votes," the latter only mentions "opinions." The "votes" in question were those cast in the Legislative Assembly in January 1793 on whether to sentence Louis XVI to death or to a milder sentence. In exile, Louis XVIII had initially (1795) threatened to punish those who voted for the death sentence, but as early as 1797, he "disclaimed any idea of vengeance, even against the Regicides."[12] As several of the senators were among the regicides, they had an obvious interest in including an amnesty for their vote in their initial statement. I do not know why they failed to do so, but they soon amended the mistake.

Article 66 of the Charter asserts that "the punishment of confiscation is abolished." This has often been seen as a magnanimous act of the new regime, to distance itself from the lawless practices of its predecessors. In Vaclav Havel's words, "We are not like them." Benjamin Constant said that the article "was the most beautiful part of the Charter."[13] The fact that the article can be traced back to the senatorial draft of April 6 suggests another interpretation, namely, that the senators used the bargaining power conferred on them by Alexander to protect their own properties. This was the reading offered by Bonald in 1816: "We are not making any mistakes about the motive for so much humanity [among those who wanted to abolish confiscation]. Those who inspired the abolition of confiscation . . . were themselves gorged with confiscated property and feared that one day the law from which they had profited so much would be turned against them."[14] The two interpretations are not mutually exclusive. There is a natural fit between the desire for reconciliation that often (although far from always) animates incoming leaders and the desire for immunity in the outgoing ones.

[11] Ibid., p. 94.
[12] Mansel (1999), p. 117.
[13] Gorce (1926), p. 17.
[14] Nettement (1860), vol. 3, pp. 570–71.

The first Restoration lasted one year. The new regime initiated no trials or extensive purges of officials left over from its revolutionary and imperial predecessors. Some measures, discussed in Section IV, were taken for the restitution of careers and properties. The process was cut short, however, by Napoleon's return and the Hundred Days (March–June 1815). After Waterloo, the return of the Bourbons was no more automatic than it had been in 1814, but this option won out over the others – the same as in 1814 minus Bernadotte – because Wellington threw himself behind it. Before returning to Paris, Louis XVIII issued two proclamations. On June 25, he promised to reestablish the Charter, "to reward the good, and to apply [*mettre en exécution*] the existing legislation against the guilty." Although the promise to abstain from retroactive legislation suggested that the scope might not be too wide, the vagueness of the language was ominous. The French forces in Paris might prefer to fight rather than capitulate and then be repressed.[15] Thus, Talleyrand (backed by Wellington) persuaded Louis XVIII to issue the Cambrai Proclamation of June 28, in which he drew a distinction between the "instigators and authors of this terrible plot" and those who were merely "misguided" [*égarés*]. While the latter would be pardoned, the former would be "designated for the vengeance of the laws by the two chambers, which I intend to assemble immediately." He also imposed a cutoff date for the pardons, which would cover only acts committed after March 23 (the day of his departure from France) and before June 26 (the day of his arrival in Cambrai). The opportunists who had joined Napoleon during the Hundred Days, but left the ship when it was clear that it was sinking, would go free; the diehards would not. The date of March 23 was inadequately chosen as Napoleon's entry into Paris, and the first rallyings to his cause occurred on March 20. Fouché himself, in fact, joined him on that day.

For those who might plausibly be seen as diehards or "instigators," the Cambrai Proclamation was obviously insufficient. In the talks on the peace convention that was signed on July 3, the French commissioners negotiated on behalf of the provisional government dominated by Fouché. They were instructed to insist on Article XII, which asserted that all inhabitants of the capital "will continue to enjoy all their rights and freedoms and will not be harassed or investigated in any way with regard to the functions they occupy or may have occupied or their political behavior and opinions." Wellington was happy to grant this demand, as in his mind the immunity would only constrain the allies, but not the King when his

[15] Houssaye (1906), p. 146.

authority was substituted for theirs. His interlocutors may, however, have deluded themselves (or been deluded by Fouché) into thinking that the clause offered them a blanket amnesty.[16]

The Allies, in fact, decided to force the pace or, rather, to force Louis XVIII to do so: "The English and Russian governments, which ... prior to the return of the King to Paris had tried to keep the party of emigration out of his councils, now allied themselves with this party in demanding punishments and proscriptions."[17] On July 13, the allied ministers asked Talleyrand which measures the government was planning to take "against the members of the Bonaparte family and other individuals whose presence was notoriously incompatible with the public order." Talleyrand advised the King to refer the allies to the Cambrai Proclamation, according to which the guilty would be designated by the legislature. As he writes in his memoirs, he "hoped that by delaying the measure, time would come to our help in softening it, if not have it rejected altogether."[18] Yet Fouché persuaded the King to implement the minimal measure needed to satisfy the Allies, claiming that by sacrificing fifty or sixty individuals, one would save the lives of a thousand.[19] I return to the implementation of this measure.

The first peace settlement in 1814 did not impose heavy financial costs on France. Although the Charter committed Louis XVIII to assume all of Napoleon's debts, the Allies did not – despite the wish of Prussia – impose war indemnities on the country. In 1815, the situation was entirely different. Although Wellington prevented the Prussian general Blücher from carrying out what one might call his "Morgenthau plan *avant la lettre*" (see Chapter 7), France had to pay heavy war indemnities and pay for the upkeep of the occupying armies. Taken together, these costs were roughly equivalent to the amount later paid out to the émigrés and therefore a main obstacle to an early reimbursement. It does not seem that the Allies intervened in questions of reparation and restitution, as they had done in 1814. In an official note dated November 1815, Wellington asserts "that the King will endure if the courtiers and his family do not force him to take measures that would seriously disturb the purchasers of *biens nationaux*,"[20] but I have not seen it suggested that he exercised any kind of pressure on the French government.

[16] Ibid, pp. 299–300, 574–75; Nettement (1860), vol. 3, pp. 62–67.
[17] Houssaye (1906), p. 425.
[18] Talleyrand (1967), vol. 3, p. 251.
[19] Houssaye (1906), p. 427.
[20] Gain (1928), vol. 1, p. 227.

III. RETRIBUTIONS

In the First Restoration, there were no trials, no political justice, and only minimal purges in the public administration.[21] These policies were imposed by Louis XVIII against the wishes of the ultraroyalists, "who were out for revenge, violence and blood. The last thing they wanted was for the Restoration to be as mild, rational and conciliatory as Louis XVIII intended."[22] In the second Restoration, they came back with a vengeance, and for vengeance.

Ceding to the combined demands of the Allies and the émigrés for punishments and proscriptions, Fouché drew up a list of the guilty. Its exact composition is unknown, but it was apparently or allegedly intended to make the whole measure unworkable. According to one account, "Fouché made a very numerous list and asserted that the measure would not bring any advantage if it was not executed at that scale; by this means he intended to bring about a complete abandonment of proscription."[23] According to his biographer, "he first had the idea of causing the measure to fail, by generalizing it in the most exaggerated manner; thus he drew up a ridiculous list of proscriptions in order to discredit the decree and block its application by making it burlesque."[24] Be this as it may, the list was redrawn a number of times by the government, until on July 24, a decree announced that nineteen officers would be brought before a military council, whereas thirty-eight other individuals would be assigned to house arrest until the legislature could designate those who would either be proscribed or brought before the courts. Of the fifty-seven, thirty-one had assisted Napoleon in his March to Paris or accepted functions in his administration before March 23, whereas the remaining twenty-six were designated in violation of the Cambrai Proclamation. Some of them were singled out because they were regicides, others because they had offended the royal family or Fouché in some way.[25] The list was generally viewed as both overinclusive and underinclusive. Many of those named were obscure and their wrongdoings doubtful. At the same time, many of the grand dignitaries of Napoleon's regime, beginning with Fouché himself, were not included. The farcical aspect of the events hardly needs underlining.

[21] For the purges, see Sauvigny (1999), p. 78; Mansel (1999), p. 203; and especially Tulard (1977), pp. 51–54.

[22] Mansel (1999), p. 209.

[23] Contemporary accounts cited in Houssaye (1906), p. 428 n. 3.

[24] Madelin (1945), vol. 2, p. 455.

[25] Houssaye (1906), pp. 430–33.

Assisted by Fouché, who was not particularly eager to pursue his recent accomplices, most of the designated officers fled the country or went into hiding. One of them (Lavallette) was condemned to death by an ordinary tribunal (*cour d'assises*) but managed to escape. Another (Labedoyère) was condemned to death by a military council. The most famous, Maréchal Ney, was taken before a military council, which declared itself incompetent to try him. According to a general who later supervised his execution, the members of the council, "being almost as guilty as the accused, would not have dared to impose the death sentence." Commenting on this remark, Henry Houssaye writes that "given the miserable weakness of human nature, the suspicion hovering over them would rather have induced them to be severe."[26] When Ney was tried by the newly appointed upper house of the legislature, he invoked Article XII of the peace treaty, claiming that it granted immunity beyond the period of occupation. The appeal was unsuccessful; he was condemned to death and executed.

Although the government had expected, wished, and maneuvered for an assembly of moderates,[27] the elections to the lower house had returned an ultraroyalist assembly, "la chambre introuvable." When the deputies met on October 7, their dissatisfaction with the decree of July 24 soon became evident. Following the general mood of the country, they wanted much stronger measures:

> Hand the leaders of the conspiracy over to the courts; deny the right to vote and a fortiori to be elected to those who had been part of the assemblies of the Hundred Days; establish lists of indignity for admission to public office of those who had played an active role in the recent events; remove from France, by a temporary banishment, the most compromised persons whose presence might prove dangerous; replace the personnel of the administration; dissolve the imperial courts and establish the judicial institutions *de novo*; make the functionaries of the imperial regime under the Hundred Days pay twice or thrice the normal amount of taxes, so that the war indemnities would weigh more heavily on those who had provoked the war; finally ban in perpetuity the regicides who, having been treated so mildly by Louis XVIII on his first return, had then sworn an oath to the [constitution enacted during the Hundred Days] banishing the Bourbons in perpetuity from the French territory.[28]

[26] Ibid., p. 571. See also Chap. 8.VI.

[27] Sauvigny (1999), p. 124; Houssaye (1906), pp. 528–29.

[28] Nettement (1860), vol. 3, pp. 269–70. A variant of the proposal to have the functionaries pay higher taxes was that the Treasury could sue the responsible parties to fund the indemnity payments (ibid., p. 454). The proposal was rejected as incompatible with the Article of the Charter that asserted that confiscations were abolished.

The main motivation for these and other drastic proposals was sheer anger toward those who were seen as having brought ruin and humiliation to the country. In the parliamentary debates, some offered the subtler argument that because the decree of July 24 had been perceived as blocking action in the courts, "ardent populations had substituted excesses of fury and vengeance for the justice that was refused them."[29] Many of the deputies also opposed the idea of enacting a bill of attainder against named individuals. They wanted measures that were phrased in abstract and general terms, notably the proscription of the so-called *régicides relaps* – 143 individuals who had compounded the vote to execute Louis XVI with the more recent betrayal of his younger brother.

The law that was adopted on January 7, 1816, offered a general amnesty for those who had taken part, directly or indirectly, in the "rebellion and usurpation" of Napoleon, with two classes of exceptions. First, the assembly upheld the decree of July 24, with the modification that the King might remove some of the named persons from the list.[30] Second, the assembly overwhelmingly voted to banish the *régicides relaps*. More draconian measures, which would have condemned 850 individuals to deportation or death and confiscated their fortunes, were rejected by a margin of nine votes in a secret ballot. Rejected also was a proposal to extend the amnesty to royalists charged with crimes against individuals in the South and the West.[31] The debates and the outcome were heavily shaped by extraparliamentary events. After the execution of Ney on December 7, the King's Minister Richelieu thought that his relatively lenient proposition (with no proviso for the regicides) might pass, since the thirst of the gods had been slaked: "He may have had in mind the animal tamers who go into the cage only when the ferocious animals have just had a meal."[32] Two weeks later, however, the evasion of Lavallette "had the effect of exasperating the chamber and making it amend the amnesty proposition in a more rigorous sense."[33]

While it took six months for parliament to reach a decision, private justice was more expeditious. In July and August 1815, several hundred suspect individuals were killed in the South of France by royalist gangs and the clandestine royalist society Les Chevaliers de la Foi, closely linked to the ultraroyalist Duc d'Angoulême, the son of the King's brother. In

[29] Ibid., p. 312.
[30] On this "amendement Roncherolles," see ibid., pp. 465–66.
[31] Resnick (1966), p. 75 n. 31.
[32] Houssaye (1906), p. 592; see also Nettement (1860), vol. 3, pp. 425–26.
[33] Houssaye (1906), p. 590; see also Nettement (1860), vol. 3, pp. 445–50.

many places, Angoulême's influence led to a system of dual and competing authorities, with the officials appointed from Paris confronting those backed by Angoulême and the ultraroyalist groups.[34] In Toulouse, a Paris-designated mayoral candidate, who had served in the office during the Empire and the first Restoration but resigned during the Hundred Days, was blocked by the Chevaliers de la Foi because he had refused to cooperate with them in April 1814.[35] In Nîmes, the authority of the prefect appointed by the king was undermined by subprefects and mayors appointed by Angoulême.[36] There is even evidence that "some members of the ultra-royalist leadership in Toulouse wished to make Angoulême's government of the Midi a center of authority for a secessionist South, a new 'Kingdom of Aquitaine.'"[37]

In Provence, "lawless action in this period [just after Waterloo] was directed not only at supporters of Napoleon but also at those whose misdeeds dated from the years of the Revolution."[38] The Napoleonic officials "who did not flee were often forced to purchase their freedom in ransom or 'insurance' from organized gangs."[39] In Avignon, a man who killed a Bonapartist was jailed, but freed by a crowd the next day.[40] In Toulouse,

> [m]any who were not suspect for their revolutionary past were under suspicion for having joined clubs of Bonapartists organized during the Hundred Days. Affiliation with these fédérations, however, had not been a purely personal decision or for that matter a voluntary one. Napoleon's government had supported them actively, and in the South had tried to bring pressure to join on both the purchasers of nationalized properties and public officeholders.[41]

The royalist repressions often had a religious aspect. In the Gard, where Protestants had benefited heavily from Napoleon's measures, "Protestant women were singled out for a strange beating. Skirts were lifted and the women paddled with a board whose protruding spikes formed a fleur-de-lys. Up to 49 women were victims of this scourging, and at least two died."[42] In Nîmes, "the threat to Protestant life and property . . . from the

[34] Sauvigny (1999), p. 120, draws attention to the many parallels between this situation and that which obtained in France in the fall of 1944.
[35] Resnick (1966), pp. 25–26.
[36] Ibid., pp. 49–50.
[37] Ibid., p. 117.
[38] Ibid., pp. 9–10.
[39] Ibid., p. 11.
[40] Ibid., p. 18.
[41] Ibid., p. 29.
[42] Ibid., p. 52.

incoming royalist bands, abetted by the royalist authorities, forced hundreds of Protestants to leave the city. A threat by [the police commissioner] to confiscate the property of those who did not return by July 28 failed to stem the exodus."[43] Thus, their property was looted if they stayed, confiscated if they left. The military commander appointed by Angoulême did not try to interfere. In a report to the War Ministry, he omitted the religious aspect of the massacres when he wrote that "[t]he people immolated in the streets are Bonapartists and revolutionaries. The people has only preempted [*dévancé*] the law that would have struck them."[44] Here, the argument is not that private justice is necessary since legal justice will not be done, but that private justice is acceptable since it only carries out more speedily what the courts would do later in any case.

Louis XVIII had difficulties getting the situation under control until he recalled Angoulême to Paris and issued a statement criticizing those who "under the pretext of turning themselves into ministers of public vengeance, had satisfied their private hatreds and vengeances.... The guilty must fall under the sword of the law and not under the weight of private acts of revenge."[45] His main concern, however, was to restore the authority of the state, not to show clemency.

In the West of France, the white terror was generally bloodless[46] and took mainly the form of harassing purchasers of nationalized properties.[47] Although the biens nationaux were a less frequent source of conflict in the South, they figured there as well. Thus, in Toulon the "white terror" sought out "purchasers of nationalized property during the Revolution as well as men who had remained in office during the Hundred Days."[48] There was in fact an overlap between the two sins of having purchased nationalized property and having served Napoleon, who had even gone so far as to favor for appointments to public office those who possessed biens nationaux.[49] In this way, the questions of retribution and reparations were closely linked. The initial demand for restitution of biens nationaux became a matter not only of justice but also of revenge.[50] When ultimately the solution was chosen to indemnify the original owners, rather than

43 Ibid., pp. 54–55.
44 Houssaye (1906), p. 471.
45 Nettement (1860), vol. 3, p. 220.
46 Houssaye (1906), p. 549, cites one killing. Gabory (1989), p. 867, says that "not a drop of blood was spilled."
47 Houssaye (1906), p. 549.
48 Ibid., p. 17.
49 Gain (1928), vol. 1, p. 212.
50 Ibid., pp. 221–31.

return their property, some royalists argued that as a matter of "legitimate vengeance," the indemnity should be paid by the purchasers.[51]

The Second Restoration, unlike the first, carried out vast purges in the public sector. As the government thought, with some justification, that its earlier failure to purge was a major cause of Napoleon's return to power, it was determined not to repeat the mistake. It has been estimated that fifty thousand to eighty thousand functionaries, a quarter to a third of the total, were dismissed.[52] The basic criterion was whether an official had sworn the oath to Napoleon during the Hundred Days.[53] Among the twenty-three appeals courts in the country, nineteen lost a total of 294 magistrates, including 15 presiding judges.[54] Extensive measures were also taken to "break bonapartism in the University."[55] In the Army, the Minister of War created a classification of officers in fourteen categories, with descending chances of retaining their positions.[56] As this is the most fine-grained classification of incriminating acts I have come across in any case of transitional justice,[57] it is worthwhile reproducing in full:

(1) 206 officers and military officials who had left the Army within twenty days of Napoleon's arrival in Paris;
(2) 103 individuals who, without leaving the Army, had refused to swear an oath of loyalty to Napoleon;
(3) 5 officers who had taken the oath but redeemed themselves by leaving the Army;
(4) 107 officers who had joined Napoleon, but then left the Army before the return of the King;
(5) 22 officers who had been dismissed by Napoleon, but not for motives that could harm their reputation;
(6) 709 officers who had remained in service, but against whom the offices of the ministries contained denunciations accusing them of being attached to the King;
(7) 511 officers who were not in active service when Napoleon took power, and made no request to go back into service before the return of the King;

[51] Ibid., p. 492.

[52] The number seems large, yet Chateaubriand (1816), pp. 484–86, claimed that the purges were unjust because they were partial and arbitrary, and argued that the government should either have proceeded to a "large purge" or made no purge at all.

[53] Sauvigny (1999), p. 136.

[54] Royer (2001), p. 495 n; Ponteil (1966), p. 43.

[55] Gerbod (1977), pp. 89–90.

[56] Vidalenc (1977), pp. 64–65. Houssaye (1906), p. 564, gives a slightly different summary.

[57] The scheme for evaluating the behavior of French prefects during the German occupation (see Chap. 4) was even more detailed, but it was not implemented.

(8) 480 officers who had retained their position [*destination*] without soliciting a new one;
(9) 2,001 officers whose service had been purely passive [*sédentaire*];
(10) 729 officers and military officials who, after the departure of the King, had received promotions or rewards that the King had accorded them;
(11) 2,139 officers and military officials who had followed Bonaparte until the return of the King to Paris;
(12) 37 officers in the preceding category who had also signed petitions to Napoleon;
(13) 41 officers who had commanded revolutionary battalions or partisan bodies;
(14) 612 officers who were grouped in seven particularly reprehensible categories:
   1. Those who declared themselves for Bonaparte in the twenty days that preceded the departure of the King;
   2. Those who on their own initiative hoisted Bonaparte's banner;
   3. Those who had repressed or punished faithful servants of the King;
   4. Commanders of forts who refused to give up their places when it was clear that the King ordered them to do so;
   5. Those who had marched against the royal troops in the interior;
   6. Those who had insulted the effigy of the King or the Princes, or decorations they had previously received from His Majesty;
   7. Officers on half pay who had voluntarily left their homes to join Bonaparte in his march on Paris.

Although the overall logic of culpability behind this ranking is somewhat opaque, many of the distinctions make clear sense. It was worse to attack the King than to defend oneself against him. It was better not to swear an oath to Napoleon while serving in his Army than taking the oath and then leaving it. To have been dismissed by Napoleon was more compelling proof of innocence than to have been denounced as a royalist.

IV. REPARATIONS

The restored Bourbon regime offered reparation to its supporters for loss of property and, to a smaller extent, loss of career opportunities. Personal suffering, through jail or exile, went uncompensated. Loyal supporters of the King were sometimes rewarded by positions at the court or in the administration, but there was no general scheme to compensate them.

Career restitution seems to have been most important in the Navy. On May 25, 1814, the Ministry of the Marine issued a decree that allowed émigré officers to return to the service at one rank above the one they had when they left it.[58] Many officers were not content with this, however. Instead, they

> aimed at a grade corresponding to their seniority. Vitrolles [secretary of the King's Council] tells that one day Malouet, Secretary of the Navy, brought to the Council the petition of a former officer of the royal navy who had not seen service since 1789, at which time he was a mere cadet; he nevertheless demanded nothing less than the grade of rear admiral, arguing that this would have been his position had his career taken its normal course. "Answer him," said Vitrolles, who understood the logic of his reasoning, "that he has only forgotten one essential fact: that he would have been killed in the battle of Trafalgar."[59]

The issue of reparations for loss of property was far more consequential. There were two kinds of confiscated property, "biens de première origine" confiscated from the Church and "biens de seconde origine" confiscated from individuals. These included mainly émigrés (426,000 confiscations) but also those who had been condemned by the revolutionary tribunals (15,000) or been deported (16,000).[60] The number of émigrés and deported may have been around 200,000.[61] The total number of individuals who were ultimately indemnified was about 25,000. The gap between the numbers has several explanations. Many had not been dispossessed because they possessed nothing or had sold off their property before leaving the country. Others had lost movable property or annuities, which were not indemnified. Some had been able to recover their properties, and some were dead without leaving heirs.

In the abstract, the salient issues were the following. (i) Should reparative measures be limited to individuals or also include the corporate property of the Church? (ii) Should the measures be limited to landed property or be extended to movable property, annuities, and so on? (iii) Should they be limited to confiscated properties, or be extended to destroyed (real) or devalued (personal) properties? (iv) Should goods that had been confiscated but not sold off be returned to the former owners? (v) Should goods that had been confiscated but sold off be the subject of restitution,

[58] Nettement (1860), vol. 1, p. 462.

[59] Sauvigny (1999), p. 79. The former officer calculated his rank in a counterfactual world in which neither the Revolution of 1789 nor the Napoleonic wars had occurred. In his response, Vitrolles relied on a counterfactual world in which the officer had not emigrated during the revolution but had gone on to fight in the Napoleonic wars. The latter counterfactual, involving less extensive rewriting of history, is the more relevant one.

[60] Gain (1928), vol. 1, p. 543.

[61] Ibid., vol. 2, p. 178, which is also the source for the following statements.

monetary compensation, or both? (The last solution would imply restitution to the original owners and compensation to the purchasers.) (vi) If compensation were chosen, how would the funds be raised? (vii) If compensation were chosen, should it be framed as a measure of justice, grace, or social reconciliation?

Some of these questions had been resolved politically. In the 1801 Concordat with Napoleon, the Pope committed himself and his successors to respect the sale of confiscated Church goods.[62] The Charter extended this provision to individually held properties. These measures did not prevent former owners or their associates from trying to take justice into their own hands. Parish priests sometimes refused to give the last rites to purchasers of biens nationaux unless they had given up their property before dying.[63] These were isolated instances, as was also the behavior of the Minister of War, who told a general that he would employ him only if he returned the émigré properties that he had bought at third hand.[64] A more general and widespread phenomenon was the harassment to which the purchasers were often exposed, not only by their neighbors, who envied them the cheaply acquired properties, but also by former owners who had come back to settle in the vicinity. This process began before the Restorations, when Napoleon allowed some of the émigrés to come back. They might buy back their properties, if they could afford to, or offer to "ratify" the sales at a price if they could not. Because of the uncertainty surrounding their fate and the stigma associated with their acquisition, the biens nationaux were often severely undervalued. By offering to ratify the sale, the former owner could benefit himself as well as the purchaser, whose destigmatized property would now appreciate in value. In the Vendée and other places, former owners also instigated systematic persecution of the purchasers.[65] The harassments and the depreciation continued and intensified after the Restorations, notably the Second.

By a law of December 5, 1814, properties confiscated from the émigrés that remained in the hands of the state were returned to their former owners. The bulk of the properties (95 percent) was 350,000 hectares of forest, of which almost half belonged to the Duc d'Orléans and the Prince de Condé. An alternative solution, to allocate unsold properties proportionally to *all* former owners, whether their properties had been sold off

[62] Godechot (1998), p. 715.
[63] Gain (1928), vol. 1, pp. 99, 330.
[64] Ibid., p. 99.
[65] Ibid., pp. 57–59.

or not, was not contemplated at the time.[66] Unsold Church properties were treated differently. Although the ultraroyalist parliament in 1815 voted to return unsold Church goods, the King, who needed to sell off Church forests to cover the budget deficit, refused to give his sanction to the law.[67] When the question of indemnifying owners of sold property came up, nobody suggested that Church goods might be included. Thus, compared to individual owners, the Church lost out twice.

Although the issue of indemnifying individual owners whose property had been sold off was raised during the First Restoration, the debates were cut short by the Hundred Days. In the Second Restoration, financial constraints excluded immediate indemnification. Although many vindictive émigrés now demanded full restitution, that solution was excluded by the Charter and by the King's realization that it would have brought about civil war. Whereas the Charter had merely guaranteed the property of the new owners, the government now made it a crime to question it. On October 31, 1815, parliament adopted a proposal to "punish for sedition all persons who spread or accredit alarming rumors concerning the inviolability of the so-called national properties or about the re-establishment of the tithe or of feudal dues." Although the law was directed against the liberal opposition, which wanted to keep alive the anxieties of the purchasers from which it drew political benefits, it was also severely criticized by the ultraroyalists.[68]

The biens nationaux were a festering wound. Their existence was viewed as doubly unjust: because of the injustice of the original confiscation and because of the artificially low prices at which they had been acquired (they had been paid for in devalued paper money). In addition, neighbors who had not had the same good luck as the purchasers were often envious. Because of their origin and because of political uncertainty about the future, their prices remained artificially low, creating problems for resale and mortgaging. The purchasers were in an anomalous situation: Although not wrongdoers, they were the beneficiaries of wrongdoing. Because of the hostility of the ultras, which the liberals had an interest in presenting as even more pervasive than it was, they lived in a state of permanent anxiety. They wanted "not only to enjoy their property in security and tranquillity, but with honor."[69] (A telling detail is that

[66] It was put forward later (ibid., p. 137 n. 3) just as it had been contemplated earlier by Napoleon (ibid., p. 44).
[67] Ibid., pp. 238–47.
[68] Ibid., p. 232.
[69] Ibid., p. 343.

until the end of the nineteenth century, archivists refused to communicate the names of purchasers to scholars in order to protect the honor of families that might be compromised by the acquisition of biens nationaux.)[70] Their psychology was complex, and even tortured. One historian says that "[t]here are some forms of remorse which become twisted and turn into hatred. The history of the Restoration can be summarized in the famous saying: 'Whoever has offended cannot forgive.'"[71] Commenting on this observation, another historian asserts that "it would be more correct to say that the purchaser, looked down upon and despised by the former owner, envied and ridiculed by his neighbor, retreated into a defiant isolation vis-à-vis the regime and, until 1830, gladly posed as a victim."[72]

The original owners had an obvious interest in being indemnified. The purchasers wanted to possess with honor and to enjoy the higher property values induced by destigmatization. The government favored indemnification, because it expected higher income from registration taxes on property sales when properties simultaneously rose in value and found more buyers. More importantly, it wanted to pacify the émigrés as well as the purchasers for whom unpacified owners represented a constant threat. Only the small liberal opposition had an interest in keeping the conflict alive.[73] It is not surprising, therefore, that the government took the initiative to indemnify the owners once the finances had been restored. Shortly before his death in 1824, Louis XVIII prepared indemnity legislation, which was implemented by his brother, Charles X, in 1825. It took the form of *le milliard des émigrés,* a billion francs to be distributed in the form of annuities among roughly twenty-five thousand returned émigrés or heirs of émigrés. Although the capitalized value of these annuities may have been of the same order of magnitude as what the state had received from the sale of the properties, the fact that they had usually been sold at artificially low prices implied that the owners got substantially less than the real value of what they had lost.

These procedures gave rise to a number of objections on the grounds of unfair discrimination. Many objected that it was arbitrary to compensate

[70] Ibid., p. 349.

[71] Gorce (1926), pp. 162–63.

[72] Gain (1928), vol. 1, p. 348.

[73] This is not quite accurate. "If the purchasers became reassured before the financial situation allowed the payment of the indemnity, it would lose one of its two raisons d'être; the émigrés therefore had an interest in maintaining the uncertainty, keeping the crisis alive, and pushing for the depreciation of biens nationaux by means of absurd campaigns" (ibid., p. 160).

for the loss of real property but not for the loss of personal property. To rebut this argument, one pamphleteer

> tried to justify the privilege accorded to the émigrés, the only victims of the Revolution who will be indemnified: in the first place, haven't they suffered more? Also, even if one does not recognize the rights of suffering [les droits du malheur], one may concede that there are some evils whose undoing matters more for the *common interest* and *public morality*; "who will deny, for instance that the disrespect and violation for landed property requires a prompt indemnification, because the whole society rests on the principle of its inviolability.... The community suffers much less from the violation of twenty pieces of movable property than from a single attack on landed property. I am not saying that there is nothing grand or noble in the possession of coins, or that gold is cosmopolitan, that money commands no patriotism; I am only saying that all the generous sentiments and all the beautiful and honorable affections that bind us to the land arise from landed property."[74]

This preterition is as transparent as the classical example of the genre, Cicero's *In Verrem*. The claim being made is clearly that "cosmopolitan" Jewish financiers who had seen their fortune confiscated during the Revolution had no moral claims to compensation. There is an added twist to this part of the story, in that the milliard des émigrés was funded by a scheme for converting annuities that was widely and to some extent correctly seen as discriminating against *rentiers*.[75] Not only were former owners of movable property excluded from compensation, but current owners of such property also had to fund those who were to be compensated. The idea of having the purchasers of biens nationaux fund the indemnity, either because they had paid too little for them in the first place or because they could afford to pay now that their property values would go up, came to nothing.[76]

The argument that compensation could be justified by suffering was a dangerous one, since it invited the question of who really suffered most under the Revolution. In the Vendée, where many had lost property in fighting against the Revolution, there was relatively little compensation. Rather than leaving their country and seeing their property confiscated, they stayed to fight and see their houses burn. Technically, therefore, many of them did not fall under the 1825 law. Although Louis XVIII had promised in 1818 that their day would come, it never did. To weaken the obvious moral credentials of these martyrs of the counterrevolution,

74 Summary and quotation in ibid., vol. 2, p. 12.

75 For a lucid exposition, see Sauvigny (1999), pp. 373–74.

76 Gain (1928), vol. 1, pp. 492–504.

defenders of the law drew a distinction between two kinds of suffering, productive and unproductive. "The State did not enrich itself by the ruin of other victims of the Revolution, whereas the treasury could use the proceeds from the sale of émigré property for public spending."[77] This argument would, however, have justified compensation for confiscated movable property. Hence, neither the argument from suffering nor the argument from productivity singled out real estate owners as uniquely worthy of compensation.

The *rapporteur* of the 1825 law to the Chamber of Deputies, M. de Martignac, tackled the problem of selectivity head-on. Wasn't it impossible, he asked rhetorically, to compensate all those who had been ruined and unjust to compensate only a few?[78]

> There is no doubt, he answered, that the reparations cannot match the destructions. The riches of France now that it has reestablished order and legitimacy would not suffice to compensate for the losses suffered by a country impoverished by anarchy and license.
>
> "If, however, among the evils wrought by the Revolution, there are some that justice singles out as the most serious and odious, and reason as the most fatal, and if there are some whose origin is an attack on the most sacred rights, and whose trace remains a persistent cause of divisions and hatred, should our inability to heal all evils prevent us from applying to some of them a remedy that is within our power?" The émigrés are privileged in their misery: they have lived through the same torments as others, and suffered like them from bankruptcy and war, but in addition they have been struck by the horrible force of confiscation.
>
> By its very nature, confiscation requires a reparation. It was not an *established punishment,* but an *exercise of vengeance,* which shook society to its foundations. "It is essential and in everybody's interest to set a memorable example to express that a great injustice will, sooner or later, receive a great reparation."[79]

The rapporteur of the parliamentary commission for the law, M. Pardessus, also asked who "would dare to pretend that the multitude of injustices that were carried out in the people's name dispenses with the need to repair any of them," and repeated that the confiscation "heaped up on the head of those who were affected and their family all the losses that have only been partially borne by the other citizens."[80] In the debates, Benjamin Constant argued for a radically different view: "The *rentiers* have suffered as much as, or more than, the honorable men one is now

[77] Ibid., p. 434; see also p. 487. For the factual and moral complexities of the issues, see also Gabory (1989), pp. 913–32.

[78] Gain (1928), vol. 1, p. 512.

[79] Summary and quotation from ibid., pp. 562–63.

[80] Ibid., vol. 1, p. 570.

trying to assist. They have not only been cut down [*réduits*], but have suffered the Terror, the military requisitions, and all the calamities that have come down upon France."[81] In this perspective, the émigrés were fortunate because they had been spared the storms that had passed over their country.

Were the compensations measures of legal justice or of grace?[82] On the former hypothesis, past entitlements are decisive. On the latter, present needs are more important. (As we have seen, the debate was further complicated by the frequent references to and comparisons of past *sufferings*.) In his report to the Chamber of Deputies, M. de Martignac took a firm stand in favor of viewing the measure as one of grace rather than justice, arguing that because of the long time that had passed and the uncertainty of the legal situation, the legal heirs could not appeal to any legitimate expectations to inherit: "The aim of the law is to assist the children or the closest relatives of the dispossessed."[83] Strictly speaking, of course, expectations have nothing to do with legal justice, which respects windfall gains no less than others. In some cases, however, present needs may seem more compelling than the fulfillment of legal duties that do not go together with legitimate expectations, especially when strict compliance with legal justice would be financially ruinous. As one speaker said, either the debt is due in justice and has to be fully repaid, which would "perhaps absorb the totality of the territorial capital of France," or it is not, in which case "it is only appropriate to allocate assistance."[84]

The 1825 law was adopted, in secret ballots, by 159 votes against 63 in the upper house, and with 221 against 130 in the lower house. It has been assessed that among the members of the upper house, about 150 had a direct personal interest in the matter, as dispossessed émigrés or as their heirs.[85] The implementation of the law was left to courts and administrative agencies, which carried out their enormous task with great

[81] Ibid., p. 582.

[82] Ibid., vol. 1, pp. 293, 371, 450, 482, 567, 573, 618; vol. 2, p. 255.

[83] Ibid., vol. 1, p. 567. The premise for the statement is a distinction between "the true family of the émigré" and "the representatives of the heirs, who would often be strangers to the former owner."

[84] Ibid., p. 371.

[85] Ibid., vol. 2, pp. 222–23. When Maréchal de Macdonald in 1814 made the first proposal to indemnify the former owners whose goods had been sold off, malicious critics argued that he was motivated by the desire to enhance the value of an émigré property he had acquired. Having tried in vain to purchase the ratification of the sale by the former owner, the Duc de Broglie, he now resorted to a "general measure" to achieve the same interested goal (ibid., vol. 1, p. 190).

conscientiousness. Their impartiality and willingness to respect the letter of the law, rather than any supposed "émigré spirit," can be brought out by two examples. Even common criminals benefited from the legislation if they had been condemned by revolutionary tribunals rather than by ordinary courts.[86] Two sisters of St. Just, the embodiment of the Terror, received a small indemnity.[87]

The matter did not end with the vote. The indemnification was partially canceled after the July Revolution of 1830, in spite of the fact that Louis Philippe (the former Duc d'Orléans) had been one of its main beneficiaries. In the 1848 Revolution, one of the demands of the radicals was for the repayment of the milliards des émigrés – to confiscate the 1825 compensation for the 1792 confiscation! In 1851, two deputies even proposed confiscation with payment of accrued interest.[88] Although these proposals came to nothing, the fact that they were made and had a central place on the radical platform is revelatory of how some segments of the population viewed the 1789 Revolution. Other segments, to be sure, viewed it very differently. It is an extraordinary fact that in many parts of France, the opprobrium attached to the biens nationaux persisted into the twentieth century. Georges Lefebvre reports that "a little before the [First World] war, in Fromelles, a peasant pointed out to me the heirs of purchasers [of biens nationaux] as possessors of stolen goods, which even today he would not buy."[89] In 1923, Emile Gabory could write about the Vendée that "the question of the nationally sold properties still prevents cordial relations among certain families."[90]

V. SUMMARY

As in the previous chapter, I conclude by summarizing aspects of the narrative in a more conceptual form.

The two Restorations were negotiated transitions, carried out under the auspices of the Allied powers. The latter also supervised transitional justice, partly (in 1814) by forcing the incoming Bourbons to pull their punches, partly (in 1815) by insisting on a purge of supporters of Napoleon.

The Napoleonic senators who were entrusted with the task of carrying out the transition in 1814 acted on self-serving motives when they insisted on an amnesty

[86] Ibid., vol. 2, pp. 114–15.
[87] Ibid., p. 231.
[88] Ibid., p. 382.
[89] Lefebvre (1924), p. 468 n. 2.
[90] Gabory (1989), p. 1063.

for past political acts and opinions, the abolition of confiscation as a mode of punishment, and the inviolability of properties that had been confiscated under the Revolution and sold off to private individuals. On the first two counts, their wishes probably coincided with Louis XVIII's desire for social peace and reconciliation. On the last count, only the support of Tsar Alexander's bayonets enabled the senators to get their way.

Self-interest may also have motivated some of those who proposed or voted for indemnification of the former owners of nationalized property. Once restitution had been excluded, former owners clearly had an interest in compensation. Those who had purchased their property had a convergent interest, as indemnification would lift the uncertainty and suspicion surrounding their holdings and thus enhance their value. Only the liberals had an opposing interest, since they depended on (and promoted) the anxieties of the purchasers.

At various times, the following reparative measures were proposed: (i) the solution that was finally adopted, namely, to indemnify the original owners with public funds and leave the confiscated properties in the hands of the new owners; (ii) the same as (i), except that the indemnification would be funded by the new owners; (iii) the proposal to return confiscated properties directly to the old owners; (iv) the same as (iii), with the additional measure of compensating the new owners.

Many aspects of the reparation scheme were perceived as morally arbitrary. (i) Those whose properties had not been sold off got them back, whereas others merely obtained financial compensation. (ii) Confiscated church properties were not returned, even when they had not been sold off. (iii) Compensation covered only the confiscation of *real* property, not of personal property. (iv) Compensation covered only the *confiscation* of real property, not the destruction of real property.

The various reparation schemes were defended by a number of arguments. (i) For most émigrés, reparation was strictly a matter of entitlement. (ii) For some of them, restitution of their property or having indemnification funded by the purchasers was also a punitive measure toward the latter. (iii) To justify differential treatment of different groups of victims of the Revolution, it was argued that priority should be given to those who had suffered the most. (iv) Some also argued that priority should be based on present need, rather than on entitlements or past sufferings. (v) Many argued that priority should be given to the repair of wrongdoings from which the state had benefited, thus excluding compensation for destroyed property.

On June 28, 1815, Louis XVIII declared that he would delegate retributive measures to parliament. Under pressure from the Allies and the émigrés, he was nevertheless forced to take immediate but limited measures on July 24. When the elections, to his surprise and dismay, returned an ultraroyalist Chamber of Deputies, they forced him to take the further step of proscribing all the *régicides relaps,* and nearly succeeded in imposing even more radical measures. Among the émigrés, the fury in 1815 against those who had joined Napoleon during the Hundred Days was stronger than the demand in 1814 for punishment of the regicides from 1793.

The government carried out vast purges in the public administration. Napoleon's return had been much facilitated by the fact that many of his followers had been left in place, and the government did not want to make the same mistake a second time.

In the "white terror" of the summer of 1815, several hundred individuals were killed and many more mistreated in various ways. For a while, Louis XVIII lost control over the country, as his nephew established a rival administration in the South.

3

The Larger Universe of Cases

I. INTRODUCTION

In this chapter I discuss some thirty-odd further cases of transitional justice. With three exceptions, they all took place in transitions to democracy in the twentieth century.[1] The list of cases is not complete, notably because of the omission of recent and ongoing Asian processes (Cambodia, East Timor, and South Korea). Also, some factual statements in the text may need to be corrected and updated in the light of continuous developments.[2] In future studies of the topic, the unfolding process of transitional justice in Iraq may warrant an extensive discussion that I cannot offer here. I believe, however, that together with the two previous chapters, the cases I do consider provide sufficient material for the conceptual and causal analyses in Part II.

There are no important episodes of transitional justice in new democracies between the Athenian episodes and the mid–twentieth

[1] The three volumes of Kritz (1995) provide fundamental, even if incomplete, source material. Collections of case studies include Herz (1982b), Henke and Woller (1991), Roth-Arriaza (1995), McAdams (1997), Larsen (1998), Deák, Gross, and Judt (2000), and Elster (in press). The most comprehensive country studies (in languages I read) are of France (Novick 1968), Belgium (Huyse and Dhondt 1993), Denmark (in the exceptionally rich study by Tamm 1984), Italy (Woller 1996), and the ex-GDR (Quint 1997). The last is one of the very few books that cover all three main aspects of transitional justice: trials, purges, and compensation. Other outstanding studies that are extensively cited in the present volume are Müller (1991), Sa'adah (1998), Pross (1998), McAdams (2001), Frei (2002), and Bancaud (2002).

[2] The fortnightly newsletter published by the International Center for Transitional Justice (http://www.ictj.org/) provides constant updates.

century.[3] Contrary to appearances, perhaps, the French Revolution did not punish the former elites for past wrongdoings, nor compensate the peasantry for what they had suffered. The charges laid against the aristocrats during the Terror were based on what they had done *after* the Revolution, namely, conspiring with foreign countries and planning an invasion of France. It is also inaccurate to say[4] that the abolition of feudal dues was a "reparation" of past injustice. The decrees of August 4, 1789, aimed at eliminating injustice for the future, without any additional compensation for past injustice. To the extent that the Revolution is relevant for transitional justice, it is only through the later attempts to punish its agents and undo its actions.

One might ask whether the German "transition to democracy" after World War I should be included in the universe of cases. Under pressure from the Allies, the new democratic Germany tried forty-five officers for war crimes, with minimal results.[5] There were no purges in the public sector.[6] Although there were extensive reparations, these did not, for the most part, take the form of compensation to individual victims. Belgian victims of German atrocities were not compensated, for instance. One must question, moreover, the sincerity of the German conversion to democracy. According to Gordon Craig, the Germans "adopted democracy as a means of persuading the Allies to grant Germany lighter peace terms, and when the victorious powers in Paris refused to oblige, they reverted to their true sentiments with a vengeance."[7] In fact, not just democracy but even the decentralized form of government may have been adopted for these strategic reasons.[8] As there was no serious effort to carry out either transitional justice or a transition to democracy in a very meaningful sense, I shall not include the creation of the Weimar Republic among my cases here. I shall nevertheless have occasion to discuss the transition

[3] There was limited transitional justice in the Second Spanish Republic of 1931 (Payne 1993, pp. 40–42).

[4] As does Diesbach (1998), p. 35.

[5] Horne and Kramer (2001), pp. 340–55; Bass (2001), Chap. 3.

[6] Craig (1981), p. 419.

[7] Ibid., p. 415. Conversely, after the fall of France in the summer of 1940, the Pétain government may have thought that the country could obtain more favorable terms of peace if it adopted a semidictatorial regime (Paxton 1997, pp. 52–53, 195).

[8] Expounding the ideas of Max Weber, who was drawn into work on the constitution while also serving as an expert adviser to the German delegation at Versailles, Mommsen (1984), p. 335, writes that "[t]o start with a radically unitarist constitution was in Weber's view inexpedient from the point of view of foreign policy. He feared that it would elicit distrust with the Entente governments [France and Britain] and therefore might well move them to impose even harsher peace conditions."

after 1918, in light of its importance as a negative model for transitional justice after 1945.

In the rest of the chapter I proceed as follows. Section II presents a further case of restoration of monarchy (England 1660) and two cases of transition to independence (the United States in 1783 and Algeria in 1962). The subsequent sections III through VII consider five geographical and chronological clusters of transition to democracy in the twentieth century: Western Europe and Japan after 1945, Southern Europe around 1975, Latin America in the 1980s, Eastern Europe after 1989, and Africa from 1979 to 1994. Section VIII proposes some classifications of the case studies, based on the endogenous or exogenous nature of the pre-transitional regime and of transitional justice, the duration of the pre-transitional regime, and the duration of transitional justice.

II. RESTORATION OF MONARCHY AND TRANSITION TO INDEPENDENCE

The restoration of the French monarchy that I discussed in Chapter 2 had a close English predecessor. Just as the execution of Charles I in 1649 parallels that of Louis XVI in 1793, there are similarities between the measures of retribution and reparation carried out after the restoration of the monarchies. Important differences also emerge.

In the Declaration of Breda dated April 4, 1660 – the analogue of the Cambrai Proclamation on June 28, 1815, by Louis XVIII – the future Charles II provided assurances for those who thought they might have something to fear from the restoration of monarchy. "Excepting only such persons as shall hereafter be excepted by parliament," he promised that "no crime whatsoever committed against us or our royal father before the publication of this shall ever rise in judgment or be brought in question against any of them, to the least endamagement of them either in their lives, liberties or estates." He went on to say that

> because, in the continued distractions of so many years and so many and great revolutions, many grants and purchases of estates have been made, to and by many officers, soldiers and others, who are now possessed of the same, and who may be liable to actions at law upon several titles, we are likewise willing that all such differences, and all things relating to such grants, sales and purchases, shall be determined in parliament, which can best provide for the just satisfaction of all men who are concerned.

The day after Charles II was declared King, a Bill of Oblivion and Indemnity was introduced in parliament to make good the promises of the

Breda Declaration.[9] General Monck, who introduced the Bill, proposed that only five persons be excepted from the general amnesty, reflecting the King's desire for minimal retribution. Over the next months the Lords and Commons debated the exceptions, "the one House safeguarding those the other would penalize."[10] In the end, there were four categories of exception. Thirty-three regicides, out of more than sixty who had been considered at various stages, were designated for execution. A further nineteen were imprisoned under threat of execution. Seven were subject to "Pains, Penalties, and Forfeitures (not extending to Life)." Finally, twenty persons were disqualified from holding public office. While these debates were going on, a royal proclamation encouraged the regicides to surrender "under Pain of being excepted from any Pardon or Indemnity both for their respective Lives and Estates." Those concerned were understandably reluctant to do so, however, as "the continuing debates in the two Houses, and the unpredictability of their tempers, offered no assurances that surrender would be to their advantage. The Commons held that those who gave themselves up should be shown mercy; the Lords disagreed."[11] The regicides had no reason to believe that the King could *deliver* on his implicit promise of immunity, since that matter was to be decided by parliament.

The Breda Declaration had also referred "all things relating to such grants, sales and purchases" to parliament. In practice, the matter was so complex that much of it had to be further relegated to the courts.[12] Three kinds of property had been confiscated during the Interregnum: crown land, church land, and land belonging to individual supporters of Charles I. Unlike what happened in the French Revolution, the property of the last group had not been taken outright, but confiscated if they were unwilling or unable to pay the fines imposed on them for their "delinquency" (i.e., support of Charles I). Needless to say, these supporters now expected to be rewarded for their loyalty. At the same time, those who had bought their properties also had legitimate expectations, since while in exile, "Charles appears to have assumed that a full restoration of land would follow his return. In order to encourage his potential friends, he [promised] compensation to all who made a timely show of loyalty to him for what they might lose by such a Restoration."[13] Purchasers of crown and church

[9] The following draws on Keeble (2002).

[10] Ibid., p. 72.

[11] Ibid., p. 74.

[12] The following draws on Thirsk (1954). The article contains a wealth of suggestive information, only a small part of which is sampled here.

[13] Ibid., pp. 315–16.

lands received fair compensation. Former and new owners of privately held land were left to fight it out in the courts: "Royalists regained their land in all but exceptional circumstances,"[14] such as when "royalists had prejudiced their titles by confirming [at a price] sales to purchasers during the Interregnum."[15] Also, those who had sold land to pay their fines did not get it back. When land was restituted, those who had bought it were sometimes compensated in the form of favorable leases, but "it is impossible to tell" how often this happened.[16] If the property had changed hands more than once, the secondhand buyers who were forced to return it were able to sue the first purchasers for compensation and sometimes succeeded, sometimes not.

When countries under colonial rule undertake and succeed in a war of independence, they usually target indigenous collaborators with the colonial power for punishment. After the end of the hostilities, that power may or may not try to ease the situation of their former allies. As examples, I shall briefly consider the American and Algerian wars of independence. In the American war, the indigenous collaborators were the loyalists or "Tories"; in Algeria, the "harkis." In each case, they amounted to about 15 percent of the population, that is, substantially more than the proportion of collaborators with the enemy in German-occupied countries in World War II. Although loyalists and harkis were assured protection by the respective peace treaties, these were poorly observed in America (at least before 1787) and ignored in Algeria. Although these cases differ in many ways from the other episodes discussed in this book, they throw light on psychological and political mechanisms that are also at work in the other instances.

In these protracted civil wars, neutrality was not an option. In 1954, the very first tract issued by the Algerian Liberation Front (FLN) stated: "To stay away from [*se désintéresser de*] the struggle is a crime."[17] The French military as well as the insurgents tried to force the population to take sides. The French might initiate contact with an uncommitted Algerian, expecting that this would compromise him so much in the eyes of the FLN that the only safe course was to become a harki under French protection.[18] The FLN would deliberately single out Algerian or French moderates for

[14] Ibid., p. 323.

[15] Ibid., p. 324.

[16] Ibid., p. 327.

[17] Hamoumou (1993), pp. 133–34. Cp. the statement cited in Chap. 4, that "the silence of [Jean] Giono [during the German occupation of France] was in itself a crime."

[18] Ibid., p. 165.

assassination.[19] In America, too, "[i]ndifference and neutrality were [not] tenable positions."[20] After the first years of the war,

> [t]o become the object of persecution, it was no longer necessary that an address or protest be signed or a pamphlet written or a violent sentiment uttered against the revolutionary government. If the position or religious creed, or relationship of a person seemed in any way to indicate Tory sympathy, he must clearly and publicly demonstrate his allegiance to the popular cause.[21]

Those who did not were liable to social ostracism and, in many cases, tarring and feathering.[22] After the victories at Trenton and Princeton, Washington "commanded all persons who had accepted Lord Howe's recent offer of protection, either to retire within the British lines or take an oath of allegiance to the United States."[23] In fact, "military commanders on either side issued proclamations . . . urging or demanding an oath."[24]

The transitions to independence were embodied in peace treaties. The Anglo-American treaty of 1783 states:

> It is agreed that Congress shall earnestly recommend it to the legislatures of the respective states to provide for the restitution of all estates, rights, and properties, which have been confiscated belonging to real British subjects; and also of the estates, rights, and properties of persons resident in districts in the possession on his Majesty's arms and who have not borne arms against the said United States. And that persons of any other description shall have free liberty to go to any part or parts of any of the thirteen United States and therein to remain twelve months unmolested in their endeavors to obtain the restitution of such of their estates, rights, and properties as may have been confiscated; and that Congress shall also earnestly recommend to the several states a reconsideration and revision of all acts or laws regarding the premises, so as to render the said laws or acts perfectly consistent not only with justice and equity but with that spirit of conciliation which on the return of the blessings of peace should universally prevail. And that Congress shall also earnestly recommend to the several states that the estates, rights, and properties, of such last mentioned persons shall be restored to them, they refunding to any persons who may be now in possession the bona fide price (where any has been given) which such persons may have paid on purchasing any of the said lands, rights, or properties since the confiscation.

These were compromise formulations, the British having wanted more than mere recommendations. Most states were slow to follow them, and

[19] Ibid., pp. 181–82.
[20] Van Tyne (2001), p. 76.
[21] Ibid., p. 61.
[22] Ibid., pp. 61, 241, 295.
[23] Ibid., p. 129.
[24] Ibid, p. 141.

some continued to enact new anti-Loyalist measures. In Massachusetts, "bills for amnesty and repeal of all laws contrary to the treaty were introduced seven times from 1784 to 1785, [but] they invariably died in debate or were tabled."[25] In New York, the legislature passed a law in 1784 that "levied a tax on areas of the state within British lines during the war. The act's preamble argued that all inhabitants enjoyed 'the blessing derived from freedom and independence,' but not everyone had 'sustained [the] many and heavy burdens and expenses in prosecuting the late war.'"[26] Beginning in 1785, however,

> Alexander Hamilton in New York, Benjamin Rush in Pennsylvania and Aedanus Burke in South Carolina each mounted public campaigns to restore property and political rights to most former loyalists. They argued that public vengeance was a self-inflicted wound on the American body politic, that a fragile republican polity would ill-afford the corrosive effects of such recriminations and retribution. By 1787 most states, needing the commercial skills of departed loyalist merchants, began repealing anti-Tory legislation.[27]

From 1783 to 1789, a British commission "heard 3,225 claims for property and income lost on account of claimants' loyalty to the Crown during the Revolution, and ... granted compensation to 2,291 claimants. ... The compensation of more than three million pounds amounted to 37 per cent of the successful claimants' estimates of their losses."[28]

The 1962 Evian agreement said that

> [n]o one shall be the object of police measures or legal measures, disciplinary sanctions or any kind of discrimination on grounds of opinions that were expressed on the occasion of events in Algeria that occurred before the date of the referendum on self-determination, or for acts committed on the occasion of the same events before the day of the proclamation of a cease-fire. No Algerian can be forced to leave Algerian territory, nor be prevented from leaving it.

The agreement, which did not include any effective guarantees for the safety of harkis, was not respected.[29] The number of harkis massacred remains unknown, but estimates vary from 10,000 to 150,000.[30] Among the motives cited for the killings are the spontaneous desire for vengeance in the population, the desire of late recruits to the movement to show

[25] Maas (1994), p. 68.

[26] Tiedemann (1994), p. 80.

[27] Calhoon (1991), pp. 258–59.

[28] Ibid., p. 259.

[29] As Monika Nalepa points out to me, it might have been better for the harkis if the agreement had included legal procedures for trying them.

[30] Pervillé (2002), pp. 243–45.

their patriotism,[31] and a tendency for the different fractions of the FLN to overbid each other in vindictiveness.[32] The French government did nothing to stop the killings, and very little to accommodate harkis who desired to leave the country for France. In 1783, by contrast, between 60,000 and 80,000 American loyalists were able to leave for other parts of British America.[33]

III. WESTERN EUROPE AND JAPAN

The modern history of justice after transitions to democracy begins essentially with the defeat of Germany, Italy, and Japan in 1945. In Germany, the processes of transitional justice began immediately after the war and continue into the present.[34] Of the twenty-two Nazi officials tried by the four-power International Military Tribunal in Nuremberg, three were acquitted, seven were sentenced to prison, and the others received the death penalty. Other trials were conducted separately by the four powers in their occupational zones. American military tribunals convicted 1,814 German war criminals (450 received death sentences), British tribunals 1,085 (240 death sentences), French 2,107 (104 death sentences). About half of the death sentences were commuted. Later, the Germans themselves took over the task of trying crimes from the Nazi period: "In 1996 the federal minister of justice... reported that cases against 5,570 individuals accused of crimes related to National Socialist rule were still pending. The minister reported further than 106,178 individual cases had been investigated since 1945, resulting in 6,494 unreversed convictions."[35]

A vast purge process (denazification) was also set in motion, but scaled down when it turned out to be impracticable. This process, too, was turned over to the Germans themselves, who showed little interest in coming to terms with their past. By February 1947, the German tribunals had processed only slightly more than half of the 11,674,152 completed screening questionnaires (*Fragebogen*). Of these 6 million individuals, only 168,696 had been brought before a tribunal. Of these, only 339 had been classified as major offenders, 3,612 as offenders, and 13,708 as lesser offenders. The rest were either classified as "fellow travelers" (*Mitläufer*)

[31] Hamoumou (1993), p. 250.
[32] Pervillé (2002), pp. 218–20, favors this explanation.
[33] Calhoon (1991), p. 259; Moore (1984).
[34] For an overview, see Cohen (in press).
[35] Sa'adah (1998), p. 175.

or exonerated. A total of 2,018 had been sentenced to a period of internment. De facto, denazification turned into a "machine for political rehabilitation."[36] The failure of denazification is perhaps best seen in the total absence of a purge of the West German judiciary system inherited en bloc from the Nazi period.[37]

Legislation to compensate the victims of the Nazi regime was also adopted, first under Allied auspices and then by the West German parliament.[38] The Federal Restitution Law of 1956 (further discussed in Chapter 6) created an elaborate compensation scheme for victims of the Nazi regime. By 1965, a total of 3 million claims had been processed, of which roughly two-thirds were from non-German nationals.[39] By 1986, a total of 77 billion DM had been paid out.[40] Claims by slave laborers and forced laborers, who did not fall under this law, met initially with little success.[41] In the 1990s, however, German firms and the German government contributed to an 8 billion DM fund for these victims.[42] West Germany also paid 3 billion DM in reparations to Israel.[43]

In the Soviet occupational zone, things worked out differently. Soviet Directive 201 from August 1947 demanded the prosecution, among others, of those who "by spreading tendentious rumors have put the peace of the German people or of the world in danger," a phrase that was intended and understood as a signal opening for the punishment of anti-Communists.[44] (For reciprocal reasons, Communists were denied the benefits of compensation legislation in West Germany.) According to official sources, 520,000 former Nazi Party members were dismissed from their jobs in the public sector.[45] The actual number is probably smaller, but there is no doubt that these purges were more extensive than those in the other occupational zones.

Transitional justice in Italy began earlier and ended earlier than in any other country engaged on either side in World War II. After the fall of Mussolini in July 1943, the Badoglio government passed a first purge law on December 28 of that year. The centerpiece of the purge legislation

36 Frei (2002), p. 38.
37 Müller (1991); Friedrich (1998).
38 Pross (1998).
39 Pross (1998), Appendix B, Table 3.
40 Ibid., Table 8.
41 Ferencz (2002).
42 Eizenstat (2003), p. 264.
43 Sagi (1986).
44 Welsh (1991), p. 93.
45 Ibid., p. 95.

was the Law of July 27, 1944, followed by the "Nenni law" adopted on November 14, 1945, and the amnesty law of June 22, 1946. The process was complicated by the existence of two successive regimes, the fascist regime that lasted from 1922 to 1943 and the German puppet republic of Salò that was established in northern Italy after Mussolini's fall and was incomparably more savage than the former. The Law of July 27, 1944, explicitly stated that fighting against Salò was an extenuating circumstance for complicity in fascist crimes; the article "created an obvious escape clause that existed only to be utilized; and it was."[46] The matter is further complicated by the fact that some areas were subject to purges and trials three times in succession, as the lines of military conflict moved north: first by the resistance movement, then by the Allied military government, and finally by the Italian government.[47] There was extensive "wild justice," amounting to about ten to twelve thousand lawless killings by partisans.[48] The coalitional politics of the major parties made for inconsistent policies. As Minister of Justice, the Communist leader Togliatti enacted amnesty legislation as part of his attempt to win over middle-class and agrarian groups, only to repudiate the law when his party left the government.[49] Although the law exempted especially atrocious crimes from the amnesty, the wording was so vague that the court of appeal could and did acquit persons who had committed horrible acts on the grounds that others had done things that were even worse.[50]

In Japan, as in Germany, there were several sets of proceedings. The institution corresponding to the Nuremberg Court was the International Military Tribunal of the Far East in Tokyo.[51] Comprised of justices from eleven allied nations, it judged twenty-eight high-ranking Japanese officials. In contrast to Nuremberg, there were no acquittals. In addition, each of the Allies created its own military tribunal to judge individual atrocities committed against their personnel. General MacArthur, for instance, established a War Crimes Branch of the American Army in Yokohama that tried more than 1,000 suspects, of whom 200 were acquitted, while 124

[46] Domenico (1991), p. 77.
[47] Woller (1996), pp. 145–89.
[48] Ibid., p. 280.
[49] Ibid., p. 385.
[50] Ibid., pp. 388–89.
[51] For comparisons between Nuremberg and Tokyo, see Cohen (1999) and Dower (1999), pp. 454–61.

were sentenced to hang and 622 to life imprisonment.[52] As this tribunal was under American jurisdiction, the sentences could be and in some cases were appealed to the U.S. Supreme Court. Both the Tokyo and the Yokohama courts have been severely criticized for violations of due process and for being essentially a form of victors' justice.[53] Some 200,000 individuals, mostly former officers, were prohibited, usually on a provisional basis, from holding public office.[54] With the emergence of the Cold War, these individuals were "gradually 'depurged,' while on the other side of the coin the radical left was subjected to the 'Red' purges."[55]

Transitional justice was also carried out in the countries that had been under German occupation during the war (Belgium, Denmark, France, Holland, Norway) or had otherwise collaborated with Germany (Austria, Hungary).[56] Except for France, where some 10,000 lawless killings took place,[57] there was little wild or private justice. There was a great deal of variation in the modalities and the scope of transitional justice in these countries. One simple statistic is the proportion of the population that suffered some kind of legal punishment, including the loss of civil rights:[58]

Austria	Belgium	Denmark	France	Holland	Hungary	Norway
0.2%	1.2%	0.3%	0.25%	1%	0.3%	2%

The higher numbers for Belgium, Holland, and Norway are due in part to the fact that in these countries, members of Nazi organizations were automatically considered guilty. In general, fewer women than men were

52 Harries and Harries (1987), p. 101.

53 For Tokyo, see Minear (2001); for Yokohama, see Taylor (1981).

54 Dower (1999), p. 82.

55 Ibid., pp. 525–26; Tiedemann (1982), p. 201.

56 In Greece, transitional justice was soon eclipsed by the civil war (Paschis and Papadimitriou 1998).

57 This is a highly contested and politicized number. For different sides of the debate, see Amouroux (1999), Chap. 2 and Rousso (2001). A detailed account by a nonprofessional historian is in Bourdrel (1988, 1991). As in Italy, many of these killings took place in the context of an ongoing war, and may have served military rather than (or as well as) retributive purposes. Also, some may have been motivated by private malice and carried out under the cover of the resistance.

58 The following tables are based on Deák in press (Austria), Huyse and Dhondt 1993 (Belgium), Tamm 1984 (Denmark), Rousso 2001 (France), Mason 1952 (Holland), Karsai 2000 (Hungary), and Justis-og politidepartementet 1962 (Norway). For reasons related to imperfect data collection and ambiguous definitions, the numbers are only approximate.

sentenced.[59] Another statistic, virtually uncorrelated with the first, is the number (per million of population) of executed death sentences:

Austria	Belgium	Denmark	France	Holland	Hungary	Norway
4	30	11	39	4	16	10

Some of these countries adopted a novel charge, "national indignity," a form of low-grade treason punished by "national degradation," that is, the loss of civil and political rights. In France,[60] the disqualifications included loss of the right to vote and to hold elective office; a ban on public employment; exclusion from leading functions in semipublic corporations, banks as well as newspapers and radio; and exclusion from the legal and teaching professions. As a result of pressure from the Communist party, the law on national degradation also allowed for the confiscation of the past *and future* property of the concerned individual. In Belgium, the disqualifications included loss of political rights, but also of the right to exercise the professions of doctor, lawyer, priest, journalist, or teacher, as well as exclusion from leading functions in any organization whatsoever.[61] These unusually severe Belgian measures amounted to a kind of "civic death."[62]

In France and Belgium, the loss of civil rights could occur by two mechanisms: It could be imposed directly or be the consequence of convictions in a criminal trial. In Italy and Holland, only the first mechanism was used. When the first postfascist Badoglio government adopted a law on "punishment of fascist crimes and behaviors" on June 1, 1944, it created a new category of the "excluded," those who had "violated the basic principles of public and private law, equity and decency." Sanctions included the loss of the right to work in certain professions and, in severe

59 In Denmark, 5% (Tamm 1984, pp. 776–77); in Belgium, 12% (Huyse and Dhondt 1993, p. 205); in Norway, 35% (Justis-og Politidepartementet 1962, p. 110); in Holland, 25% (Rominj and Hirschfeld 1991, p. 289). The high Norwegian percentage may be due to the fact that almost half the sentences took the form of plea-bargained fines by passive party members. The Dutch data are percentages of those interned, not of those convicted. I have not found national data for the other countries. Amouroux (1999), p. 90, refers to several *départements* in which a majority of the indicted were women, but does not give rates of conviction. In Denmark, women represented 30% of the convicted informers (Tamm 1984, p. 273). In France, women were a substantial majority among the convicted informers in two *départements* (Burrin 1995, p. 215). In one Danish case, a death sentence was commuted, against the wishes of the convicted woman, to spare the feelings of the members of the executing platoon (Tamm 1984, p. 355).

60 For a full discussion, see Simonin (2003).

61 Huyse and Dhondt (1993), pp. 30–33.

62 Ibid., p. 30.

cases, forced labor.[63] In Holland, courts could deprive collaborators of the right to vote and to be elected, to serve in the armed forces, to hold government positions, and to exercise certain occupations. As a separate measure, loss of citizenship and hence of property was imposed on 40,000 Dutch men and, as an automatic consequence, on their wives.[64]

In Norway and Denmark, only the second mechanism was used. The Norwegian legislation was draconian, including the loss of the right to own real estate, but the practice was generally lenient.[65] In Denmark, those convicted of collaboration with the Germans lost their right to vote and to be elected, to perform military service, to work in the public service, to work as lawyer or doctor or in any other accredited occupation, to work as teacher or priest, and to have any administrative or financial involvement with the movie, theater, or newspaper business.[66] Further variations arose in the duration of disqualifications, ranging from five years to life, and in whether they could be applied separately or only en bloc.

In all these countries, there were also dismissals in the public sector. Exact numbers are hard to come by. In France, about 2 percent of the 1 million to 1.5 million public functionaries were sanctioned, about half by dismissal.[67] Overall, Denmark seems to have been the most lenient and Belgium the most severe country in this respect. In France, Belgium, and Norway, these sanctions were at the lowest end of a *cascade of punishments*. Punishment at a higher level entailed punishment at lower levels, but the latter could also occur in the absence of the former. Moreover, exclusion from professional organizations could be the effect or, more surprisingly, the cause of other sanctions. Thus in Belgium, those who had been excluded from their professional associations were automatically deprived of certain rights for their lifetime.[68] Conversely, the punishment of national degradation included a ban on membership in professional associations.[69] In these countries, taken together, one observed all the links set out in Figure 3.1.

[63] Woller (1996), p. 123. The law was superseded by the Bonomi government's law of July 26, 1944.

[64] Mason (1952), pp. 64–68.

[65] Justis-og Politidepartementet (1962), pp. 426–29.

[66] Kritz (1995), vol. 3, p. 377.

[67] Rousso (2001), pp. 532–33.

[68] Huyse and Dhondt (1993), p. 54.

[69] Ibid., p. 30.

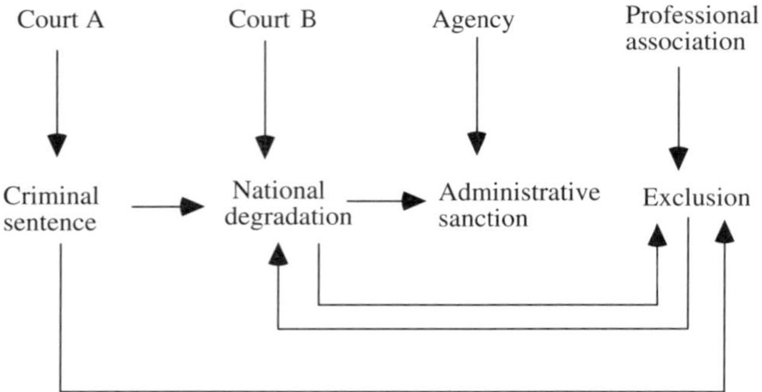

FIGURE 3.1

Measures of restitution and compensation were also undertaken. In France and Norway, public commissions have evaluated the economic losses imposed upon Jews in these countries, and the extent to which they were matched by reparations after the war. In France, the compensation for expropriated firms to Jews and their heirs that was made immediately after the war turned out to have been surprisingly adequate. Of the confiscated properties, 75 percent were restituted, representing 90–95 percent of the value of the total.[70] In Norway, the majority members of the commission estimated restitution and compensation to 60 percent of the losses.[71] In Austria, two historians discovered in 2000 that "[o]f the 34,780 Jewish businesses registered with the Nazis in 1938, only 4,300, almost all large and valuable enterprises, were Aryanized and, after the war, either returned or compensated for to their owners. The great bulk, some 30,000 small businesses, mostly shops, had been completely destroyed with no compensation ever having been paid."[72]

IV. SOUTHERN EUROPE

The next cluster of transitions to democracy occurred in the mid-1970s, with the fall of the dictatorships in Portugal, Greece, and Spain. Whereas the 1945 transitions all stemmed from the same cause, the end of World War II, the temporal coincidence of these South European transitions seems to have been an accident. In Portugal, the coup orchestrated by junior and midrank officers on April 25, 1974, set in motion a zigzag

70 Prost, Skoutelsky, and Etienne (2000), p. 173.
71 NOU (1997), p. 62.
72 Eizenstat (2003), p. 302.

course of purges and counterpurges.[73] As in Italy in 1944–45, agents of the fascist regime and members of the economic elite were indiscriminately targeted for exile, purges, and jail. As in France in 1945, transitional justice and nationalization went hand in hand. A few years later, most of the purges were undone by new legislation. In 1997, parliament passed a law compensating opponents of the fascist regime for their years in exile or underground.[74]

After the fall of the Greek military regime in July 1974, the incoming Karamanlis government

> quickly implemented a program of 'dejuntaification.' By one account, [Karamanlis] dismissed or replaced over 100, 000 people in the military, in government down to the local level, and in state organizations.... Within six months, criminal proceedings were initiated against more than one hundred former officials for participation in the 1967 Polytechnic incident [when thousands of students were arrested and many killed or injured], or torture of detainees. The torture trials of the military police gained the most public attention; by December 1976, the Greek government stated that more than 400 such trials had taken place across the country.[75]

An important feature of these trials is that they were "prompted by the cumulative pressure of civil suits brought by several former prisoners against their torturers in the absence of public prosecution."[76] The ambiguous course of justice is also shown by the fact that "no compensation was given to the victims of torturers, although employees of the state who had been dismissed by the junta were reinstated where possible or had their pensions updated or restored."[77]

The Spanish case is unique among transitions to democracy, in that there was a deliberate and consensual decision to abstain from transitional justice. In July 1976, the government declared a partial amnesty that freed approximately four hundred political prisoners. Next, "[t]he Amnesty Law of October 1977, one of the first political measures approved by the new democratic government with the support of a parliamentary majority, achieved two things. First, most political prisoners were released, including persons accused of blood crimes. Second, a 'full stop' was approved to prevent the trial of members of the outgoing regime." The law "allowed civil servants to recover their jobs and pensions, but

[73] Pinto (1998).
[74] Pinto (2001), p. 87.
[75] Editorial summary in Kritz (1995), vol. 2, p. 242.
[76] Psomiades (1982), p. 264.
[77] Ibid., p. 265.

did not indemnify either military officers or civil servants for salaries lost after being fired from their jobs."[78] The archives of the secret police were sealed (why not burned?). The law was part of a broader transitional pact, which also included the legalization of the Communist Party and the consensual adoption of a new constitution. Although sometimes used as a model, by members of the Hungarian opposition[79] or by the leaders of Solidarity in Poland,[80] this consensual decision to ignore the past has in fact had no direct imitators. Both in Hungary and Poland, lustration procedures were set in place that were hardly compatible with the Spanish model. In fact, the Spanish "disremembering" may itself be coming to an end. In 2002, claims for reparation were "being prepared on behalf of over 250,000 Spanish Republican prisoners employed as forced laborers" during the Civil War.[81]

V. LATIN AMERICA

The 1980s saw transitions to democracy in many Latin American countries. These transitions were mostly negotiated by outgoing military regimes, which tried, often successfully, to ensure immunity for themselves. Some of the new democracies established truth commissions that would identify the victims, usually without naming the wrongdoers. Some countries undertook compensation of the victims based on the information produced by these commissions. In several countries the situation is still fluid, and amnesties may well be overturned or circumvented.

Argentina is one of two countries in the region where officers were prosecuted, convicted, and eventually sent to jail. Following the defeat in the Falklands War, the demoralized military regime organized free presidential elections in 1983. To achieve his twin aims of holding the military responsible and integrating them into the new democracy, incoming President Alfonsín engaged in secret negotiations with the military leaders: "The military would hand in a list of thirty or so names of officers they were willing to judge and convict in exchange for the suppression of what they perceived as a campaign to destroy the armed forces. Another important feature of the exchange was the Presidency's determination to pardon those convicted for human rights violations before the end of his

[78] Aguilar (2001), pp. 102, 103.
[79] Huntington (1991), p. 127.
[80] Walicki (1997), pp. 189–90.
[81] Eizenstat (2003), p. 351.

term, namely in 1989."[82] When the military reneged on the bargain and refused to judge their own, jurisdiction was transferred to civil courts. At the same time, Alfonsín discovered that in a democracy, parliaments and courts may refuse to honor elite bargains of this kind. In the end, some high-ranking officers went to jail, whereas most benefited from a "Full Stop" and notably from a "Due Obedience Law," which was passed, probably as part of another bargain, after a military uprising in protest against the numerous indictments.

As a parallel track, the Argentine government created the National Commission of the Disappeared, which documented nine thousand persons who had "been disappeared." (The official number has since been raised to twelve thousand. Other sources indicate still larger numbers.)[83] Although the Commission itself did not name perpetrators, someone inside it leaked 1,351 names to the press. The named wrongdoers could suffer serious consequences in their everyday life. One navy captain who was well known for his brutal acts "has suffered dozen of attacks in recent years by strangers on the street or people who say he tortured them and their relatives."[84] Later, these files became the core of a reparations program that entitled family members of a disappeared person to receive $220,000 as a lump-sum payment. In recent years, innovative legal moves, such as "truth trials" and cases brought against those who kidnapped children of victims, have brought about a revival of transitional justice.[85] At the time of this writing, the lower house of Congress and the Senate had annulled the "Full Stop" and "Due Obedience" laws, and a final decision by the Supreme Court was awaited.

Bolivia is the other country in which, after long delays, some military officers were sent to jail.[86] In 1982, the last and most oppressive of four successive military regimes was overthrown. In 1984, two leftist parties took the initiative to hold the leaders accountable. After a delay of two years, Congress decided to present a formal indictment against the dictator, García Meca, and fifty-five of his collaborators to the Supreme Court. Seven years later, the Court managed to overcome a series of politically motivated obstructions and handed down prison sentences against Meca, members of his government, and paramilitary agents. Of the forty-eight

[82] Acuña (in press).

[83] Ibid.

[84] *New York Times*, August 12, 1997.

[85] http://www.hrw.org/reports/2001/argentina/argen1201-01.htm provides continuously updated information.

[86] The following account is based on Mayorga (1997) and Human Rights Watch (1993).

who were convicted, only eleven were apprehended; the others remained fugitives. The Truth Commission that had been established in 1982 collected testimony on 155 disappearances that took place between 1967 and 1982, but was dismantled before it could complete its investi gations.[87]

In Brazil, the generals enacted a self-amnesty law in 1979, which remained in force after a protracted transition to democracy that was finally completed with the election of President Cardoso in 1990. Although Brazil never had an official truth commission, the Archdiocese of São Paulo secretly prepared a report on "Torture in Brazil" that received wide attention when it was published in July 1985. Five months later, the Archdiocese published a list of 444 torturers. Because of the amnesty, these "had little more to suffer than the people's contempt."[88] The continuing preoccupation with the wrongdoings by the military regime is reflected in the 1995 decision by parliament to have the families of political militants indemnified with $100,000–$150,000 each. By 1998, compensation had been given to survivors in 148 of 234 cases.[89] Attempts to have the amnesty law overturned have so far been unsuccessful.

In Chile, the military junta that was in power from 1973 to 1990 has tried very hard to make itself immune to prosecutions. In 1978, the junta enacted a self-amnesty law covering all criminal acts committed during the state of siege (from the 1973 coup to 1978). In 1980 it promulgated a constitution that was intended to cement the basic features of the authoritarian regime for the indefinite future.[90] Through an extraordinary set of interlocking appointment mechanisms, an institutional bloc consisting of the Senate, the National Security Council, the Constitutional Tribunal, and the Supreme Court has been able to obstruct democratic reforms as well as transitional justice.[91] When a 1988 plebiscite failed to confirm General Pinochet in power and a presidential election in 1989 voted the democratic candidate Aylwin into office, the Supreme Court

[87] Hayner (2001), p. 53.

[88] Wechsler (1998), p. 76.

[89] Brito (2001), p. 141.

[90] Barros (2002).

[91] The Supreme Court, which at the time of the quasi-democratic transition in 1990 consisted mainly of Pinochet appointees, had a decisive influence in filling its own vacancies. Of the seven judges of the Constitutional Tribunal, three had to be Supreme Court justices, two were appointed by the National Security Council, and one was appointed by the Senate. In addition to thirty-two elected senators, there were nine "designated senators," of whom two were chosen by and from the Supreme Court and four by the National Security Council.

systematically blocked his attempts to investigate crimes from the period not covered by the amnesty law.[92]

As a substitute measure, Aylwin created a truth commission that documented three thousand human rights violations and recommended extensive reparations. Although the report did not name perpetrators, "the Communist party paper, *El Siglo,* published a list of the names of human rights violators."[93] A 1992 law established compensation in the form of a monthly payment of $370 to the relatives of each victim. One year later, parliament adopted legislation to compensate fifty-eight thousand former public sector employees who had been dismissed for political reasons. At the same time, judges pursued the "Aylwin doctrine" that allowed courts to engage in fact-finding about past crimes (similar to the Argentinean truth trials), even though prosecutions were blocked by the 1978 amnesty.[94] More recently, the investigation of General Pinochet came to an end on July 1, 2002, when the Supreme Court dismissed the case against him, ruling that he was mentally unfit to stand trial.

In Mexico, there has not been any political transition in the usual sense of the term. Yet when the candidate of PRI (Institutional Revolutionary Party), which had been governing since 1929, lost the 2000 presidential elections to the candidate of the PAN (National Action Party), a center-right political party, it amounted to a fundamental within-regime change. Although the one-party rule was the result of electoral choices rather than inscribed in the constitution, the lack of alternation in power and the repressive ruling techniques made the PRI regime semidictatorial during much of its existence. The government undertook a "dirty war," including forced disappearances and torture, against groups deemed "subversives." An investigative commission was established in 1993, but to little effect until the last PRI president Zedillo granted it economic and political independence. By November 2001, it had documented 532 cases of human rights abuses, often naming the officials involved (most of whom were dead). When the new president, Vicente Fox, took power in 2000, he appointed a Special Prosecutor for Political Crimes of the Past. So far, no prosecutions have been initiated. Some officers involved in the dirty war have been convicted by military tribunals, but for drug trafficking, rather than for human rights violations.

[92] Brito (1997), pp. 174–84.

[93] Ibid., p. 162.

[94] Brito (2001), pp. 132–33; Acuña (in press).

In Uruguay, the military regime that was established in 1973 handed over power to a democratically elected president in 1985. By many accounts, the transition was preceded by a secret agreement (the Naval Club Pact) that there would be no prosecution for human rights violations. Since the amnesty was not part of the National Pacification Law adopted after the transition, many cases were initiated against military officers. Although the Supreme Military Tribunal, supported by the government, claimed jurisdiction over these cases, the Supreme Court ruled in favor of the civil judiciary. Three bills were presented in Congress to limit or prevent prosecutions, but all of them failed. Following another secret meeting of the president, the minister of defense, and the leaders of the two main political parties, parliament adopted amnesty legislation two weeks before thirteen military officers were due to appear in court. Three years later, the law was upheld in a national referendum. An official truth commission produced a lame report, whereas a nongovernmental commission produced massive documentation of abuses. In 1985, parliament enacted legislation "for the rehabilitation of 10,500 public employees, and extended retirement benefits to 6,000 people."[95] On April 27, 2003, Uruguayan President Jorge Batlle announced that the government would pay reparations to families of people who died while in the custody of the military dictatorship between 1973 and 1985, as well as to victims of guerrilla groups.

VI. EASTERN EUROPE

In the spring of 1989, Round Table Talks and subsequent elections in Poland triggered a domino process of transitions to (more or less) democratic regimes.[96] In chronological order, the transitions took place in Poland, Hungary, East Germany (GDR), Czechoslovakia, Romania, and Bulgaria.[97] The country that for most of them had been their nominal

[95] Brito (1997), p. 1225.

[96] This section draws heavily on research assistance by Monika Nalepa.

[97] Because of its marginal and uncertain status, I do not treat the transition in Albania. I also bracket transitional justice in the Baltic states. I leave aside Slovakia, since it "seems to have chosen to ignore the past" (Schwartz 2000, p. 219). In September 2002, however, the Slovakian government reached an agreement with the Slovak Jewish community to create a fund of $18 million to be used for community purposes and individual compensation (Eizenstat 2003, p. 367). Also, at the time of writing, Slovakia was just beginning to investigate the files of the security police, which will be transferred to the equivalent of Poland's Institute for National Remembrance (Monika Nalepa, personal communication).

ally and de facto oppressor, the Soviet Union, also underwent an uneven course toward democracy. The extent of transitional justice varies a great deal across the region. Broadly speaking, purges and reparations have been most extensive in Czechoslovakia and the Czech Republic and least important in Romania. In all countries, there have been relatively few trials. As for the Soviet Union, one might claim that its most important moment of coming to terms with the past occurred during the process of destalinization, rather than in the later process of decommunization.[98] As in Mexico in 2000, this was a within-regime change rather than a regime transition.

Compared to transitional justice in Western Europe after World War II – and to the magnitude of the crimes[99] – there have been relatively few trials in the postcommunist transitions. Although some regime leaders have been prosecuted, convictions have not always followed. In Bulgaria, the general secretary of the Communist Party received a seven-year prison sentence for embezzlement in 1992, but was acquitted by the Supreme Court in 1996. In 1997, three members of the Politburo in the former GDR were sentenced to jail sentences ranging from three to six and a half years for their responsibility in the shootings at the Berlin Wall. Earlier, three members of the National Defense Council had received comparable sentences for their involvement in these killings. A second trial of three Politburo members in 2000 resulted in their acquittal on grounds further discussed in Chapter 5. In Romania, the dictator and his wife were executed in an extralegal killing. In Poland, protracted trials of General Jaruzelski for ordering the police to shoot on demonstrators in 1970 and of General Kiszczak for ordering police to shoot on miners protesting martial law in 1981 have still not produced verdicts.[100] In the Czech Republic, two former Ministers of the Interior under the communist regime were charged in 2001 with abuse of power. One was acquitted, and the trial of the other was interrupted because of his bad health. In 2002, Prague City Court acquitted the former senior communist leaders Milos Jakes and Jozef Lenart of treason charges for conspiring with Soviet

98 For discussions, see Smith (1995a) and Adler (2001).

99 See the documentation in Courtois et al. (1997). One must not, however, conflate the overall comparison between Nazi and Communist crimes with the comparison between Nazi Germany and the Soviet satellite countries. As emphasized by Rottleuthner (1994), GDR wrongdoings, for instance, were vastly less serious than those of the Third Reich.

100 Jaruzelski asserts, however, that he would have preferred to serve a three-year prison sentence and go back to private life, rather than having to spend most of his remaining life in court as defendant or witness (Wiktor Osiatynski, personal communication).

occupiers after the 1968 Warsaw Pact invasion that crushed the reformist Prague Spring movement. In Hungary, there have been no trials of major communist leaders.

Nor has there been extensive prosecution against lower officials. With regard to the former GDR, "as of March 31, 1999, 22,765 investigations were opened, leading to the opening of just 565 criminal court cases. Verdicts were reached in 211 cases, of which just 20 cases resulted in actual prison sentences.... Border guards who were sentenced in court for having committed intentional homicides were, almost without exception, punished with suspended prison terms."[101] Although "Czech state prosecutors have charged some 100 comrades with crimes relating to the abuse of power in the former Czechoslovakia – from physical and mental torture to assassinations of communist opponents – only five verdicts have been handed down by Czech courts [between 1989 and 1999]."[102] In Hungary, prosecution of those responsible for massacres in the 1956 uprising was initially blocked when the Constitutional Court struck down legislation extending the statutes of limitation. When the issue was reframed in terms of international conventions, which are not subject to statutes of limitation, some trials were initiated and convictions obtained – more than forty years after the uprising and ten years after the transition. In Bulgaria, trials that had been initiated in 1993 against four officials who had been running a labor camp under brutal conditions seem to have been suspended following the murder of a key witness in September 1994. In Poland, twelve officials of the secret service were condemned to prison sentences ranging from four to nine years.

The purges in the public sector of the postcommunist societies took several forms. In the former GDR, one observed the traditional practice of dismissing tainted officials. By 1992, fully 50 percent of the former judges and prosecutors had lost their jobs.[103] By 1997, 42,000 officials had been dismissed because of their collaboration with the state security services (Stasi).[104] Beginning with Czechoslovakia, the other countries in the region adopted a new method, "lustration." Three years after the passage of the lustration law in 1991, the Czech Interior Ministry had

[101] Offe and Poppe (in press).

[102] Remias (1999).

[103] Offe (1996), p. 95.

[104] McAdams (2001), p. 73. Koehler (1999), p. 8, cites Joachim Gauck, the federal commissioner in charge of the Stasi archives, as estimating the number of full-time Stasi employees at 274,000 and "unofficial collaborators" at around 500,000. Offe and Poppe (in press) cite the numbers of 91,000 and 174,000 for these two categories.

received about 240,000 requests for screening. Of the 237,000 certificates that were issued, 4 percent stated that the individual had collaborated with or been an agent of the state security services. In these two countries, then, purges attained, respectively, one out of four hundred and one out of a thousand in the population.

The motivation – at least the official one – for lustration is to prevent high-ranking communist officials or collaborators with the security services from serving in important functions in the new regimes. This may entail dismissal, ineligibility, or simply exposure. When relying on dismissal and ineligibility, lustration combines features of classical purges with the sanction of "national degradation" used in West European countries after 1945. Reliance on exposure is a more innovative model. In Hungary, high officials are screened by a secret panel of judges, who can offer them the choice between resigning and having their past misdeeds made public. In Poland, candidates for high elective or appointive office have to declare whether they were "conscious collaborators" between 1945 and 1990. If they admit it, no further action is taken, except that the record is made public. Voters or hierarchical superiors then decide how to respond to the information. Candidates who falsely deny that they collaborated are banned from public office for ten years.[105]

There have been very extensive processes of restitution throughout the region.[106] In all countries except Poland (where private farms were never abolished), restitution of agricultural land was a major issue. In the former GDR, the Unification Treaty states that land confiscated by the Nazis between 1933 and 1945 (which was not restituted by the communist government) or by the East German government after 1949 should be given back to the former owners. Exempt from restitution was land that had been nationalized during the Soviet occupation from 1945 to

[105] A similar system of "self-purging" was adopted in South Africa (see Section VII). An early precedent was a proposal (not implemented) made in August 1944 by Mauro Scoccimarro, a Communist who was responsible for purges in the Italian administration. He proposed that all officials above a certain level should be retired with generous pensions, with the possibility of appeal. If they won the appeal, they would be reinstated; if they lost, they would lose not only their job but their pension as well (Woller 1996, pp. 191–92). For a comparison between these "incentive-based" screening procedures and the more usual "evidence-based" procedures, see Nalepa (2003a).

[106] See notably Quint (1997) and Pogany (1997). A good, brief survey with a valuable conceptual discussion is found in Heller and Serkin (1999), pp. 1399–1412. In actual practice, land restitution in the former communist countries has often been a complex and ambiguous process, as documented in the essays in Hann (2003). In many regions, collectivist forms of agriculture have been recreated.

1949, including large estates in Prussia. In Czechoslovakia and the Czech Republic, in-kind restitution of land has been a high priority for the new regime. In 2001 the Czech government claimed that 1.2 million hectares of arable land, or nearly one-third of the country's total, had been given back to private owners. In Bulgaria, by the end of 2000 5.68 million hectares (99 percent of the land identified for restitution) had been restituted to the former owners and their heirs. In Hungary, compensation vouchers were distributed to (among others) dispossessed owners, who could use them to buy state-owned and cooperatively held land. By 1996, about-one third of all cultivated land had been auctioned off to some six hundred thousand individuals. In Romania, it has been estimated that following legislation in 2000, 2.5 million hectares will be returned. In several countries, large properties belonging to the precommunist elite have been restituted to the owners, who include Vaclav Havel and former King Simeon of Bulgaria.

Those who suffered under communism for other reasons than loss of property have also been compensated to varying extents.[107] In Bulgaria, the 1991 "Law on Political and Civil Rehabilitation of Oppressed Persons" granted compensation to eight categories of victims, including "the heirs of persons who died, committed suicide or disappeared in connection with forced changes of name," that is, ethnic Turks who were forced to take Bulgarian names. Political prisoners in the former GDR could receive 300 DM for each month of imprisonment. In Czechoslovakia, a 1992 law granted those who had been interned for political reasons between 1948 and 1954 a monthly supplement to their pension; if they were deceased, their survivors received a lump-sum payment. A 1997 law offered more generous compensation, proportionally to the time spent in detention. In Poland, a law from 1991 granted compensation to "persons repressed for their activity aimed at achieving Poland's independence," but arbitrarily excluded those handed over to the Soviet secret police. This restriction was lifted by 1993 legislation. By 1996, Poland had paid out about $125 million in reparations to former political prisoners and their heirs.

VII. AFRICA

Among African transitions, I first consider those that took place in Rhodesia (1979) and South Africa (1994). In both countries, a white economic elite remained after the transition, which was largely shaped to safeguard

[107] See Pogany (1997), Chap. 8, for a survey.

their interests. I then summarize the main features of transitional justice in Ethiopia after 1991.

In Rhodesia, as in Spain in 1978 and Uruguay in 1989, there was a conscious decision to abstain from transitional justice. The Lancaster House Agreement that laid down the terms for the Rhodesian transition did not contain an amnesty clause,[108] but during his interregnum as governor, Christopher Soames signed amnesty ordinances ensuring that no prosecution could take place for any acts done either by members of the former government or by persons acting in opposition to it. At independence, Prime Minister Mugabe gave a speech in which he agreed to "draw a line through the past," in order to achieve reconciliation and reassure foreign investors. According to the agreement, the government could not forcibly expropriate privately owned farmland for a period of ten years. In return, Britain agreed to share the cost of buying land sold voluntarily to the government for redistribution.

In South Africa, the Truth and Reconciliation Commission that was set up as part of the negotiated transition to democracy represents a unique way of coming to terms with the past.[109] The Commission was established in December 1995 and delivered an interim report in 1998. The Amnesty Subcommittee of the Commission is still hearing and deciding cases. In addition to this subcommittee, which is concerned with applications for amnesty for crimes carried out under apartheid, the Commission has subcommittees on Reparation and Rehabilitation and on Human Rights Violations. By 1998, the latter had identified about fifteen thousand victims. On this basis, the former has recommended that each victim get an amount between $2,000 and $3,000 each year for six years. Thirteen and a half thousand victims have received a total of $5.5 million in emergency assistance.[110] On April 17, 2003, President Mbeki announced that the government will pay approximately $85 million in reparations to more than nineteen thousand apartheid victims who testified before the Truth and Reconciliation Commission. Each will receive a one-time payment of about $3,900. There has been no land reform to undo the massive dispossession of Africans by the 1913 Land Act, and no compensation for the forcible removal of the black population under apartheid.

[108] Contrary to what is asserted by Carver (1995), p. 253.

[109] The five volumes of TRC (1999) provide documentation of the Commission's work. An update is provided on the Commission's website, http://www.doj.gov.za/trc/index.html.

[110] Knox and Monaghan (2002), p. 56. In August 2002, a class-action lawsuit brought by victims of apartheid against up to a hundred companies, including Swiss and American banks, was initiated.

The procedure for granting amnesty is somewhat similar to the Polish mechanism for lustration. Amnesty (immunity to criminal and civil proceedings) would be granted to applicants who could show that their acts had been (i) motivated by political goals rather than by malice or desire for gain, and (ii) proportional to the occasion that triggered them.[111] The applicant would also have to provide full information about the crime, including evidence about the chain of command. As a person who did not apply for amnesty risked prosecution or litigation, the mechanism established an incentive for wrongdoers to come forward if they could plausibly claim to satisfy conditions (i) and (ii) and were willing to tell the full truth. Since amnesty hearings documented wrongdoings in great detail and invariably named the perpetrators, some might be deterred from applying by the anticipation of public disapproval. By the end of 2000, there had been 7,112 applications for amnesty, of which 849 had been granted and 5,392 rejected. The rejections concerned, for the most part, common criminals who used the amnesty procedure as a longshot attempt to gain freedom. By one assessment, "perpetrators did not come forward in great numbers, showing their faith in the unlikelihood of future prosecutions."[112]

The transition in Ethiopia began when the Dergue regime led by President Mengistu fell in 1991. When the United Front (EPRDF) that overthrew him entered the capital in May of that year, it immediately detained several thousand Dergue officials, and many were arrested later. Trials began in 1994; in 2001, the special prosecutor announced that they would come to an end in 2004. By 2003, Ethiopian courts had handed down 1,181 verdicts, including 375 acquittals out of 6,180 cases, with some 2,200 suspects still held in prison and the rest being tried in absentia. The trials are proceeding at an exceptionally slow pace. Thus, when the former Olympian gold medalist Mamo Wolde received a six-year prison sentence in January 2002 for his responsibility in a 1978 killing, he had already spent nine years in pretrial detention and was released immediately. Some death sentences have been handed down, but it is not clear whether any have been executed. The country also initiated administrative purges, some of them carried out by Grievance Hearing Committees in government offices. Members of the judiciary, including 16 of 33 judges on the Supreme Court and about half of 143 judges on the high

[111] Hayner (2001), p. 260, notes that in practice, "lack of proportionality was rarely the reason for rejecting an application."

[112] Wilson (2001a), p. 210.

courts, were automatically excluded qua members of the Workers' Party of Ethiopia.[113]

VIII. CLASSIFYING THE CASES

In classifying these episodes, we can pay attention to the nature and duration of the *autocratic regime,* and to the nature and duration of the *process of transitional justice* itself. The regime as well as the process may be endogenous or exogenous. They may also be of short or of long duration. The place of a given episode of transitional justice on these dimensions can affect the political and emotional dynamics in a number of ways that will be explored in later chapters.

The autocratic regime that preceded the transition to democracy may either have originated within the nation itself, or been imposed by a foreign power.[114] The process of transitional justice may be either initiated by the new regime or carried out under the supervision of a foreign power. Combining the two dichotomies, we may classify the episodes as shown in Table 3.1.

Some cases are ambiguous, or may require some comments:

- We do not know the extent to which the oligarchy that was overthrown in 403 was a puppet Spartan regime, nor the extent to which transitional justice was imposed by Sparta.
- Transitional justice in the French Restorations was partly endogenous, notably with regard to purges and indemnification.
- Italy and Austria might have a place in all four cells of the table. The Salò regime was imposed by the Germans. Although the *Anschluss* of Austria was technically an invasion, the ensuing regime had strong national support. In both countries, purges and trials were carried out by the Allied military government as well as by the national one.
- Over time, transitional justice in Germany after 1945 became increasingly endogenous and, as a result, increasingly lenient.
- Bulgaria was unlike other Eastern European countries in that the Soviets were not seen as an occupying force, due to the positive image

[113] Haile (2000), p. 29.

[114] Or both. Thus, "[m]uch of the difference between [the] public reactions [to regime atrocities] stems from the types of wartime administrations encountered in each nation: native regime or collaborationist. Germany's government was native; France's was collaborationist. Italy from 1922 until 1945 experienced both" (Domenico 1991, p. 145).

TABLE 3.1

	Endogenous Transitional Justice	Exogenous Transitional Justice
Endogenous autocratic regime	English Restoration	
	Latin America	Athens 403 B.C.
	South Africa	Germany 1945
	Bulgaria	Japan 1945
	Romania	France 1814
	Ethiopia	France 1815
	Hungary 1945	Austria 1945
	Greece	Rhodesia
	Italy	
	Spain	
	Athens 411 B.C.	
Exogenous autocratic regime	United States 1783	
	Algeria 1962	
	Poland	Former GDR
	Hungary 1989	
	Czechoslovakia	
	Countries occupied by Germany during World War II	

of Russia as having liberated the country from "the Turkish yoke" in 1878.

- Romania, too, was special. Once a faithful member of the communist bloc, the country later gained full independence.
- Transitional justice for the former East Germany is the most complex case. The transition itself was endogenous: The regime collapsed from within. The reunification treaty, too, was a voluntary agreement between two sovereign states. The former East Germany, although not coextensive with the regime that was to judge it, was at least included in it. Yet in practice, the former East Germans were judged by former West Germans and within the legal and constitutional framework that unified Germany inherited from West Germany. In one sense, nevertheless, the trials were endogenous, since the unification treaty laid down that any acts to be tried had to be defined as crimes according to the penal codes of both countries.

In some ways, the most interesting cases are the doubly endogenous cases (the upper left-hand cell) in which a society has to come to terms *with itself*. After the transition, leaders and agents of the old regime are still part of the fabric of society. Whether directly, by their access to means of violence or to the voting booth, or indirectly, by their importance for economic reconstruction and development, they may be able to influence the treatment that is meted out to them. In a metaphor that I have also used to describe the process of constitution making in new democracies,[115] society has to *rebuild itself in the open sea,* using the materials at hand, however flawed they may be. Even when judges, for instance, were deeply involved with the predemocratic regime, there may be no practical alternative to using them, or the least compromised among them, to judge that regime itself.

Moreover, pre-transition regimes, as well as the process of transitional justice under the new regime, may be of variable duration. Consider first the pre-transitional regime (or regimes).[116] The First and the Second French Restorations were separated by the Hundred Days. Each of the two Athenian oligarchies that I discussed in Chapter 2 was in power for less than a year. At the other extreme, the USSR endured for almost 75 years. Intermediate cases are Mexico (70 years), GDR (57 years), the apartheid regime in South Africa (45 years), Portugal (44 years), Eastern Europe (ca. 40 years), Spain (40 years), Chile (26 years), France before the First Restoration (25 years), Italy (23 years), Brazil (20 years), Bolivia (18 years), Ethiopia (17 years), Uruguay (12 years), West Germany (12 years), England before the Restoration (11 years), Argentina (7 years), Greece (7 years), and the countries occupied by Germany during World War II (5 years). When the predemocratic regime has been of short duration, memories of wrongdoing and suffering tend to be vivid and (other things being equal) emotions correspondingly strong. If it has been of long duration, the intensity of emotion and of the demand for retribution will depend (other things being equal) on when the worst atrocities took place.

Consider next the temporal dimension of transitional justice itself. In *immediate transitional justice,* proceedings begin shortly after the transition and come to an end within, say, five years. There are three contrasting cases. In *protracted transitional justice* the process starts up immediately, but then goes on for a long time until the issues are resolved. This pattern

[115] Elster (1993a).

[116] The following numbers are subject to some caveats. If one dates the onset of state injustice to the 1913 Land Act, the South African regime is the longest lasting. In Hungary, nondemocratic regimes were in place for seventy years, with a brief episode of democracy in the middle. For the last ten years of authoritarian leadership, Brazil was undergoing a "long transition" to democracy (Linz and Stepan 1996, pp. 167–69).

is found in Bolivia, Ethiopia, Germany after 1945, and most postcommunist countries. In *second-wave transitional justice,* we can distinguish three stages. After a process of immediate transitional justice, there is a latency period during which no action is taken, until, decades later, new proceedings are initiated.[117] The Papon and Touvier trials in France, as well as the recent process of compensating Jewish bank account holders and slave workers, fall in this category. The reopening of cases against Argentinean officers may soon provide another example. In *postponed transitional justice,* the *first* actions are undertaken (say) ten years or more after the transition. The prosecution of Pinochet is a paradigmatic example. The 1825 law that established compensation to the French émigrés for property confiscated under the Revolution was enacted ten years after the Second Restoration.

One might ask if there is a correlation between these two temporal variables. Other things being equal, the shorter the duration of the autocratic regime, the more vivid the memories of wrongdoings, the more urgent therefore the emotional demand for retribution, and the more immediate therefore the start-up of transitional justice. The ceteris paribus clause sweeps too many factors under the carpet, however. I'm not saying that each case has its own dynamic, so that we have to fall back on "thick description." As we shall see, there are many shared mechanisms in the universe of cases, but they are at a lower level of abstraction.

117 The best study is Rousso (1990).

PART II

ANALYTICS OF TRANSITIONAL JUSTICE

In Part II, I try to impose some structure on the cases I surveyed in Part I. It is clearly time to delineate the idea of transitional justice in a more conceptual manner. This I try to do in Chapter 4. In the rest of the book, I offer elements of explanation to account for variations in transitional justice across time and space. I first discuss how the fate of wrongdoers (Chapter 5) and victims (Chapter 6) is determined by the priorities of legislatures, courts, and administrative agencies. In the following three chapters, I step back to consider the broader economic, social, and political forces that constrain and shape these decisions. The constraints are the topic of Chapter 7. In Chapter 8, I consider the emotional motivations that are pervasive in most cases of transitional justice. Chapter 9 considers the politics of transitional justice, whether based on interest or ideological motivations.

I do not aim at presenting a "theory of transitional justice." As in my earlier work on local justice, I have found the context-dependence of the phenomena to be an insuperable obstacle to generalizations. The closest I come to a "law" of transitional justice is that the intensity of the demand for retribution decreases both with the time interval between the wrongdoings and the transition and with the interval between the transition and the trials (Chapter 8). Yet even here, we find that counteracting mechanisms may keep memory and resentment alive for a century or more. I do aim at some generality, however, in the sense of trying to identify recurring patterns of behavior.[1] In Chapter 5, I discuss the pervasive importance of counterfactual reasoning in generating justifications

[1] I defend this procedure in Chapter 1 of Elster (1999).

and excuses for alleged wrongdoings. I also try to identify some profiles of wrongdoers, together with the most common legal reactions to them. In Chapter 6, the tension among entitlement, past suffering, and present need, as competing justifications for reparation for wrongdoings, provides a unifying theme. Chapter 7 is more of a ragbag of mechanisms, in which the constraints imposed by negotiations and by several kinds of scarcity stand out. Chapter 8 provides a more systematic analysis of the relations among the passage of time, memory, emotion, and the demand for retribution. In Chapter 9, finally, I try to discuss the role of politics in transitional justice at several levels, ranging from short-term electoral tactics to long-term conservative or revolutionary strategies.

4

The Structure of Transitional Justice

I. INTRODUCTION

To compare and explain cases of transitional justice, we must first define the comparanda and explananda. This is the purpose of the present chapter. The most difficult task is to spell out the role of "justice" in transitional justice. In Section II I consider justice as a *motivation* – the desire for justice to be done – and its complex relations to other motivations that may animate the actors in this context. The topic of Section III is justice as an *institution*. The main challenge here is to identify criteria that allow us to distinguish *legal justice* – the main topic of the present book – from *political justice*. In Section IV I distinguish among *levels* of transitional justice, which may involve – as executors or targets – individuals, corporate actors, states, or supranational entities. In Section V I discuss categories of *agents* involved in transitional justice, focusing on cases in which one person belongs, simultaneously or successively, to more than one category. In Section VI, finally, I try to identify the key *decisions* of transitional justice that have to be made by the incoming leaders. These decisions will reappear as the dependent variables in the last three chapters.

II. THE MOTIVATION OF JUSTICE

The main task of this book is to discuss why processes of transitional justice have taken different forms in different transitions, and why they have sometimes been absent altogether. This is a *positive* or explanatory task. As I said in the Preface, I mainly eschew normative issues of what should be done or what should have been done. Yet this distinction between positive and normative approaches is somewhat misleading. In deciding how to deal with wrongdoers and victims from the earlier regime, the leaders of the incoming regime are often influenced by their ideas about what is required by justice. The normative conceptions of justice held by the agents of transitional justice can enter into the explanation of the decisions they reach.

In this perspective, the analysis of transitional justice is part of the *empirical study of justice.* Another subject that has been studied under this heading is "local justice," that is, the study of how institutions allocate scarce goods and necessary burdens, such as allocation of organs for transplantation or selection of young men for military service.[1] One may also ask how conceptions of justice have entered into the adoption of electoral systems, for example, the extension of suffrage or the design of electoral districts.[2] Considerations of fairness and justice may also play a role in wage bargaining.[3] In addition to such real-life studies, there is a large experimental literature on perceptions of fairness and their role in explaining behavior.[4]

Generally speaking, these studies address one or several of three tasks. In all cases, we need (i) to *identify* the conceptions of justice and fairness held by the agents we are considering. Although it is hard to define what counts as a conception of justice in the abstract, we may distinguish the concern with justice from other motivations by formal criteria, such as impartiality and universality. (Even conceptions that violate *impartiality,* in the sense that they allow an agent to give more weight to people close to him or her than to others, may still count as a conception of justice if they respect *universality,* in the sense of agreeing that other agents are entitled to claim the same privilege for those close to *them.*)[5] These criteria may be satisfied by many different substantive conceptions of justice, be they egalitarian, utilitarian, rights-based, or others. I shall often refer to them by the generic term of *reason.*

Once we have identified the conception of justice held by an agent, we can look either for (ii) its upstream *causes* or for (iii) its downstream *consequences,* notably the impact on behavior. Considering (ii), there are numerous studies relating subjective ideas about justice to properties of the individuals who hold them, such as age, gender, and nationality. There are

[1] Elster (1992a, 1995).
[2] See, for instance, Keyssar (2000).
[3] Elster (1989).
[4] See, for instance, the large literature on Ultimatum Games, surveyed in Camerer (2003).
[5] Nagel (1991).

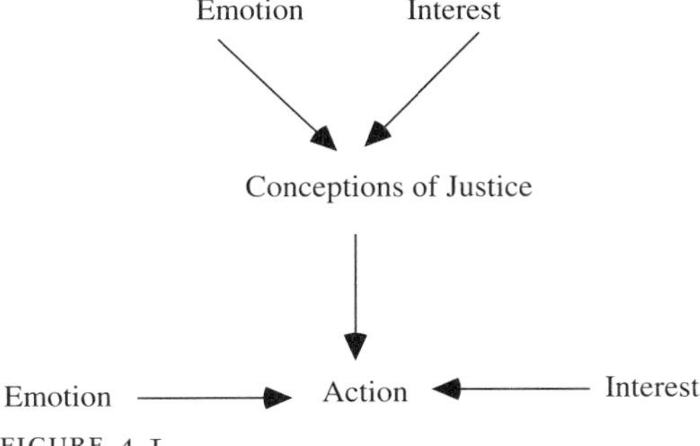

FIGURE 4.1

also studies that try to identify context-specific conceptions of justice, by arguing, for instance, that ideas of fairness that seem appropriate among friends differ from those that are adopted in the context of the family. Finally, we may seek the causes of these ideas in other motivations of the agent, notably in the interest of the agents or in their emotions. This will be my focus here.

Considering (iii), we may find that subjective conceptions of justice matter little for actual behavior. They may be mere "Sunday beliefs" that command subjective assent without inducing action to bring about a just state of affairs. In other cases, we may find that the desire to see justice done provides the main explanation of the agent's behavior. In still other cases, we may find that justice coexists with other causally efficacious motivations, such as emotion or self-interest, so that the action that is finally taken owes something to each. If we abstract from the other factors mentioned in the previous paragraph, questions (ii) and (iii) may be captured by Figure 4.1. (Arrows represent *possible* causal relations. In any given case, they may or may not operate.)

I adopt this trichotomy of motivations – reason, interest, and emotion – from the seventeenth-century French moralists, notably La Bruyère.[6] In the context of transitional justice, they may be illustrated by a mid-1783 letter from New York Chancellor Robert Livingston to Alexander Hamilton:

> I seriously lament with you, the violent spirit of persecution which prevails here and dread its consequences upon the wealth, commerce & future tranquillity of the state. I am the more hurt at it because it appears to me almost unmixed with *purer patriotic motives*. In some few it is a blind spirit of *revenge & resentment,* but in more it is the most *sordid interest*.[7]

[6] Elster (1999), Chap. 2.

[7] Cited from McDonald (1982), p. 75.

The phrases I have italicized correspond to reason, emotion, and interest, respectively. Even if we rarely find them so explicitly held up against each other, these motivations are pretty near universal in transitional justice. In the French Restoration, for instance, former owners who demanded restitution in kind could be motivated by the sacred rights of property in the abstract (reason), by a desire to take revenge on the purchasers (emotion), and by a desire to get their property back (interest). Although we may suspect that the first motive was little more than window dressing for the second and third, the suspicion is somewhat undermined when we observe a former *monarchien* from 1789, Bergasse, who was neither noble nor émigré, making the same principled argument for restitution in kind.[8] In Czechoslovakia after 1989, too, libertarian thinkers who demanded restitution in kind as a matter of principle did not themselves expect to benefit personally. It follows that if those who *do* stand to benefit argue from impartial principles, we cannot assume that they are merely being hypocritical. To decide whether they are, we would have to look at their behavior in other contexts.

The desire to see justice done is not simply one motivation among many that may animate the actors of transitional justice. In most societies, there is a *normative hierarchy of motivations* that induce meta-motivations over first-order motivations. In ancient Greece, for instance, the most valued motive was the desire to promote the good of the *polis*; the second-ranked that of taking revenge on an enemy; the third-ranked that of pursuing one's self-interest; and the least valued that of envy. Given a hierarchy of motivations, those who act on a low-ranked motivation often tend to present it to themselves or to others as a higher-ranking one. At the same time, they want, as far as possible, to perform the *action* that their real motivation suggests to them. A person may be motivated by self-interest *and* by a desire not to appear to himself or to others as motivated by self-interest. (For other examples, substitute "vanity," "envy," or "revenge" for "self-interest" in the previous sentence.) As I have discussed elsewhere, people use a remarkable array of stratagems to satisfy their first-order motivations and their meta-motivations at the same time.[9]

[8] Gain (1928), vol. 1, p. 444.

[9] Elster (1999), Chap. 5. The idea of meta-motivations is unrelated to the concept of meta-preferences introduced by Sen (1977). An example of Sen's approach would be a person with two *different* preference orderings, one for eating over dieting and one for dieting over eating, and a meta-preference favoring the latter. Following La Bruyère's insight that "Men are very vain, and of all things hate to be thought so" (*Characters* XI.65), a meta-motivation could amount to a preference for dieting over eating on grounds of health over having *the same* preference ordering on grounds of vanity.

In transitional justice, an emotionally based desire for revenge may in one sense be stronger than the desire to carry out impartial justice. In turbulent times of transition, what Madison called "the mild voice of reason" may find it difficult to get a hearing. At the same time, because of its higher rank in the normative hierarchy, individuals under the sway of other motivations may be *deferential* toward reason and want to have it on their side. As Seneca said, "Reason wishes the decision that it gives to be just; anger wishes to have the decision which it has given seem the just decision."[10] In transitional justice, this general deferential attitude is reinforced by a more specific mechanism. Often, the incoming leaders want to show that "We are not like them" (Havel). When they set out to deal with the lawless practices of the past, they do not want to do it in a lawless manner.[11] Their desire to demarcate themselves from the old regime may constrain, however, the satisfaction of their desire to punish the agents of the regime. It may be impossible, for instance, to punish what appears to be obvious acts of wrongdoing without introducing retroactive legislation, thus embracing the lawless practices of the previous regime. As we shall see in Chapter 8, a common response to this tension is to try to have it both ways, by using subterfuge to disguise the retroactive character of punitive legislation.

In the present book, the operation of reason in transitional justice is the topic of Chapters 5 and 6, which consider how courts and legislatures try to differentiate among putative wrongdoers and victims on the basis of impartial arguments, or at least using arguments presented with a claim to being impartial. The operation of emotion is the topic of Chapter 8. In Chapter 9, on the politics of transitional justice, I consider several types of interest: that of wrongdoers in avoiding prosecution, that of victims in obtaining compensation, and that of political parties in increasing their share of the electorate. In many cases, interest fuses with reason and passion in producing political *ideologies*. After 1945, many former Nazis believed passionately that since they had acted in the interest of the nation by defending it against "Bolshevism," they should be rewarded

[10] *On Anger* (I.xviii).

[11] If the new democratic leaders have grown up inside the autocratic regime, it may be hard to shed the habits of the past (Kuk 2001, p. 336). Destalinization provides an example. During a short period (between 1953 and 1956), it was permissible not to quote Stalin, but soon people were discouraged to do so, in accordance with the Stalinist axiom that whatever is not obligatory is forbidden (Elster 1993b, Chap. 2). See also Chapter 8 for expressions in France and Denmark of the idea that wrongdoers cannot expect to be treated better than they treated others, as well as Chapter 7 for Morgenthau's similar views on Germany.

rather than punished. Although the external observer has no difficulty in diagnosing a strong component of bad faith in this attitude, one must be careful not to reduce it to mere group interest. By contrast, the attitude of the post-Communists is much closer to the naked pursuit of interest.

III. THE INSTITUTIONS OF JUSTICE

We may distinguish three institutional forms of justice: legal justice, administrative justice, and political justice. Better perhaps, we may conceptualize the institutions of justice as a *continuum*, with pure legal justice at one end and pure political justice at the other. Administrative justice may be closer to the legal or to the political end of the spectrum, depending on the extent to which the officials to be purged have the benefit of due process. Moreover, legal justice may be impure and still recognizably legal. Also, some forms of political justice share important features with legal justice.

What I shall call "pure political justice" occurs when the executive branch of the new government (or an occupying power) unilaterally and without the possibility of appeal designates the wrongdoers and decides what shall be done with them.[12] A paradigm case is the decision of the Allied powers in 1815 to sentence Napoleon to exile at St. Helena.[13] The list of individuals to be proscribed that was drawn up by the French government on July 24, 1815, was intended as a measure of this kind, although in the end, it was not used as the main basis for action. At the end of World War II, many political leaders and activists were against the idea of meting out legal justice to the Nazi leaders. The British government proposed to draw up a list of fifty or a hundred individuals who could be shot at sight.[14] Stalin proposed, maybe half-jokingly, that the number should be one thousand times as large.[15] In the United States, associates of Henry Morgenthau proposed twenty-five hundred summary executions.[16] In

[12] One might also include the power of the executive to decide the fate of the wrongdoers once they have been designated as guilty by another organ of government. In 1945, de Gaulle, for instance, used his powers of grace very extensively (Bancaud 2002, p. 70).

[13] Bass (2000), Chap. 2.

[14] Ibid., p. 181.

[15] Taylor (1992), p. 30.

[16] U.S. Senate (1967), p. 483.

France, two high magistrates in the resistance proposed a reintroduction of the revolutionary penalty (established during the Terror) of declaring some individuals outlaws who could be slain with impunity by anyone.[17] None of these proposals came to anything.

In France in 1944–45, the *préfets* and the departmental liberation committees, emanating respectively from the national government and from the resistance, were often capable of bypassing, ignoring, or undermining the action of the ordinary courts. If a politically suspect person had been acquitted by the court or received a nonsuit, the préfet, taking a leaf from the book of the Vichy government,[18] could subject him to internment or house arrest, "not merely to protect him from popular vengeance" but as a measure of incapacitation or punishment.[19] The liberation committees could request and often obtain, through the action of the *Commissaire de la République,* the transfer of local judges who were deemed insufficiently rigorous in their practices.[20] There is a subtle but important difference between these forms of political interference with the law and the political screening of judges that was observed in many countries. When judges are appointed on the basis of their political records *before* the trials take place, they are free to follow the law and their conscience. When they are replaced or their decisions ignored *after* an acquittal or a nonsuit, the situation is closer to pure political justice.

Pure political justice may also take the form of *show trials,* where the appearance of legality is a mere fiction because the outcome is a foregone conclusion. In the negotiations among the Allied powers over the Nuremberg process, the Soviets essentially wanted a show trial where the only role of the tribunal would be to decide the *degree* of guilt of the major war criminals.[21] In the end, the trials conformed to legal justice in two essential respects: adherence to due process and uncertainty about the outcome (as shown by the fact that three of twenty-three defendants were acquitted).[22] By contrast, the Tokyo trials deviated from legal justice in both respects. Except for Napoleon's exile, the Tokyo proceedings are

[17] Bancaud (2002), p. 363.

[18] Ibid., p. 423.

[19] Ibid., pp. 60–61, 293.

[20] Ibid., pp. 295–300.

[21] Marrus (1997), pp. 47–48.

[22] Acquittals are not definite proof, however, that we are not dealing with a show trial. In the Riom trials under Vichy, one of the accused was destined for acquittal in order to show the impartiality of the justice system (Bancaud 2002, p. 395).

perhaps the closest approximation to pure political justice in the universe of cases. Although the phrase "victors' justice" has been used about other transitions as well,[23] here it takes on its full derogatory sense.[24] On a smaller scale, the same can be said about the Yokohama trials.[25] In other transitions, the incoming regime has not even bothered with show trials. Instead, leaders and agents of the outgoing regime have simply been executed, whether for the sake of revenge or incapacitation. Examples include Russia in 1917[26] and Romania in 1989.[27]

At the other end of the spectrum, "pure legal justice" may be characterized by four features. First, the laws should be as *unambiguous* as possible, to reduce the scope for judicial interpretation. Needless to say, there will always be some room for judicial discretion. Yet in the typical case, the freedom of judges and officials to decide what the law *implies* is much smaller than the freedom of legislators to decide what the law shall *be*. The Italian amnesty law of July 22, 1946, offers an example of a law phrased in terms so ambiguous that it hardly constrained the judges at all.[28] Another example is provided by the German amnesty law of December 19, 1949, which among other things granted amnesty for "sentences for actions taken on a political basis after 8 May 1945 and that can be attributed to the special political circumstances of recent years."

[23] Some form of victors' justice is not only inevitable but may even be desirable. The alternative to victors' justice, namely, to choose jurors and judges among those who remained neutral or passive under the autocratic regime, is hardly a superior solution (Andenæs 1980, p. 261). As I note in Chapter 8, neutrals may try to pacify their guilty conscience by imposing excessively severe sentences.

[24] Minear (2001); Gower (1999), Chap. 15; Harries and Harries (1987), Chap. 13.

[25] Taylor (1981); Cohen (1999).

[26] Kirchheimer (1961), p. 96 n, summarizes an entry in Trotsky's diary that "tells why a trial against the czar, reviewing the sum total of the czarist regime's policies, could not be carried out. There were three reasons: the uncertain course of the civil war; the need to show both friends and foes that there was no way back; and a point emphasized by Lenin, that judicial proceedings would not allow the execution of the family members, who by necessity must fall victim to 'the principle of dynastic succession.'"

[27] The executioners, being ideologically close to Ceausescu, may have used his murder to protect themselves, hoping that the public's demand for vengeance would be saturated after the execution (Monika Nalepa, personal communication). Along the same lines, the reason why Mussolini failed to use his power of grace to prevent the execution of his son-in-law Ciano may have been his awareness that if "the Nazi Germans were satiated by the blood of others," he might be spared himself (Bosworth 2002, p. 17). I return to the theme of the "thirst of the gods" in Chapter 8.

[28] Woller (1996), pp. 382–83. The law exempted from amnesty people in "high" positions and those who had committed "unusually cruel" acts, without specifying the meaning of these terms.

As one politician remarked, "I can commit a deed from political motives. But what is a political basis?"[29]

Second, the judiciary should be *insulated* from the other branches of government. Beyond a narrow range of offenses, there is no room for military courts. Professional judges should be assigned randomly to cases in order to prevent the government from selecting "reliable" judges to try "delicate" cases.[30] Lay judges and jurors should also be chosen randomly from the population at large. In the trials after 1945 of collaborators with the Germans, this principle was, as we shall see, routinely violated. The role of the legislature should be limited to the enactment of laws in which proper names never occur. In other words, acts of attainder – a procedure in which parliament passes judicial sentence on an accused person as if it were a court of law – are not allowed. This principle was violated in the English Restoration, but partly respected in the French.

Third, judges and jurors should be *unbiased* when interpreting the law. At a minimum, they should not distort the meaning of the law to justify a decision they have already reached for extralegal reasons. While bias may be produced by lack of insulation, it can also occur on its own. In transitional justice, judges and jurors, no less than legislators, illustrate Seneca's dictum that "anger wishes to have the decision which it has given seem the just decision." In such cases, bias results in excessive severity.[31] In other cases, it may produce excessive leniency, the most notorious example being the ex-Nazi judges in post-1945 Germany who were to judge Nazi criminals. To take one example among the many cited by Ingo Müller in his disturbing book *Hitler's Justice*, officials who had handed over prison inmates to the Gestapo and the concentration camps were acquitted as "unwitting tools" who had not understood what they were doing: "It was admittedly true that the Ministry's correspondence had frequently referred to the prisoner's 'annihilation,' but in the view of the Wiesbaden Country Court, their 'awareness that the word "annihilation" was being

[29] Frei (2002), p. 17. The vagueness was intentional. The original impetus behind this provision was a request by the Center Party to grant amnesty for "offenses related to enthusiasm for the democratic idea or opposition to surmounted National Socialism." In addition to covering crimes committed *against* Nazis, the vague formulation that was eventually adopted also covered crimes committed *by* them.

[30] See, for instance, Kirchheimer (1961), p. 217 n. 88.

[31] Sometimes the bias may work against itself, however, as when the prosecutor's office decides for a nonsuit, rather than exposing an individual to the "Russian roulette" of a jury trial (Berlière 2001, p. 336).

used did not in and of itself... represent a sufficient basis to conclude that the defendants knew or suspected the killings were taking place.'"[32]

Finally, legal justice must adhere to principles of *due process,* notably:

- adversarial and public hearings
- the right to choose one's own lawyer
- the right to appeal
- no retroactive legislation or retroactive application of the law
- respect for statutes of limitations
- determination of individual guilt
- a presumption of innocence that places the burden of proof on the prosecution
- the right to a speedy hearing (justice delayed is justice denied)
- the right to due deliberation (justice expedited is also justice denied).

As I document toward the end of the chapter, these requirements are routinely violated in transitional justice. Later chapters will show that such abridgments sometimes occur for good reasons, sometimes not.

The extent to which this ideal type is approximated in reality depends on the type of society and on the nature of the situation. In "law-abiding societies" during "normal times," violations of the criteria I have enumerated are rare. In societies where the rule of law is poorly established or in exceptional circumstances, violations happen more frequently. Political transitions belong to these exceptional circumstances (wartime is another). Among the transitions I discussed in Part I, even those that took place in normally law-abiding societies violated one or usually several of the criteria. As we shall see, violations may be unavoidable and on occasion even desirable, and even when they are neither they may be understandable and perhaps forgivable. When many violations accumulate or where core criteria are violated, there comes a point, however, when legal justice is replaced by political justice.

As an operational indicator, this point occurs when an observer can predict the outcome of all trials with full certainty. Legal justice requires that outcomes be, to some extent, shrouded in uncertainty. Prosecutors will, to be sure, choose cases they think they can win, yet knowing they might lose. As noted, the uncertainty may stem from the vagueness of the law rather than from the procedural hurdles of due process. We may nevertheless use uncertainty of outcome as a minimal indicator of a functioning legal justice system. Because of this feature of legal justice, it may be badly

[32] Müller (1991), p. 251.

suited to political aims: "Of the manifold devices to rid the regime of political foes, the judicial inquest obtains neither the quickest nor by any means the most certain results."[33] In fact, "sustaining a tribunal means surrendering control over the outcome to a set of unwieldy rules designed for other occasions, and to a group of rule-obsessed lawyers."[34] The gains in legitimacy may or may not offset the costs of delay and uncertainty. Attempts to have it both ways are difficult to pull off. Referring to courts-martial of the Vichy militia and to the American trials for Japanese war crimes, Otto Kirchheimer writes that "in each case the tribunal sought the mechanical certainty of the result while trying to partake – illegitimately – in the creative suspense of a result which can legitimately originate only in the unfolding of the trial itself."[35] Referring to the Riom trials of Léon Blum and others under Vichy, Alain Bancaud writes that "the use of closed proceedings . . . has the drawback of canceling what justified recourse to the legal system, viz. the benefits of a process that promises to shed 'full light' and to show that the accusers have nothing to hide."[36]

Political justice differs from political interventions in legal justice, as when judges or jurors are selected on political grounds. The second Athenian transition in 403 B.C. was unique in that the courts were deliberately stacked in favor of the outgoing rather than the incoming regime. In Hungary after World War II, "[t]he People's Courts were made up of delegated representatives of the anti-fascist coalition. Only the presiding judge was a professional."[37] In Austria, "[t]he composition of the People's Courts was less revolutionary than that of their Hungarian equivalents: here three of the six judges were professionals."[38] In France, members of the first High Court that judged prominent collaborators were drawn at random from two lists, one consisting of fifty deputies or senators who had held office on September 1, 1939, and the other of fifty members chosen by the consultative national assembly. After the election of a constituent national assembly in October 1945, a second High Court was created whose members were drawn randomly from a list containing deputies in proportion to the representation of the political parties in the assembly.[39] In many countries that were occupied by or collaborated with Germany, lay judges

33 Kirchheimer (1961), p. 359.
34 Bass (2000), p. 6.
35 Kirchheimer (1961), p. 340.
36 Bancaud (2002), p. 396.
37 Déak (in press).
38 Ibid.
39 Noguères (1965).

and jurors were either selected or screened by the resistance.[40] The political element in the composition of these bodies is compatible with legal justice in the minimal sense. It may reduce the uncertainty of outcomes, but does not eliminate it. The very political French High Court, for instance, pronounced nonsuits or acquittals in 45 out of 108 cases. I discuss some of these decisions later in this chapter.

In the universe of cases, the trial of Pierre Laval before the High Court nevertheless stands out as a borderline case between legal and political justice.[41] The president of the tribunal "proved totally incapable of either keeping order in the tumultuous courtroom or controlling his own outbursts."[42] During a break in the third session, the parliamentary jurors openly insulted Laval and asked for "twelve bullets." Laval protested, "Before I am judged!" to which a juror responded, "You have already been judged by France."[43] An observer commented that "French justice is discredited. Laval has won the last round."[44] By judging him according to procedures uncomfortably similar to those of Vichy,[45] the jurors sacrificed the goal of demarcating themselves from the lawless practices of the predecessor regime for the goal of punishing its leaders.

I have emphasized that a functioning legal system is a source of uncertainty. *Full certainty exists only in show trials.* A functioning democracy, too, is a pervasive source of uncertainty. As Adam Przeworski has emphasized, a crucial feature of democracy is that nobody can be fully certain ex ante that their party will win the election.[46] *That certainty exists only in sham elections.* Even a constitutional monarchy is subject to the uncertainty generated by elections and assemblies. In 1815, the first government of Louis XVIII counted on the elections to return a moderate assembly that would

[40] This was the case in Denmark (Tamm 1984, pp. 131–37), France (Novick 1968, pp. 151–52), Italy (Woller 1996, pp. 225, 296, 326), and Holland (Mason 1952, p. 72). In Belgium, too, members of the resistance claimed a central place in judging the collaborators, but were met with the argument that "Heroes are not made for judging" (Huyse and Dhondt 1993, p. 90). (For a further comparison of the *qualités de résistants* and the *qualités de magistrats*, see also de Gaulle's first Minister of Justice, François de Menthon, cited in Bancaud 2002, p. 135.) Bancaud (2002), p. 388, notes a surprising reason why "Vichy judges" were deemed undesirable by the resistance: They had shown themselves too reluctant to impose the death sentence under the occupation!

[41] Stenographic transcripts in *Le procès Laval* (1946).

[42] Novick (1968), p. 177.

[43] *Le procès Laval,* p. 207.

[44] Cited in Novick (1968), p. 177.

[45] Comparing the Riom trial with that of Laval, Bancaud (2002), p. 399, writes that the latter was an even "more exorbitant judicial farce" than the former.

[46] Przeworski (1988).

support its policies, but instead it had to step down before the ultraroyalist *chambre introuvable.* Once an assembly has been elected, its decisions may be hard to predict unless there are both party discipline and public voting. In the chambre introuvable, neither condition obtained. In the debates over the amnesty law passed in January 1816, there was uncertainty up to the last minute. In the English Restoration, the extensive uncertainty about whom parliament would exempt from the general amnesty kept many from following the King's orders to give themselves up.

I am not saying that these cases amount to legal justice simply by virtue of not being instances of "pure" political justice. I am merely making the point that if the executive decides to delegate political justice to parliament rather than carrying it out directly, it may be as frustrated as if it hands the task over to the courts. The potential targets for punishment do not have the benefits of unbiased judges and due process, but they may benefit from having friends in parliament who are biased in their favor (and suffer from having foes biased against them). In transitional justice, such political infighting may even take place in the context of a legal trial. The Nuremberg Charter stated that "the Tribunal shall take decisions by a majority vote and in case the votes are evenly divided, the vote of the President shall be decisive: provided always that convictions and sentences shall only be imposed by affirmative votes of at least three [out of four] members of the Tribunal." Some implications of this strange voting scheme appear in the account of the sentencing of Rudolf Hess:

> Lawrence and Nikitchenko thought Hess guilty on all four counts. Biddle and de Vabres voted for only Counts One and Two; since there was equal division on Counts Three and Four and unanimity on Counts One and Two, the latter prevailed. This result was of small account compared to the votes on the penalty – de Vabres for twenty years' imprisonment, Biddle and Lawrence for a life sentence, Nikitchenko for death. De Vabres stuck to his guns, so the impasse could be rectified only if Biddle and Lawrence joined de Vabres or if they and Nikitchenko joined forces. Biddle wrote: 'We finally – except French – agree on life sentence.' Presumably Nikitchenko feared that Biddle and Lawrence might join de Vabres, producing only a twenty-year penalty for the Russians' most hated bugaboo.[47]

A reasonable voting scheme would simply have excluded the twenty-year penalty, since three of the four members wanted a heavier sentence. As the rules stood, however, Nikitchenko had to guess whether the British

[47] Taylor (1992), p. 560.

and American judges had the death sentence as their second or third preference. On another occasion,

> De Vabres found Schacht guilty on Counts One and Two, but felt his subsequent mitigating actions required a prison sentence of only five years. Lawrence was... strongly for acquittal, as were both Birkett [UK] and Parker [United States], but Biddle would convict Schacht on Count One and put him in prison for life. Nikitchenko was... for the death penalty, but now saw that Schacht would go free unless something broke. He consulted Biddle on "how much we have to go down" in order to join with de Vabres. Finally, a deal was made for the penalty of eight years.... The next morning Lawrence called Biddle aside and told him that de Vabres had decided that Schacht should be acquitted, which of course put the judges back in the impasse. The reason? The previous day (September 12) Papen had been acquitted by a two to two impasse between Biddle and Lawrence for acquittal versus de Vabres and Nikitchenko for conviction and a light penalty. Fritzsche was then acquitted by three votes, with Nikitchenko dissenting. Biddle described de Vabres's reasons vis-à-vis Schacht: "His reasons are that he would have voted to convict all defendants, since in some measure all are responsible, and since Papen and Fritzsche are acquitted, Schacht, who is far less responsible than Papen, should be acquitted. Unity of judgment demands acquittal of all three."[48]

Administrative justice, that is, purges in the public administration, is close to legal justice if sanctions can be appealed to a court. In Italy by the end of 1946, for instance, 2,895 out of 3,200 dismissals of higher functionaries had been reversed on appeal to an administrative court.[49] Purge procedures in the first instance may also have elements of due process. In France in 1944, these guarantees were weaker for dismissals undertaken as part of a purge than for ordinary administrative dismissals. In the latter case, the functionary had the right to inspect (but not to make a copy of) the whole dossier that had been established against him. In the former, he only had the right to be told the grievance against him so that he could prepare his defense.[50] Prior to 1875, however, dismissals for political motives were entirely excluded from French administrative jurisprudence.[51] Thus, the vast purges of 1815 were essentially acts of pure political justice.

In most of the book I discuss institutions that are closer to the legal justice end of the continuum. I also consider practices that are closer to the other end, notably if they are established under a pretense of conforming to the rule of law. Show trials are often held "in the shadow of the law," in

[48] Ibid., p. 564.
[49] Woller (1996), pp. 370–71.
[50] Goyard (1977), pp. 14, 34.
[51] Ibid., p. 23.

the sense that the need to *appear* to be constrained by legality may impose some limits on the arbitrariness and lawlessness of the procedures. The Riom trials, for instance, were cut short on Hitler's direct order because they provided the occasion for brilliant defense speeches that were, in fact, acts of accusation.[52]

IV. LEVELS OF TRANSITIONAL JUSTICE

Transitional justice can involve several levels: supranational institutions, nation-states, corporate actors, and individuals. In this book, the main focus is on measures of transitional justice that (i) are enacted by a state and (ii) target wrongdoers and victims who are citizens of that state. I shall also have occasion, however, to discuss some of the other cases.

Supranational institutions include the Nuremberg War Crimes Tribunal, the International War Crimes Tribunal for the Far East, and the International Criminal Tribunals for Rwanda and for the former Yugoslavia.[53] The latter two tribunals differ from the other cases discussed in this book in that they represent neither successors nor winners but the international community. I shall not, therefore, consider them further. Let me note, nevertheless, a common feature of transitional justice after Bosnia and after World War II. In 1944, the publication by the *Wall Street Journal* of the Morgenthau plan (see Chapter 7) to impose a "Carthaginian peace" on Germany triggered accusations by Thomas Dewey, Roosevelt's rival for the upcoming presidential elections, that Goebbels had used the plan to "terrify the Germans into fanatical resistance."[54] In Bosnia, France and Britain "saw the issue of war criminals as a potential impediment to making peace in ex-Yugoslavia, binding the hands of policymakers who might have to cut a deal with criminal leaders."[55] By implication, refusing to deal might prolong the war. The analogy is imperfect, since in World War II the Allies excluded a negotiated peace. What is common to the two cases is that anticipation of harsh justice after the transition can delay the transition by stiffening the will to resist of dictatorial leaders.[56]

52 Lacouture (1977), pp. 469–81.

53 In addition to these courts that deal with criminal cases, the European High Court in Strasbourg has been seized with several cases involving restitution of confiscated properties in former communist countries (see *Le Monde* 2003).

54 Beschloss (2002), p. 160.

55 Bass (2000), p. 211.

56 See also note 62 to Chapter 7.

After a war, the victorious states may demand reparations from the losers or punish them, individually or collectively. The aim of reparations may in fact also be retribution or deterrence, rather than simply compensation. In 1945, the Allies eventually chose the path of punishing individual Nazi leaders, rather than adopting the Morgenthau plan that would have punished the German people collectively, by setting the living standard of Germany back to that of 1810 (Chapter 7). If one believes, as Morgenthau did, that the "Nazi regime is *not* an excrescence on an otherwise healthy society but an organic growth out of the German body politic,"[57] then each and every German bore responsibility for the war and deserved to be punished. Whereas anger is triggered by what individuals *do*, hatred is caused by beliefs about what they *are* (Chapter 8). Morgenthau's beliefs about the German national character were less radical than Nazi beliefs about the Jewish racial character, but had some of the same essentialist features. Just as a basic premise of anti-Semitism is that "the Jew could not be changed, that a Jew remained a Jew,"[58] "Morgenthau was sure that the Germans were a war-loving race, and possibly incurable."[59]

Corporate actors include organizations (political parties or churches), economic enterprises, professional associations, and municipalities. In some cases they may be targets of transitional justice; in others they may be dispensers of justice. (They may also be denied justice, as happened to the French Catholic Church after 1815.) In a still ongoing process in Eastern Europe, assets confiscated from religious communities by the Communist regime have been returned. In the Czech Republic, Prime Minister Klaus refused to promote legislation for the return of communal Jewish property, because he feared that it would trigger compensation demands from the Sudetengermans and from the Catholic Church. In 2000,

[57] U.S. Senate (1967), p. 599. See also Beschloss (2002), p. 52: "Unlike other American officials, Morgenthau refused to separate the German people from their evil government. He was an original believer in collective guilt for German war crimes."

[58] Hilberg (1985), p. 21.

[59] Beschloss (2002), p. 71, citing a contemporary account. There are several essentialist theories about Germans. There is the Goldhagen (1996) thesis that Germans are intrinsically anti-Semitic. There is the Arendt (1994) thesis that Germans are intrinsically obedient and conformist: Had they received orders to kill all the Poles or all the Frenchmen, they would have done so as well (Novick 1999, p. 137, citing Bauer 1992). (As noted by Novick 1999, p. 245, however, the disturbing findings in Milgram 1974 suggest that under the appropriate circumstances, *anyone* might be induced to harm *anyone*.) Finally, there is the Morgenthau thesis that the Germans are intrinsically aggressive.

the Czech parliament nevertheless decided to return Jewish property that remained in the hands of the state.[60] In Romania, a law from 1997 ordered the return of communal Jewish property that had been confiscated during World War II, returned when Romania switched allegiance to the Allies, and confiscated again four years later. In Poland, the authorities "have contended that restitution should be limited by reference to the religious needs of Poland's current Jewish community,"[61] which is less than one-tenth of 1 percent of the prewar Jewish population. In Bulgaria, the Supreme Court ordered the return of a profitable hotel in Sofia that was previously owned by the Jewish community, but seven years later the government was still ignoring the decision.[62] In Hungary, the Church Property Act passed in 1991 has created many problems, particularly when property has been returned to the Catholic Church in regions where most Catholics were ethnic Germans who were expelled after the war. The return of one of the two high schools in a town to the Evangelical Church shows that "while restitution may remedy an historical wrong it can also create new problems and, ironically, injustice."[63] I return to that issue in Chapter 6.

The recent negotiations involving Swiss banks, Italian insurance companies, and German firms that benefited from Nazi wrongdoings also involved corporate actors rather than individuals.[64] The extent to which current managers of these institutions benefited personally from actions taken by their predecessors fifty-odd years earlier is impossible to ascertain, and almost certainly irrelevant to their behavior. By contrast, they may be held responsible as individuals for their procrastinating and obfuscating behavior during the later negotiations. In practice, however, that responsibility devolved on the firms that employed them. The Swiss banks, in particular, had to pay what amounts to punitive damages for what they did and said in the 1990s, in addition to reparation for what they did in the 1940s.

Punishment of wrongdoers may involve three levels of actors, as illustrated in Figure 3.1 in Chapter 3. Three-level patterns are also found in restitution, when property is taken from individuals and later allocated by the state to a corporate actor representing those individuals if,

60 Pogany (1997), Chap. 9; Eizenstat (2003), Chap. 1.
61 Pogany (1997), p. 190.
62 Eizenstat (2003), p. 38.
63 Pogany (1997), p. 196.
64 For surveys, see Authers and Wolffe (2002) and Eizenstat (2003).

as in the case of many victims of the Holocaust, they left no heirs. The peace treaties with Hungary and Romania that were established at the Paris Peace Conference in 1947 incorporated clauses "which would require the transfer of heirless and unclaimed property belonging to persecuted persons, organisations or communities to bodies representing the dispossessed."[65] In 1999, the Norwegian parliament allocated 150 million Norwegian crowns ($20 million) to the Jewish communities, to supplement the insufficient compensation for Aryanized Jewish property that was given after 1945. Conversely, when property taken from individuals ended up in the possession of a corporate actor such as the Communist Party, the state could return it to the original owners.[66]

Corporate actors may carry out purges of their members or employees. To take only one profession, in Norway and Denmark after 1945, collaborating journalists were purged by the press associations. In Denmark, a professional purge inquiry was even held behind closed doors during the occupation.[67] In Belgium, journalists were prominent targets of state action. France and Holland present intermediate cases. In Holland, journalists came before a state-appointed purge board made up mostly of resistance journalists and a few judges.[68] In France, an ordinance of March 1945 authorized the commission that delivered the indispensable professional card for journalists to refuse it for shorter or longer periods to those who had been active in collaborationist journals.[69]

Private firms, too, might carry out internal purges of their employees. In Belgium, some managers, spontaneously or under pressure, dismissed

65 Eizenstat (2003), p. 175. The clauses were never implemented.

66 "A highly symbolic case dealing with restitution of expropriated private property is again in the hands of the Chairman of the Housing and Urban Development Office (URMiM). Under his scrutiny is the site of the former communist party headquarters where a leading Warsaw newspaper was located before the war. . . . This case is charged with emotion in light of the original public good that this parcel's nationalization was to have served and its subsequent appropriation by the apparatus of communist power. In another legal dispute over the nationalization of property, foreign-based descendants of the prominent Tarnowski family are seeking title to personal assets seized during the postwar expropriation of their land holdings in eastern Poland. Many of these personal possessions are currently held by the district museums in Rzeszow and Lancut as well as the National Library" (Polish news bulletin, March 20, 2002).

67 Tamm (1984), p. 602.

68 Mason (1952), p. 108. This was the general pattern in the Dutch professional purges. In Belgium, apart from journalists, the main procedure was the internal purge.

69 Delporte (1999), pp. 399–400.

employees who were under judicial investigation.[70] In Holland after liberation,

> the need was felt to purge industrial plants and other enterprises. In many instances workers refused to work alongside "impure" elements. Consequently, internal Purge Boards were soon improvised in most plants and bigger businesses, staffed by workers and employees with good resistance records. These boards advised sanctions, usually dismissals, to the employers, who almost always carried out such suggestions. Although no decree had confirmed the legality of these private Purge Boards, they appeared to work satisfactorily.[71]

Finally, no picture would be complete without a discussion of "private justice," carried out by individuals against other individuals. It can take the form of extralegal killings, as in France after 1815 or in France and Italy at the end of World War II. In Belgium in 1944–45, there was widespread looting, which received a semiofficial endorsement when the government suspended a decree from 1795 that would have enabled collaborators to receive compensation for damage to their property.[72] It can also take the form of deliberate and public humiliation, by tarring and feathering collaborators,[73] forcing them to drink castor oil in public until it takes effect,[74] or cutting the hair of women who had engaged in "horizontal collaboration" with the enemy.[75] During the White Terror in 1815, there was extensive harassment of royalists and Protestants (Chapter 2). As in cases of "vindictive rape,"[76] many of these abuses were not triggered by any specific actions on the part of the victims, but by their membership in a hated category. In Latin America, amnestied officers who are known to have participated in torture or disappearances have been met with informal social ostracism. Those convicted for collaboration may receive the same treatment after serving their sentence, and their children may suffer the scorn of their classmates.

70 Huyse and Dhondt (1993), p. 56.

71 Mason (1952), p. 100.

72 Huyse and Dhondt (1993), pp. 50–51.

73 As noted in Chapter 3, this was a standard treatment of loyalists during and to some extent after the American War of Independence. It also occurred occasionally in the liberation of France in 1944.

74 Woller (1996), p. 281.

75 This is the topic of the path-breaking and myth-breaking work of Virgili (2000).

76 On rapes by the Prussian troops in France after Napoleon's second abdication in 1815, see Houssaye (1906), pp. 492–94. An estimated 2 million German women were raped by Soviet soldiers in the end stages of World War II (Beevor 2002, p. 410).

Private justice may also be seen as a substitute for, or preemption of, legal justice. In the 1815 debates in the French parliament, some argued, as we saw in Chapter 2, that unless one allowed for unconstrained legal justice rather than the limited political justice embodied in the declaration of July 24, the population might take justice into its own hands. In a comment on the massacres during the White Terror in Nîmes in 1815, a local officer argued that private justice was acceptable since it only carried out more speedily what the courts would do later in any case. Unofficial blacklists also belong in this category. In France, the first of many successive blacklists of writers was established in March 1943. Later, not only were new names added to the list, but some were also deleted.[77] In the spring of 1998, an unknown organization in Lublin (Poland) published the names of 119 persons who had allegedly cooperated with the militia before 1989. Two of the named individuals killed themselves.[78]

Conversely, legal actions may be shaped by the perceived need to preempt and prevent private justice. In Marseilles in 1815, those suspected of Jacobinism or Bonapartism were sent to the Château d'If for their own protection.[79] In France in 1944, many spontaneous killings were the result of "frustration at the slowness of official justice"; hence, the "new *commissaires* and prefects did their best to appease popular anger by the rapid institution of courts-martial."[80] In Belgium, Denmark, and France, the large number of internments of dubious legality was justified at the time by the need to protect suspected individuals from private justice.[81] In Denmark, the reintroduction of the death penalty was justified by the need to prevent private executions.[82] In such cases, first-best justice is replaced by second-best procedures to prevent third-best outcomes.

Private and legal justice may interact through the mechanism of *denunciation*. Although it is more common in autocratic regimes than in their democratic successors,[83] democratic transitions may also offer the opportunity for disinterested as well as interested denunciations.[84] The following story about Albert Soboul, a Jacobin historian of the French

77 Sapiro (2003), pp. 244–49.

78 Kuk (2001), p. 209.

79 Houssaye (1906), p. 147. Edmond Dantès, by contrast, was sent to the Château d'If to prevent him from revealing the Bonapartist leanings of the father of a prominent judge.

80 Novick (1968), p. 72; also Lottman (1986), pp. 110, 179, 182–83, 201.

81 Huyse and Dhondt (1993), pp. 105–6; Tamm (1984), p. 105; Lottman (1986), pp. 135–36.

82 Tamm (1984), p. 75.

83 The essays in Fitzpatrick and Cellately (1997) give many examples of denunciation in totalitarian regimes, but none from democracies.

84 For this distinction, see Kozlov (1997).

Revolution and a lifelong Communist, may provide an example.[85] Soboul joined the communist resistance movement in 1940–41. On December 5, 1944, he sent a letter to the academic purge board of Montpellier, where he had been teaching before he was discharged in 1942, in which he denounced another professor, Lucien Tesnières, as responsible for his dismissal. The charge rested on a letter that Tesnières had written to Soboul in September 1941, threatening to denounce him to the public prosecutor for not having returned borrowed books to the university library of which he was the director. The denunciation by Soboul for having been denounced proved to be unfounded. We can only speculate about the underlying personal motives.

V. THE AGENTS OF TRANSITIONAL JUSTICE

To understand the processes and outcomes of transitional justice, we should first identify the agents who are involved. The wrongdoings carried out by the earlier regime create three kinds of agents. First, there are the *wrongdoers,* the perpetrators of wrongs on behalf of the autocratic regime. Second, there are the *victims* who suffered from the wrongdoings. Third, there are the *beneficiaries* of wrongdoing. To these we may add the category of *helpers,*[86] who tried to alleviate or prevent the wrongdoings while they were taking place, and that of *resisters,* who fought or opposed the wrongdoers while these were still in power. A further category is that of the *neutrals,* who were neither wrongdoers, victims, helpers, nor resisters.[87] After the transition there emerge organizers and advocates of transitional justice, or *promoters,* as I shall call them for brevity. These include the political actors who decide to proceed with purges, trials, and reparation, and the lay elements (jurors, liberation committees, and the like) who may be involved in implementing their decisions. More broadly, I also include among the promoters those who are most vocal in demanding justice. Judges and prosecutors, too, if politically motivated, may fall in this category. Finally, there are those we may think of as *wreckers* of

[85] Singer (1997), pp. 208–9.

[86] I limit myself to those who helped victims who were not also resisters. Those who help members of the resistance more or less automatically become members themselves. For some brief remarks on those who helped the Jews during World War II, see Hilberg (1992), pp. 212–14.

[87] For some purposes, it may be useful to subdivide neutrals into *attentistes,* who wait before committing themselves to the winning side, and those who simply want to avoid any kind of commitment.

transitional justice, that is, the individuals who try to oppose, obstruct, or delay the process. Altogether, then, we may distinguish eight relevant categories of agents. In Chapters 5 and 6 I discuss two of them – wrongdoers and victims – in more detail.

To bring out the moral, legal, and political complexities of the situation, I shall give examples showing that a given individual may appear in more than one category, successively or simultaneously. Anticipating the analyses in Chapter 5 of excuses and mitigating factors, I shall deal most extensively with wrongdoers who claim the status of either resister or victim as an extenuating circumstance. I shall also discuss more briefly, sometimes referring to later chapters, how resisters may come to be seen as wrongdoers, how resisters and victims may or may not overlap, how wrongdoers and beneficiaries of wrongdoing may or may not overlap, how neutrals may be viewed either as wrongdoers or as resisters, how wrongdoers and resisters may overlap with wreckers, and how the class of promoters may overlap with those of victims, resisters, beneficiaries, neutrals, and even wrongdoers. Altogether I shall discuss *eleven different role combinations*.

(1) Someone who committed or benefited from acts of wrongdoing at one time may later become a resister. After the transition, these individuals will often have a morally and legally ambiguous status. One reason that Albert Speer escaped execution at Nuremberg was that, in the words of the Tribunal,

> in mitigation it must be recognized that in the closing stages of the war he was one of the few men who had the courage to tell Hitler that the war was lost and to take steps to prevent the senseless destruction of production facilities, both in occupied territories and in Germany. He carried out his opposition to Hitler's scorched earth program in some of the Western countries and in Germany by deliberately sabotaging it at considerable personal risk.[88]

By and large, however, there were few surviving turncoats in the Third Reich. The members of the July 20, 1944, conspiracy against Hitler were

[88] http://www.yale.edu/lawweb/avalon/imt/proc/judspeer.htm. With respect to Seyss-Inquart, the Tribunal found that "in certain cases Seyss-Inquart opposed the extreme measures used by ... other agencies, as when he was largely successful in preventing the Army from carrying out a scorched earth policy, and urged the Higher SS and Police Leaders to reduce the number of hostages to be shot" (http://www.yale.edu/lawweb/avalon/imt/proc/judseyss.htm). Seyss-Inquart was nonetheless condemned to death and executed. Whether the different treatments were due to Speer's crimes being smaller or his redemptive acts being more important is hard to tell.

all executed on the spot. I shall focus instead on transitional justice in France after the liberation, when many Vichy collaborators claimed *actes de résistance* or *faits de résistance* as extenuating circumstances. I limit myself to the courts that, because they dealt with a relatively small number of cases, have been most extensively studied, the High Court of Justice, which tried high-ranking Vichy officials, and the Jury of Honor, which decided on the eligibility for public office of the deputies and senators who held office in 1940 and voted plenary powers to Pétain.

The French law on national indignity of December 26, 1944, stated that those condemned to national degradation might have their sentence lifted if "at some date posterior to the actions held against them they had rehabilitated and distinguished themselves by military action against Germany and its allies or by active, efficacious and sustained participation in the resistance against the occupant or [the Vichy] government." Many of those brought before the High Court were charged, among other things, with national indignity. In its decisions, the Court relied on a very broad interpretation, going well beyond the normal meaning of the words, of the requirement of "active, efficacious and sustained participation." In one case, the mere nondisclosure of activities of the resistance was seen as an "act" of resistance.[89] In another, a single heroic act in August 1944 was enough. In some cases, an important basis for alleging participation in the resistance was the expression of German dissatisfaction with the person in question.[90] Often, relatively small services rendered to the resistance seem to have offset heavy involvement in the repressive apparatus of Vichy. Moreover, there may have been a tendency to rewrite history, when individuals who changed behavior after (say) 1942 claimed that they had actually been playing a "double game" from the beginning.[91]

In the French trials and debates after liberation, the idea of "compensation" was sometimes stretched very far. As just indicated, the basic principle was that to atone for wrongdoing, an act had to take place *after* the actions held against the wrongdoers. In some cases, however, the High Court viewed heroic behavior in World War I as an extenuating circumstance that might offset later wrongdoings.[92] In their attempts to

[89] Chauvy (2003), p. 230.

[90] Chauvy (2003), pp. 113, 122, 135, 158, 160. Paxton (1997), p. 341 n.6, notes that General de la Porte du Theil was acquitted after the liberation because the Germans had deported him in the mistaken belief that he was a *résistant* rather than merely a Vichy nationalist; see also Chauvy (2003), p. 174.

[91] Paxton (1997), p. 90; see also ibid., pp. 14–16, and Baruch (1997), p. 429.

[92] Chauvy (2003), pp. 141, 180.

persuade de Gaulle to commute the death sentence of Robert Brasillach, François Mauriac and others invoked the fact that Brasillach's *father* – *mort pour la patrie* in November 1914 – had "paid in advance" for the wrongdoings of his son.[93] An even more original compensatory argument was offered in a 1944 report emanating from the bar of Aix-en-Provence, claiming that since the errors of some of its members were redeemed by the courage of others, no purge was needed.[94] In addition, as I shall now argue, the High Court was willing to accept as compensation for earlier wrongdoings behavior whose sole purpose may have been to establish that excuse.[95]

After Pearl Harbor, the invasion of North Africa, Stalingrad, and the invasion of Sicily, many regime leaders and supporters in German-occupied countries began to suspect that their time was measured. For those who had not compromised themselves too much, there was a clear incentive for opportunistic or strategic changes of mind and behavior.[96] As noted in Chapter 3, the Italian law of July 27, 1944, had the prospective purpose of inducing collaborators with the fascist regime to redeem themselves by joining the struggle against the Nazi republic of Salò. Although the French law of December 26, 1944, was technically backward looking, it is probable that some legislation of this kind had been anticipated and to some extent guided preliberation behavior.[97] In the spring of 1944, the press magnate Jean Prouvost successfully tried to "redeem [*racheter*] his behavior" by handing over large sums of money to the resistance in exchange for receipts that he was later able to produce at his trial before the

93 Lacouture (1980), vol. 2, pp. 203, 208.

94 Israël (2003), p. 215.

95 To show how such strategic behavior is incompatible with genuine redemption, we may draw an analogy to religious salvation. The religions that accept that good works may lead to salvation usually stipulate that the works have to be performed "for love and fear of God" and not for the *sake* of salvation. Redemption, like salvation, is essentially a by-product (Elster 1983, Chap. 2). The difference is that unlike God, courts can be fooled.

96 I am not considering the turncoats or weathervanes who simply adjust their behavior under the new regime, sometimes rewriting history in the process. Two amusing anthologies, which juxtapose statements made by prominent individuals under successive regimes, are Eymery (1815) and Orion (1948). From the former, we may cite the astronomer Laplace, who dedicated the first edition of his *Exposition du système du monde* to Napoleon and the second to Louis XVIII. From the latter, the texts written by Wladimir d'Ormesson in 1940 and in 1944 provide particularly good examples of weathervane opportunism.

97 Some organizations in the resistance told compromised high functionaries that they could improve their prospects by unconditional adherence to the movement (Baruch 1997, p. 514). Other organizations opposed this practice of "privileging efficiency over morality" (ibid.).

High Court.[98] Another accused person produced a dramatic letter of resignation (addressed to Laval) from January 1944, "perhaps written with the ulterior motive that it might be used some day to justify his conduct and attitude."[99] A third was acquitted because of his heroic (if pointless) behavior in August 1944, when "he succeeded . . . in hoisting the Tricolor on the roof of the Renault factory while under SS fire that killed the patriot accompanying him."[100] Among others tried before the High Court, several who were acquitted because of *faits de résistance* had joined the movement only when it seemed likely that the Germans were losing the war.[101]

Robert Paxton argues that the French were, in general, very slow to realize that Germany would be defeated.[102] If that was indeed the case, we would not expect much opportunistic side switching, or only in the very last stages.[103] The exact distribution of beliefs and its change over time are, of course, impossible to establish. Various behavioral indicators reported by Philippe Burrin suggest, however, that by the end of 1943 at least, investment in a German victory had ceased to look profitable. Whereas in the first quarter of 1943, most young Frenchmen commanded to work in Germany obeyed the summons, disobedience had become the rule by the end of the year.[104] Similarly, the proportion of high school students who chose German as a foreign language (or whose parents chose it for them) doubled from 1939 to 1942, while falling rapidly thereafter.[105] Finally, many publishers who eagerly signed up for the right to translate German

[98] Chauvy (2003), pp. 162–63. Several bankers, too, tried to redeem themselves by large cash donations to the resistance in 1944 (Burrin 1995, pp. 281–82). Toward the end of the war, the resistance refused several offers of monetary assistance from high regime officials (Bloch-Lainé and Gruson 1996, p. 174), an issue that caused internal controversies similar to those mentioned in the previous note.

[99] Chauvy (2003), pp. 162–63, p. 228.

[100] Ibid., p. 168.

[101] Ibid., pp. 83, 145, 245.

[102] Paxton (1997), pp. 337–39.

[103] Subtler forms of opportunism depended on uncertainty about the outcome of the war, rather than on the conviction that Germany would lose (see, for instance, Baruch 1997, p. 519). In practice, it may be next to impossible to distinguish belief-based and value-based decisions to join the resistance. Some may have taken that decision because the prospects of a German victory seemed increasingly dim, and others because the behavior of the occupying power and its puppet regime became increasingly harsh. If I understand him correctly, François Bloch-Lainé (in Bloch-Lainé and Gruson 1996, pp. 74, 130, 134) suggests that many higher functionaries disguised their opportunistic belief-based change of behavior as a principled value-based one.

[104] Burrin (1995), p. 194.

[105] Ibid., pp. 304–5.

books chose not to use the option, in some cases presumably because they saw the writing on the wall. One publisher, Albin Michel, bought the rights to fourteen books but published only one.[106]

There are also other robust indicators that the French were very much aware of the difference between someone who joined the resistance in 1941 and someone who waited until 1943 or 1944. One is an undated document recently published by Marc Olivier Baruch, proposing a very detailed point system for blaming or exonerating members of the French prefectoral corps.[107] Although the scheme was not implemented, it reflects the perceived importance of the timing of resistance. The other is the behavior of the Jury of Honor established by the law of April 6, 1945, regulating the purge of the parliamentarians.

The proposal published by Baruch distinguishes fourteen dimensions of behavior or of career development. For each dimension, the functionary could receive positive or negative points, which presumably were to be added up to yield an overall evaluation. Because of the intrinsic interest of the document, I shall provide a (selective) summary that goes beyond the mere issue of timing.

(i) The document makes no distinction between Jews and Freemasons. Protecting the one or the other group receives the same number of points (+1) and persecuting the one or the other the same number (−2). Although this symmetry reflects the language of the regime, it appears clearly inappropriate in retrospect.
(ii) The number of points awarded for joining the resistance is finely graded according to the time of entry: +7 points for those who entered before November 1942, +4 for those who entered between November 1942 and September 1943, +3 for those who entered between September 1943 and May 1944, and +1.5 for those who entered after May 1944.
(iii) The number of points awarded for exercising a leading function in the resistance in the same periods were, respectively, +10, +7, +4, and +2.
(iv) To have "done nothing for the resistance" counted as 0 (rather than as a negative factor).

106 Ibid., p. 333. Another behavioral indicator is provided by the stock exchange movements (Destrem and Destrem 2003, p. 90).

107 Baruch (2003), pp. 164–69. For a discussion of point systems in the context of local justice, see Elster (1992a), Chapter 3.

(v) One positive point was awarded for having received no promotion under Vichy, normal promotion counting as 0, and exceptionally rapid promotion as −1.
(vi) A neutral attitude toward the Vichy militia and similar organizations generated one negative point, whereas mere hostility counted as 0. Open struggle was awarded one-half point.
(vii) Negative points were awarded for having held important posts in the Vichy government, with larger negative numbers corresponding both to later periods and to higher office. Thus, being a close personal associate (*intuitu personae*) of the head of the state or of the government before November 1942 generated the same number of negative points – three – as holding a leading function in a ministry after the invasion of Normandy.
(viii) Prefects appointed before the establishment of the Vichy government received one positive point, whereas appointments at later dates generated points ranging from 0 through −1 and −1.5 to −2.
(ix) Those who were discharged from their posts by Vichy received 3 positive points if they had been appointed before November 1942 and 2 positive points if they had been appointed after that date.[108]

Compared to the High Court, the Jury of Honor was also much more insistent and precise in its definition of what was to count as an act of resistance that could offset the fact of having voted for Pétain. In one of its first decisions, it laid down that

> [b]enevolent neutrality is insufficient. Insufficient is the fact of not having asked or of having refused favors of Vichy. Insufficient is the fact of having distributed forged rationing cards or of having protected some Jews. These manifestations of solidarity or sometimes of mere electoral prudence [*prévoyance*] cannot be seen as participation in the struggle against the enemy or against the usurper. The participation must have been positive and taken place before November 1942. Directly or indirectly, the person concerned must have risked his life.[109]

In requiring the redeeming actions to have been undertaken prior to November 1942, the judges "were striving to dissipate the suspicion of

[108] The dates of November 1942 and September 1943 correspond, respectively, to the invasion of North Africa (which was followed a few day later by the Germans taking full control over all French territory) and to the invasion of Sicily. Somewhat surprisingly, the German defeat at Stalingrad does not seem to have been perceived as an equally important watershed.

[109] Wieviorka (2003), p. 389.

opportunism."[110] The same motive may have been behind the requirement for the parliamentarian in question to have run a real danger, rather than merely to have performed some token acts of resistance that could later serve as an alibi. These criteria were also implemented in the later decisions. Military forms of resistance were privileged over civilian ones, except when the latter involved high risks.[111] Although the *préfets* who advised the Jury of Honor often stated that deportation to Germany was sufficient for rehabilitation, the Jury "did not consider that the hell of the concentration camps automatically conferred the right to reinstatement."[112] At that time, victimhood was not seen as tantamount to resistance.[113]

In Eastern Europe, regime collapses were so rapid and unexpected that they left no opportunity for strategic side switching. In Poland, the first and crucial Soviet domino to fall, neither the regime leadership, nor the opposition, nor foreign observers expected the triumphant victory of Solidarity in the elections of June 1989. There is nevertheless, in part of the opinion, deep skepticism toward former supporters of the regimes who turned into dissidents because of dissatisfaction with the communist policies. In the eyes of some, this change of mind (and of behavior) could never completely offset their prior acts. After the 1989 transition in Czechoslovakia, reform Communists such as Zdenek Jicinsky, who had left the party and become a dissident after the 1968 Soviet invasion, were viewed with skepticism by the "right wing" of Civic Forum. In Poland, a similar case is that of Jacek Kuron, who was in charge of setting up the communist boy scout organization in the 1950s but became disenchanted with communism and switched sides. He then spent years in prison and devoted his life to the anticommunist dissident movement, but even now his original affiliation is often brought up.

Although there was no anticipatory strategic behavior, one sometimes observes a measure of retroactive opportunism. Commenting on a bill on decommunization proposed in July 1998 by 105 members of the Polish parliament, Leszek Kuk writes:

> With the caution that characterizes the right wing of Solidarity, the conceivers of the project went to great lengths to ensure that the bans [on former

[110] Ibid.
[111] Ibid., pp. 395–96.
[112] Ibid., p. 397.
[113] Later, perceptions have changed. If one travels in France and studies the "Monuments aux Morts" erected in virtually every village and town, one can observe several additions to the list of "morts pour la France" originally established in 1945. Among the new categories are those killed in Indochina (but not in Algeria!) and those deported during World War II.

Communist officials] did not affect anyone in their own milieu. That is why the project stipulates that the repressive measures would not apply to individuals who had in the past worked in the Communist state apparatus, but then left it to embark on activities in the political opposition. Among other indicators, proof of a change of political orientation would be provided by repressive measures taken against the individuals in question before 1989, including the 48-hours detention. This was a relatively mild preventive measure, which the regime applied to political opponents among others. The detentions were decided by... bodies that were administrative rather than judiciary in nature and whose records were not kept beyond five years, implying that they do not exist anymore. In this situation it was decided that a sworn affidavit by a credible witness would be decisive. There is no doubt that this opened up easy ways of manipulation and abuse by all those who wanted at any price to rectify their political CV.[114]

(2) Conversely, resisters may come to be seen as wrongdoers, to the extent that their actions trigger retaliation by the totalitarian regime. In Italy, for instance, the official representation of the end of the war is simply one of a struggle against fascism. Yet in three villages in central and northern Italy where the Germans undertook savage reprisals in 1944, perceptions remain different, according to interviews conducted fifty years later: "[T]he hostility of part of the population of these three villages towards the partisans did not appear to weaken." The "partisans were despised in the villages because villagers regarded them as those indirectly or even 'truly' responsible for the massacre."[115] Even more indirectly, one might blame the judges, doctors, and bureaucrats who stepped down from their positions in the autocratic regime, rather than staying to prevent fanatics who would do even more wrong from taking their place (Chapter 5). Resisters may also be viewed as wrongdoers by their own organization or by rival resistance groups. For the communist resistance in France, "not only collaborators, but also *résistants* who under torture gave information to the Germans, were 'objectively' traitors and to be punished as such."[116] In Charleroi (Belgium), the entering Allied forces found "the different resistance groups engaged in rounding up Rexists and other collaborationists.... In this activity, they produced a great deal of friction, due to the fact that each resistance group had its own blacklist,

[114] Kuk (2001), p. 196.

[115] Cappelletto (2003).

[116] Novick (1968), p. 179. A Danish member of the British Secret Service, who was arrested by the Germans on his return to Denmark and informed on one of his fellow members, was sentenced to eight years in prison by a lower court but acquitted on appeal (Tamm 1984, p. 380). He had not been subject to torture, but told that he would be executed as a spy.

and occasionally the blacklist of one group would include the name of a person associated with another group."[117]

(3) The set of (alleged) victims and the set of (alleged) wrongdoers can overlap in numerous ways. Some individuals might be wrongdoers and victims at the same time, as argued by Alex Boraine about the rank and file in the South African repressive apparatus.[118] Alternatively, the claim to having been a victim might be used to defuse charges of wrongdoing. When the German Constitutional Court in 1954 decided that because of their complicity with the Third Reich, the status of civil servants in 1945 was null and void, the Supreme Court protested by asserting that as a result of this decision, the officials "would have to bear the consequences of unjust measures of which they were in fact 'victims.'"[119] Similarly, the defender in the 1963–65 trial of Auschwitz guards claimed that "these defendants too became Hitler's victims."[120] As late as "April 1969, at the beginning of the second parliamentary debate to extend the statute of limitations on murder, Günther Diehl, the government's press secretary, called men who had murdered under order 'victims of the Nazi system.'"[121]

Nazi perpetrators also claimed to be victims in a different sense – not of the Hitler regime but of the postwar processes. In 1950, a member of the Bundestag raised the question "whether a kind of 'compensation' might not be arranged for those who had been denazified at an early point, hence according to relatively strict criteria," compared to those who were assessed by later and laxer standards.[122] In the same period, "the term *Wiedergutmachung* [making good again], commonly being used to designate reparations for [Nazi persecutees], was now increasingly applied" to the reinstatement of officials dismissed during denazification:[123]

> Without a doubt, the former chief judges and Nazi functionaries considered themselves victims – with a right to *Wiedergutmachung*. The "object lesson" [*Denkzettel*] that internment had certainly meant to much of the state and societal elite had long since faded; personalities such as Scriba [a former Nazi judge seeking to be reinstated in his full pension benefits] had replaced all such lessons with a notebook full of resentment.[124]

[117] Coles and Weinberg (1992), p. 803.
[118] Boraine (2000), p. 128.
[119] Frei (2002), p. 62.
[120] Sa'adah (1998), p. 169.
[121] Ibid., p. 170.
[122] Frei (2002), p. 31.
[123] Ibid., pp. 56–57.
[124] Ibid., p. 57.

In effect, these Nazi wrongdoers presented themselves as being *doubly victims*, first of Hitler and then of the Allied powers that unjustly identified them with their victimizer.

In the Preface, I mentioned how children of Norwegian collaborators were ostracized after the war. Children born to a Norwegian mother and a member of the German occupational forces had an even more harrowing fate. Recently, their organization sued the Norwegian government for $330,000 per child in compensation for the abuses and discrimination they suffered. Although the courts rejected the claim because the statute of limitations had expired, in December 2002 the Norwegian parliament asked the government to propose a scheme to compensate the ten to twelve thousand individuals concerned. Needless to say, these children were not wrongdoers in any meaningful sense. They had not *done* anything wrong. Yet they were treated as such on the basis of what, given their ancestry, they were perceived to *be*. As in the Morgenthau plan for Germany, essentialist beliefs not very different from those of the Nazi regime were at work. The consequences for the Norwegian children were much less severe, but the attitude of their persecutors was similar.

On a larger scale, Austria has been variously viewed as victim and as co-perpetrator of Nazi atrocities. The 1943 Moscow Declaration describes Hitler's 1938 annexation of Austria as an "occupation" and Austria as "Hitler's first victim." This deeply misleading statement is belied by the enthusiasm with which the *Anschluss* was met in Austria, the ferocity of the anti-Semitism it unleashed, the large percentage of Austrians who joined the Nazi party, and the heavy representation of Austrians in the killing machinery: "Although they represented only 8 percent of the combined German-Austrian population, Austrians made up 14 percent of the SS, and 40 percent of the killing force in Auschwitz."[125] For decades, the official designation as victim enabled Austrians to live in a world of collective self-delusion, tinged with bad faith. It was "the life-lie of the republic."[126] The guilty conscience of the Austrians is reflected in the fact that by "1980 Austrian public opinion – led by [Chancellor] Kreisky – treated [the Nazi hunter Simon] Wiesenthal as a hate object."[127]

Under "mature" communism, there was a more genuine sense in which more or less everybody was at the same time victim and co-perpetrator.

[125] Eizenstat (2003), p. 281.

[126] Forster (2001), pp. 114–17.

[127] Pick (2000), p. 5; see also pp. 106–8 for the relationship between Kreisky and Wiesenthal.

Roughly speaking, everybody knew that nobody believed in the tenets of the official ideology, and yet everybody was compelled to talk and behave as if they did.[128] This system of open lies can be explained by its repressive efficacy.[129] The reason why the leaders forced people to make absurd statements in public was not to make them believe in what they said[130] but to induce a state of complicity and guilt that undermined their morality and ability to resist. Indeed, they were so hollowed out as individuals that, as a woman from the former East Germany said, "she could not just suddenly 'speak openly' or 'say what she thought.' She did not even really know precisely what she thought."[131]

Victims may also appear as wrongdoers if they collaborate with wrongdoers and facilitate their work. Thus, the "law under which Eichmann was tried had been instituted in Israel to punish Jewish collaborators. The Law for the Punishment of Nazis and their Collaborators included Nazis as a matter of form, but there was no expectation that any would be bagged. Its real target, everybody acknowledged, was collaborators among the survivors."[132] Some Jews collaborated with the Germans to gain time before they were killed, even if the price was to facilitate the killing of other Jews. In an obvious sense, they were acting under duress (see Chapter 6). The defense of John Demjanjuk, who was accused in 1986 by the Israeli government of serving as a guard in Treblinka, capitalized on this fact when it asked: "Did the Jewish guards, members of Judenrat, voluntarily (which is the main element of any crime, and in any civilized jurisdiction) guard their Jewish co-prisoners? Did, under the Nazi or Bolshevik prison regimes, any guard, particularly if he were not a Russian in the Soviet Union, or a non-German during the Nazi regime, perform his duties voluntarily and of his own free will?"

(4) Many wrongdoers derive direct material and career benefits from their actions. If they act for the sake of these benefits, they are what I shall call *opportunists* (see Chapter 5): "Already in 1933 German medical students persecuted their fellow Jewish students to rid themselves of the competition. German enterprises and their agents in banks, coveting a Jewish business, would take over their prey in unequal negotiations, assisted by

[128] See, for instance, Walder (1986), pp. 156–57.

[129] This is the explanation offered in Kolakowski (1978), vol.3, pp. 83–91.

[130] The theory of cognitive dissonance predicts, in fact, that people will adjust their beliefs to get in line with what they say only if there is no compelling stick or carrot that motivates and can be used to rationalize their utterances.

[131] Sa'adah (1998), p. 62.

[132] Novick (1999), p. 140.

regulations of the state."[133] Firms that requested slave laborers or forced laborers certainly did so because they thought they would profit. Newspaper owners in German-occupied countries who let their papers be used for German propaganda could earn monopoly profits from their collaboration. In South Africa under apartheid, the mining industry was both an instrument of oppression and its beneficiary.[134] Other connections are more indirect. Although the communist *nomenklatura* did not derive any benefits from individual acts of wrongdoing, their affluent lifestyle depended on their willingness to commit such acts. Those who were originally innocent beneficiaries of wrongdoing may themselves become wrongdoers if they refuse to return their ill-gotten gains. After 1815, the émigrés used this argument against the purchasers of *biens nationaux*; it was also widely made against the Swiss banks in the 1990s. Yet some beneficiaries are not wrongdoers, and may even be resisters. Thus, David Dyzenhaus, a vocal opponent of apartheid before its abolition, writes that "the direct benefit of the ordinary violence of apartheid to all whites was a 'cushy' lifestyle, some (including myself) living in luxury virtually unmatched in the rest of the world."[135]

Conversely, as we shall see in the next chapter, some wrongdoers derive no personal benefits from their acts. Also, they might benefit without the gains being an important part of the motivation. When Herman Göring joined the Nazi party in 1923, he could hardly have anticipated the enormous personal fortune he would amass.

(5) The lines separating neutrals from wrongdoers and resisters may be blurred. As we saw in Chapter 1, Solon enacted a law requiring that in civic strife, nobody should remain neutral. In apparent ignorance of that law, Lysias made the same argument in his speech "Against Eratosthenes." During World War II, some members of the French exile government and of the resistance demanded that all who had not fought actively against the Germans be removed from positions of authority.[136] After the liberation, a Communist writer, Claude Morgan, claimed that "the silence of [Jean] Giono was in itself a crime."[137] Many have argued that those who did nothing to help the Jews in Germany and elsewhere were "guilty bystanders," and that risking one's life to save Jews was a moral duty

[133] Hilberg (1992), p. 214.
[134] TRC (1999), vol. 4, pp. 33–36.
[135] Dyzenhaus (1998), p. 12.
[136] Singer (1997), pp. 173, 210.
[137] Todd (1996), p. 509.

rather than supererogatory behavior.[138] According to Peter Novick, the honoring of helpers – Yad Vashem Museum in Jerusalem honors more than eleven thousand non-Jews who risked their lives to save Jews during the Holocaust – must be viewed with this background: "The intention of most commemoration of the 'righteous minority' has been to damn the vast 'unrighteous majority.'"[139]

Others have argued, however, that apathy or indifference could actually be forms of resistance; specifically, that "although the overwhelming majority of the French [were] neutral" toward the anti-Jewish policies of Vichy, this "lack of cooperation could, in some cases, be viewed as a passive assistance to the Jews and a real obstacle to the anti-Jewish policies."[140] While this view corresponds to the idea that "Who is not for me is against me," the view of neutrals as wrongdoers reflects the idea that "Who is not against me is for me."

(6) Victims and resisters do not always coincide. The European Jewry that was the main victim of the Nazi regime did not, by and large, engage in resistance. One can make this statement without taking a side in the issue of whether the Jews conformed passively to a age-old tradition of compliance with the oppressor[141] or were merely deprived of the "resources and opportunities to halt the Final Solution."[142] The facts do not seem to be in dispute, only their explanation. Under communism, the bulk of the population were victims of the regime, albeit mainly in the more intangible sense of being deprived of opportunities (see Chapter 6), yet only a small minority became dissidents and virtually nobody took to arms against the regime.[143] As these cases indicate, victimhood need be neither the cause nor the effect of resistance. In other cases, victims become

[138] Novick (1999), pp. 179, 246.

[139] Ibid., p. 180.

[140] Cohen (1993), cited after Paxton (1997), p. 32. For his own part, Paxton argues (ibid.) that the "apathy made the execution of the Vichy policy easier rather than more difficult."

[141] Hilberg (1985), pp. 22–28 and passim; Arendt (1994), p. 135. On this point, as on others, Arendt's reasoning is flawed. She takes the fact that whereas 40%–50% of the 20,000 Dutch Jews who went into hiding survived the occupation, and almost nobody came back from the camps, as evidence confirming her estimate that as many as half of the Jews who died need not have done so. This is to commit the fallacy of composition, for if the hundred thousand Jews who were deported had tried to go into hiding, they would have been sharply constrained by the limited number willing to hide them.

[142] Davidowitz (1986), p. 351.

[143] In Poland, there were proposals to turn Solidarity into an "underground state," which would have been able to take repressive measures, rather than an "underground society," but they came to nothing (Monika Nalepa, personal communication).

resisters and resisters become victims. The first case is illustrated by the African National Congress and by communist resistance to Germans during World War II (after 1941). The second occurs, of course, very widely: Regimes that maintain themselves by violence are unlikely to abstain from using it against those who oppose them.

Some have argued for a moral difference between resisting and non-resisting targets of wrongdoing. In 1943, the German Communist Paul Merker wrote that

> [t]he Jewish people... had the same right to restitution for the damage done to them as did all the nations Hitler had invaded and oppressed. The Communists, by contrast, were persecuted because of what they did, not because of what they were. Those who had been punished because of their political views were not being persecuted as a "national, religious or castelike minority." They had volunteered to fight the Nazis. "Antifascist fighters" thus could not "expect material compensation for the sacrifices that result" from their voluntary commitments. Their compensation lay in "every successful battle and the final victory [over Nazism] and the erection of a democratic power."[144]

Merker is not asserting that the moral claims of victims are weaker if they were persecuted for behavior in which they engaged freely and from which they might have abstained, rather than for personal characteristics from which there was no escape. Rather, he is suggesting that the language of victimhood is inappropriate. Germans who suffered because of their resistance to Hitler were *martyrs,* not victims. To compensate for martyrdom would be somewhat like offering a religious believer financial compensation on the grounds that his fear of hell makes him chronically unhappy. Although Vaclav Havel got his family properties back, it is hard to imagine him asking to be compensated for his years in prison.

(7) Nonresisting victims and promoters may overlap. In Hungary after 1945, "so many Jews or persons affected by the anti-Jewish laws played a part in the various phases of the investigation and litigation or as judges that there is an empirical basis for the view that the essence of the whole process of retribution is that now the Jews pass judgment over the Hungarians as a revenge for the past when Hungarians passed judgment over the Jews."[145] (See also an example in the next paragraph.) Victims may also put pressure on the authorities to initiate prosecution. In Chapter 3, I mentioned how the prosecution of the Greek torturers

[144] Herf (1997), p. 52.

[145] This statement, made in 1948 by the Hungarian sociologist István Bibó, is cited with approval by Karsai (2000), p. 246.

resulted from actions by the victims. In Argentina, the "Grandmothers of the Plaza de la Maya" have been instrumental in the search for children of victims who were kidnapped under the dictatorship, and in bringing their kidnappers to justice.

(8) More frequently, resisters and promoters overlap. As mentioned, in trials after World War II, lay judges and jurors were often chosen or screened by the resistance, and may frequently have belonged to resistance movements. In France, "Vichy was judged in the High Court by those who had fought it... or by those who had suffered under it (the ordinance of July 29, 1945, opened the way to the High Court for prisoners of war and political deportees)."[146] In South Africa, the central role of the ANC in the work of the Truth and Reconciliation Commission reflected its role in the resistance to apartheid. In Eastern Europe, some of the former dissidents have been very vocal in requiring prosecution against leaders and agents of the communist regime, whereas others, acting as wreckers, have taken a conspicuously forgiving stance. In Czechoslovakia, for instance, Vaclav Benda and Vaclav Havel represent, respectively, the first and the second response. In Poland, they correspond to the right and the left wing of the former Solidarity, as personified by Jaroslaw Kaczynski and Tadeusz Mazowiecki respectively.

(9) By a mechanism further discussed in Section VI of Chapter 8, neutrals may emerge as promoters. By a different mechanism, which I consider in Section IV of Chapter 9, wrongdoers, too, may turn into promoters. More typically, of course, wrongdoers turn into wreckers. When the judges or administrators who are to dispense transitional justice were part of the machinery of the former regime, they will drag their feet, produce biased readings of the law, and otherwise obstruct the proceedings any way they can. The behavior of Fouché in 1815 is one example. In South Africa as well as in Poland, post-transition judges have resisted outside interference by appealing to the need for an independent judiciary, in spite of the complete lack of independence that most of the same judges showed under apartheid or communism.[147] In the case of Hitler's judges, the retroactive adoption of legal positivism served the same purpose: "Although it was clear to every jurist during the Nazi era... that National Socialist legal doctrines were the exact opposite of legal positivism, the claim that judges and prosecutors were merely following the law and that, after all, this was how they had been trained by their democratic

[146] Bancaud (2002), p. 112.

[147] Dyzenhaus (1998), pp. 37–38; Schwartz (2000), p. 63.

professors during the Weimar Republic became a blanket excuse for the whole profession."[148]

This tendency may operate even when the officials in question are not technically wrongdoers, in the sense that they would not themselves be targeted by the laws they are to apply. As shown by the experience from Germany,[149] France,[150] and Italy[151] after 1945, as well as of the post-communist countries,[152] former elites often display a solidarity among themselves that can bring transitional justice to a standstill. In South Africa, the negotiated transition included a statute that "formally declared the independence of the Attorney General by giving those in office tenure of their job for the rest of their working lives," in the hope that "such independence . . . would stand in the way of political pressure in the new order to prosecute the crimes committed under the old."[153]

(10) Beneficiaries, posing as victims, may act as wreckers in order to protect their ill-gotten gains. In Germany after 1945, the "Union for Honest Restitution," which organized "honest Aryanizers," managed to obtain restitution as *victims of the reparation process*. The Union "exercised a significant influence in the ranks of the CDU/CSU [the Christian Democratic Party and its Bavarian affiliate], the Bavarian party, and the FDP [the Free Democrats]. Their accomplices in the Bundestag and the press constantly managed to throw sand in the works of later restitution legislation as well, mobilizing latent hostility to the Jews."[154] In France, as further discussed in Chapter 6, a Committee of Owners of Aryanized Properties was formed after the liberation, only to be dissolved by the government.

(11) More surprisingly, beneficiaries may act as promoters. If they have benefited from the purchase of confiscated properties, they may advocate indemnification of the former owners to prevent restitution. This was, to some extent, the case of those who held biens nationaux in France after 1815. As long as the indemnity was to be paid by the state and not, as was sometimes proposed, levied on themselves, the purchasers had a

148 Müller (1991), p. 220. Liberal judges under a repressive regime may also appeal to legal positivism as a rationalization *in actu*, rather than ex post (see Dyzenhaus 1998, p. 85 and passim, and, especially, Cover 1975). On the alleged positivism of Vichy judges, see Bancaud (2002), p. 185.

149 Müller (1991); Frei (2002).

150 Israël (2003); Lesourd (2003).

151 Woller (1996), p. 88.

152 Tucker (in press).

153 Dyzenhaus (1998), pp. 128–29.

154 Pross (1998), p. 19.

dual interest in the compensation of the original owners. For one thing, compensation would remove the risk of restitution. For another, it would enhance the value of the properties whose prices remained artificially low because of their suspect origin and the political uncertainty surrounding them.

VI. THE DECISIONS OF TRANSITIONAL JUSTICE

The outcome of transitional justice is a series of legislative, administrative, and legal decisions.[155] As noted earlier, these form the explananda, or dependent variables, of subsequent chapters. In the remainder of this chapter, I survey the range of questions that typically confront the decision makers, and the range of answers they may come up with. As will become clear, many of these "decisions" did not reflect deliberate choices among alternatives. In negotiated transitions (Chapter 7), some options may be excluded by the outgoing leaders as a condition for handing over power. In other cases, some options emerge only after other solutions have been tried and found wanting.

The first question on which everything else turns is whether to address the wrongdoings of the past at all. In Chapter 3, I discussed several transitions in which the decision was made to abstain from opening up the past. In only one case, the Spanish transition of 1976–78, was this decision an endogenous and consensual one. In Brazil and Chile the abstention resulted from the self-amnesty of the military, in Rhodesia it was imposed by the British government, and in Uruguay it was chosen out of fear of how the military might react to prosecution. In the former Soviet Union, the near-total absence of transitional justice after the collapse of the communist regime was not the result of a conscious collective decision, but caused by the lack of any organized demand for justice.[156] The Charter of the First Restoration in France, which declared impunity for past opinions and votes and the inviolability of nationalized property, was to some extent imposed by the Allies.

If a new democratic regime decides to confront the past, a number of further questions arise. It may, for instance, have to *choose between justice*

[155] For a good overview, see the editorial Introduction to Herz (1982b).

[156] It is somewhat unsatisfactory to explain an absence by another absence, as in "the reason they never married is that they never met." It is probably more accurate to say that whatever incipient movements may have existed in favor of transitional justice were not strong enough to overcome the counterforces they set in motion.

and truth. (More weakly, even if nobody makes a conscious decision to grant access to the truth rather than justice, there may be an indirect causal connection between a low number of prosecutions and the providing of information about wrongdoings.)[157] Most of the twenty-odd truth commissions that have been established since 1982 have not even named the perpetrators, let alone proposed to punish them. The commission in South Africa is the major exception, but even here the knowledge of politically motivated wrongdoings does not lead to prosecution. The truth commission in El Salvador did name the wrongdoers, but parliament granted them a full amnesty five days after the report was published. In Brazil, the 444 torturers who were named by the Archdiocese of São Paulo had already been granted amnesty. In Chile and Argentina, the "truth trials" that developed in the 1990s could not, because of the amnesty laws, lead to prosecutions.

In Eastern Europe, there have been relatively few prosecutions for wrongdoings committed under communism. To some extent, a veil has been thrown over the past. At the same time, parts of the veil have been lifted by granting individuals access to their security files so that they can learn whether their relatives, friends, and co-workers spied on them under communism. In the former GDR, 3.4 million individuals had asked to see their files by 1997. In Poland, the National Remembrance Institute had by early 2002 received ten thousand applications from individuals who wanted to see their files, but it claims that budget constraints have prevented granting more than a hundred of the requests.[158] The Czech government has taken the more drastic step of making names of informers available in the public domain. On March 20, 2003, a list identifying seventy-five thousand spies and informers who had denounced friends and neighbors to the communist regime was posted on the website of the Ministry of the Interior and was also made available in print. The list revealed, in other words, that approximately 1 in every 130 Czechs had worked with the secret police.

[157] In the purge of the French press, for instance, it could happen that the sanction of temporary exclusion from the profession was inapplicable, for example, if a decision was made in June 1945 to exclude a member for six months beginning with September 1, 1944. In such cases, the Commission could demand that a list of the purged journalists be posted in all newspaper offices (Delporte 1999, pp. 397–98).

[158] The low number of applications may be due to the fact that in Poland, unlike what is the case in Germany, names of informants are blacked out in the files. This fact may in turn be due to the needs of the lustration process, which depends on individuals ignoring whether there is incriminating information about them in the files (Nalepa 2003a). See Chapter 9, Section III, for a brief comment on the budget constraints.

If the new regime decides to proceed with retributive and reparative justice, a number of further decisions will have to be taken.[159] I shall first survey *six types of substantive political decisions,* relating to the definition of wrongdoers and victims and the appropriate way of treating them, and then conclude by a discussion of the important procedural decisions that invariably force themselves upon the new authorities. Transitional justice, in fact, is characterized not only by its dramatic and traumatic substance but also by numerous deviations from due process.

(A) First, one has to decide what and who shall count as wrongdoing and wrongdoers. In Nuremberg, the main charges were crimes against peace (*jus ad bellum*), war crimes (*jus in bello*), and crimes against humanity. The Tokyo indictments were similar. In both cases, "conspiracy" to commit crimes against peace was in itself counted as a crime. The idea of conspiracy was taken in a very broad sense. When the chief American judge in Nuremberg, Francis Biddle, asked the chief British prosecutor, David Fyfe, "whether a member of the SA [Nazi storm troops] who had joined in 1921 and resigned the next year was guilty of conspiring to wage aggressive war, Fyfe replied: 'Yes, in this sense.... A man who took an active and voluntary part as a member of the SA in 1921 certainly, in supporting the Nazi Party, was supporting the published program of the Party.'"[160] In Tokyo, it has been argued, "the method of proof was ... one of inference, of inferring the existence of a conspiracy from a set of events."[161] Thus, from the fact that Japan in the early 1930s had rejected a Soviet offer of a nonaggression pact and the alleged fact that this offer had been "sincere," the tribunal inferred that "the Japanese had aggressive intentions against the Soviet Union."[162] In the Dachau, Mauthausen, and Buchenwald trials, the American prosecutors relied on the idea

[159] I am excluding the marginal issues of decisions concerning helpers and resisters. After the conclusion of the negotiations with the Swiss banks in the 1990s, the failure to compensate those who helped the Jews during the war was characterized as an "oversight" (Authers and Wolffe 2002, p. 354). As far as I know, no helpers have ever actually been rewarded or compensated for their deeds. After the fall of the oligarchs in 403, some of those who had opposed their regime were rewarded with a pay rise (Chap. 1). In Belgium and France after the liberation, being recognized officially as a (literally) card-carrying member of the resistance was a highly sought after good (Lagrou 2000). The recognition was not conceptualized as a reward, however, although it may have carried some benefits with it.

[160] Taylor (1992), p. 284.

[161] Minear (2001), p. 132.

[162] Ibid., p. 135.

of "common design" – a broadening of the notion of a conspiracy – to identify wrongdoers.[163]

Wrongdoings may involve four categories of individuals. First, there are those who *issued orders* for criminally wrongful acts to be committed. In the case of the three members of the National Defense Council of the GDR convicted for their responsibility in the border shootings, there was no smoking gun or paper trail that proved the issuing of orders, but the uncontested knowledge that "their actions would lead to death on the borders" was enough to incriminate them.[164] Second, there are those who *executed the orders*. Third, by a logical extension, one may also impute responsibility to *intermediate links* in the chain of command between those who issue orders and those who execute them. Thus in 1996, six former GDR generals were sentenced to prison terms ranging from three and a half to six and a half years for border killings. Eichmann, too, was a "conveyor belt" perpetrator.[165] Fourth, by a further extension, the conscious *facilitation* of wrongdoings, such as holding a victim down while he or she is being tortured,[166] may itself be seen as a wrongdoing. Maurice Papon was indicted (among other counts) for the "desk crime" (*crime de bureau*) of having kept a register of Jews in Bordeaux and communicated it to the German authorities.[167] Attempts to sue the national French railroad company SNCF for its role in the deportation of Jews during World War II have so far failed.[168] In countries occupied by Germany during World War II, one also had to lay down criteria for wrongful economic collaboration with the enemy, and to establish criteria for the new crimes of "national indignity" or "unpatriotic conduct."

In some cases, politically motivated wrongdoings may be excluded from prosecution. The Italian amnesty law of June 22, 1946, is one example. In the best-known case, South Africa, there has been some confusion about what counts as a political motivation. In particular, are wrongdoings committed because of racial hatred to be included in this category? In the case of the four white van Straaten brothers who had been convicted of killing two black security guards and who cited their "pure racial hatred"

[163] Greene (2003), pp. 42–43 and passim.

[164] McAdams (2001), p. 38.

[165] Arendt (1994), p. 153.

[166] In one Danish case, assisting in torture by holding the victim down led to a prison sentence of twenty years, although the torture itself would have incurred the death penalty (Tamm 1984, p. 341).

[167] *Le procès de Maurice Papon* (1998), vol. 1, p. 144.

[168] *New York Times*, March 20, 2003.

as a reason why they should be granted amnesty, the judges decided that "racism is ill-will and malice and is therefore not a political motive."[169] By contrast, four black youths who had killed a white American student, Amy Biehl, did receive the amnesty they had applied for. In the words of the amnesty subcommittee,

> As members of PASO, which was a known political organisation of students, they were active supporters of the PAC [Pan-African Congress] and subscribed to its political philosophy and its policies. By stoning company delivery vehicles and thereby making it difficult for deliveries into the townships, they were taking part in a political disturbance and contributing towards making their area ungovernable. To that extent, their activities were aimed at supporting the liberation struggle against the State. But Amy Biehl was a private citizen, and the question is why was she killed during this disturbance. Part of the answer may be that her attackers were so aroused and incited, that they lost control of themselves and got caught up in a frenzy of violence. One of the applicants said during his evidence that they all submitted to the slogan of ONE SETTLER, ONE BULLET. To them that meant that every white person was an enemy of the Black people. At that moment to them, Amy Biehl was a representative of the white community. They believed that by killing civilian whites, APLA [Azanian People's Liberation Army] was sending a serious political message to the government of the day. By intensifying such activity the political pressure on the government would increase to such an extent that it would demoralise them and compel them to hand over political power to the majority of the people of South Africa. When the conduct of the applicants is viewed in that light, it must be accepted that their crime was related to a political objective.[170]

Yet although "the attack occurred in the context of a township uprising against white domination, ... the van Straaten murders also occurred in a locale ... where many whites were organized into far-right white supremacist organizations and random acts of violence against blacks were commonplace."[171] Like the black youths, the brothers had attended political meetings without being members of a political organization or acting on its orders. In both cases, the acts also involved theft. In spite of these similarities, the committee reached opposite decisions in the two cases.

Leaders of the predemocratic regime may also be judged for *treason*, a crime that can be narrowly defined as collaboration with a foreign power or, more broadly, as any attempt to overthrow the legitimate government of the country by illegal means. The charge was widely used against high

[169] Wilson (2001b), p. 88.

[170] The quotation is taken from the website of the Truth and Reconciliation Commission: http://www.doj.gov.za/trc/decisions/1998/980728_ntamo%20openietc.htm.

[171] Wilson (2001b), p. 92.

political leaders in German-occupied countries, from Pétain and Laval to Quisling. In the former communist countries, the charge of treason has been advocated in the context of three traumatic events: the crushing of the 1956 Budapest uprising, the Soviet invasion of Czechoslovakia in 1968, and the Polish Martial Law in 1981. In Bulgaria, the issue has not come up because of the country's historically close relations with Russia. In Chile, a group of human rights organizations and relatives of victims of the Chilean military dictatorship announced in 2000 that they would file a lawsuit against Pinochet for high treason and espionage. As in the previously cited cases, this seems to rely on the narrow rather than the broad definition of treason. As I explained in Chapter 2, in 411 B.C. the oligarchs could only be charged with treason in the narrow sense because there was no basis in existing law for bringing a charge of subverting the democracy.

A delicate question is whether retribution shall be *one-sided* or *even-handed* – whether acts of wrongdoing shall include only crimes committed by agents of or collaborators with the former regime, or whether crimes committed by the opposition to the regime should also be covered. In the "Promotion of National Unity and Reconciliation Bill" that regulates the work of the South African Truth Commission, members of the liberation movement and of the state security forces are treated in an entirely symmetrical manner. At one point, Bishop Desmond Tutu "threatened to resign from the Commission unless the African National Congress formally acknowledged that it, too, was responsible for human-rights abuses."[172] The hearings on Winnie Mandela's activities made it clear that the Commission did more than pay lip service to this principle. In Argentina, President Alfonsín included among his guiding principles for prosecution that "[b]oth state and subversive terrorism should be punished."[173] Likewise, the Commission of Truth and Reconciliation in Chile was charged with investigating not only state terrorism but also subversive terrorism. Four percent of the human rights violations documented in its report fall in the latter category. In countries that had been occupied by or collaborated with Germany, unjustified killings by the resistance were not included in the formal war trials, although some victims were later formally exculpated.[174] A partial exception is Italy, where the amnesty

[172] Rosenberg (1996), p. 92.

[173] Nino (1996), p. 67.

[174] For Denmark, see Tamm (1984), Chap. 11. In France, the 1951 amnesty law included a clause that allowed victims of unofficial purges, for example, relatives of those executed by the resistance, to claim compensation. Not a single demand was registered (Lottman 1986, p. 481).

law of 1946 "not only offered the partisans who had carried out spontaneous acts of vengeance immunity from criminal prosecution, but also enabled many incriminated Fascists to return to their bourgeois lives."[175]

By contrast, when the ultraroyalist French parliament debated an amnesty law in December 1815, they rejected a proposal to extend the amnesty to royalists charged with crimes against individuals in the southern and western parts of the country. This proposal concerned, however, crimes committed *after* the transition. A newly established government may, to affirm its authority, crack down almost as hard on post-transition crimes by its supporters as on pre-transition crimes by its enemies. Thus after the liberation of France in 1944,

> [t]he Government, by a symbolic act, made it clear that it would tolerate no yielding before the threat of violence. The previous October, in Maubeuge, an angry mob had stormed the local prison demanding the execution of two collaborators whose death sentences had been commuted by General de Gaulle. The mob threatened to massacre all the other inmates of the jail if it did not receive satisfaction; the three F.F.I. [French Forces of the Interior] officers in charge did as the mob demanded. Brought to trial in Paris, the three officers were sentenced to prison terms of five to seven years. Numerous other arrests of *résistants* for unauthorized executions took place during early 1945.[176]

We may also observe evenhandedness in the treatment of crimes committed *after* the transition. In Germany, as mentioned earlier, the clause in the amnesty law of December 19, 1949, covering crimes committed after May 8, 1945, was implicitly evenhanded:

> According to the law, it was one and the same "whether it was a matter of crimes committed by former National Socialists against anti-fascists or vice versa." Whoever bribed an official to be denazified more quickly or in better fashion had acted on a political basis – but the same was true of whoever beat up a worker in the Allied-imposed industrial dismantling program, or whoever got even with a Nazi *Ortsgruppenleiter*.[177]

[175] Woller (1998), p. 543, citing contemporary statements suggesting that the law was the result of a deal between Togliatti, the Communist Minister of Justice, and the nonsocialist parties.

[176] Novick (1968), p. 77.

[177] Frei (2002), p. 21. Whereas the amnesty law represented an evenhanded treatment of different kinds of wrongdoers, a contrived kind of evenhandedness between victims and wrongdoers was observed in legislation reinstating a large number of Nazi officials in their pension and employment rights. This "Law Regulating the Legal Status of Persons Falling under Article 131 of the Basic Law" was passed on April 10, 1951, carefully synchronized with a "Law Regulating Reparations for National Socialist

(B) Next, one has to decide on how to treat the wrongdoers thus defined. The range of punishments includes execution, exile (the sanction of the regicides in 1815),[178] forced labor, imprisonment, suspended prison sentence, loss of civil and political rights, posthumous loss of "victim status,"[179] confiscations, and fines. After the 1945 transitions, the death penalty was reintroduced in several countries (Denmark, Holland, Norway) where it had previously been abolished. As noted earlier, some French officials argued for declaring certain individuals to be outlaws, an option that was also contemplated but discarded by the British government in 1943.[180] Those who were convicted of "national indignity" were punished by the loss of civil and political rights. In cases of economic collaboration, confiscation of profits often came on top of prison sentences and fines. In Holland, the wide use of plea bargaining allowed courts to impose unusual forms of punishment, such as ordering young girls to serve as maids in the families that most needed them.[181] Another innovative mode of punishment was introduced after the fall of communism, when high communist officials and collaborators with the secret service were denied access to elective or appointive office. While this measure has often been justified on forward-looking grounds, as incapacitation rather than retribution, its targets will still perceive it as a punishment. Publishing the names of wrongdoers and opening the files that identify them may also, because of the negative social consequences for the perpetrators, serve to punish them. To the extent that they do, the dichotomy between truth and justice is attenuated. The German Gauck Agency, for instance, "can best be described as a hybrid of a public archive (distributing information) and an investigative agency triggering punishment."[182]

Injustice Against Public Officials," affecting a few hundred people. This "tactless coupling" had a quite transparent motive: to ease the conscience of those who "might have considered the approach to the '131ers' as, indeed, very generous." See ibid., pp. 43–44, 53.

[178] In December 1944, the Belgian socialists produced a somewhat mind-boggling document that envisaged deportation as a punishment, but not to the Belgian Congo, since this might compromise "the moral preeminence of the white man over the indigenous population" (Huyse and Dhondt 1993, p. 123).

[179] This measure was used with respect to some of the French policemen on whom the Vichy government had conferred the status of "Victims of Duty" because of their actions against the resistance (Berlière 2001, pp. 330–31).

[180] Overy (2001), p. 6.

[181] Mason (1952), pp. 80–81. The proposal was also made (but not implemented) that those convicted of "horizontal collaboration" with the enemy should be forbidden from having extramarital sexual relations.

[182] Offe and Poppe (in press).

When economic collaboration with the Germans was treated in the regular courts, as in Belgium, Denmark, and Norway, the normal range of sanctions applied. In Holland and France, where this crime was subject to special purge boards, special sanctions were used.[183] These included, notably, the ban on occupying leading positions in a specific firm or a specific industrial branch and, in France, the publication by one or more newspapers of the other measures that had been taken. As further discussed in Chapter 7, French firms could also be punished by being prevented from making bids for public projects. In Holland, "collaborators were judged according to the general rules of patriotic conduct developed during the occupation in their respective branch of industry. These norms varied considerably in different branches of industry."[184]

(C) Even when public officials (including military officers) are not put on trial, the new regime may still decide to sanction them.[185] When old officials are replaced simply to enable the new regime to reward its followers and supporters, purges may take on the appearance of the American spoils system, with the difference that regime changes, unlike elections, occur unpredictably. When the replacement is motivated merely by the desire of the new administration to have like-minded officials implement its policies, as in France after 1848,[186] there need not be any implication that the old officials are in any way blameworthy. I do not consider these cases, but focus on those in which officials are dismissed for political faults. The goal in such cases may be either to punish officials for past harmful behavior or to prevent them from doing harm in the future. One can, to some extent, distinguish between these two motives by looking at the sanctions that are applied. If the official is demoted, transferred, or blamed, the punitive motive is likely to be more important than the preventive one. Permanent discharges may be sustained by either motivation.

The best-known or most-studied instances occurred in the German-occupied countries after 1945. In France, soldiers were held to higher standards than other parts of the population: They were obliged not only to noncooperation with Vichy but also to "the duty of resistance."[187] In Norway, some ministers who refused to follow the majority in the Church

[183] Mason (1952), p. 101; Doublet (1945), p. 96.

[184] Mason (1952), p. 103.

[185] The best conceptual and comparative studies of purges in the public administration are found in Gerbod et al. (1977).

[186] Goyard (1977), p. 20.

[187] Rousso (2001), p. 535.

who resigned collectively in 1942, had to step down after the liberation.[188] Out of forty-one local chiefs of police, all but one had to step down.[189] In Holland, the government tried to dismiss the prewar appointees to the Supreme Court for their passivity during the occupation, in contrast to the courageous attitudes of the Belgian and Norwegian Supreme Courts. However, "[t]he pre-war judges refused to accept this suspension. They pointed out that the Constitution permitted only [the Supreme Court] to dismiss judges, including its own members."[190] The government had to accept their refusal. In Denmark, criteria of "undignified national conduct" were established to purge the administration.[191] As interpreted by the courts, such conduct included stating the opinion that Germany would win the war, expressing one's satisfaction that Denmark was occupied by Germany, criticizing the Allies, stating one's sympathy with Hitler, making anti-Semitic statements, and making negative statements about the resistance and of sabotage efforts.[192] In France, such *délits d'opinion* were cited against one-third of the officials purged after the liberation.[193] Excessive zeal in dealing with the occupant was also widely used as a criterion.[194] In all these countries, the legal texts targeting public officials were phrased in very general terms, leaving a great deal of latitude for interpretation. The proposed point system for screening the French *préfets* would, had it been implemented, have been a notable exception.

In principle, sanctions for political fault differs rigorously from sanctions for professional reasons. (As noted earlier, in France the two measures have different degrees of protection by due process.) In practice, a new regime may cite professional fault as a disguise for politically motivated sanctions. This kind of "false purge"[195] occurred in the wake of German reunification, where *incompetence* as well as wrongful conduct could be cited as a ground for dismissal from public service. The German Reunification Treaty says that dismissals from public service can take place "when the employee because of lack of professional skill or of personal suitability does not correspond to the job requirements . . . or

[188] Justis-og Politidepartementet (1962), p. 439.

[189] Andenæs (1980), p. 148.

[190] Mason (1952), p. 97; see also Hirschfeld (1988), pp. 157–62.

[191] Tamm (1984), p. 520.

[192] Ibid., pp. 535–36.

[193] Rouquet (1993), p. 63. His book covers purges in the postal service and in the national education system.

[194] Bancaud (2002), p. 238; Tamm (1984), pp. 521, 545–48.

[195] Goyard (1977), pp. 33–41; see also Bancaud (2003b), p. 190.

the employee is unemployable because of lack of demand."[196] As Claus Offe notes, this allowed the German authorities to dismiss many state employees on purely technical grounds, rather than having to invoke controversial political criteria.[197] If one hesitates to dismiss a former GDR university teacher in the Department of Marxism-Leninism on political grounds, one may cite his incompetence or the lack of demand for teaching of that subject in a unified Germany. One might ask, perhaps, how many teachers of postmodern literary criticism in West Germany would pass an objective test of competence.[198]

A related kind of subterfuge occurs when purges really motivated by a desire to punish are presented as motivated by preventive aims. Raising a number of objections to the Czech and Slovak lustration law of 1992, a team of lawyers acting on behalf of several human rights organizations asserted: "No matter how often it may be denied, it is obvious that the purpose of the Act... is to punish those who have done wrong in the past by preventing them from benefiting from their wrongs by holding important state offices. That is the only explanation for this focus on the past and in many cases, the very distant past."[199] "Objective" or forward-looking criteria such as incompetence or presenting a danger for the new regime may be seen, for reasons that I mentioned briefly in Section II and further consider in Chapter 8, as more acceptable than the subjective desire for retribution.

(D) Once the decision has been taken to sanction public officials, one has to decide on concrete measures. In France, prior to the purges in 1944, the only applicable sanction was a permanent discharge from public service.[200] The decree of June 27, 1944, put in place a highly graduated system of sanctions, which included transfer, demotion, temporary release from active service, early retirement, temporary or permanent suspension of pension payments, temporary or definitive debarment, being struck from the army rolls with or without pension, temporary or permanent ban on wearing decorations and receiving the remunerations attached to them, and discharge with or without pension. In Denmark, discharged officials might receive from 1/5 to 100 percent of their pension, with all intermediate fractions (1/4, 1/3, 2/5, 1/2, 3/5, 2/3, 3/4, and 4/5) being

[196] Stern and Schmidt-Bleibtreu (1990), p. 712.
[197] Offe (1996), p. 213.
[198] Ibid., p. 214. He is not responsible for this particular example.
[199] Kritz (1995), vol. 3, p. 342.
[200] Goyard (1977), p. 24.

represented among the cases.[201] In many cases, sanctions are informal rather than formal. Those who are judged by their peers as having been somewhat too opportunistic or zealous in their relations with the autocratic regime may not have the brilliant career they had expected. Thus, in France after the liberation, an inspector of the judiciary decided that there was no point in taking disciplinary measures against a judge who had made "some remarks" in favor of Vichy: "It is enough that he has seen a colleague with less seniority be promoted ahead of him."[202] Although impossible to quantify, such informal professional ostracism is probably very common in transitional contexts. In administrations obsessed with questions of rank and precedence, they can hurt as deeply as more formal measures.

(E) To compensate victims, one must first decide what forms of suffering constitute victimhood. I shall consider this question at some length in Chapter 6. Here I only make some brief observations. First, suffering may be *material* (loss of property), *personal* (human rights violations), or *intangible* (loss of opportunities). New regimes have followed different policies in what to count as suffering for purposes of compensation. In Germany after 1945, "in contrast to indemnifications for material damage, little compensation has been paid for the hell passed in concentration camps, . . . perhaps a reflection of 'capitalist' standards of value that emphasize material rather than human loss."[203] The South African Truth and Reconciliation Commission notes in its final report that

> there had been an expectation that the Commission would investigate many of the human rights violations which were caused, for example, by the denial of freedom of movement, . . . by forced removals of people from their land, by the denial of the franchise to citizens, by the treatment of farm workers and other labor disputes, and by discrimination in such areas as education and work opportunities.[204]

Yet given the act that set it up, the Commission had no choice but to limit itself to personal sufferings, or "violations of bodily integrity," such as killings, torture and other severe ill treatments, and abduction. In Hungary after 1989, Victor Orban denounced the exclusive focus on material suffering:

> [F]ormer owners were not the only ones to suffer injustice during the past forty years. With the exception of the privileged, the whole of society was affected.

[201] Tamm (1984), p. 581.
[202] Bancaud (2003b), p. 191.
[203] Herz (1982a), p. 21.
[204] TRC (1999), vol. 5, p. 11.

> Let us just recollect that not only property was taken away from the state's citizens.... Lives, freedom, employment, opportunities for advancement and education – from the point of view of justice, these abuses were at least as important as the confiscation of property.[205]

Second, one has to define which relatives and dependents of "primary" victims to include among the "secondary" victims. The right of legal heirs to restitution of property may be unrestricted, or constrained by residency and citizenship conditions. The right of family members to receive compensation for the murder of a primary victim may be unconditional or contingent on the victim being the family breadwinner.

Third, one has to decide on the cutoff point in time. How far back shall one go?[206] In Eastern Europe, the problem arose in an acute form because of the successive processes of confiscation after 1938. In the former GDR, confiscations that took place between 1933 and 1945 and those that occurred between 1949 and 1990 were treated differently from those that happened between 1945 and 1949. In Czechoslovakia, the cutoff point was initially (1991) set to 1948, thus excluding compensation for the expropriation and expulsion of the Sudetengermans after World War II and of Jewish property before the war. A 1994 amendment to the law enabled Jews to recover property losses suffered after 1938. In Hungary, the legislators were confronted with (i) Communist expropriations, (ii) pre-Communist expropriation of large landed estates, (iii) postwar expulsion and expropriation of the ethnic Germans, and (iv) prewar confiscations of Jewish property. A law from 1991, which covered only the first category, was supplemented by legislation from 1992 that included the three others.

(F) The mode of reparation to victims varies greatly. The confiscation of landed property may be compensated by restitution of the very same land, by allocation of land of comparable quantity and quality, or by any of these procedures constrained by an upper limit on the size of the property that is allocated. As in France after 1815, monetary compensation may also be used. In Hungary, landowners (and others) have been compensated by vouchers, which they can use to bid for land in public auctions. Victims of crimes other than property right violations have been offered lump-sum compensations or pensions. In Romania and the former Soviet Union, rehabilitated political prisoners and those subject to forced

[205] Cited after Pogany (1997), p. 159. For a similar argument, see also Elster (1992b).
[206] Cowen (in press).

treatment in psychiatric institutions have (among other benefits) priority in the allocation of housing and phone installations. In East Germany, victims of Nazi persecution were also given priority for work, housing, ration cards, and the like.[207] Compensation may also take more symbolic forms, notably the invalidation of verdicts passed on regime opponents. Again, I refer the reader to Chapter 6 for more details.

The decisions I have identified by the letters A through F are *substantive* decisions that new regimes may face: whom to try, sanction, and compensate; and how to try, sanction, and compensate them. In addition, transitional justice almost invariably involves *procedural decisions* that deviate from the standards of "pure legal justice" that I listed earlier. These include, notably, the following:

> *Illegal internments.* In Denmark, France, and especially Belgium, many suspected collaborators were interned after the liberation in 1944 or 1945 without much respect for legal formalities. In Belgium, "some mayors were under strong pressure from members of the resistance and found themselves forced to give out internment orders with the name to be filled in."[208] In France, as previously noted, some prefets would adopt the Vichy practice of interning those who were acquitted by the courts or benefited from a nonsuit. As Commissaire de la République, Michel Debré used internments as a punishment by varying their duration according to the gravity of the suspect behavior.[209]
>
> *Collective guilt.* The Nuremberg trials were in part based on the concept of organizational guilt, although in practice this charge turned out to be mostly irrelevant.[210] In France, de Gaulle wanted to try the Pétain regime collectively for having signed the armistice. When his Minister of Justice threatened to resign, de Gaulle gave way.[211] The law passed by the French parliament on September 15,

[207] Timm (1997), p. 70.

[208] Huyse and Dhondt (1993), p. 102.

[209] Bergère (2003), p. 128.

[210] Taylor (1992), pp. 75, 285. He cites (ibid., p. 278) a comment by the chief American judge on the Tribunal, Francis Biddle, on the American prosecutor Robert Jackson: "Jackson takes a rigid position that knowledge has nothing to do with criminality, and that it is enough to show criminal acts by some to hold all – including charwomen apparently." The idea of organizational guilt was also criticized because of its retroactive aspects (Overy 2001, p. 49).

[211] Lottman (1986), p. 300.

1948, making it a crime to have been a member of a military unit that had committed war crimes, combined collective guilt with retroactivity.[212] In Norway, all members of the National Socialist Party were held collectively guilty of *landssvik* (betrayal of the country). Perhaps the clearest case of collective guilt in the post-1945 trials was the loss of Dutch citizenship imposed on the wives of those who had lost their citizenship because of collaboration. The Czech and Slovak lustration law of 1992 contained provisions that were criticized as being based on collective guilt and that were later struck down by the Constitutional Court.[213] The Czech Constitutional Court, however, appealed to ideas of collective guilt when it refused compensation to the Sudetengermans (see Chapter 8).

Presumption of guilt, rather than of innocence, and inverse burden of proof. French officers lost their jobs unless they could prove that they had been active in the resistance. In Belgium, it was necessary to show a "certificate of civic behavior" on a large number of occasions, for example, to enroll as a student or be inscribed on business registers. The system soon got out of hand, to the point where a former Minister of Justice wrote: "The way things are going, we can foresee the day when one has to show a certificate of civic behavior to obtain a certificate of civic behavior.... Just as under the occupation one had to prove that one was not Jewish, now there are all sorts of occasions on which one has to prove that one was not incivic."[214] In France, the CNIE (national interprofessional purge committee) delivered hundreds of "certificates of good conduct" to firms who needed them for specific transactions or recruitments.[215] On June 2, 1991, President Havel proposed that applicants for high government and state jobs in Czechoslovakia should be required to produce a certificate of noncollaboration.

212 Farmer (1999), pp. 142–43. The relevant article was abrogated in 1953, just a few days before the trial of Alsatian SS soldiers whose participation in the Oradour massacre had motivated it in the first place (ibid., p. 151).

213 For the suspect provisions, see Kritz (1995), vol. 3, pp. 313–14. For the criticism, see ibid., p. 342. For the reasoning of the Court, see ibid., pp. 362–63. When the Court struck down the provision, it was not, however, because it was based on the principle of collective guilt, but rather (as I read the decision) because it violated the presumption of innocence.

214 Huyse and Dhondt (1993), p. 42.

215 Rousso (2001), p. 571.

Biased selection of jurors and judges.[216] This phenomenon has already been extensively discussed. I also remind the reader of the unusual bias in the proceedings against the Athenian oligarchs in 403 B.C., where the special courts were stacked in favor of the *accused*. A curious instance of bias occurred in France in 1945, when de Gaulle deliberately selected two lawyers who were compromised by their relations with Vichy – one had been envisaged as president of the Riom trial and the other had expressed his hatred of Jews in the collaborationist journal *Je suis partout* – as president and prosecutor in the High Court of Justice: "Their past errors were for de Gaulle a guarantee of a certain docility."[217]

Lack of adversarial proceedings. Among the objections raised to the Czechoslovak lustration law was that "the Act does not require that the subject of a Commission hearing is entitled to the aid of counsel, to present his or her own evidence, or to refute the evidence against him."[218] In Italy after 1945, it was often difficult to find lawyers willing to defend the accused, and defense witnesses were often harassed.[219] In Germany after 1945, the opposite problem arose when the local purge boards were met with "what amounted to 'a witness strike' observed by persons who might have incriminated the defendants."[220]

Lack of appeal mechanisms. In some cases, normal appeal mechanisms are suspended or not created. In France, discharge from public service on political grounds could not be appealed prior to 1875. After the liberation, the right to appeal in criminal cases was also severely curtailed.[221] In Belgium, the denial of a certificate of civic behavior could initially not be appealed, a practice that persisted until two years after the liberation.[222] In Denmark, the law regulating war trials stated that only sentences to death or to more than ten years of prison could be appealed, except when a special

216 This refers to intentional bias. Bias may also arise accidentally, as when judges and prosecutors in the Hungarian war trials after 1945 included a large number of Jews, because, as noted by Deák (in press), "Jews alone had not been in a position to compromise themselves."

217 Roussel (2002), p. 513; see also Bancaud (2002), pp. 361–62.

218 Kritz (1995), vol. 3, p. 344.

219 Woller (1996), p. 299.

220 Herz (1982a), p. 27.

221 Bancaud (2003a), p. 94.

222 Huyse and Dhondt (1993), p. 42.

commission found that the circumstances justified an appeal.[223] In Holland, appeals were possible only when the judges of the lower courts allowed them.[224] This practice ended in 1947. In Italy, the "Nenni Law" that was adopted on November 14, 1945, established purge commissions in private enterprises whose decisions could not be appealed.[225]

Arbitrary selection of indictees. In 1815, Fouché was given the task of drawing up a list of individuals to be proscribed. He did not include himself. The American prosecutor in the Tokyo trials, Joseph Keenan, said in his opening statement that "we have no particular interest in any individual or his punishment. They are representative in a certain sense of a class or group."[226] The Emperor was not put on trial. Both Fouché and the Emperor were clearly more responsible than many of those who were indicted. When in the 1950s the German courts began to prosecute crimes from the Nazi period, there was no "systematic legal prosecution – but rather a prevalence of 'accusations by chance.' "[227]

Special courts. In some countries, the political authorities had the choice between trying cases before civilian courts and using (preexisting) military courts. This was the case, for instance, in Belgium[228] and in Argentina.[229] Both countries initially chose the military option, but in Argentina, jurisdiction was transferred to civilian courts because of the unwillingness of the Supreme Council of the Armed Forces to judge their own. In other countries, the question was whether to *create* special tribunals to deal with collaborators. In Denmark, the Council of the Resistance wanted to try the accused before special courts, partly because of skepticism toward the regular judiciary and partly to expedite the trials.[230] Under pressure

223 Tamm (1984), pp. 758–59. These restrictions applied only to the accused, not to the prosecutors.

224 Mason (1952), p. 60.

225 Woller (1996), p. 333.

226 Dower (1999), p. 464.

227 Frei (2002), p. 337. Unlike American practice, the German legal system leaves no scope for discretion to prosecutors (Davis 1971, pp. 191–95).

228 Huyse and Dhondt (1993), pp. 72–73.

229 Nino (1996), pp. 67ff.

230 Tamm (1984), p. 83. In Norway, the resistance movements strongly opposed special courts, on the grounds that they were identified with the arbitrary legal practices of the occupying power (Justis-og Politidepartementet 1962, pp. 51–52).

from civil servants, the Minister of Justice abandoned this idea after the liberation.[231] In France, martial courts and military tribunals were widely used in the first months after the liberation.[232]

Plea bargaining. In Belgium, a decree of November 10, 1945, opened for the possibility of plea bargaining, otherwise unknown in European legal systems.[233] In Holland, a similar practice was very widely used, and widely criticized because of its secretive nature.[234] In Norway, too, legislation authorizing out-of-court settlements was passed.[235] These settlements could include prison sentences up to one year (Norway) or five years (Belgium).

Retroactive legislation. In many countries, transitional justice has had to confront (or finesse) the principle of *nulla poena sine lege.* Two issues come up: whether to punish people for actions that were not criminal when committed, and whether actions that were criminal when committed can be punished more severely (e.g., by the death penalty) than laid down in the earlier law. I pursue this issue in Chapter 8. Here, let me state only that many countries have adopted retroactive laws, explicitly or surreptitiously, in their efforts to deal with the past.

Extending or canceling statutes of limitation. When an authoritarian or totalitarian regime fails to pursue crimes committed by its agents, it may seem perverse that these persons should later benefit from a statute of limitation. In Italy, both the Badoglio government and the Bonomi government that followed it passed legislation that canceled statutes of limitation for fascist crimes.[236] In West Germany, the Bundestag first extended the statutes of limitation for murder and later abolished them altogether for a more narrowly defined subset.[237] In 1993, the Czech Republic passed an "Act on the illegality of the Communist regime and resistance to it," which stipulated that "[t]he period of time from 25 February 1948 until 29 December 1989 shall not be counted as part of the limitation period for criminal acts if, due to political reasons incompatible

231 Tamm (1984), p. 119.
232 Lottman (1986), pp. 43, 107ff.
233 Huyse and Dhondt (1993), p. 134.
234 Mason (1952), pp. 79–83.
235 Justis-og Politidepartementet (1962), p. 74.
236 Woller (1996), pp. 123, 139.
237 Bark and Gress (1993), vol. 2, p. 34.

with the basic principles of the legal order of a democratic State, [a person] was not finally and validly convicted or the charges [against him] were dismissed." The law was later upheld by the Constitutional Court.[238] When the Hungarian parliament passed a similar law in 1991, it was struck down by the Constitutional Court.[239] In Bulgaria, in March 1990 (before the enactment of the new constitution), the statute of limitation was extended from twenty to thirty-five years.[240]

Shortening statutes of limitation. Conversely, the new regime may decide to put an end to prosecution before the normal statute of limitation has expired. Thus in Argentina, President Alfonsín decided in 1983 that "[t]he trials should be limited to a finite period during which public enthusiasm for such a program remained high."[241] In 1986, under pressure from the military, he had parliament enact a "full-stop law" that established a sixty-day limit for prosecution.[242] In Greece after 1974, the government set a time limit for private lawsuits against alleged torturers.[243]

Justice delayed. In some cases, notably Bolivia and Ethiopia, proceedings have taken an exceedingly long time. When (as in Ethiopia but not in Bolivia) the accused are kept in pretrial detention for many years, only to be acquitted or receive a shorter prison sentence than the time they have already spent in jail, the justice system is clearly not working as it should.

Justice expedited. Several of the measures discussed here have the effect (and were often motivated by the intention) of speeding up the pace of justice. One may also cite the practice of judging on an incomplete dossier. On November 20, 1944, Michel Debré as regional commissary of the Republic wrote to the Finance Minister that whereas basic legal principles of law would require "the totality of elements that might be provided to the court to be examined

238 Kritz (1995), vol. 3, pp. 366–68, 620–27.

239 Pataki (1995); Paczolay (1995).

240 Welsh (1996). In Bulgaria, as elsewhere in Eastern Europe, the worst atrocities took place in the Stalinist period that ended thirty-seven years before, in 1953. It is tempting, therefore, to see this measure as a preemptive strike by the Communist elite that was still in power, to prevent an extension that would render them liable to prosecution.

241 Nino (1996), p. 67.

242 Ibid., pp. 92–94.

243 Alivizatos and Diamandouros (1997), p. 37.

> carefully, it would be preferable, in my opinion, to limit oneself to facts that are certain and then leave some room for arbitrariness. I do not think that the necessity to *proceed quickly* and above all the necessity to take decisions based on elements that are certain, even if they are incomplete, can be contested."[244]

In the rest of the book I try to show how legal and administrative processes (Chapters 5 and 6) and broader social forces (Chapters 8 and 9) interact with constraints (Chapter 7) to produce these substantive and procedural decisions.

[244] Bancaud (2002), p. 373; italics added. For a sharply contrasting view, see Noguères (1965), pp. 82–83.

5

Wrongdoers

I. INTRODUCTION

We may have clear ideas about who constitute the wrongdoers in an autocratic regime, at least from a moral point of view. It is not always easy, however, to translate these moral intuitions into legal charges. Moreover, as we get to know more about individual cases, initial moral convictions may unravel. Consider the border guards who killed individuals trying to flee the former GDR. Even if we are disposed to hold them morally responsible for what they did, their legal liability is a different matter, since the reunification treaty between the two Germanys stipulates that individuals can only be accused of wrongdoing if the acts were crimes according to the legal codes of both countries at the time they were committed. Furthermore, reflecting on what it meant to be an East German who had spent his whole life under a ruthless dictatorship, a prosecutor or judge in the former West Germany might well think, "There but for an accident of geography go I." As noted in Chapter 3, the border guards almost without exception received suspended sentences.

In this chapter I attempt to carry out three tasks. In Section II, I discuss the *psychological profiles of wrongdoers* – their character, motives, and background. In Section III, I discuss *justifications for alleged wrongdoing*, that is, claims that the acts in question were in fact morally required, rather than morally wrong. In Section IV, I consider *excuses and mitigations for wrongdoing*, that is, claims that culpability for wrongful acts is removed or reduced because of special features of the situation. Some of these claims are visibly self-serving, others compellingly plausible, while still others raise genuine moral dilemmas. I do not, however, focus on the normative validity of the claims. In line with the general positive or explanatory approach of the present study, I only offer a catalogue raisonné of claims of justification, excuses, and mitigating circumstances, together with some observations on their causal efficacy in explaining the decisions of courts and other actors.

II. PROFILES OF WRONGDOERS

I draw on five scholarly studies to construct a typology of wrongdoers.[1] Although I believe that *three* categories – fanatics, opportunists, and conformists – are especially robust and important, I end up distinguishing among *seven* kinds of wrongdoers, further nuances being cited in the footnotes. In a more refined typology, François Bloch-Lainé enumerates *fifteen* different reasons why higher French functionaries collaborated with the Germans.[2] As the discussion illustrates, the ensemble of human motivations is a pie that can be sliced in many ways, partly because of the complexity of mental states and partly because of the inadequacy of language. Hence, I do not aim at the impossible goal of providing a canonical classification, based on exhaustive and mutually exclusive categories.

In the only book known to me that is devoted exclusively to this topic, Lothar Fritze distinguishes four categories of wrongdoers in the former GDR: those who acted with a good conscience, opportunists, conformists, and collaborators.[3] The first category has two subdivisions: those who are positively convinced that they are doing the right thing, and those who merely have no doubts about the morality of their behavior. The former correspond to what I shall call the *fanatics*. The latter tend to be *accomplices*

[1] The *agents* of transitional justice may also offer their own typologies. Thus Frei (2002), p. 29, cites a spokesman for the Social Democratic Party as asserting in 1950 that "a large portion of the people favored the [Nazi] regime out of 'error'; others went along out of delusion, or greed, or complacency in imitating seemingly cleverer people; and more than a few 'indeed truly out of authentic idealism.'" Frei argues that the blanket concept of "error" is unilluminating and was essentially used apologetically. The category of greed corresponds to the idea of opportunism discussed later in this chapter. The idealists (and perhaps the deluded?) are what I call fanatics. Despite the verbal similarity, the category of imitators differs from that of conformists on which I rely. People conform mostly out of pressure, but imitation is more voluntary.

[2] In Bloch-Lainé and Gruson (1996), pp. 256–58. A leitmotiv in this book is how French officials, many of them graduates and sometimes valedictorians of the Ecole Polytechnique, were eager to find technically optimal solutions to the complex problems created by the occupation (the "bridge-over-the-river-Kwai" syndrome).

[3] Fritze (1998). Acute as his analyses are, the paucity of concrete examples makes them somewhat marginal for my purposes.

of wrongdoing, rather than its authors.[4] In the following, I ignore the second subcategory, because in practice it is hard to distinguish it from that of the conformists. Both opportunists and conformists act in the knowledge that what they do is wrong, but whereas the former take the initiative to act, the latter simply tend to yield to (even mild) pressure. The opportunist is a careerist, whereas the conformist merely wants to maintain his or her livelihood.[5] Collaborators are (roughly speaking) those who embrace wrongdoing because they believe it is the lesser evil.[6] To the extent that they are justified in their belief, they are in fact not wrongdoers at all (see Section III) and, hence, will be ignored in the construction of the typology.

In an analysis of actors involved in the destruction of the European Jews, Raul Hilberg first makes a distinction between the established administration and the newcomers in Hitler's regime. Concerning the former, he emphasizes the need for *zeal*: "[M]uch more was required of a bureaucrat than automatic implementation of anti-Jewish measures. Without his timely proposals and initiatives, the process would have been crippled."[7] Concerning the latter, he differentiates among three motivations:

> For some, particularly individuals with flexibility and ambition, a position in the new sector was an alternate, promising career created by circumstances. Others had struggled unsuccessfully in an organization and found in the party or a party-dominated organization a concrete realization of their undiscovered talents. Still others were accomplished men who exchanged an attainment or profession for the new movement, because Nazism had become an all-consuming element in their lives.[8]

These are, respectively, opportunists, losers, and fanatics. Opportunists and losers have in common that they join the rank of wrongdoers because of the benefits it provides them, the difference being that opportunists are looking for material gains and the losers mainly for psychological rewards.

4 Ibid., pp. 103–5.
5 Ibid., pp. 260–61.
6 Ibid., pp. 302–10.
7 Hilberg (1992), p. 25. In fact, the requirement of initiative, of "working towards the Führer" (Kershaw 1999, p. 529), may have characterized the bureaucracy as a whole, newcomers as well as the old elite. Arendt (1994), pp. 136–37, refers to this attitude as the Nazi version of the categorical imperative: Act in such a way that the Führer, if he knew, would approve.
8 Hilberg (1992), p. 39. Hanich (1998), pp. 382–83, refers to a very similar classification of Austrian Nazis produced in 1947 by the Austrian Research Institute for Politics and Economics, with the added category of "German-Nationalists" who in 1938 saw the fulfillment of their dream of the great German Fatherland.

According to Hilberg, Eichmann was a loser. Among the Norwegian collaborators with the Germans during World War II, many belonged to this category – pathetic prewar figures who suddenly found themselves in high office.

Fanatics, by contrast, are not motivated by the desire for personal benefits. Some member of the SS killing units (*Einsatzgruppen*) "had status and prospects in society, but chose Security Police work out of conviction."[9] These were the *Unbedingte*, unconditional believers who formed the backbone of the regime.[10] Although they endlessly emphasized the need for decisiveness and ruthlessness,[11] they were not predominantly sadists. On the contrary, Hannah Arendt asserts, a systematic effort was made to weed out sadists from the Einsatzgruppen.[12] Himmler also took the problem of corruption in the SS very seriously: "A man could not be an idealist and at the same time stuff his pockets, make love to Jewish women, or engage in drunken orgies."[13] In the regular army, too, a good soldier was someone who had to "overcome himself" to kill Jews. Acting on a desire to kill would be "an abnormal act, worthy perhaps of an 'Eastern European' (such as a Romanian)."[14]

An official history of "civil affairs" – military administration of occupied territories – in World War II proposes the following classification of Fascist officeholders in Italy:

> First, there were the nonpolitical conformists (who had joined the party to keep their job); second, the political opportunists (who had joined primarily to get a job); third, the presumptive scoundrels. The last were not determined to be scoundrels by technically correct judicial process but by popular indictment: especially in the smaller towns, the Italian populace tended to riot or to threaten riot if certain Fascist officials were not promptly dismissed.[15]

The category of scoundrels is not useful for my purposes here. Again, a crucial distinction is made between opportunists and conformists,

9 Hilberg (1992), p. 44.
10 Wildt (2002).
11 Ibid., pp. 137–42.
12 Arendt (1994), p. 105. Hilberg (1992), pp. 53–54, says, more weakly, that sadistic "behavior was not particularly welcomed, but neither was it prosecuted"; also Hilberg (1985), pp. 904–5.
13 Hilberg (1985), p. 905.
14 Ibid., p. 326. Hitler, too, made a distinction between an anti-Semitism of emotion and an anti-Semitism of reason (Hilberg 1992, p. 5). Those motivated by the latter allegedly had to *overcome* their (humanitarian) emotions.
15 Coles and Weinberg (1992), pp. 373–74.

the latter joining the party to retain their job rather than to get one.[16]

In a study of "the concept of administrative purging," Claude Goyard classifies public officials sanctioned for collaboration with the Vichy regime in four categories:

1. *Mediocre profiteers* who ran after any kind of material benefit to be found in the circumstances of war or of the economic regulations in force....
2. *Concealed malefactors,* denunciators or slanderers who stayed in the shadows while trying to harm their colleagues or fellow citizens....
3. *Hotheaded or excited ideologues* who exerted themselves for the Vichy government or the collaborationist cause, happy to find themselves *united* against the Third Republic which they abhorred....
4. A final category, by far the most numerous. which includes all the amorphous and apathetic, the *imprudent* and the *rash,* whether by temperament or by lack of discernment, who, having one day gone too far in their private speech, did not know how to retreat in time.[17]

In addition to opportunists and fanatics, there now enters the category of *the malicious,* who use the occupying regime to promote their private grudges. The fourth category in this scheme has a somewhat residual character, combining as it does the apathetic and the rash. If we focus on the latter part of the characterization, however, the fault of individuals in this group seems to lie in lack of judgment and of prudence, rather than in being animated by a reprehensible motive. This rings true, and not only with respect to public officials. In countries occupied by Germany, for instance, it often happened that individuals betrayed resistance members by negligent rather than deliberate action;[18] remember also the American warning during World War II, "Loose lips sink ships." Defeatists – those who without any bad motives expressed the belief that the autocratic regime was there to stay and that resistance was pointless – also belong here. Let us refer to these individuals as *the thoughtless.*

[16] This distinction is also drawn by Bloch-Lainé and Gruson (1996), p. 54. A clear illustration may be taken from the behavior of Dutch policemen during the German occupation. While some participated in actions against the resistance or in roundups of Jews out of fear of losing their jobs (or worse) if they refused, others were motivated by the substantial "catch bonuses" (Hirschfeld 1988, pp. 171–79).

[17] Goyard (1977), pp. 31–32.

[18] Tamm (1984), p.382, cites a case in which a man who witnessed what he suspected (correctly) to be a weapons transport by the resistance told his wife, who told a neighbor, who told an acquaintance (who acted as driver for the Germans), who told the Germans. They were all indicted in the lower court, but acquitted because the evidence was not found to be conclusive. On appeal, the neighbor was convicted to eight years in prison. For other examples, see Bloch-Lainé and Gruson (1996), pp. 174–75.

Philippe Burrin studied a sample of 648 French men and women who were convicted of national indignity, on grounds of membership in a collaborationist movement, by the special courts instituted for that purpose. He provides fine-grained information about the age, profession, and political past of the individuals concerned, as well as the time of entry into and, when applicable, exit from the movement. Although his main purpose is sociological rather than psychological, he offers some comments on the motivations of these low-grade traitors. He finds that in one case out of five, and even one out of four among those who joined a movement in 1942, *interest,* notably in better relations with the occupying forces, was an important motivation. In one case out of ten, and in one of three among those who joined in 1943–44, he finds motives such as "the search for protection, the influence or even the coercion exercised by a family member or a superior."[19] These categories seem to correspond, at least roughly, to those of opportunism and conformism.

The most important motive in Burrin's sample, however, was *conviction,* "which explains the adherence of 75% on average, 80% of those who joined in 1941, and only 41% of those who joined in 1944."[20] The convictions in question include support of Pétain, anticommunism, and various ideas of social justice. While many anticommunists were fanatics, the other two convictions did not (I assume) take this extreme form. Wrongdoers may be *principled* without being fanatics. Given the other data Burrin presents, I conjecture that many of the early principled adherents came from the upper middle class. They tended to be "first in, first out,"[21] adjusting their behavior to changing realities. I also conjecture that those who joined from conviction in 1944 were militant anti-Communists.

We can now regroup these seven categories as follows:

Opportunists, losers, and the malicious are all animated by *desire for gain.* Opportunists seek material gain, and losers seek the psychic benefits of appearing important in their own eyes and in those of others, while the malicious seek the satisfaction of seeing their enemies or rivals brought down. Although the category of losers overlaps with that of the malicious,[22] neither group can be subsumed under the other.

Conformists are motivated by the *fear of material loss.* This is not the simple equivalent of the desire for material gain, since for most people, the sacrifice of a career is much more momentous than the opportunity to build one.

19 Burrin (1995), p. 437.

20 Ibid.

21 Ibid., p. 435.

22 Thus Burrin (1995), p. 215, explains the predominance of women among convicted informers by the fact that "denunciations are the weapons of the weak."

Fanatics and the principled are like these four groups in that they are *motivated by consequences,* but unlike them in that their main motivation does not derive from the consequences for themselves. The principled differ from the fanatics in their willingness to change course once they discover that the cause is worthless or badly served. Some wrongdoers who turn into resisters fall into this category.[23] The thoughtless are unlike all the other groups, in that the grounds for blaming them *do not include motivations* at all.

In most autocratic regimes, the rank and file of wrongdoers are probably to be found among the conformists and the thoughtless, supported or cemented by the presence of the principled. The elite wrongdoers, as it were, are the fanatics. Opportunists and the malicious are parasites on the wrongdoing regime, rather than its driving or sustaining forces. When the regime is being run mainly by opportunists, as in the final stages of the German Democratic Republic, its days are numbered. These statements, to be sure, are very general, perhaps excessively so. The psychology of political wrongdoing and of political wrongdoers is an undeveloped field, to say the least, and so I have had to rely on my overall impressions rather than on specific studies. Although the legal literature and court decisions offer some insights (which I explore later) into the psychology of wrongdoers, they do not amount to a positive analysis of motivation. Nor can they help us understand *systems of wrongdoing,* in which differently motivated agents incite, exploit, and supplement one another.[24] We can get a glimpse of local constellations through Jean Guéhenno's description of the participants in a "patriotic ceremony" under Vichy, where we meet the "local pharmacist who for two years has been taking his revenge for not having had any influence in the rest of his life"; the mayor, an old member of the Radical Party, "who does not want to miss the Legion of Honor"; and the schoolteacher, who "is afraid of losing his job." The organizer of these events was the Minister of Former Combatants, Xavier Vallat, a true fanatic who based his rule on such alliances of losers, opportunists, and conformists.[25]

I shall argue in Chapter 8 that different types of wrongdoers elicit different emotional reactions. Conformists and the thoughtless induce anger or indignation, fanatics and the malicious trigger hatred, opportunists

[23] In the terminology of note 103 to Chapter 4, their change of mind is value-based, whereas that of the opportunists is belief-based.

[24] For the somewhat related case of interaction among different motivations in generating collective action, see Elster (1989), Chap. 5. The main common feature with systems of wrongdoing is the presence of some agents who are not motivated merely by their own advantage.

[25] Paxton (1997), p. 242.

and losers prompt contempt. Whereas conformists and the thoughtless cause these specific emotions because of what they *do*, actors in the other categories generate emotional reactions because of what they *are*. Among the latter, fanatics and the malicious make us hate them because they are evil; opportunists and losers make us despise them because they are weak. I shall also argue that specific legal reactions to wrongdoing correspond closely to the spontaneous action tendencies associated with these emotions.

III. JUSTIFICATIONS FOR ALLEGED WRONGDOING

I distinguish between justifications, excuses, and mitigating circumstances.[26] When an alleged wrongdoing is justified, it is shown to be not a wrongdoing at all. To kill one person to save ten may be justified – not merely permissible but even mandatory (i.e., not doing so would be wrong). When a wrongdoing is excused, the excuse removes culpability from the action. To kill in self-defense may excuse the killing. Mitigating circumstances reduce but do not remove the culpability of the agent. From the early common law onward, "while the impact of provocation was to mitigate the killing to manslaughter, the effect of a valid claim of self-preservation was to excuse the killing."[27]

I am concerned only with excuses and justifications offered with a claim to *legal* validity. When actors excuse or justify their actions to look good in their own eyes[28] of in those of others,[29] rather than to avoid punishment, they often adopt strategies that would not be accepted by a court of law. Thus, the excuses that "others did it too" or that "others did things that were even worse"[30] may be psychologically effective,[31] but

[26] Fletcher (1978), p. 356.

[27] Ibid., p. 352.

[28] This is the focus of Snyder, Higgins, and Stucky (1983); see also S. Cohen (2001), Chap. 4.

[29] This is the focus of Benoit (1995).

[30] "In their own minds many German officers imagined gradations of guilt: someone who had killed a thousand people felt he would do well admitting to only killing three.... As a skillful interrogator, [the American officer Paul] Guth used that tendency to advantage, knowing that in the eyes of the tribunal killing three or three thousand bore the same consequences" (Greene 2003, p. 163).

[31] Snyder, Higgins, and Stucky (1983), pp. 50, 87. As they also note (p. 54), the claim that others did it too may result from an *attributive projection*, "whereby the person is aware of possessing an undesirable characteristic and therefore 'defensively' projects this characteristic onto other people." Thus, the conscious awareness that "I did something

legally they carry no weight.[32] Such *factual* claims about what others did cannot exculpate or justify. By contrast, *counterfactual* claims about the behavior of others may be legally relevant for questions of guilt. There are, as we shall see, a number of counterfactual arguments that have been used to justify or excuse apparently or allegedly wrongful behavior. The most important are the following:

- The lesser evil justification (I): If I hadn't done it, someone else would have done it, with even worse outcomes.
- The lesser evil justification (II): If I hadn't done it, something else would have happened, with even worse outcomes.
- The instrumentality justification: If I hadn't done it, I would not have been able to act effectively against the oppressive regime.
- The fungibility excuse: If I hadn't done it, someone else would have.
- The duress excuse: If I hadn't done it, I would have been killed or otherwise seriously harmed.
- The futility excuse: If I had refused to do it, it would have made no difference.

Many justifications are based on the counterfactual claim that "If I had stepped down, somebody else, worse than me, would have taken my place."[33] This lesser-evil claim was, for instance, the "standard excuse" of members of the SS[34] and the "classic excuse" of many of the politicians and high functionaries tried before the French High Court.[35] No doubt such claims are sometimes self-serving, but they may also have a core of truth. In Holland, for instance, civil servants who decided to stay in place after the German invasion could rely on secret government instructions

bad" prompts the unconscious inference to "Others did it too," enabling the subject to conclude, "What I did wasn't so bad after all."

32 If other known offenders are not prosecuted, however, the claim may have some relevance (Davis 1971, pp. 167–70).

33 Arendt (1994), p. 145, mentions a related counterfactual excuse: "[A] murderer who could prove that he had not killed as many people as he could have killed would have a marvelous alibi." She imputes this defense to the "moderate wing of the S.S." at the end of WW II. Literally speaking, the excuse is absurd unless supplemented by a claim that others in the same position would have killed more people.

34 Bark and Gress (1993), vol. 1, p. 77.

35 Chauvy (2003), p. 239; see also ibid., pp. 148, 159, 251, 266. The last reference is to René Bousquet, in whose case the High Court made the important observation that the lesser-evil argument might not be valid if the greater evil was supposed to be direct German intervention. Even if the Germans were more *inclined* to take severe measures, their lack of knowledge of the French situation made them less *able* to act effectively. Matters were different if a functionary remained in his post in order to avoid being replaced by a diehard *French* collaborator (for an example, see ibid., p. 277).

from 1937, saying that (with important qualifications) "in the event of an enemy occupation, civil servants had to stay at their posts in the interest of the population." Since the "highest-ranking civil servants assumed that direct German rule would be more radical and cruel, a less desirable option," they mostly remained in office. Later, "as the German occupation policy became more radical and the administrators became a tool toward this end, the policy of the lesser evil lost favor with the public."[36] In France, functionaries who desired to step down might be asked by the resistance to remain in place and, as a result, be acquitted of charges of collaboration after the liberation.[37]

Consider also the role of the judges who implemented and legitimated the inhumane policies of the predemocratic regime. In France during the German occupation, only one (eccentric) judge refused to take the oath to Pétain.[38] Many argued that it should indeed be taken, "since the alternative was to see captured *résistants* come before a judiciary even more Pétainized than it already was.... Frequently it had been a question of passing an unjust sentence short of death lest the case – or future cases – be taken out of the judge's hand and put in those of a Vichy fanatic."[39] Since acquittal might be followed by internment or deportation, whereas a severe sentence could be used by the Germans as a criterion in the selection of hostages, judges looked for "intermediary solutions," sometimes at the request of the defense.[40] Judges who stepped down were compared to deserting soldiers, or to doctors who refuse to soothe the pain of the patient when they cannot heal him.[41] In Denmark, too, judges collaborated with the Germans to prevent the occupying power from simply taking the judicial system into their own hands, which would have had predictably worse outcomes for the population.[42] Along similar lines, during

36 Rominj (2000), pp. 178–79; see also Hirschfeld (1988), e.g., pp. 141, 150, 211. Hirschfeld emphasizes the ambiguity of the instructions, which allowed many officials to use them after the liberation to defend their conduct.

37 Chauvy (2003), pp. 124–26, 148. Baruch (1997), pp. 504–6, emphasizes the ambiguity of the situation of these functionaries, who might be criticized by the German occupational forces for their lack of cooperation and by the exile government for remaining in place.

38 More generally, and not surprisingly (Tocqueville 1968, p. 597), the *résistants de la première heure* tended to be nonconformists (Baruch 1997, p. 453).

39 Novick (1968), pp. 85–86; see also Bancaud (2002), pp. 414–33.

40 Bancaud (2002), pp. 423–24.

41 Ibid., p. 421.

42 Tamm (1984), p. 36. More unusually, some Danish judges who had reservations about deviations from due process in the trials of *collaborators* nevertheless agreed to serve, since otherwise "there would have been a preponderance of the most punitive judges" (ibid., p. 134).

the apartheid era, a South African human rights lawyer asserted that "If we . . . argue that moral judges should resign, we can no longer pray, when we go into court as defense counsel, or even as the accused, that we find a moral judge on the Bench."[43] These justifications seem generally to have been effective in blocking prosecution.

The claims of civil servants in the Third Reich "that they stayed in their jobs for no other reason than to 'mitigate' matters and to prevent 'real Nazis' from taking over their posts"[44] are more controversial. The case of Hans Globke, the éminence grise of Konrad Adenauer when he was Chancellor of West Germany, may be cited here. The standard version of his story is as follows. As an official commentator on and interpreter of the 1935 Nuremberg racial laws, Globke was prima facie unacceptable in high office in the Federal Republic. "Adenauer, however, believed that Globke had done his best to give the laws the mildest possible interpretation,"[45] and Globke himself claimed that "he had remained in his post to try to prevent worse things from happening."[46] Things appear in a different perspective, however, when we learn from the 1985 edition of Hilberg's *The Destruction of the European Jews* that

> [o]n December 23, 1932, even as party men interested in exposing and isolating the Jews were demanding that Jews have only Jewish names, an official of the Prussian Interior Ministry, Hans Globke, wrote a directive, for internal use only, to prohibit approval of name changes that were sought by Jews who might have "wished to disguise their Jewish descent."[47]

Behavior that may seem excusable and even justified as a response to circumstances outside one's control is less acceptable when it is shown to have been proactive. In the first (1961) edition of Hilberg's book, there is no reference to Globke's pre-Hitler behavior. Had the facts been known at the time, he might not have been retained by Adenauer – or he might still have been.

In a German court case from the late 1940s,

> a group of physicians were indicted for intentionally killing hospital patients. Their defense was that they were carrying out orders to perform euthanasia on

43 Dyzenhaus (1998), p. 57.

44 Arendt (1994), p. 12; see also Overy (2001), pp. 158–73.

45 Bark and Gress (1993), vol. 1, p. 247.

46 Herf (1997), p. 290.

47 Hilberg (1985), p. 33. The document in question belonged to the Central Archives of the GDR, which could hardly be expected to be unbiased, but I assume Hilberg would not have cited it unless he was confident of its authenticity. On the "East German anti-Globke campaigns," see also Frei (2002), p. 333 n. 53.

mentally ill patients and that further, they did so only because they believed that they could save many patients by falsely warranting that the patients were curable. They believed, presumably on reasonable grounds, that if they did not participate in the killings, loyal party members would do so, with a much higher toll of innocent lives.[48]

The High Court for the British occupational zone recognized that the justification might in principle be valid, but added that "the burden of proof would be on the defense to prove that their conduct resulted in a net savings of life."[49] Inasmuch as the Court found the defendants guilty, it presumably did not think they had satisfied this requirement.

A variant of this counterfactual justification in Eastern Europe after 1989 was that "if we hadn't been rigorous in repressing opposition, the Soviets would have intervened, with much worse results." When the Polish parliamentary committee that investigated the possibility of prosecuting the authors of the 1981 martial law decided to drop the case, this argument may have been one of their main reasons.[50] The chief responsible party, General Jaruzelski, did not want to rely heavily on this rationale, however. Although he did claim that martial law was the lesser evil, this was so (he said) in comparison not only with foreign invasion but also with the economic anarchy that was threatening to ruin the country. This case has an additional feature of some interest. It seems likely today that the Soviet Union would, in fact, not have intervened had Jaruzelski failed to impose martial law. Yet after the transition, "the majority of legal scholars in Poland took the position that even an erroneous judgment about such a danger could not be punished, provided merely that it did not stem from rashness or neglect."[51] Even erroneous beliefs may excuse (but not justify)[52] if they are well grounded in the evidence obtainable at the time of action.

A justification of this general kind was also offered in 1951 by I. G. Farben when sued by Norbert Wollheim, who had worked for the corporation as a slave laborer during the war: "In fact, said the defendant, if the inmates had not been employed they would have been killed even

48 Fletcher (1978), p. 853.

49 Ibid., pp. 546–47.

50 Walicki (1997), pp. 206–15.

51 Ibid., pp. 214–15; see also Fletcher (1978), p. 696 (a mistaken but reasonable claim of justification can serve as an excuse). One should keep in mind that even if the Soviets had no intention of intervening, it was in their interest to make the Polish leadership believe that they would.

52 According to Fletcher (1978), p. 696, a reasonable but mistaken claim of justification can excuse, but not justify.

sooner. The implication was that Wollheim should have been grateful to Farben that he was still alive."[53] The argument raises a general question, which applies to many other justifications as well: Can behavior be justified by its predictable good consequences when these were not part of the motivation for that behavior and would not by themselves have been sufficient to induce it?[54]

After World War II, many who were accused of economic collaboration with the enemy appealed to counterfactuals in their defense. In Norway, owners of newspapers that had adapted to the occupation defended themselves by saying that a completely German-dominated press would have had a negative impact on public opinion.[55] (The investigative commission reached the opposite conclusion: The German propaganda would have been less harmful if it had been exposed openly as such.) An enterprise that produced for the Germans might claim that more harm to the country would have been done had the factories been dismantled, machinery shipped to Germany, and workers conscripted into the German labor service. In Belgium, the memory of World War I, during which transfer of industrial equipment to Germany had caused massive unemployment, provided a lesser-evil argument for the collaborationist policy of the "bankers' consortium."[56] Alternatively, if the machines had been idle, they would have deteriorated and not been available for postwar reconstruction; also, there would have been no occasions for sabotage and slow-down actions.[57] Again, one might ask (but perhaps not be able to answer) whether these effects of collaboration entered into the motivation of the acts.

An amazing counterfactual was also used after World War II to justify the granting of pensions to former SS officers. Although the provision was limited to those who could prove "that they served only in functions such as those of the regular army," the Federal Social Court of Cassel got around the problem by stating that "[a]nyone who saw service during the Second World War as a member of an SS combat unit (*Waffen-SS*) of a kind that, had these units not existed, *would have been performed by regular soldiers,* is to be considered, as a rule at least, to have performed service

[53] Ferencz (2002), p. 36; see also ibid., p. 103.

[54] This is in a way the inverse of the "double effect" question: Can behavior be justified in spite of its predictable bad consequences as long as these were not part of its motivation?

[55] Hjeltnes (1990), p. 105.

[56] Witte and Craeybeckx (1987), p. 254; see also Conway (2000), p. 147.

[57] Mason (1952), p. 103; Tamm (1984), p. 486; Andenæs (1980), pp. 134–42; de Rochebrune and Hazera (1995), pp. 320–28. As early as 1943, the Danish resistance movement warned against listening to these arguments (Tamm 1984, p. 101).

similar to that in the regular army." In this way "the court recognized even the guard duty of the Second SS Death's Head regiment at Dachau as 'service similar to that in the regular army.'"[58] A somewhat similar counterfactual argument has also been used to extend, rather than shrink, the circle of wrongdoers. On December 17, 1942, the Belgian exile government decided that henceforward the crime of "bearing arms against Belgium" would such include menial tasks as chauffeuring or cleaning German barracks, since if Belgians had not performed them they would have devolved on the German occupying force.[59] Anyone who released enemy forces from other work so that they were free to fight was as guilty as anyone who actually fought himself, just as any SS member who performed duties that would otherwise have been performed by the regular army was as innocent as a member of a regular fighting unit.

What I called the "instrumentality justification" rests on the claim that working *for* the oppressive regime was a necessary condition for being in a position to work *against* it. In German-occupied countries, for instance, an agent who collaborated with the Gestapo in his official capacity might claim that he did so only in order to obtain information that he could convey to the resistance. To gain credibility with the Germans, he might have to perform actions that, taken by themselves, would have made him liable to punishment after the war. In Norway, a much-discussed case concerned a police inspector who had a central responsibility in the deportation of the Norwegian Jews, while at the same time providing information to the resistance about the plans of the Gestapo.[60] After he had been acquitted in a lower court, the Supreme Court sent the case back for a new lower court trial, which resulted in a new acquittal. The reasoning of the court in the second trial rested on an extension of the argument from necessity. By analogical reasoning, the court said, assisting in the deportation of Jews in order to be in a position to help the resistance could be seen as taking part in collective self-defense, assuming (as did the court) that the benefit to the resistance offset the harm to the Jews.[61] The facts of the case were obscure, however, as were the motives of the defendant. He seems to have

58 Müller (1991), p. 207; my italics.

59 Huyse and Dhondt (1993), p. 64.

60 Sveri (1982). I am grateful to Hans Fredrik Dahl for bringing this case to my attention.

61 The argument may rest on the essential fungibility of lower officials. If the policeman had refused to obey orders to round up the Jews, someone else would have done it. Hence, one has to compare the assistance that only he could give to the resistance and the marginal harm (compared to the person who would have taken his place) he did to the Jews. It might even be the case that this marginal contribution to the harm was negative, if his replacement would have acted more harshly.

invoked, at various points, the double-game or camouflage argument, the duress excuse that he would have been punished by the Germans if he had refused to obey, and the lesser-evil justification that he had to remain in his post to prevent penetration of the police by the Nazi militia.[62]

In France after liberation, the double-game argument was very widely used and abused.[63] In genuine cases, officials had been told by the exile government or the resistance to remain in place, because they could be more useful there than by taking to the maquis.[64] (The Norwegian policeman had not sought this kind of approval.) In many spurious cases, collaborating officials simply claimed that they had also performed patriotic acts. The commissions investigating claims by civil servants to have worked for Vichy only to be able to work at the same time for the resistance "required that an organic connection between the two be shown; mere parallel activity was not acceptable as a justification."[65] Beyond that, they would presumably have to show that the gain from one activity offset the harm caused by the other and that this "net benefit" is why they had remained in place.

The presence of an *enemy* may also be used to justify what might, in isolation, appear to be wrongdoing. Downplaying the Holocaust, many Germans justified atrocities on the Eastern Front by the necessity of fighting Bolshevism. As a British observer wrote, "the [West] Germans regard part of their historical mission as having been for many centuries the defense of European civilization against Asiatic barbarism."[66] Hence, some suggested, instead of prosecuting them, the Allies should be grateful for what they had done. As the Cold War induced the Western powers to show greater leniency toward the war criminals, Germans might infer that their argument had been tacitly if belatedly accepted. In East Germany, the Nazi past was used to establish a "justification for imposing a postwar dictatorship on an untrustworthy and dishonored people."[67] Latin American dictators have routinely, and sometimes sincerely, tried to justify their

[62] Søbye (2003), pp. 136–40.

[63] See notably Baruch (1997), pp. 513–18.

[64] Baruch (1997), p. 432.

[65] Novick (1968), p. 89.

[66] Schwartz (1991), p. 218.

[67] Herf (1997), p. 24. Here, as elsewhere in his book, Herf errs by taking the antifascist rhetoric of the GDR at face value. The Communist rule was just as repressive in countries that had not proved themselves to be "untrustworthy and dishonored." Monika Nalepa (personal communication) suggests that in these other countries, the lack of anti-Communist violence may be explained by the desire of the oppostion to avoid giving the Communists an excuse for persisting in their repressive behavior.

repression by invoking the need to counter communism, terrorism, and guerrilla violence. In Chile, "the military were . . . quite proud of what they had done. . . . They felt that 'they had participated in a heroic historic act.'"[68] A difficulty with the "internal enemy" justification for atrocities is that the enemy may be the effect, rather than the cause, of the wrongdoings. In South Africa, for instance, apartheid violence preceded the armed resistance to it.

IV. EXCUSES AND MITIGATIONS

I treat excuses and mitigations together, the former being, as it were, a limiting case of the latter. Duress, for instance, is defined in the American Model Penal Code by the criterion that "a person of reasonable firmness in his situation would have been unable to resist" the urge to commit a wrongdoing.[69] A paradigmatic case is the agent's well-grounded belief that he would be killed if he did not obey an order to execute a wrongful killing. Yet even well-grounded beliefs come in degrees, and there must be some level of subjective probability at which the belief ceases to provide a complete excuse, without instantly losing *all* relevance for the degree of culpability.

It may be uncertain or debatable whether a given feature of a wrongdoer, such as his motivation or talent, should be seen as aggravating or as extenuating. In the following, I discuss cases in which motivations of fanaticism and opportunism are cited to either effect. In 1944, a famous disagreement opposed de Gaulle to François Mauriac over the issue of whether the great talent of the writer Robert Brasillach made him more or less culpable.[70] In Norway, the same question came up in the debate over the guilt of Knut Hamsun.[71] The self-defense of another writer who espoused the Nazi doctrine, Heidegger's dictum that *Wer gross denkt, muss gross irren* ("Great thinkers make great mistakes"), could also be used to condemn him. The issues of talent and motivation may be related – presumably courts would not see the talent of an opportunist as an extenuating circumstance.[72]

[68] Brito (1997), p. 63.
[69] Fletcher (1978), p. 831.
[70] Sapiro (2003), p. 252.
[71] See Dahl (in press) for comments on the Hamsun trial.
[72] While nothing indicates that Heidegger was an opportunist, his student Gadamer might qualify. Although never a member of the Nazi Party, Gadamer "did enroll in a Nazi indoctrination camp in 1935, once it became clear that doing so would open certain academic

In Section V of Chapter 4 I considered some typical excuses or mitigating factors, such as the claim of some wrongdoers to be redeemed by later acts of resistance or the claim of others to have been victims themselves of the oppressive regime. Without any attempt to be systematic or exhaustive,[73] I now proceed to discuss other commonly used arguments. As with justifications, many excuses rely on counterfactuals. First, there is the common claim that "if I hadn't done it, somebody else would have." In their defense, Eichmann as well as Papon claimed that they were merely fungible cogs in the machinery of extermination and as such not personally responsible.[74] In Eichmann's case, the excuse was questioned when the prosecution in Jerusalem showed that in July 1944, he ignored orders by Admiral Horthy to stop deportation of the Jews and prevented Jewish officials from informing Horthy about his disobedience until it was too late.[75] Zealous behavior – going beyond the call of duty – can indeed be used to rebut the excuse of fungibility. In purges of the public administration in German-occupied countries, the criterion of excessive zeal in dealing with the occupying power was routinely used to this effect. The argument is more complicated when applied to the Third Reich, where, as noted, zeal was the norm and lack of initiative might have triggered sanctions.

A second counterfactual excuse is that of *duress*: "If I had refused to do it, I would have been killed." The relevance of this claim is particularly dubious when the agent in question is ordered to carry out the act in question by a group of which he is himself a member, rather than a subordinate. As we saw in Chapter 2, this is one of the points that Lysias made in his speech "Against Erastothenes." The duress defense was also routinely offered by those who carried out Nazi or Communist atrocities. In a famous decision from 1964, a German court recognized duress as an

doors" (McLemee 2003). After the war, in the Soviet occupational zone, "Gadamer's lectures began to make enthusiastic references to the dictatorship of the proletariat" (ibid.).

[73] I ignore, in particular, the "superior order" defense, which has been extensively discussed in the literature on war crimes (e.g., Osiel 1999).

[74] Arendt (1994), p. 289, argues: "If the defendant excuses himself on the ground that he acted not as a man but as a mere functionary whose functions could just as easily have been carried out by anyone else, it is as if a criminal pointed to the statistics on crime – which set forth that so-and-so many crimes per day are committed in such-and-such a place – and declared that he only did what was statistically expected, that it was mere accident that he did it and not somebody else, since after all somebody had to do it." This reasoning is, of course, totally confused.

[75] Arendt (1994), p. 201.

excuse for the mass murder of Jews in White Russia.[76] Objectively, this excuse may have been groundless. Commenting on Nazi exterminations, Christopher Browning writes that "in the past forty-five years no defense attorney or defendant in any of the hundreds of postwar trials has been able to document a single case in which refusal to obey an order to kill unarmed civilians resulted in the allegedly inevitable dire punishment."[77] In the 1963–65 trials of the Auschwitz guards, one defendant, Mulka, said that he would have been signing his own death warrant if he had refused to obey: "The court took care to explore the plausibility of Mulka's fear: the evidence suggested that camp officers who refused orders could expect to be transferred to the front and/or to a punishment battalion, but no other penalties were likely."[78] Yet can we be sure that, subjectively, the guards did not *believe* that they would be shot if they refused to obey?[79] If they believed, non-self-servingly,[80] that they would, they might claim that they were "forced" to kill.[81]

Duress, defined as the inability to resist, may not merely be a function of the threat or danger the person faces. Individuals might differ in their abilities to resist, not merely because of their personal characteristics but also because of their position or specific features of the situation. The French legal code, for instance, states that for duress to be established, "it must be of such a nature to 'make an impression on a reasonable person,' taking into account the condition of the individual involved."[82]

[76] 1964 NJW 730. The doctrine established by that decision is that the actor is excused when the only way he can save his life is at the expense of the lives of several or even many others (http://www.benediktweiten.de/strafrecht/Entsch_Notstand_Fall_m_Lsg.htm).

[77] Browning (1992), p. 170.

[78] Sa'adah (1998), p. 169. Some may, of course, have perceived transfer to the front as the near equivalent of a death sentence. Even if that prospect cannot serve as an excuse, it might (as noted earlier) be a mitigating circumstance.

[79] Browning (1992), pp. 170–71, considers this question and answers it in the negative for the Battalion 101 that is the main topic of his book. Since "[b]y SS standards, [the commander of this battalion] was a patriotic German but traditional and overly sentimental" (ibid., p. 164), matters may have been different elsewhere.

[80] Frei (2002), p. 90, implies that such beliefs and the claims based on them were in fact typically self-serving.

[81] A story told by the foremost historian of the Norwegian war trials, Johs. Andenæs (1978, pp. 187–88), is relevant here. He cites a letter he received from a former collaborator, who recounts how he refused a request from a superior in the Nazi hierarchy to serve on one of the infamous special courts. When told that he might suffer the death penalty for his refusal, he replied that he might also risk the death penalty if he accepted, and that it would be better for his posthumous reputation if he were sentenced by the Nazi Party than by the resistance. The superior was shaken by the reply, and later also refused to serve on these courts.

[82] Novick (1968), p. 194.

On the basis of the last proviso, Georges Vedel argued that the French deputies who voted full powers to Marshal Pétain on July 10, 1940, were not acting under duress, since "a representative of the nation must be assumed to be less easily constrained than an ordinary citizen."[83] In an implicit polemic against the acquittal for mass murder of Jews in White Russia, George Fletcher argues that any purely agent-centered conception of duress is mistaken because it "focuses simply on the side of the pressure exerted on the defendant, without considering the relationship between the threat to the defendant and the act he must commit.... If the cost in human lives is sufficiently high we could properly expect someone to resist threats to his own life."[84] Presumably he means that knowledge of the high cost to others will have a *causal* force in enabling the agent to resist, not merely a moral force.[85]

In German law after World War II, "the instigator is an accessory rather than a perpetrator."[86] At the same time, if the person who pulls the trigger acts under orders *and* under duress, believing he would be killed if he did not kill, he would also be regarded as an accessory.[87] The implication that there might be perpetrator-less crimes eventually "led the academic community almost unanimously to reject" the underlying theory.[88] For courts reluctant to call anyone a murderer, however, the doctrine was very useful:

> The Hannover County Court found a former Nazi who had personally killed several people guilty as an "accomplice to murder" – that is, someone who had provided assistance to the actual perpetrator. It then sentenced his superior officer, who had given the orders and should logically have been held responsible, for having "incited to murder." Since there was no one else between them in the chain, these crimes remained "murders" without a "murderer." On November 15, 1951, the Mönchengladbach County Court also found someone who had given an order to kill guilty of "inciting to murder" but acquitted the man who had carried it out, since he had acted under duress.[89]

A third variety of counterfactual excuses relies on the pointlessness, rather than on the dangers, of breaking ranks. Whereas the defense "If I hadn't done it, someone else would have" relies on the futility of *exit,* this

[83] Ibid.
[84] Fletcher (1978), pp. 832–33.
[85] For illuminating remarks on the idea of inability to resist, see Watson (1999).
[86] Fletcher (1978), p. 644.
[87] Ibid., pp. 657–58.
[88] Ibid., p. 659; also Walther (1995), p. 106.
[89] Müller (1991), p. 249. I have not verified whether the Hannover case also involved duress.

excuse rests on the futility of *voice*.[90] In the trial of the Auschwitz guards, Mulka claimed that "he knew that resistance would be both futile and fatal."[91] In the 1996 trial of seven former members of the East German Politburo, "the indictment held [that] they must have known they had the power in their hands to do more to secure the rights 'to life and freedom' of the GDR's citizens. However, the prosecutors charged, they consciously failed to take advantage of this possibility 'to work to achieve a humanization of the border regime and thereby prevent the killing and wounding of escapees.'"[92] One of the accused, Günter Schabowski, responded that

> under the conditions existing at that time in the GDR he could not realistically have done anything to alter the prevailing policy at the Wall. "Any effort to move in this direction under the then-existing conditions would have immediately been perceived as an attempt to call into question the general line [of the party] and the personal authority of the general secretary. This would not have had the slightest chance of working in the politburo or in any other body."[93]

In his case, the excuse was not accepted. In the second Politburo trial in 2000, however, two of the three accused were acquitted on the grounds that they "would not have been able to prevent people from getting killed at the Wall." The third was acquitted because he had actually "tried to achieve an easing of the border regulations that could in the long run have led to an end of the exodus." (It is not clear that these two arguments are consistent with each other.)

Further defenses rely on what might be called accidents of time and space. *Time-related* excuses or mitigating circumstances include the following:

"I was young then."
"It was so long ago."
"I only collaborated for a short time."
"I only collaborated in the early stages of the repressive regime."
"I only collaborated in the late stages of the repressive regime."
"I am so old now that I should be spared."

The low age of the offender at the time of the (most recent) offense is clearly relevant. Among the Alsatians on trial for their participation

[90] For these categories, see Hirschman (1972).
[91] Sa'adah (1998), p. 169.
[92] McAdams (2001), p. 48.
[93] Ibid., p. 49.

in the Oradour massacre, "eight... had been under eighteen years at the time they were drafted into the German army, only to be transferred to the SS a few weeks later."[94] At the time of their trial, the mayor of the Alsatian town Colmar "questioned how much heroism one can expect of teenagers."[95] In 1952, the only former Wehrmacht officer serving in the West German parliament published an article in which he proposed amnesty for war criminals over sixty and under twenty-eight,[96] implicitly raising the age of criminal responsibility to twenty-one years.

The time interval between the deeds and the trial has two separate effects. As we shall see in Chapter 8, the emotional intensity of the general demand for retribution may depend on how long ago the worst excesses took place. One may also argue on more principled grounds that a given offense should be treated more leniently if it lies in the distant past. Thus, one justification of statutes of limitation is that the offender may in a real, if elusive, sense no longer be "the same person" twenty or forty years later.[97] Even when there is no formal statute of limitations, decisions may be affected by this factor. In Germany after reunification, court decisions led to legislation in 1996 prohibiting the release of files to prospective employers if the individual's contact with the secret police ended before December 31, 1975.[98] With regard to dismissal from official service, several German Länder argued that the *duration* of contact was also relevant,[99] presumably because a short-lived collaboration suggests a momentary weakness, rather than a deeper flaw.

The timing of wrongdoing matters because of the light it throws on the motives of the wrongdoers. Opportunists will support a regime of wrongdoing only when its prospects look good. Fanatics may support it even when the prospects are uncertain (at its inception) or bleak (toward the end). Although there are, as we shall see, many exceptions, opportunists seem in general to be treated more leniently than fanatics. We should expect, therefore, those who join an organization of wrongdoers before it assumes power, or when it is about to lose it, to be sentenced more severely than those who join the regime in its heyday. This expectation is

94 Farmer (1999), p. 140.
95 Ibid., p. 153.
96 Frei (2002), p. 206.
97 Nino (1996), p. 182, citing Parfit (1984).
98 McAdams (2001), p. 83.
99 Sa'adah (1998), p. 219.

clearly borne out in post-1945 Germany. In Brandenburg (in the Soviet occupational zone),

> [t]he date when an individual joined a National Socialist organization was [a] significant piece of evidence considered by the [denazification] commissions. Entrance before 1933 was particularly incriminating as it evidenced active support for National Socialism before Hitler assumed the chancellorship.... Party Members who entered in 1933 could often convincingly claim that they had joined in the general rush of excitement following Hitler's assumption of power, and that, like so many unpoliticals and nominal party members, they did not have the courage to break publicly with the party despite their disenchantment. Those who joined the party from 1937 onward were the least incriminated; 1937 was a key year because that was when the NSDAP [Nazi Party] began to compel individuals to join.[100]

In the denazification of the American occupational zone, all who had joined the party before May 1, 1937, were classified as "offenders," the second-most serious category of wrongdoers.[101] In the British zone, "dismissal [from public service] was inevitable for anyone who had joined the NSDAP or the SA or the SS before April 1, 1933."[102] As the party did not admit new members between 1933 and 1937, practices in the three zones were essentially the same. (The French did not rely on this criterion in the zone they administered.)

In countries occupied by Germany during World War II, early collaboration was usually treated more leniently. In Holland, economic "collaboration in the last years was considered more serious than in the beginning of the occupation."[103] The same was true of Norway.[104] In France, too, "there was a tendency to excuse simple Pétainism in the first months of the Vichy Regime, but never after November 1942."[105] In Denmark, the lawyers in the resistance took a different position from the civil servants. The latter wanted more rigorous criteria to apply for collaboration after August 29, 1943, when the Germans assumed direct rule over the country, than for the first years of the war. The former wanted equal rigor to be applied for the whole period of occupation, claiming that it would be wrong to absolve "the largest and most dangerous group of traitors – those who were astute enough to leave the sinking ship on

[100] Vogt (2000), p. 212.
[101] Vollnhals (1998), p. 162.
[102] Ibid., p. 171.
[103] Mason (1952), p. 103.
[104] Andenæs (1980), pp. 137–38.
[105] Novick (1968), p. 89.

August 29."[106] In the end, the resistance lawyers got their way, with some exceptions.

These patterns could have varying explanations. In Norway, the confusion reigning immediately after the German invasion made it seem more excusable to 'join at that time than later, when the resistance had been established.[107] The reason why economic collaboration was judged more harshly if it took place toward the end of the war may also be that by that time, it was more crucial to the Germans and therefore did more harm to the Allies. Unusually, the Danes in the resistance seem to have thought the opportunists not only more numerous but also more dangerous than the diehards who would stay to the bitter end. The Danish civil servants and the French resistance presumably thought that it was more reprehensible to collaborate with the more repressive end-stage regimes that emerged as Germany's prospects were dimming. Thus in France, "Russian victories in the East led many fanatical anti-Communists at Vichy to second the German war effort in order to save Europe from 'Bolshevization.'"[108] Late-stage collaboration would be more severely punished, therefore, as it was associated with both fanaticism and severity of repression. By contrast, as noted in Chapter 4, opportunists might to some extent have redeemed themselves by turning against the regime.

Old age may affect sentencing, either by itself or in combination with the ailments that come with age. A ten-year prison sentence is worse when the condemned person is eighty than when he is forty; hence, for equal crimes, the former should get shorter time in prison. When a French court sent Maurice Papon to prison for ten years at the age of eighty-seven, it was actuarially close to a sentence for life. The case against Erick Honecker was dismissed because of his illness. "If the trial were allowed to become an 'end in itself' [*Selbstzweck*]... the FRG would be as guilty of violating the basic rights of its citizens as was the GDR. 'The individual,' as the judges put it, '[would] become a simple object of state measures,' and a fundamental distinction between the two political orders would be obscured."[109] In the case of Auguste Pinochet as well, the main issue has been his mental competence, rather than his age per se.

[106] Tamm (1984), pp. 91–92.

[107] Andenæs (1980), pp. 137–38.

[108] Novick (1968), p. 12.

[109] McAdams (2001), p. 38. This seems an overstatement of a valid point. Trying a dying criminal may violate his dignity, but on a scale from 0 to 10 it's probably around 1, whereas the GDR routinely committed violations of level 7 or 8.

Space, too, matters. Those who live in a border region between an occupying nation and an occupied nation may, because of their torn loyalties or forced collaboration, receive a more lenient treatment. In Denmark, the draft law dealing with those who had served in the German army contained a passage that "the sentence can be reduced for Danish citizens who are part of the German minority in Southern Jutland." This formulation was not retained in the final law of June 1, 1945, but a more general clause that allowed for reduced sentencing or even dropping of charges was clearly motivated by the situation of this group.[110] In the legislative debates, a deputy from the region said that those who had fought on the Eastern Front should benefit from mitigating circumstances because they had at least the courage of their convictions, unlike those who had joined one of the local militias.[111] Because the practice of the courts failed to reflect the intention of the legislators, the law was clarified by an addition of June 29, 1946.

After the victory in France in 1940, Germany proceeded to a de facto annexation of Alsace-Lorraine.[112] Military service in the German armed forces became obligatory for all men born between 1920 and 1924. Although forty thousand deserted or escaped to other parts of France, one hundred sixty thousand were mobilized. When on February 13, 1953, a Bordeaux court condemned thirteen Alsatian ex-SS soldiers for their role in the massacre in Oradour-sur-Glane, legislation was immediately introduced to give full amnesty to those who had been forcibly incorporated into the German armies. The controversial law was supported by de Gaulle, who asked, "What French person will not understand the inflamed suffering of Alsace?" The law was passed on February 18 with 319 votes against 211 and 83 abstentions, and three days later, the thirteen Alsatians left their prison. The excuse was not that the Alsatians had shown the courage of their convictions, but that they had joined the German army under duress.

Consider finally the subjective conditions for guilt, or *mens rea*. There are two main questions: motive and knowledge. With regard to motives,

110 Tamm (1984), p. 417.

111 Ibid., pp. 417–18. The former, he said, "felt they were Germans, they were Nazis. They felt under an obligation, and drew the consequences from it." By implication, the latter had less honorable motives. It seems, however, that the reason the minority leaders established one of the militias was to comply with German demands for volunteers in a way that would limit the number of recruits to active war service (ibid., p. 411). When these leaders were tried, however, this fact was not cited as a mitigating circumstance for the charge of having established the militia (ibid., p. 431).

112 The following draws on Farmer (1999), Chap. 5.

we may refer back to the classification of wrongdoers offered at the beginning of the chapter. It seems clear that the conformists and the thoughtless, when punished at all, are viewed more leniently than the others. Conformists may claim – or rather it may be claimed on their behalf[113] – that they were the victims of *moral confusion*. In long-standing dictatorial regimes, the sense of morality may be undermined among those who have not known any other political order. In defending the Italian amnesty law of June 22, 1946, the Communist Minister of Justice, Togliatti, argued that as "every free voice of criticism of the tyrannical government was forbidden" under the fascist regime, "it became very difficult, above all for the younger generation, to distinguish between right and wrong."[114] In the trial of the Auschwitz guards, the court cited as a mitigating circumstance that National Socialism had created "an unexampled spiritual confusion,... bring[ing] into question previous values and [erasing] the boundaries between right and wrong."[115] Concerning the trials of the GDR border guards, it was similarly argued that "given the indoctrination of the soldiers, their socialist upbringing since childhood and the approval of the use of firearms in the GDR, it was impossible to claim that their obedience to orders was obviously contrary to the law."[116] As noted, the guards almost invariably received suspended sentences.

Among the agents of the Nazi or Communist regimes, should the fanatic or the opportunist be punished more severely? In other words, is the personal commitment to an inhumane ideology an aggravating or an extenuating circumstance? In the Fourth *Provinciale,* Pascal heaps scorn on the Jesuits who teach that one cannot sin if one does not know that what one is doing is wrong. Yet the Jesuits were writing for hardened sinners who wanted to be able to enjoy the pleasures of the flesh without paying the price of damnation, not for dedicated ideologues who were willing to risk their lives for the perverse causes they believed in. An argument could be made that those who join the same evil causes and perform the same evil acts merely for their career advantage or economic gain are even more debased. Thus in Denmark, the Attorney General said, in a speech to the judges' association in October 1945, that acting as drivers for the

113 We may distinguish between excusatory and exculpatory defenses, the former being the reasons that can intelligibly be given by the agent himself, and the latter those that make sense only when made by third parties. The excuses for fanaticism and conformism fall in the latter category, whereas the counterfactual and time-related excuses fall in the former.

114 Woller (1996), p. 382.

115 Sa'adah (1998), p. 171.

116 Marxen and Werle (1999), p. 21.

Germans or performing similar paid work was "almost worse from the ethical point of view" than doing active duty as soldiers. Those who engaged in the former activities "had no conviction they were fighting for; it was all a question of money."[117] This, it seems, was also the reasoning of Danish courts when they judged that use of the death penalty for informers was justified if (i) the consequences of the denunciation were serious and (ii) the motive was mere economic gain.[118]

A preference (if one may call it that) for fanaticism over opportunism was also manifested in the High Court trial of the virulently anti-Semitic French politician Xavier Vallat. In his speech to the jury, the prosecutor said that "even if there were elements of fanaticism in Vallat's behavior, it was not dictated by 'a low and self-interested motivation.' This is what allowed him not to go so far as to require 'the extreme sanction' while demanding a 'severe punishment.'"[119] In the trial against members of the GDR National Defense Council, the lower court judge, Boss, "chose to take mitigating circumstances into account in sentencing Kessler, Streletz, and Albrecht to milder jail terms than those requested by the prosecution. Without excusing the officials' actions, he pointed out . . . that the defendants had themselves been 'prisoners of German postwar history and *prisoners of their own political convictions*.'"[120] This amounts to saying that fanaticism is an extenuating circumstance.

The converse (and probably more common) argument was made in Germany after the war, when the Socialist leader Carlo Schmid asked for the early release from prison of a prewar friend, Martin Sandberger, who "had admitted direct responsibility for the shooting of 'around 350' communists and had not denied the murder of Jews by his [SS] Mobile killing unit."[121] Sandberger, Schmid explained, was not "a raving fanatic." "Without the intervention of National Socialism," Schmid said, "Sandberger would have become a diligent, industrious, assiduous official like many others; he would have tried to build his career upon special and striking accomplishments, since he was very openly ambitious. This ambition also prompted him to join the SS and SD. He saw these party organizations as offering him the best prospects of quickly rising to positions in which he could distinguish himself."[122] In the second

[117] Tamm (1984), p. 294.
[118] Ibid., p. 382.
[119] Chauvy (2003), p. 180.
[120] McAdams (2001), p. 40; italics added.
[121] Frei (2002), p. 227.
[122] Ibid.

French Restoration, too, the opportunists who joined Napoleon during the Hundred Days were treated more leniently than the diehards who had made it possible for him to return.

The motives of *torturers* may also be seen as relevant for their sentencing. After World War II, the Italian Corte di Cazzatione reversed a number of convictions for gruesome crimes on the grounds that there were others that were still worse.[123] Thus,

> a most unfortunate and grotesque distinction was drawn between "ordinary" tortures and tortures that were particularly "atrocious." Using this formula the courts were able to pardon the following crimes: the multiple rape of a woman partisan; a partisan tied to a roof who was punched and kicked like a punch-bag; electric torture on the genitals applied though a field telephone. On this last case, the Corte di Cazzatione . . . ruled that the tortures "took place only for intimidatory purposes and not through bestial insensibility."[124]

In the Danish trials of collaborators after World War II, this priority was reversed. Those who mistreated or killed individuals for personal motives or pique were less likely to get the death penalty than those who did so to serve German interests.[125] The worst Danish torturer escaped execution because the Supreme Court found that his actions were due to "sadistic perversion of sexual drives,"[126] rather than to an instrumental purpose. The mentally disturbed cannot be evil.

Concerning *informers,* Denmark established a disjunctive criterion for guilt that was partly objective (depending on outcomes) and partly subjective (depending on intentions). The law of June 1, 1945, authorized the death sentence for informing "if the act had as a consequence loss of life, harm to body or health, or deprivation of liberty . . . *or* if such consequences were intended."[127] Thus, informers could be executed even if the person betrayed had not been arrested.[128] In Belgium[129] and in Holland, the severity of sentencing for informers increased with the severity of consequences for the denounced person. Dutch informers could be executed only if their action had led to the death of the person they informed on.[130] In a rather extraordinary decision concerning the former GDR, a German

[123] Woller (1996), pp. 388–89.
[124] Ginsborg (1990), p. 92.
[125] Tamm (1984), pp. 321–22, 345.
[126] Ibid., p. 353.
[127] Cited after Tamm (1984), p. 757 (my italics). In his discussion of the law, Tamm (ibid., p. 129) omits the second disjunct.
[128] Mason (1952), p. 177 n. 4.
[129] Huyse and Dhondt (1993), p. 66.
[130] Mason (1952), p. 63.

court found that lack of objective harm allowed an inference to the lack of intent to harm:

In [a] decision on February 15, 1996, involving the fate of a notary who had briefly collaborated with the [State Security Police], the [Federal Constitutional Court] found... restrictive language to define the grounds that would constitute a loss of confidence in someone's capacity for public service. The judges contended that fairness to the accused entailed taking explicitly into account "whether, by way of example, the transmission of information of a denunciatory character had the intention or expectation that it would [promote] inhumane consequences or circumstances incompatible with the rule of law." In this case, evidently, it did not. Because there was no evidence that the individual in question had inflicted any harm on the family on whom he had written reports ("no one was hurt [by his activities]" they noted), the court overturned the ruling that had led to the notary's original dismissal.[131]

Beliefs, too, matter. We have seen that beliefs about what would happen to oneself if one disobeyed orders could be relevant to the issue of guilt. Similarly, beliefs about the consequences for others matter. In the High Command case at Nuremberg, the tribunal "insisted on the indispensability of *actual knowledge*" of atrocities,[132] in contradistinction to the International Military Tribunal for the Far East, which relied on strict liability. An initial proposal at Nuremberg that voluntary membership in a criminal organization be sufficient to prove guilt was expanded by requiring that the defendant *knew* that the organization engaged in crime.[133]

Between actual knowledge and strict liability there are the two modal categories of "should have known" and "could have known." In the trial of the Auschwitz guards, the court noted as an extenuating circumstance that although the accused, Mulka, "should have known that he risked being drawn into criminal acts [it is not certain] that he actually considered that he might be misused for criminal purposes."[134] In Holland, there were divergent interpretations of the condition that the accused must have

wittingly acted against the interest of the Dutch nation.... Even the *Hoge Autoriteiten* [high courts] did not agree. The *Hoge Autoriteit* at 's-Hertogenbosch decided that "wittingly" applied only where the accused *knew* that he acted against the interests of the Dutch people; the fact that he *could have known* was not enough. The *Hoge Autoriteit* at the Hague stated that "*should have known*" was sufficient.[135]

[131] McAdams (2001), pp. 82–83.
[132] Cohen (1999), p. 67.
[133] Taylor (1992), p. 557.
[134] Sa'adah (1998), pp. 169–70.
[135] Mason (1952), pp. 74–75.

In Denmark, the resistance-based commission that produced the first legislative draft wanted to replace the strict test of actual knowledge by the weaker test of "should have known,"[136] but the proposal was not adopted in the final legislation.[137]

The issues of motive and beliefs interact or overlap. Although the intention to do harm differs from the belief that harm will result as a by-product of actions performed for other motives, courts may be reluctant to see any relevant difference. Anglo-American law, for instance, tends to ignore the difference between inflicting harm purposefully and doing so knowingly.[138] In other legal systems, the latter has been viewed as the lesser offense, although not necessarily in wartime. Thus in 1942, the Belgian exile government moved the frontiers of guilt by changing the *mens rea* for wrongdoing. While the law originally required an *intention* to harm the country for an act to qualify as criminal collaboration with the enemy, it now merely required that the agent had acted in ways that he *knew* would involve risk for the country or for his compatriots.[139] Whereas the earlier definition only covered fanatics who wanted to impose harm, the latter also included opportunists who were indifferent about or at least undeterred by any harm they might cause.[140]

Earlier, I considered the relation between *actual and intended* consequences in assessing the wrongness of acts. The same issue arises with respect to the relation between *actual and foreseen* consequences. Consider, for instance, the actions that Jewish slave laborers brought against the Krupp armaments producers in a protracted litigation beginning in 1954. In 1949, the head of the firm, Alfried Krupp von Bohlen, had been convicted by a Nuremberg court of three American judges for its use of slave labor during the war. In its judgment, the court cited, among other charges, the shipment by Krupp of female Hungarian slave workers to Buchenwald in the last days of the war. The court added that "nothing further has been discovered about the fate of the young Hungarian Jewesses of the Krupp firm," implying that they had been killed. Krupp was released from prison two years later, in a decision by the American High Commissioner for Germany, John McCloy, that has been variously described as a move in the fight against communism and as "an excellent

136 Tamm (1984), p. 79.

137 For the category of "should have known," see also Fritze (1998), pp. 96–103.

138 Fletcher (1978), pp. 257–58.

139 Huyse and Dhondt (1993), p. 64.

140 Thus Pierre Laval, while not a visceral anti-Semite, was indifferent about the fate of the Jews and willing to sacrifice them without hesitation (Burrin 1995, p. 82).

weapon for Communist propaganda."[141] Later, it turned out that among the claimants for compensation were four hundred Hungarian women cited in the 1949 judgment. Krupp's lawyer reacted with indignation, claiming that "This error... certainly contributed to the high term of imprisonment to which Herr von Bohlen was sentenced and which he to a considerable extent served. For this there is no restitution."[142] This was to ignore, however, that it was Krupp

> who had approved the transfer from [the Krupp factory in] Essen back to the concentration camp, knowing fully that the SS had said they would never allow the inmates to fall in Allied hands alive. The fact that the prisoners were not murdered in Buchenwald, as everyone who knew the circumstances might rightfully have expected, was not thanks to any effort on Krupp's part to save them.[143]

There is a strong intuition that the women's good luck, which was also Krupp's good luck, is morally irrelevant for his punishment. Intuition may seem weaker in the following case: "One businessman, sentenced to prison because his firm had contracted to build gas chambers, had his conviction overturned because it turned out that his firm hadn't gotten the contract after all: his bad luck in the early forties; his good luck in the late forties."[144] It is not easy, though, to nail down the morally relevant difference between the two cases. In both, an attempted act of wrongdoing was aborted merely because of decisions made by another party. The decision by Krupp to hand over the women comes closer, however, to fulfilling the criterion of being the "last proximate step" toward commission of the offense, which is sometimes used to establish guilt for attempted crimes.[145] In the case of the gas chamber contractor, it seems true that "if the plan had not been interrupted, he might have changed his mind at some moment before consummation of the offense."[146]

[141] Schwartz (1991), p. 173, paraphrasing the general (Telford Taylor) who had presided over Krupp's indictment. See also Novick (1999), p. 92.
[142] Ferencz (2002), p. 99. I assume that "restitution" is a translation of *Wiedergutmachung*, i.e., "making good again."
[143] Ibid.
[144] Novick (1999), p. 90.
[145] Fletcher (1978), pp. 139–40.
[146] Ibid., p. 189.

6

Victims

I. INTRODUCTION

Acts of wrongdoing that cause suffering can elicit two reactions in the victim (or in third parties). First, there may be a desire to impose a corresponding suffering on the wrongdoer: an eye for an eye. Second, there may be a desire for the harm to be undone, at least to some extent or as far as possible. As shown by the institution of "Wergeld," these two ways of restoring an equilibrium can serve as substitutes for each other. In ancient Teutonic and Old English law, according to the *Oxford English Dictionary,* Wergeld was "the price set upon a man according to his rank, paid by way of compensation or fine in cases of homicide and certain other crimes to free the offender from further obligation or punishment."[1] Conversely, one might think of punishment as a substitute for compensation if the wrongdoer is unable to pay the Wergeld. Yet in modern legal systems, punishment is not justified by the needs of the victims. Reparation for victims of wrongdoing is uncoupled from punishment of the wrongdoer.[2]

The process of compensation may nevertheless be wholly or partly shaped by punitive intentions. In the French Restoration, some émigrés

[1] Whereas compensation was paid to relatives, fines were paid to the King (Hurnard 1969, Chap. 1).

[2] Yet in transitional justice there may sometimes appear to be a coupling. According to McAdams (2001), p. 138, "By emphasizing restitutions and reparations, [Adenauer] may have hoped to deflect attention from his government's decision to refrain from making criminal trials or purges of former Nazi officials a central feature of its *Vergangenheitsbewältigung.*" (For an objection to this argument, see Herf 1997, p. 7.; see also Chap. 9.) It has also been argued that the Chilean reparations have served as a substitute for retribution; some who were entitled to them have refused them as "blood money."

wanted to punish the purchasers of their properties by having them fund the indemnity. Although the preference in post-Communist Czechoslovakia for in-kind restitution over monetary compensation or voucher schemes may have been overdetermined, one motive was to prevent properties from falling into the hands of the former nomenklatura.[3] Similarly, Ady Steg, vice chairman of the Mattéoli Commission that investigated the restitution to French Jews after World War II, made a distinction between Swiss and French bankers. The $1.25 billion settlement with the Swiss banks was justified by the fact that "the Swiss had lied, shredded documents, and hidden information, he said. They deserved the public castigation and the demands for large, rough justice payments. In contrast, he argued, the French deserved better from their Jewish accusers."[4]

The idea of undoing harm is extremely elusive.[5] Since life does not have an "Undo" button, one might try instead to bring about the state that would have obtained today had the original harm not occurred. On reflection, however, this end-state criterion is inadequate, since it does not take account of the suffering that occurred in the interval between the time the wrongdoing took place and the present. Even if I get my farm back in the state of improvement to which I would have brought it had it remained in my possession, I might still want to be compensated for the years during which I was unable to enjoy the fruits of private farming and had to work in the coal mines instead. If I have suffered damage to health and body, it may even be impossible to create the counterfactual end state. In that case, I might need compensation not only for past suffering but also for reduced earning capacities and perhaps also for reduced capacity for enjoying life. Maybe we could say that the victim is entitled to the lifetime sum of happiness that he could have expected to achieve, given his initial circumstances, had the harm not been done. But as a victim, I might refuse to be compensated on the basis of what the average person in my position would have achieved. Even if very few members of my social group go to college, I might want to receive compensation for being denied the opportunity to do so.

I shall have the occasion to refer to some of these normative issues, to the extent that they form part of the background of actual processes of reparation and compensation. My main task, however, is to classify types

[3] Cepl (1991), p. 583.

[4] Cited after Authers and Wolffe (2002), p. 155. Note that the Swiss banks were punished not for what they "did then" (during the war) but for what they "say now" (when the matter came up fifty years later).

[5] See Cowen (in press) for a penetrating discussion.

of suffering and modes of reparation and, when possible, to suggest an explanation of why some victims received compensation (and in which form) and others did not (or received less). In Section II, I consider *material suffering*, that is, the loss of real or personal property. In Section III, the topic is *personal suffering*, that is, harm to life, body, or liberty. In Section IV, I discuss *intangible suffering*, that is, loss or lack of opportunities.[6] I conclude in Section V with a discussion of questions of evidence and burden of proof in compensation cases.

II. MATERIAL SUFFERING

Property can be real or personal; if personal, it can take the form of physical objects or financial assets. One form of material suffering is the *destruction* of property. When the transition is preceded by external or internal warfare, as in the years following the French Revolution or in World War II, there is often extensive loss or destruction of property. In Norway, for instance, it was calculated that the country lost 14 percent of its physical capital during World War II.[7] Homes and what they contain may be destroyed by air raids or scorched-earth tactics. For reasons discussed later, destroyed property has usually been compensated at a relatively low rate. I shall focus, therefore, on the *confiscation* of property.

As a first example, we may consider the fate of the French Jews during World War II.[8] About fifty thousand enterprises and buildings were Aryanized, that is, sequestered and set under administration by the Commissariat Général aux Questions Juives for the purpose of liquidation or, preferably, resale to "Aryans." By the end of the war, more than half of the properties were still under this administration because of slowness and occasional obstruction,[9] the difficulty of determining whether a buyer

[6] Conceptually, the two last categories overlap. Imprisonment is a form of personal suffering. Being unable to go abroad is an intangible suffering, but it can also be seen as being imprisoned in one's own country. Under communism, even life outside jail was like being in prison. If you tried to escape, you could get shot. Similarly, the first and the third categories overlap. When, as under communism, people are unfree to sell their labor power, is their property partially confiscated or are their opportunities curtailed? In spite of such ambiguities, I believe the classification is robust enough to be useful.

[7] NOU (1997), p. 39.

[8] The following draws on *Mission d'étude* (2000) and Prost, Skoutelsky, and Etienne (2000).

[9] See Bancaud (2002) for a general discussion of the semilegalism of Vichy. In line with his analysis, Prost, Skoutelsky, and Etienne (2000), p. 24, note that because "the CGQJ [General Commissariat for Jewish Questions] laid claim to all the external signs of legality

was really Aryan, and the reluctance of purchasers to buy properties with a contested origin and uncertain future. (See also Chapter 2 on a similar phenomenon in the French Restoration.) The Germans also carried out looting on a grand scale, transferring works of art and furniture to Germany. On July 21, 1944, for instance, two railway wagons containing forty-three pianos left Paris for Silesia and Frankfurt an der Oder.[10] One might have thought that at this stage of the war, the Germans would have had better uses for their rail equipment. By 1946, 2,043 pianos had been recovered. Also, "hundreds of paintings stolen from wealthy Jews by the Nazis made their way to France's great national collections and remained there for decades."[11] Jewish bank accounts were blocked, and French Jews had to pay a collective fine of one billion francs in retaliation for assassinations of German soldiers.

Consider next expropriations of private property in the former GDR.[12] The first took place under the Soviet occupational regime, when more than seven thousand private firms and estates, totaling 2.5 million hectares, were nationalized. The main (but not only) targets of the reform were the aristocratic Junkers, who were seen as deeply responsible for the rise of Nazism; hence, "the dissolution of these centers of economic power would assist in preventing the rise of similar movements in the future."[13] (As we shall see in Chapter 7, the same idea, on a larger scale, was used to argue for the *political* dismembering of Germany.) The expropriated properties were then distributed to individual farmers in small plots, which could be inherited but neither sold nor leased. Under the GDR regime, these small holdings, together with other individually held plots, were consolidated into collective farms. The industrial firms that had been spared by the Soviet measures remained in private hands until 1972, when they were expropriated by the state. In addition, houses and other property of those who had fled to the West were either expropriated or put under the administration of the state. In the legislation enacted after reunification, "the concept of 'expropriated property' is not limited to property actually taken by confiscatory decree. Rather it can also include property acquired by the state 'as a result of economic coercion.'"[14]

to accomplish its iniquities, [it was] sometimes forced to limit them." For a discussion of this "civilizing force of hypocrisy," see Elster (1999), Chap. 5.

10 *Mission d'étude* (2000), p. 94.

11 Eizenstat (2003), p. 287.

12 The following draws on Quint (1997), Chap. 11.

13 Ibid., p. 126.

14 Ibid., p. 129.

Describing more individual cases would soon run into diminishing marginal returns. Let me move on, therefore, to measures of reparation, and first consider the case of destroyed property. As mentioned, there seems to be a tendency for this kind of loss to be less generously compensated than confiscated property. In France after 1815, the Vendéens who had fought for the King and seen their properties destroyed received little compensation, whereas the émigrés, who had put personal security above loyalty to the King and had their properties confiscated, were indemnified. As we saw in Chapter 2, the argument for making this distinction was that the state had not benefited from property destruction as it had from property confiscation. Instead of (relatively) full compensation to some and none to others, one might have chosen partial compensation to all, but this was not the course taken.

After 1945, several German-occupied countries enacted legislation compensating individuals for destroyed property. The conceptual bases for these measures were, however, need and solidarity, rather than entitlement. The French law of October 28, 1946,

> did not indemnify the loss of "sumptuary" elements, the legal definition of which is not easy. One has to put oneself in the context of the postwar years, a time of extreme penury in a France where after four years of occupation and generalized looting, allied bombardments and destructions due to the struggles of the Liberation, everything had to be rebuilt. The sumptuary was thus opposed to the necessary. For instance, neither jewelry nor works of art were indemnified.[15]

In Norway, too, the principle of *regressive compensation* for war damages was well established: "The purpose of the legislation was to assist survivors for purposes of reconstruction, not to recreate prewar fortunes."[16] There was "a general feeling that the whole country had suffered, and a certain reluctance to compare sufferings."[17]

The distinction between destroyed and confiscated property also arose in the final negotiations, in 2000, about how to divide the 10 billion DM that the German government and companies had agreed between them to pay to hitherto neglected victims of the Nazi regime. The two main dimensions were compensation for workers forcibly employed by German firms during the war versus property-related compensations. Within the first category there were important subdivisions that will concern us later. Within the second, there was a tension between Jewish claims for

[15] *Mission d'étude* (2000), p. 150.
[16] NOU (1997), p. 47.
[17] Ibid., p. 39.

compensation for looted bank accounts and unpaid insurance policies, on the one hand, and East European claims for compensation for war property damage, on the other:

> The Eastern Europeans claimed they had a right to share the property payments, because their homes had been destroyed by Nazi troops.... For the Jewish groups, that argument was nothing less than offensive. Their property claims were based on racially motivated plunder – the so-called aryanization of Jewish businesses and financial assets. Of course the Eastern Europeans had lost property, but their homes were destroyed as part of the wider war – just as British homes were flattened by German air raids.[18]

The argument of the Jewish groups might rest on a distinction between intended victims and collateral victims, the former having stronger claims to compensation than the latter. In that case, those who had their homes destroyed in terror bombings would also have a strong claim. Alternatively, the privileged nature of the Jewish victims could rest on the racial nature of the intentions, rather than on intentionality per se. Nobody seems to have used the argument from the French Restoration that whereas somebody benefited from the plunder of Jewish assets, nobody gained from the destruction of East European homes. As these brief comments show, the matter is complex, but the arguments I have cited all go in the same direction. The claims of destroyed property are weaker than those of confiscated property.[19]

Let me now turn to the latter claims, and first address the thorny issue of *dual ownership* that often arises in cases of confiscation.[20] If the state sells the confiscated holdings to private individuals who buy them in good faith, the new owners will soon come to see their property as legally and morally valid. To return the property to the original owners would be to

[18] Authers and Wolffe (2002), p. 232. The final settlement awarded 150 million DM for claims where the taking of property was racially motivated, 50 million for all other property claims, and 150 million for insurance claims.

[19] For an exception, see Dreyfus (2003), p. 317. In the decision he describes, the reluctance to give priority to those who had their property confiscated over those who had it destroyed by air raids is combined with a claim that public opinion would react to compensation of individuals in the former group who already had important financial resources at their disposal. Hence, the refusal to give priority to confiscated property may have been an expression of solidarity with the worst off or, since many of the potential beneficiaries were rich Jewish bankers, a disguised form of anti-Semitism.

[20] A related issue is that of dual entitlement to a position. If a Jew had been dismissed from his functions in a bank and another taken his place, could he later reclaim his position? When this question arose in France after the liberation, it was resolved by ad hoc procedures, rather than by a legal text (Dreyfus 2003, pp. 301–2).

commit one injustice in trying to repair another. The question was clearly stated by John Stuart Mill:

> Possession which has not been legally questioned within a moderate number of years, ought to be, as by the laws of all nations it is, a complete title. Even when the acquisition was wrongful, the dispossession, after a generation has elapsed, of the probably *bona fide* possessors, would generally be a greater injustice, and almost always a greater private and public mischief, than leaving the original wrong without atonement. It may seem hard, that a claim, originally just, should be defeated by mere lapse of time; but there is a time after which, (even looking at the individual case, and without regard to the general effect on the security of persons) the balance of hardship turns the other way. With the injustices of men, as with the convulsions and disasters of nature, the longer they remain unrepaired, the greater become the obstacles to repairing them, arising from the aftergrowths which would have to be torn up or broken through.[21]

Although the injustice of the original wrong does not disappear, the injustice and social dislocations caused by repairing it increase with time and may ultimately come to dominate the initial injustice. With one possible exception, Mill's claim is confirmed by the historical cases of dual ownership. When (and only when) something like a generation has passed since the wrongful acquisition are the new owners allowed to retain their property. This was the case in the French Restoration and in the former GDR after 1990, when the unification treaty stipulated that an exception to the return of confiscated property arises when the new owners have acquired it "in an honest manner."[22] In the English Restoration, by contrast, the property was by and large returned to the original owners. In Norway after 1945, "Jews [and others] could claim their property back regardless of whether the purchaser had acquired it in good faith."[23] In France, a Committee of Owners of Aryanized Properties, which tried to defend the *droits acquis,* was dissolved by a decree from January 1945.[24] The possible exception is the supposed Athenian decision in 403 B.C. to let confiscated goods remain in the hands of those who had bought them. The episode is shrouded in uncertainty, but if that is indeed what happened, it testifies strongly to the desire for reconciliation and social peace among the returning democrats.

[21] Mill (1987), p. 220.

[22] Quint (1997), p. 131. By far the largest numbers of GDR citizens were tenants rather than houseowners. They received no protection in the treaty. As a result, "the massive shift of residential property . . . has led to extraordinary social dislocations" (ibid., p. 133) of the kind that in Mill's eyes would have counted against restitution.

[23] NOU (1997), p. 20.

[24] Prost, Skoutelsky, and Etienne (2000), p. 57.

Let me anticipate the argument of Chapter 8 to note that the emergence of an "aftergrowth" that would complicate restitution is not the only effect of the passage of time. To the extent that demands for restitution have an emotional component, as they often do, and that emotions decay with time, as they also tend to do, we have another reason for expecting restitution to be less frequent as time goes on. In practice, it is sometimes hard to separate the "aftergrowth mechanism" (which leads to increased opposition to restitution) from the "emotional-decay mechanism" (which leads to decreased demand for restitution). In the French Restoration, when for reasons that I discuss in Chapter 8 the emotions decayed slowly, the decision to abstain from restitution could be traced directly to the social dislocations it would have created. The converse case may be illustrated by the reactions observed in 1972 when a Norwegian law professor proposed that the state confiscate the large forest properties near Oslo of a wealthy individual whose ancestors acquired them by allegedly dubious means in the eighteenth century.[25] Although the social dislocations would have been minimal, the idea was viewed as a mere curiosity.

When confiscated property remains in the hands of the state or devolves on corporate actors, the strong conflict pitting individual owner against individual owner does not arise. In these cases, we might expect, and do indeed observe, restitution in kind even after a long passage of time. This was the case of the unsold properties (mainly forests) that were returned to the owners by the French law of December 1814. The same outcome was observed in Czechoslovakia after 1989, in spite of "the initial preference of the government for financial compensation for former owners rather than restitution in kind."[26] According to the Bulgarian law of December 20, 1990, real property confiscated under communism, if in possession of the state, was to be returned to the persons from whom it had been confiscated or their legal heirs. If the property was not in possession of the state, the victims were to be compensated with property of equal value or the monetary equivalent. Although Poland has not adopted legislation on the topic, a draft law from 1993 would allow for restitution in kind in cases "where the property was still owned by the state, where it had been transferred free of charge to co-operatives, or where it was used for public purposes. In other cases, either a substitute property or 'reprivatisation bonds' were authorised."[27] Even in the case of corporate

[25] Fleischer (1972).

[26] Cepl (1991).

[27] Pogany (1997), pp. 154–55. These other cases would presumably include dual individual ownership.

property, however, the passage of time makes a difference. Thus, after the fall of communism, the demand for the return of collectivized land has been much less vocal in the former Soviet Union, where land was socialized in the 1930s, than in Eastern Europe.[28]

Restitution in kind is backward looking and rights-based. The alternative solution – compensation – is forward looking and utilitarian. From an economic point of view, "the transfer of assets ... to the original owners or their heirs does not seem to represent the most rational or productive use of state-owned property."[29] Thus, the German "Unification treaty provided that a former owner can be denied a return of expropriated property if the property is needed for urgent investment uses that would yield general economic benefits in Eastern Germany."[30] The owner must accept the proceeds of the sale or other compensation. This was also the reasoning of the Hungarian Constitutional Court in the First Compensation Case when it ruled, using an explicitly forward-looking argument, that favoring original landowners was justified if and only if "it can be proved that with the preferential treatment of former owners the distribution of state property will yield a more favourable overall social result than equal treatment would."[31]

The amount of compensation for confiscated property is rarely "full." In the French Restoration, the émigrés received roughly what the state had received from the sale of their property, but substantially less than its value. In Hungary after 1990, former owners were compensated in vouchers, which could be used to acquire state-owned property, rather than in cash. Moreover, "full compensation was payable only in respect of items [i.e., vouchers] worth up to 200,000 forints (£1,574 at the June 1991 rate of exchange). Items valued in excess of that sum were subject to partial compensation on a degressive scale up to a maximum of 5 million forints per person and per item of property."[32] As with the payment of war damages, the regressive scale could be justified both on egalitarian grounds and on grounds of scarcity of resources. Egalitarian arguments were probably also behind the size constraints on in-kind restitution in several East European countries. In Romania, for instance, the 1991 law on restitution stated that no owner would receive more than ten hectares

[28] Hann (2004).
[29] Pogany (1997), p. 150; also Heller and Serkin (1999), pp. 141–42.
[30] Quint (1997), p. 129.
[31] Cited from the decision reproduced in Sólyom and Brunner (2000), p. 114.
[32] Pogany (1997), p. 163.

or less than one-half hectare. In 1999, the upper limit was extended to fifty hectares.

A controversial issue is whether those entitled to reparation have to satisfy requirements of citizenship or residence. The Bulgarian law of December 20, 1990, stipulated that if former owners were foreign citizens or Bulgarian citizens permanently residing abroad, they could only receive monetary compensation, not in-kind restitution. The Czechoslovak parliament passed a similar law in May 1991, but it was struck down by the Czech Constitutional Court in 1995. Other compensation laws with similar restrictions were also struck down. In Romania, a law passed in 1994 limited compensation to Romanian citizens who were resident in the country. Former owners living abroad would have six months in which to return to Romania and register their claims. In Poland, the Sejm passed a law that allowed for restitution or compensation, but limited it to Polish citizens only. (The limiting clause had been eliminated by the Senate, but reinserted by the Sejm.) The law was vetoed by the President, on the grounds that it would cause excessive strains on the budget (the expected costs were about $11 billion), as well as create "social divisions" in the country.

III. PERSONAL SUFFERING

In an autocratic regime, even those who are not the target of overt repressive measures may suffer from everyday harassment and petty persecution. Victims or resisters may spend years in prison or camps, where they are not merely deprived of liberty but often mistreated as well. During World War II, many persons were rounded up as "forced laborers" or "slave laborers" for German firms, the former being non-Jewish workers from Eastern Europe and the latter mainly Jewish workers who were taken from concentration camps or ghettos and literally worked to death. Actually, "the Jewish concentration camp workers were less than slaves. Slavemasters care for their human property and try to preserve it; it was the Nazi plan and intention that the Jews would be used up and then burned."[33] In addition to their physical suffering, they were subject to the mental anguish of being under a death sentence. Extreme cases of personal suffering may be caused by rape, torture, and medical experiments on human beings. Death, too, may count as a suffering if it entitles dependents to compensation.

[33] Ferencz (2002), p. xxv.

Compensation for personal suffering may be regulated by a number of criteria. Some categories of suffering may be excluded altogether. Some categories of victims (as defined by other criteria than their mode of suffering) may be excluded altogether. Some categories of victims receive compensation at a uniform rate regardless of their circumstances. Others are compensated in greater or smaller amounts as a function of their past or present circumstances. In the following, I give examples of all these procedures. Many of the issues can be illustrated by the distinction between slave laborers and forced laborers in World War II. In 1999, multilateral negotiations[34] led to a settlement by which German industry and the German government would pay 8 billion DM in compensation for involuntary labor, 1 billion for property losses, and 1 billion to endow a "Future Fund" and to cover legal and administrative costs. I have already mentioned the disagreements concerning confiscated versus destroyed properties. More salient, however, was the conflict opposing spokespersons for forced laborers and slave laborers.

Slightly more than half of the 242,000 slave laborers were Jews, the others being mainly Russians and Poles. Almost all of the 1.26 million forced laborers were non-Jewish, most of them Poles.[35] According to one account, "[a]ll sides agreed there should be a differential between the Jewish and the non-Jewish payments. After all, forced laborers were deported, beaten and incarcerated, but slave laborers were victims of attempted murder."[36] There was agreement that the slave laborers should receive more, but the exact ratio was controversial. The East Europeans proposed a two-to-one proportion, whereas the Jewish negotiators demanded four to one. According to one account, this generated a compromise solution of a three-to-one ratio.[37] According to another, the solution was found almost by accident, when the same number (1.812 billion) "appeared twice on [the lawyers'] chart – once beside the [Jewish] Claims Conference, the other times beside the Poles.... An equal number was the only political solution possible."[38] When there is a prominent focal-point solution, it

[34] They involved American class-action lawyers, German industry, the German and American governments, East European politicians, the Jewish Claims Conference, and the World Jewish Congress. Vivid accounts are given in Authers and Wolffe (2002) and Eizenstat (2003).

[35] Eizenstat (2003), pp. 206, 239–40.

[36] Authers and Wolffe (2002), p. 205. If the proportions I just cited are accurate, this stark opposition cannot be.

[37] Eizenstat (2003), p. 264.

[38] Authers and Wolffe (2002), p. 243.

can break a deadlock in bargaining.[39] The presence of two focal points may *cause* a deadlock.[40] In the present case, however, there seems to have been a miraculous coincidence of two focal-point principles: split the difference and equal division.

These negotiations confirm the claim that the Holocaust serves as "moral capital" for the Jews and for Israel.[41] When arguing for higher rates of compensation for slave laborers, one Jewish lawyer (and Auschwitz survivor) said to another (who had lost ten relatives to the Nazis), "You are a disgrace to the memory of the Holocaust and your father. You are equating slave and forced labor. You should be ashamed of yourself."[42] The substance behind this rhetorical argument is presumably that the slave laborers suffered more because they knew they were destined for death, and therefore should be compensated more. This devaluation of the claims of the forced laborers was reinforced by the German negotiators, who insisted that there was a long tradition for East European workers to come to Germany to help out with the harvest, and that many of them were happy to be on German farms rather than in their own countries. For some reason, these negotiators did not "see the difference between voluntary and coerced agricultural work."[43]

The question may arise, however, whether past *suffering* or present and future *need* is the most relevant ground for compensation. Suppose there are two victims. One suffered badly in the past, but recovered and is now in the normal mental and physical state for his age, and capable of earning a normal income. The other suffered less in the past, but did not recover and is now unable to work. If our aim is to compensate for past welfare loss, we might give priority to the first. If it is to ensure future welfare, the second might have the stronger claim. This question, which came up in the French Restoration, has been important in the debates over the compensation for Nazi wrongdoings. When the first German compensation law was enacted in 1953, the most prominent advocate of victims' right to reparation, Otto Küster, "criticized not only government officials but also representatives of the political parties for insisting on need as the sole basis for compensation. Küster pointed out that the persecutees insisted that they had a special right based on their special situation: they

[39] Schelling (1960), Chap. 3.
[40] Raiffa (1982), p. 54.
[41] Novick (1999), p. 156, citing David Singer of the American Jewish Committee.
[42] Authers and Wolffe (2002), p. 231.
[43] Ibid., p. 238; see also pp. 208, 218, 221.

were due compensation for their sufferings."[44] In the early I. G. Farben cases, both the length of past suffering and the acuity of present need were used to allocate the fixed sum that had been negotiated between the company and the Jewish Claims Conference. Initially, each slave laborer who had worked for more than six months was given 5,000 DM, while those who had worked less received 2,500 DM.[45] Later, supplementary payments were given to widows, minor children, the aged receiving public assistance, and other needy persons. Also, "specific standards of need had to be established for different countries, since an allocation based on deutsche marks would have a different impact depending on the rate of exchange and the local living standard."[46] Thus, relatively few requests were approved from the United States, "with its higher standard of living and relatively generous welfare system."[47]

In the 1999 negotiations about compensation to slave laborers and forced laborers on a vastly larger scale,[48] the chief negotiator for the German companies, Manfred Gentz, argued for many of the same criteria that the Claims Conference had used 40 years earlier. Stuart Eizenstat recounts this phase of the negotiations as follows:

> As Gentz described it, only forced and slave laborers who were now needy would be permitted to recover monetary compensation, for there was "no moral obligation if they are not needy." His colleague, Michael Janssen of Degussa, said that German industry did not want to pay Holocaust survivors who were now medical doctors. When I explained that the purpose was to pay people for their hardship in the past, regardless of their success since the war, Gentz replied, "Why should we pay for suffering sixty years ago?" In addition, Gentz insisted that the German companies would cover only people who had been deported into the Third Reich's 1937 borders and who were confined in guarded camps, neatly cutting out Austria and the Sudetenlands and excluding the forced workers relocated within their own countries to work for the Germans. His rationale: "We want to give money to those who lived under the worst conditions, so this means the deported and those who lived in prisonlike conditions." ... The [German] companies wanted the victims paid on a scale according to where they now lived – less for those in Eastern Europe (where most of the survivors lived) than those in the United States, Western Europe, or Israel. As Gentz put it indelicately, 5,000

44 Lüdtke (1993), p. 565; see also Pross (1998), p. 41.

45 Ferencz (2002), p. 54.

46 Ibid., p. 62.

47 Ibid., p. 63. The comment is puzzling, since a higher general standard of living would presumably count in favor of *higher* rates of compensation.

48 The total amount was about 8 billion DM, whereas the combined earlier payments from I. G. Farben, Krupp, Siemens, AEG, and Rheinmetall amounted to about 52 million DM (figures not adjusted for inflation).

German marks would not mean much to "a rich Jew in New York" but would make a great deal of difference to a Ukrainian pensioner.[49]

Gentz also proposed to limit compensation to those who had worked at least six months in forced labor.[50] The arguments, if reported correctly, are obviously inconsistent. One cannot at one and the same time argue that past suffering is irrelevant *and* that it should be weighted by its intensity and duration. In response, the class-action lawyers "attacked every single one of Gentz's suggestions. The requirement of a minimum six months' labor would be unacceptable to any court. Assessing victims' needs would undermine the desire for equal treatment in compensation payments. Changing payments according to living standards was 'arbitrary and unfair,' and contrary to 'humanitarian principles.'"[51] Although each of these assertions could be challenged, not only on grounds of principle but also by recalling that the criteria Gentz suggested had previously been used by the Claims Conference, he did not get his way. The reason his proposals caused an uproar was probably that his concern was too obviously to limit the total amount of compensation, not (as in the case of the Claims Conference) to decide on the optimal allocation of a fixed amount. Criteria that could be reasonable in themselves become odious when used as a disguise for economic interest.

The German Federal Restitution Law of 1956 (building on the law from 1953) also made fine differentiations among victims.[52] In addition to material and intangible harms, the law covered three categories of personal suffering: harm to life, harm to body and health, and harm to freedom. Those entitled to compensation included Germans who had suffered harm as a result of persecution "on the grounds of political opposition, race, religion, or worldview." Yet some categories were excluded. Gypsies (Roma and Sintis) were not eligible for compensation, since in 1956 the Supreme Court found that "despite the appearance of racial-ideology points of view, it as not race as such that formed the grounds for the measures taken, but the Gypsies' antisocial characteristics." Even when the court reversed its decision a few years later, those who sought compensation for compulsory sterilization received no satisfaction, since this surgical intervention had not caused any diminution in the ability to earn a living.[53] Communists could be denied compensation as enemies of "the

[49] Eizenstat (2003), pp. 232–33.

[50] Ausser and Wolffe (2002), p. 208.

[51] Ibid., p. 209.

[52] The following draws on Pross (1998), Chap. 2.

[53] Lewy (2000), p. 204.

free democratic order." Moreover, "those sentenced to more than three years' imprisonment after May 1948 were not entitled to compensation." Thus, a woman whose life had been ruined through Nazi persecution, physically and financially, was denied compensation because in her desperate situation she committed several thefts and, by virtue of the sentencing requirements for recidivism, was given three and a half years in prison. Victims could also be denied compensation if they "purposefully or negligently provided incorrect or misleading information" about their case. The fragile idea of "negligently providing misleading information" is representative of the harshness of the legislation: "Having just functioned as a mass murderer, [the German state] now felt it could judge who was worthy or unworthy of reparation" for the crimes it had committed.[54]

IV. INTANGIBLE SUFFERING

This category consists of the lack or loss of *opportunities*. Under an autocratic regime, certain opportunities may be denied to all citizens, denied to specific groups, or restricted to a privileged elite. Under the Revolution and Napoleon, French émigré officers were blocked in their career advancement. Under the Nazi regime, Jews were denied entry into (among others) the legal and military professions. Under communism, people were not allowed to sell their labor power and others were not allowed to buy it. Opportunities for travel abroad and access to higher education were reserved for the nomenklatura and their children. Under apartheid, the opportunities of blacks were curtailed in numerous ways.

Intuitively, it might seem strange to refer to each and every denial of an opportunity as suffering on a par with material or personal suffering. If a person does not *want* to take up a certain opportunity, such as embarking on a legal career, his or her welfare is the same whether or not that opportunity is in fact available. Yet there are several reasons for counting denial of opportunities as a harm. If that person *knows* that he is being denied the opportunity of a legal career, he can never be quite certain whether his lack of desire for it is shaped by the fact that it is unavailable to him ("sour grapes"). That gnawing uncertainty counts as a harm. Being singled out as unworthy in some respect is also a form of harm. (This effect does not obtain if the good is denied to everybody.) Finally, one might take the more radical step and argue that opportunities for welfare, rather than welfare itself, is the morally relevant issue. I return to that question later.

54 Ibid., p. 55.

Most reparation schemes do not include compensation for denial of opportunities. In Hungary, the Second Compensation Law passed in 1992 addressed (among other issues) the question of compensation for harm done to Jews during World War II. As Istvan Pogany writes,

> the law provides compensation only for interferences with *property* rights after 1 May 1939. It applies to government takings authorised by the Second Jewish Law but does not extend to other and far-reaching interferences with the economic life of the Jewish community.... However, the economic consequence of expelling Jews from certain sectors of employment... was at least as severe, for the individuals concerned and for their families, as the confiscation of property proved for others.[55]

Note that Pogany does not address the harm imposed on those in the younger generation who were prevented from *entering* these sectors of employment. The same focus on actual losses is found in the Federal Restitution law passed by the West German parliament in 1956. The law included, among its eight categories of grounds for compensation, both harm to career advancement and harm to economic advancement. Yet with an exception that I italicize, the harms are actual losses (compared to a preexisting baseline), rather than opportunities forgone (compared to a counterfactual baseline). The harms include "revocation of admission to legal practice, layoffs from the civil service... or a private business, reduced income, *prevention* or interruption of education or training."[56]

Peter Quint might seem to take a more evenhanded approach when he cites both "*dismissal* from employment in retaliation for filing an application to leave the GDR" and "*exclusion* from an advanced high school on political grounds" as typical cases of political discrimination for which compensation might be claimed.[57] Elsewhere, he refers to compensation for "the *interruption or denial* of a chosen career."[58] Yet the focus on a *chosen* career implies that the denial is in fact a form of interruption. To be excluded from a high school differs from not being admitted.

There are several reasons why the focus tends, albeit with some ambiguity, to be on lost opportunities rather than on opportunities forgone. The general phenomenon of loss aversion implies that actual losses loom larger than forgone gains.[59] Also, "the problems of proof, as well as the

[55] Pogany (1997), p. 171.
[56] Pross (1998), p. 51.
[57] Quint (1997), p. 224; italics added.
[58] Ibid., p. 225; italics added.
[59] Kahneman and Tversky (1979).

difficulties of measuring the ultimate consequences of the claimed discrimination, [are] daunting."[60] A bureaucracy does not deal easily with counterfactual claims of this nature. Damage to property and body can be measured and quantified in a natural way. The likelihood that I would have taken up an opportunity that was blocked to me, and my likely degree of success in that career, do not lend themselves to objective quantification. The loss of preexisting career options that the agent had in fact already chosen falls somewhere in between. Although he might later have gone on to do something else or become a failure in his chosen profession, there is a presumption in his favor that does not exist in the purely counterfactual case. This presumption is of course rebuttable, as shown by the story cited in Chapter 2 of the French émigré naval officer who wanted to be promoted to admiral after the Restoration.

But there may be a deeper reason as well. It can be brought out by citing an article by Ernst Ehrmann in *Die Zeit* from 1964. As stated in a summary by Christian Pross, Ehrmann

> felt that the demands of the persecutee organizations would lead to an enormous number of new trials and proceedings: "In the still-closed world of the persecuted, especially the emigrants, it's buzzing like a beehive. New desires are being awakened." Increasing the sum, for example, for interference with education for "the peculiar people, the Gypsies" was completely out of place, as Gypsies placed no value on education and thus did not need to be compensated for lost educational opportunities.[61]

The argument, for all its unpleasant overtones, is related to recent debates over the relative importance of desires and opportunities in ranking social states.[62] There are strong reasons against ranking states merely on the basis of preference satisfaction and against basing compensation merely on the basis of unfulfilled desires. There might be too much compensation, if people report desires they do not really have. There might be too little, if they adjust their desires to their opportunities ("sour grapes"). Yet the proposal to rank states merely on the basis of the opportunities they offer, and to base compensation merely on blocked opportunities, is also problematic. Is opportunity Set A really better than Set B if the two are identical, except that in A one individual has an opportunity that she does not want to take up? *Couldn't Set A in fact be worse,* if it involves the wasteful provision of a costly opportunity to someone who is not going

[60] Quint (1997), p. 224.
[61] Pross (1998), p. 63.
[62] See, for instance, Le Grand (1992) for an example-studded exposition.

to make use of it? And if that individual is deprived of that opportunity, ought she to be compensated for the loss?

V. THE BURDEN OF PROOF

Before loss of property can be compensated, the legal claim to property must be established. If damage to health is to be compensated on the grounds of reduced income-earning capacity, it must be shown that the reduction is causally related to the original harm. To compensate a person for a lack of opportunity, one might require proof that the option would actually have been chosen had it been available. I ignore the more intractable third issue, and focus on the evidence needed to justify reparation for material or personal suffering.

By and large, courts and agencies tend to demand strict, individualized evidence before they authorize compensation. The burden of proof is on the person making the request. In criminal cases, the law is usually concerned with avoiding false convictions. Wrongdoers are given the benefit of the doubt because it is better for ten guilty to be let free than for one innocent to be convicted. There is no equally explicit principle underlying administrative decisions, but the main emphasis has usually been on the need to avoid paying compensation to those not entitled, rather than to avoid denying them to those who are entitled. This normal tendency for bureaucratic tightfistedness may, however, come into conflict with the dictates of compassion and atonement. Also, the demand for rigorous proof of victimization may, for some victims, add to their burden.

The case of forced sales of Jewish property in Germany and German-occupied countries is a case in point. Whereas many Jewish firms and other properties were simply confiscated, others were sold under duress at below-market prices, perhaps to enable the owner to flee the country. The question is how to establish that the situation was one of duress. In Austria, "the burden of proof lay with the victim, who was required to show that the transfer was the result of persecution. In contrast, German law assumed such transfers took place under duress."[63] In France after the liberation, the initial project of the Ministry of Justice was very favorable to the purchasers of Jewish properties. It was "strongly criticized by the judicial committee [of the provisional government] headed by René Cassin, which especially criticized it for demanding of those whose properties had been spoliated that they offer proof of duress [*violence*] in cases

[63] Authers and Wolffe (2002), p. 311.

where they had given their consent to the act."[64] The later ordinance of April 21, 1945, states that any transfers made with the consent of the interested party are "presumed to have taken place under duress" if they occurred after June 16, 1940.[65]

In a Norwegian case from 1949, an agency had to decide how to treat a claim by a Jewish survivor of the Holocaust for restitution of property. All the members of his family had perished in the camps, the order of their deaths being (i) unknown and (ii) relevant for the amount to which he was entitled. Among the solutions that might have been chosen, the agency opted for the one least favorable to the claimant.[66] In recent negotiations between the French and American governments, the French negotiators "found it 'abhorrent' for Jewish survivors to recover funds based solely on their religious affiliation, and not on hard evidence that they or their families had personally lost assets in French banks."[67] Under pressure, however, they admitted a concern to avoid false negatives and granted the possibility of making payments on a claimant's "intimate and personal conviction" of entitlement.[68] Here, as in the actions against the Swiss banks, the question was how to frame demands based on "rough justice" – legally uncertain but morally compelling claims.

To use a stylized example, suppose it is known that there were a hundred victims in a certain category. Two hundred come forward to claim compensation, but because of lack of evidence, there is no way of verifying their claims. Should one grant full compensation to all, award half compensation to all, or deny compensation to all? The outcome of the French and Swiss negotiations can perhaps be said to be in the spirit of the second solution. This was also the spirit in which ancient Jewish law resolved the question faced by the Norwegian agency:

> There are . . . a few cases in which there is in effect equal probability on opposing sides, because of symmetry in evidence. . . . "A house collapsed on a man and his wife. The husband's heirs say, 'The woman died first and the husband afterward'; the woman's heirs say, 'The husband died first and the wife afterward.' . . . Bar Koppara [second century A.D.] taught: 'Since these are heirs and those are heirs, they divide the inheritance.'"[69]

[64] Prost, Skoutelsky, and Etienne (2000), p. 68.

[65] Ibid., p. 69.

[66] NOU (1997), p. 110.

[67] Eizenstat (2003), p. 307. As he describes it, the French reaction was due not to lack of generosity but to deeply ingrained legalism.

[68] Ibid., p. 330.

[69] Franklin (2001), p. 6.

In this case, there is a fixed rather than adjustable total to be divided but, to repeat, the spirit of compromise is similar.

The allocation of compensation for personal suffering may, as noted, depend on the duration and intensity of past suffering or on the acuity of need in the present. In some compensation schemes, however, neither past suffering nor present need, singly or in combination, suffice for entitlement. Compensation will be provided only if there is a *causal link* between past harm and present need. In the language used to implement the 1956 German Restitution law, one had to estimate the "persecution-induced reduction in earning capacity." A decision by a Düsseldorf court shows the tortuous causal diagnostics involved:

> If it is assumed that a complaint that was substantially caused by persecution, and is thus eligible for a full pension, would have emerged later to the same extent or an extent that can be precisely determined, at a time that can be precisely estimated, through harms independent of persecution in conjunction with the genetic predisposition, this overtaking causality must be established with a probability bordering on certainty. No grounds for a reduction in pension exists if the complaint was substantially caused by persecution at the moment it appeared, but, as a result of a special predisposition in the patient, it irregularly failed to abate, as long as it is not established that this predisposition would have become manifest even without persecution.[70]

Thus, although causal preemption is grounds for denying a pension, it is not denied if the injury is triggered by persecution and then maintained by a disposition, unless it can be shown that the latter would have caused the injury even without the trigger.

In a harrowing account, Christian Pross shows how the medical examiners, many of them former Nazi Party members, systematically used causal analysis or pseudoanalysis to minimize the extent of "deserving victimhood." Thus,

> medical evaluators required so-called bridge symptoms to prove persecution-induced complaints. The persecutee had to submit reports proving that signs of the complaint had emerged immediately after the persecution and had lasted through the years until the time of the examination assessment. This requirement by the German examining doctors flew in the face of all scientific fact. In Denmark and France, extensive studies in the early 1950s had already established that many chronic psychological and somatic illnesses in persecutees appeared only after a symptom-free latency period lasting many years. This had also been known in the Federal Republic since the mid 1950s.[71]

[70] Pross (1998), p. 74.
[71] Ibid., p. 78.

The case of Herr W. is also typical.[72] He was eleven years old in 1933, popular with everyone at school. Then "everything changed overnight" and in October 1934, W. and his parents emigrated to Palestine. After many problems, he emigrated to the United States in 1957, where he had more problems. In a piece of quasi-Nietzschean diagnosis, one doctor found that

> Herr W. had been traumatized not by mistreatment as about of ten to twelve years of age, but as a small child, due to the separation of his parents, the loss of his biological father, and a troubled relationship with his stepfather. The doctor concluded that if W.'s childhood had been happy, the discrimination at age ten should not have made any difference. On the contrary it should have toughened him. Such social discrimination "does not lead to psychological harm; it is more likely to strengthen the ability to cope with life."

Along similar lines, a psychiatrist found a "woman, who had spent three years in Auschwitz, to have a psychopathic personality with a tendency toward abnormal processing of experience and an inability to deal with life, as general medical experience showed that a normal person would have overcome this burden six months after liberation at the latest."[73] Moral reactions apart, the reasoning is flawed by *the aversion to admitting uncertainty* that is characteristic of poorly developed disciplines, such as clinical psychology and psychiatry. In addition, the medical examinations could be iatrogenic,[74] as the victims "were forced to recall their experiences, with destructive consequences for many."[75] Thus, according

[72] Ibid., p. 122ff.

[73] Ibid., p. 96.

[74] The related issue of "pension neurosis" is also worth mentioning. In the wake of World War II, psychiatrists in Great Britain, France, and Germany developed a theory to the effect that the payment of pensions for war neuroses tended to perpetuate the symptoms: "The effect of pensions and allowances on war neurotics had already been noticed during the war. 'The whole therapy was so vitiated by the pension system,' the respected British psychotherapist T. A. Ross wrote of his work between 1917 and 1921, 'that it was impossible to gauge the value of any form of treatment.' Ross found that, as men got better, the thought of losing their allowance (and with it a guaranteed livelihood) would cause their hysterical symptoms to return or new symptoms to appear. . . . Other liberal-minded doctors agreed. Bernard Hart warned that it was very dangerous for there to be a relationship between symptoms and pensions. Consciously or not, as long as a pension depended on the existence of symptoms, recovery would be impeded" (Sheppard 2000, p. 151). After 1945, German doctors continued to rely on this theory to deny compensation to victims of Nazi persecution (Pross 1998, pp. 84–85).

[75] Ibid., p. 55, p. 141. He also quotes (p. 96) the following statement: "We must not forget the constant rousing of memories, aggressions, and resentments caused by the restitution process – the endless difficulties of producing witness statements and documents on damage to property and education, proof of persecution as such, the dealing with

to the New York psychoanalyst Kurt Eissler, "The patient should actually receive compensation for the agitation and degradation suffered in the course of the reparations procedure."[76] In such cases, the phrase "burden of proof" takes on a literal sense.

In an equally harrowing study, Ingo Müller details a number of cases in which German courts went to unbelievable lengths to deny reparation. In one case, a man who had been arrested when he was sixteen for opposing National Socialism was denied reparations because of his love of jazz: Given his age, "he could . . . certainly not express sensible opinions relating to political matters. On the contrary . . . his fondness for outlandish music proved clearly that he had not reached a degree of maturity which would permit one to speak of reasoned judgment."[77] As in another case involving a woman who was denied a disability pension on the grounds that her offense had been personal rather than political, "the fact that the Third Reich itself had treated [the] actions as a political offense was supposedly irrelevant."[78] In a third case, a Social Democrat had been jailed for refusing to serve in the army and later, when he was drafted, for refusing to lay minefields because he was unwilling to have anything to do with lethal weapons. His demand for reparation was rejected

> on the grounds that his actions had indeed been politically motivated, but that resistance to the Third Reich could "be regarded as rightful, and accordingly a government action punishing this resistance be regarded as injustice in the legal sense . . . only if the chances of success for this act of resistance were such as to make it a serious and practical attempt to eliminate existing unjust conditions."[79]

In other words, Don Quixotes and Kantians need not apply.

medical disagreements on the backs of the persecutees, the slowness of the process and the sometimes insistent narrow-mindedness of the restitution bureaucracy that led to new illnesses."

[76] Ibid., p. 106.

[77] Müller (1991), p. 263.

[78] Ibid., p. 265.

[79] Ibid., p. 265.

7

Constraints

I. INTRODUCTION

In the present chapter, I consider how the modalities of transition may constrain the substantive and procedural decisions of transitional justice. In some cases, they do so by making some options absolutely unfeasible ("hard constraints"). More frequently, they do so by affecting the trade-offs between justice and other goals, such as economic reconstruction or survival of the new regime ("soft constraints").

I shall proceed as follows. In Section II, I discuss how transitional justice may be constrained by the negotiations that establish the new regime. In Section III, some aspects of transitional justice in Germany in 1945 are considered in some detail. In Section IV, I discuss economic constraints on transitional justice. I conclude in Section V by considering the tension between various desiderata of transitional justice that may make it impossible to satisfy all of them at the same time.

II. THE CONSTRAINTS OF NEGOTIATED TRANSITIONS

The leaders of an incoming regime may not be free to implement transitional justice as they please, if the transition was ushered in by negotiations that included provisions of amnesty or clemency. In fact, it is hard to see why outgoing leaders would ever relinquish power voluntarily unless they were assured that their persons, and preferably their property, were secure. The main question of the present section concerns the *basis* of that assurance. Although I focus on twentieth-century negotiated transitions, I begin with some earlier cases.

The first instance of a negotiated transition is the restoration of Athenian democracy in 403 B.C. As explained in Chapter 1, we do not know the details of the tripartite negotiations among oligarchs, democrats, and Spartans, nor the extent to which these negotiations forced the democrats to pull their punches more than they would otherwise have done. Their behavior in the years following the transition suggest that the moderation was at least to some extent chosen, rather than imposed.

As explained in Chapter 2, the First and Second French Restorations also emerged from negotiated settlements between outgoing and incoming elites. As in Athens, these negotiations were supervised by a third party. In 1814, the Allied powers forced Louis XVIII to adopt a more moderate policy, notably with regard to property restitution, than he would have preferred to do. In 1815, the Allies played a more complex role. First, they supported Talleyrand when he persuaded Louis XVIII to issue the Cambrai Proclamation of June 28 that promised immunity for most supporters of Napoleon and delegated retributive measures to parliament. Later, however, they pushed the government to enact immediate measures in the decree of July 24. Between these two events, they had also held out an ambiguous promise of immunity in the negotiations over a peace convention. Although the French negotiators may have thought they had obtained a permanent amnesty, the relevant article in fact only protected them until the return of Louis XVIII.

I want to draw attention to two features of the events in 1815. First, the delegation of retributive measures to the future parliament was no doubt motivated, at least on Talleyrand's part, by the expectation that the elections would return a moderate assembly. Presumably he also hoped that it would still the anxieties of some who might otherwise have resisted the transition. His hopes were thwarted when the elections produced an ultraroyalist parliament bent on vengeance. Second, the Allies were able to negotiate a bloodless settlement by a suitably ambiguous promise, which might later be interpreted in a different spirit from how it was understood by the losers. When judging Maréchal Ney, the upper house of parliament rejected the interpretation of Article XII of the peace convention that would have protected him from prosecution.

The Greek transition of 1974 came about in a somewhat similar manner. In the trials of the Greek military, the Court of Appeal accepted a retroactive interpretation of an ambiguously worded amnesty decree, which the military had believed gave them impunity.[1] The importance

[1] Alivizatos and Diamandouros (1997), pp. 43–44.

of the issue is brought out by the following comment: "[T]o the extent that the phrasing of the amnesty decree appeared to include principals of the authoritarian regime and thus provided them with an additional incentive to remain quiescent, it afforded the incoming civilian leadership precious breathing space during which to proceed with the implementation of its democratization strategy."[2] Although the incoming president, Karamanlis, later "vehemently denied the existence of any understanding involving the outgoing regime,"[3] the issue remains open.

These observations can be related to what I said in Chapter 4 about legislatures and courts as *sources of uncertainty*. Those who listened to Talleyrand may have agreed to a peaceful transition in part because they expected a legislature that would not punish them. Those who signed the peace convention on July 3, 1815, may have done so because they thought Article XII provided them with a legally valid protection. Similarly, the Greek officers agreed to step down because they thought themselves protected by the amnesty decree. Under conditions of democracy and the rule of law, however, negotiators may be *unable to deliver* on any promises they might make on behalf of future legislatures and courts. Moreover, they cannot guarantee the behavior of their own successors. Even when those who negotiate on behalf of the incoming forces are in charge of the first or provisional government following the transition, they may be replaced by others who do not necessarily feel bound by their promises.

The incoming forces often have two conflicting desires: for a peaceful transition and for transitional justice.[4] When negotiating with the outgoing leaders to achieve the first goal, they may have to sacrifice the second. If the negotiators believe that they will form the first government and remain in power for some time (and the belief is shared by their interlocutors), promises of amnesty or immunity may be rendered credible by their concern for their reputation. Other credibility-enhancing mechanisms, based on military or economic power, are discussed later in the chapter. Here, I only want to mention that an incoming elite may bootstrap itself into credibility, as it were, by laying its reputation on the line. We know from wage bargaining that union leaders often exploit their known concern for their reputation by making public demands or threats that might not have been credible if made behind closed doors. This argument does not

[2] Ibid., p. 59 n. 42.

[3] Ibid.

[4] The following is indebted to very helpful conversations with, and suggestions by, Monika Nalepa.

apply directly to negotiated transitions, in which the bargaining mostly does take place behind closed doors.[5] In fact, the very existence of a bargaining process may be hidden, as it was in Argentina and Uruguay in the mid-1980s. Yet the negotiators may care sufficiently about their reputation among fellow members of the incoming and outgoing elites to be motivated to keep their word. In the Polish 1989 transition, for instance, the phrase *pacta sunt servanda* (promises are to be kept) was a constant refrain on both sides of the bargaining table. This mechanism will fail, however, if the outgoing elite believes that after the transition, the negotiators will be replaced by others who are not bound by their promises. It may also fail to generate an agreement if the old elite believes that future courts and legislatures may take an independent stance. Perversely, promises of immunity are more credible if the courts are so corrupt and entangled in the old regime that vigorous prosecution is unlikely.

If the negotiated settlement is supervised or mediated by a third party, as in Athens in 403 B.C. and in France in 1814 and 1815, additional mechanisms of credibility may come into play. The third party may offer asylum for the outgoing elite, or threaten the incoming elite with sanctions if they fail to respect the promise of amnesty. The exile option for the Athenian oligarchs may be seen as an instance of the first strategy. Later in this section I cite the role of the American ambassador to Hungary in 1989 as a possible instance of the second. The problem, of course, is that the issue of credibility is then shifted onto the third party. In the asylum case, the credibility of protection is enhanced if, as in Athens in 403 B.C., there are close relations between the outgoing elite and the third party.[6] If, however, a democratic country offers to serve as a broker in negotiations between outgoing autocrats and incoming democrats, its promises to the former may lack credibility. Here, too, the concern of the third party for its reputation may make the difference, especially if its role and its promises are in the public domain.

These general comments will serve as background for a discussion of negotiated transitions in Latin America, in postcommunist societies, and in South Africa. In Argentina and Uruguay, the promises of immunity were made credible by the control the outgoing elite retained over the armed forces. Yet because the deals were struck in secret, compliance was not automatic. In Argentina, President Alfonsín promised that only a limited

[5] Even in apparent exceptions such as the Hungarian and Bulgarian Round Table Talks in 1989–1990, it is likely that some deals were struck behind the scenes.

[6] Sutter (1995), p. 121 n. 10.

number of officers would have to be tried, and that even these would be granted an amnesty at the end of his term. Later, however, both the legislature and the courts threw spanners in his wheel. First, the Senate passed a law "explicitly [providing] that abhorrent or atrocious acts rebut the presumption of mistake about the legitimacy of the orders. This . . . condition thwarted Alfonsín's strategy, transforming a narrow, implicit exception to a bright-line rule into a broader, explicit means to rebut the presumption."[7] Later, a dramatic demonstration of judicial independence occurred after parliament passed a "full-stop law" on December 23, 1986, establishing a sixty-day limit for initiating prosecutions: "When the full-stop law became operative, courts all over the country, even those in the interior which had been rather dormant, became frantic with activity, even skipping the usual summer judicial vacation in January,"[8] on which Alfonsín probably counted. When the military showed signs of unrest, Alfonsín pushed through a "due obedience law" that created an "almost irrefutable defense for middle- and lower-rank officers."[9]

A very similar sequence occurred in Uruguay. In 1984, an explicit or implicit deal was struck to assure the military that the incoming government would protect them from prosecution.[10] In 1985, the first cases against military officers came to the courts. The military, supported by the new government, claimed that the cases fell under the jurisdiction of the military tribunals, but in June 1986, the Supreme Court ruled in favor of the civilian courts. Parliament, too, refused to honor the pact: "Between October 1985 and December 1986, three bills were presented to Congress to limit or prevent prosecutions. All three failed."[11] Under strong pressure from the military, parliament finally passed an amnesty law on December 21, 1986. As in Argentina, the deal was finally respected, but only when return to military rule seemed imminent.

In the East European transitions, the outgoing elite lost all or almost all of their power base, retaining, at most, potentially damaging information. They had few credible threats at their disposal to assure their future. Nor could the negotiators for the opposition in the Round Table Talks make credible promises on behalf of their successors or the new institutions

[7] Nino (1996), p. 75.
[8] Ibid., p. 94.
[9] Ibid., p. 100.
[10] Gillespie (1991), p. 176, and Brito (1997), pp. 74–78, argue that the deal was tacit rather than explicit. Other commentators seem to think it was closer to the explicit end of the spectrum.
[11] Brito (2001), pp. 128–29.

that there would be no vindictive legislation. Yet in several countries, some kind of understanding was probably reached. Concerning Poland, Wiktor Osiatynski writes that "[a]lthough the Solidarity side at the Round Table claims that they did not make any deals with the communists, the personal security of the latter was presumed. Such was the effect of the 'bold line' with which Prime Minister Tadeusz Mazowiecki promised to divide the post-communist future from the communist past."[12] This suggests that a very implicit deal may have been struck. Along the same lines, Adam Michnik is quoted as saying, "If I didn't tell [General Czeslaw] Kiszczak at the Roundtable that he would be judged if I came to power, it would be deeply wrong of me to demand it now."[13] Kiszczak was eventually put on trial several times, however, most recently in 2001.

The question also came up in 1992 when the Olszewski government released a list of alleged secret police collaborators. Mazowiecki and his followers opposed publication of the files, perhaps because of

> a lingering feeling . . . that the files should remain closed as a way of upholding the bargain reached at the roundtable talks with the communist party, which had made a roundabout contribution to Poland's transition to democracy by surrendering power. The party had upheld its end of the deal; and it would be changing the rules of the game now to start raking through the past.[14]

Yet as the publication of the list shows, the implicit promises of the Round Table negotiations lost their force when the negotiators lost office. The left wing of Solidarity could not count on the right wing's respecting the promises made at the Round Table, partly because the right wing had no important presence in the negotiations and therefore little reputation to lose, and partly because its position was intrinsically (or strategically) more vindictive. I return to this question in Section III of Chapter 9.

There is some evidence that the Hungarian Round Table Talks in 1989 also included explicit or implicit agreements on the limits to transitional justice. Reform Communists have claimed that a law passed in 1991 to suspend the statute of limitations for certain crimes violated the "gentleman's agreement" that had been made during the Round Table Talks between the government and the opposition in 1989.[15] (Although the

[12] Osiatynski (1991), p. 841.

[13] Halmai and Scheppele (1997), p. 179. The description of the atmosphere at the Round Table Talks given by Osiatynski (1996) is consistent with this remark. Along the same lines, see Kuk (2001), p. 194.

[14] Winton (1992), pp. 17–18.

[15] Kritz (1995), vol. 2, p. 650. See also the dispatch "Parliament Debate on Secret Service Proposal" from the Hungarian News Agency, November 13, 1991.

Constitutional Court struck the law down, the alleged promise played no role in its decision.) In 1999, the Hungarian Association of '56 Rebels asked a court in Budapest to freeze the ex-Communist Party's assets and properties as part of a civil prosecution. The chairman of the association said that "[i]n 1990, there was a cosy deal among the political elite that the Communists would not be brought to account. We are putting an end to that – even if we have to do it through a civil case."[16] People knowledgeable about the atmosphere at the Round Table Talks assert that the process of working together to bring about a viable compromise created an implicit trust that would later prevent the winners from prosecuting the losers.[17] In addition, the reputation effect may have operated.

Other mechanisms may also have been at work. The American ambassador to Hungary during the Round Table Talks recalls that he personally promised that "neither [the Secretary General of the Communist Party] nor incumbents like him would be jailed or persecuted in the future."[18] Presumably, the promise was based on an implicit threat to the opposition of withholding economic assistance if they nevertheless went ahead and prosecuted their former persecutors. The Hungarian Communists also adopted indirect strategies to the same end. In the Round Table Talks, the proposal to create a Constitutional Court came from the Communist side, not, as one might have expected, from the opposition. Apparently, "the Communists wanted a strong court because they hoped it would protect them against reprisals if they lost power."[19] One Communist delegate to the Round Table Talks said that "we thought that this was one of the institutions which would later be able to prevent a turning against the constitution, a jettisoning of the institution, the creation of all sorts of laws seeking revenge."[20] Thus, in addition to the protection they might receive from their own corrupt courts, the Hungarian Communists also benefited from the highly principled attitude of the new legal institutions.

The transition in Czechoslovakia had elements of negotiation that enabled the Communists to retain control over the Ministry of the Interior long enough to destroy some files.[21] It is impossible to tell whether the

[16] *Sunday Telegraph* (London), July 25, 1999.
[17] András Bozóki (personal communication).
[18] Tökés (1996), p. 300; see also p. 395.
[19] Schwartz (2000), p. 77.
[20] Cited after Schiemann (1998).
[21] Calda (1996), pp. 159–60, 163. He claims that negotiations occurred only because Civic Forum underestimated the weakness of the Communist regime.

allocation of this ministry to the Communists amounted to an implicit deal over transitional justice.[22] In Bulgaria, too, transitional justice was indirectly shaped by the negotiations between the regime and the opposition. Transitional justice was never genuinely discussed – although raised several times by the opposition – in the Bulgarian Round Table Talks.[23] Yet indirectly, the prospects for prosecution and restitution were affected by the electoral laws adopted in these talks. Whereas the opposition wanted proportional representation, the Communists, whose candidates had greater visibility, wanted 75 percent of the deputies to be chosen by majority voting in single-seat districts. The compromise was a mixed system in which each voter cast two votes, one for a party list and one for a single candidate. As a result, the Communist Party won a clear majority in the constituent parliament, which it used to "include in the Constitution measures to protect itself and its property against future hostile regimes."[24]

In the process of German reunification, two principles were adopted that later were important constraints on transitional justice. First, expropriations that had taken place under Soviet occupation between 1945 and 1949 were to be exempt from restitution. This clause has been widely seen as imposed by the Soviet Union as a condition for accepting reunification. Second, the "unification treaty maintained in force the Basic Laws' constitutional clause forbidding ex post facto prosecutions; this decision may reflect in part the leverage communist elites still possessed as unification arrangements were being negotiated."[25] There is little evidence to support these claims about a causal link between the reunification negotiations and transitional justice.[26] Concerning the first, there is even some evidence to the contrary.[27] Moreover, the logic of the arguments is questionable. It is not clear why nonrestitution of the properties would be in the interest of the Soviet Union. Although the East German leaders certainly had an interest in minimizing the scope of prosecution, it is not clear that they

[22] Monika Nalepa (personal communication) suggests that in Poland, too, the fact that the Communists retained control over the Ministry of Military Affairs is an indicator that a deal had been struck. This is confirmed by my meeting in 1992 with a centrally placed Polish politician, who asserted that Kiszczak had protected himself by taking with him incriminating files on the Church.

[23] Kolarova and Dimitrov (1996), p. 194.

[24] Schwartz (2000), p. 168.

[25] Sa'adah (1998), p. 177.

[26] Neither of two standard works on German reunification (Maier 1997; Zelikov and Rice 1997) indicates that transitional justice was on the agenda of the negotiations.

[27] Quint (1997), p. 139.

retained any kind of leverage at that stage in the transition. This being said, until convincing alternative explanations are forthcoming, one cannot exclude that these limits on transitional justice were imposed by the Soviet or East German governments as conditions for reunification.

In the South African negotiations, the National Party tried initially to entrench the power of the white minority through a variety of constitutional means, which included high thresholds for amendments, an upper house that would give disproportionate representation for minority groups, and a guaranteed presence with veto power in the Cabinet.[28] If they had succeeded, they might have used these powers to block transitional justice. When this indirect strategy failed, they used their bargaining power to negotiate severe limits on reparations and prosecutions. The 1994 Interim Constitution, which was negotiated under the clear threat that the apartheid regime might refuse to hand over power if its demands were not met, allowed for restitution of land, but only for dispossessions after June 13, 1913. This was the date of the Land Act that allotted 13 percent of the land, mostly marginal in quality, to the African 70 percent of the country.[29] The Interim Constitution also asserted that "amnesty shall be granted in respect of acts, omissions and offenses associated with political objectives and committed in the course of the conflicts of the past." In the mandate of the Truth and Reconciliation Commission that was established in 1995, the amnesty was embedded in a more complicated set of procedures, which made it possible to prosecute some wrongdoings from the apartheid era. The Commission's mandate also included recommendations for reparations to the victims of "gross" human rights violations, carefully defined (I assume) to exclude the regime's resettlement of large parts of the population by force.

We may ask whether the African National Congress (ANC) would have agreed to these sharply restricted forms of retribution and restitution if they had not been constrained by the apparatus of repression controlled by the white elite. The fact that they respected the agreed-upon arrangements after these constraints have been lifted suggests that they might have chosen them in any case. They might have decided to pull their punches for the sake of social reconciliation. They might also have decided to eschew large-scale prosecution because of the huge practical problems it would have created,[30] and to limit the class of victims eligible for compensation

[28] Spitz and Chaskalson (2000), pp. 25, 27, 43; also Steytler (1995), p. 67.

[29] Asmal, Asmal, and Roberts (1997), p. 7.

[30] Boraine (2000), p. 285.

to match what the state could afford to pay out. Finally, and in my view most importantly, the sheer economic power of the white elite might have deterred the ANC from seeking large-scale transitional justice. Because the international capital market is extremely sensitive to signs of social and political instability, the ANC would have known that prosecution of wrongdoers from the apartheid era or extensive redistribution of land could trigger the disaster scenario that was later played out in Zimbabwe. Hence, the ANC might have chosen moderation even had it not been imposed on them.

If unconstrained, the ANC would almost certainly not, however, have chosen the "evenhanded" policy of the Truth and Reconciliation Commission. Although the ANC had proved itself remarkably willing to crack down on its own members for human rights violations, through two internal truth commissions in 1992 and 1993, the idea that perpetrators and victims of apartheid were somehow on a par would have been abhorrent to them. Many ANC members, including the later President of the country Thabo Mbeki, strongly criticized the Commission for its "artificial evenhandedness."[31] Evenhanded treatment of perpetrators and victims is, in fact, limited to negotiated transitions, other examples being the truth commissions of Argentina, Chile, El Salvador, and Guatemala. Over and above the desire for immunity, it often seems important for the outgoing elite to create an appearance that its human rights violations were justified by those of the opposition.

This kind of evenhanded punishment is never seen after regime defeat or regime collapse. Winners do not punish their own. In 1945 as in 1919, the Germans responded to accusations of war crimes by playing the tu quoque argument to the hilt, but with little success.[32] In Denmark, there has been much speculation about a deal between the resistance movement and the politicians to grant immunity for the four hundred killings of informers by members of the resistance, but the evidence is thin.[33] The fact is, however, that there were no prosecutions, neither in Denmark nor in any of the other countries occupied by Germany. In France, numerous arrests of résistants for unauthorized executions took place during

[31] Ibid., Chap. 9.

[32] For 1919, see Horne and Kramer (2001), pp. 334–35. For 1945, see Taylor (1992), pp. 409, 554. In Nuremberg, the defender of Admirals Raeder and Doenitz succeeded in getting Admiral Nimitz to state that he, too, had engaged in sinking merchant ships without warning. Although this admission did not lead to an indictment of Nimitz, it did affect the verdict of the German admirals.

[33] Tamm (1984), Chap. 11.

early 1945.[34] They were all, however, accused of carrying out revenge killings *after* the liberation, rather than of unjustified murders during the occupation. In the former Communist countries there was virtually no armed opposition to the regimes and, hence, no killings to be prosecuted or amnestied.

III. THE CASE OF GERMANY

Transitional justice in Germany after World War II was subject to multiple, if ambiguous, constraints. Among the Allies, some thought that draconian punishment of the German people, notably by destroying its means of production, would also be the best means to prevent a resurgence of German militarism. Others argued that the latter goal imposed strict limits on the punitive measures to be taken, and that a "Carthaginian peace" would be counterproductive. Still others (sometimes the same individuals) argued that it was absurd to punish Germany by destroying its industrial might at a time when Western Europe was in desperate need of economic resources. Finally, the emerging communist threat led the Allies to moderate their initial severity.

Most obviously, limits to prosecution and compensation were imposed by the perceived need to have a strong Germany as a buffer against the aggressive intentions of the Soviet Union. During World War I, Churchill "warned Lloyd George's War Cabinet that they 'might have to build up the German army' and 'get Germany on her legs again' to stop Bolshevism."[35] In nearly identical terms, he told Anthony Eden in October 1943, "We mustn't weaken Germany too much – we may need her against Russia."[36] At that time, and for the next few years, this was a minority opinion. (Later, as we shall see, Churchill was quite willing to impose a Carthaginian peace on Germany.) Yet from 1947 onward, "the basic priority of U.S. policy in West Germany was shifting from punishment of the Nazis to economic reconstruction in the general interest of West European security against the Soviet threat. Thus the new Secretary of Defense, James Forrestal, in August 1947 ordered [General Lucius] Clay to cease denazification procedures."[37] Restitution, too, was truncated

[34] Novick (1968), p. 77; Amouroux (1999), pp. 499–526.
[35] Beschloss (2002), p. 123.
[36] Ibid., p. 124.
[37] Bark and Gress (1993), vol. 1, p. 78. The shift from exogenous to endogenous transitional justice, together with the return to democracy, might have produced the same effect even if the Cold War had never taken place (Herf 1997, p. 209).

because of Cold War concerns. The Swiss, for instance, "got away [with their obstructionist attitude] because of the Cold War. Reparations had become secondary to the need to rebuild Europe and especially Germany's frontline states in the war against Stalin's aggressive Communist empire in Eastern Europe."[38] And it is no accident that the second-wave transitional justice that finally compensated slave laborers and forced laborers employed by German firms occurred only after the collapse of communism.

In 1944–45, however, American attitudes toward the Soviet Union were far more positive, or even naive. Secretary of War Stimson, for instance, "who equated the OGPU [the Soviet Secret Police] with the Gestapo, was horrified at Soviet domestic terror. 'Stalin recently promised his people a constitution with a bill of rights like our own,' Stimson wrote. 'It seems to me now that our success in getting him to carry out this promised reform, which will necessarily mean the abolition of the secret police, lies at the foundation of our success.'"[39] At this stage, attitudes toward the USSR did not interfere with the debates in the Roosevelt administration over transitional justice, where an intense struggle opposed Stimson to Henry Morgenthau, Secretary of the Treasury. In the end, Stimson had his way. The Nuremberg trials in 1945–46 took place largely along the lines he had been advocating. The draconian economic measures advocated by Morgenthau were eventually abandoned in favor of economic reconstruction. The political justice he had proposed was replaced by legal justice.

Much of the evidence for the early stages of this development is to be found in an extraordinary document known as "the Morgenthau diary" on Germany. It is not really a diary, but a collection of official documents, draft memoranda, recorded conversations of staff meetings and telephone calls, and sundry other documents that Morgenthau had gathered and kept while in office. They were published in 1967 by the Internal Security Subcommittee of the Committee on the Judiciary of the U.S. Senate. The committee and the subcommittee were both chaired by James O. Eastland, a Senator from Mississippi who held extreme anti-Semitic and antiblack views,[40] as well as being strongly anticommunist. He entrusted the editing of the document to Anthony Kubek, Professor of History at Dallas University, who later showed up among the Holocaust deniers in the *Journal of*

[38] Eizenstat (2003), pp. 106–7.
[39] Bass (2000), p. 156.
[40] Caro (2002), pp. 103, 767.

Historical Review.[41] Because of Morgenthau's close working relationship with Harry Dexter White, an alleged but not proven Communist agent,[42] Kubek argued that Morgenthau's plan to de-industrialize Germany was motivated by a desire to leave the country open for a Communist takeover. Stimson saw the plan as purely vindictive and motivated by Morgenthau's Jewishness.[43] I return to the latter issue in Chapter 8.

Morgenthau's policy toward individual Nazi leaders was to dispense with trials altogether. He preferred a list to be drawn up of perhaps twenty-five hundred individuals who, when apprehended, could be executed immediately. The British, too, were initially in favor of summary executions of a smaller number of individuals, but could not agree among themselves about whom to include. A second aspect of Morgenthau's policy can be traced back to a 1943 memorandum by two Treasury officials. The key idea was that by "taking away Germany's facilities for the production of synthetic gasoline and nitrogen, and by prohibiting it from accumulating stockpiles of raw materials essential for the prosecution of a war, we will render Germany impotent, militarily speaking, *regardless of what the will of the people in that country might be*."[44] The phrase that I have italicized expresses the intention to act on the objective opportunities for warfare of the German people, not on their subjective belligerency. Later, Morgenthau and his staff expanded considerably on this proposal: The coal mines in the Ruhr should be flooded or dynamited and sealed for fifty years to make the Germans "impotent to wage future wars."[45] The Germans should be prohibited from developing any kind of industry that could be converted into military production (ploughshares into swords): "If you have a bicycle, you can have an airplane.... If you have a baby carriage, you can have an airplane."[46]

[41] A paper by Kubek on the Morgenthau diaries is available at http://www.codoh.com/germany/GERMORGEN.HTML. A recent book in the same revisionist/negationist vein is Dietrich (2002).

[42] Skidelsky (2001), pp. 256–63; see also Boughton (2000).

[43] Bass (2000), pp. 166. These two criticisms antedate the Cold War. In U.S. Senate (1967), p. 664, White refers to a conversation of September 28, 1944, with Professor Lerner of Williams College in which the latter said he was in favor of the Morgenthau proposal but predicted opposition on two grounds, "one, that this is a method of increasing the strength of Russia and the danger of Russia.... Secondly, he said that there would be the feeling that the Jews were just trying to be vindictive, because of the fact that they have suffered at Hitler's hands."

[44] U.S. Senate (1967), p. 354.

[45] Ibid., p. 489. The fifty-year seal is mentioned on p. 882.

[46] Ibid., pp. 876–77.

Morgenthau's plan for dismantling German industry was adopted at the Quebec meeting between Roosevelt and Churchill in mid-September 1944. Although Churchill was initially opposed to and apparently revolted by the plan, he was persuaded by the argument that Britain would benefit from the elimination of German competition; there may also have been a quid pro quo in the form of British acceptance of the plan in exchange for lend-lease aid.[47] The "Directive on Germany" issued at Quebec stated that since "the Germans have devastated a large portion of the industries of Russia and other neighboring allies ... it is only in accordance with justice that these injured countries should be entitled to receive the machinery they require in order to repair the losses they have suffered." Reparations by the transfer of capital goods could thus be doubly motivated as just compensation to the victims of the Nazi regime *and* as a strike at Germany's industrial and military capacity. By contrast, if one had followed the policy adopted after World War I and funded reparations out of ongoing production, that capacity would have had to remain in place. In conclusion, the Directive stated: "This program for eliminating the war-making industries in the Ruhr and the Saar is looking forward to converting Germany into a country primarily agricultural and pastoral in character." Morgenthau claims that Roosevelt wanted Germany to be set back to 1810: "People could get along without bathrooms and still be perfectly happy."[48] His own attitude was more brutal: "I don't care what happens to the population."[49] "Let them stew in their own juice."[50]

Industrial dismantling was Morgenthau's main strategy. As a backup, he also proposed political dismemberment (as well as the breakup of the Junker estates). In addition to Germany ceding territories to neighboring countries,[51] he proposed the division of Germany into a Northern and a Southern part, each of them organized as a "confederation of states, with emphasis on states' rights and a large degree of local autonomy."[52]

47 Skidelsky (2001), pp. 362–64; Rees (1973), Chap. 16.

48 U.S. Senate (1967), p. 536.

49 Ibid., p. 488.

50 Ibid., p. 492.

51 Treasury officials made some extravagant proposals in this respect. According to one memorandum, "[t]he area given to France would contain approximately 2 million; to Poland 6 million; and to the Netherlands and Belgium 12–13 million" (U.S. Senate 1967, p. 456). According to a later proposal, "Denmark should be given the territories between its present borders and the International Zone, north of the Kiel Canal" (ibid., p. 463). The final version retained only concessions to France and Poland.

52 U.S. Senate (1967), p. 550.

In a later document, one of the authors of the 1943 memorandum added that this strategy "alone would not suffice since political developments several decades hence may make a reunion of the several German states possible. In that case the reunited Germany would immediately possess a huge industrial potential unless the Ruhr industry were destroyed."[53] In the end, the Allies imposed a moderate physical dismantling and a moderate political decentralization.

Although Morgenthau mainly wanted to eliminate Germany's capacity for aggressive war, he also wanted to influence its will. We must distinguish between two levels of will formation. First, there is the desire of individual Germans to wage aggressive war. Second, there is the formation of a national policy through the aggregation of individual preferences. The strategy of political decentralization was aimed at the capacity for aggregating individual wills. In Morgenthau's mind, this strategy had to be supplemented by measures aimed at changing the attitudes of individual Germans. As a summary of a discussion with Stimson, Morgenthau dictated the following on August 23:

> So I said, "If you let the young children of today be brought up by SS troopers who are indoctrinated with Hitlerism, aren't you simply going to raise another generation of Germans who will want to wage war?" He said that was true. Then I said, "Don't you think the thing to do is to take a leaf from Hitler's book and completely remove these children from their parents and make them wards of the state, and have ex-U.S. Army officers, English Army officers and Russian Army officers run these schools, and have these children learn the true spirit of democracy?"[54]

The statements cited so far argue that two separate sets of measures will be required, one to act on the capacity of the Germans and one to act on their will. Later, Morgenthau suggested that the Allies might exploit the mechanism of "adaptive preferences":[55] By acting on the opportunities of the Germans, one might at the same time shape their desires. In a response to Stimson's criticism of his plan, he wrote that

> whether the spark of hope for world conquest . . . will be kept alive will not depend upon how "soft" or "hard" the Germans think we have treated them. The spark will flame if the German people feel that it is still within their power to conquer the world. The spark will die once the German people realize that making their aim in life the conquest of other peoples is futile.[56]

[53] Ibid., p. 602.
[54] Ibid., p. 426.
[55] Elster (1983), Chap. 3.
[56] U.S. Senate (1967), p. 632.

Stimson's views of these matters were very different.[57] He was strongly in favor of subjecting the Nazi leaders to legal trials rather than summary execution, and equally strongly against the dismantling plan. He first set out his views in two pre-Quebec memoranda to Roosevelt, one responding to a proposal from the Secretary of State, Cordell Hull, and the other responding to the Morgenthau plan. To Hull's argument[58] that the German standard of living should be kept at a subsistence level, Stimson replied that

> if this means the edge of poverty, [it] would mean condemning the German people to a condition of servitude, in which, no matter how hard, or effectively a man works, he could not materially increase his economic position in the world. Such a program would, I believe, create tensions and resentments far outweighing any immediate advantage of security and *would tend to obscure the guilt of the Nazis* and the viciousness of their doctrines and their acts.... Such methods, in my opinion, do not prevent war; they tend to breed war.[59]

The phrase that I have italicized echoes statements Stimson had made a few days earlier in a conversation with John McCloy:

> We should always have in mind the necessity of punishing effectively enough to bring home to the German people the wrongdoing done in their name, and thus prevent similar conduct in the future, without depriving them of the hope of a future respected German community.... Remember this punishment is for the purpose of prevention and not for vengeance. An element in prevention is to secure in the person punished the conviction of guilt.[60]

Although Stimson here argues for punishment as a form of prevention, the causal link he suggests does not go through special or general deterrence. The mechanism of deterrence takes individual motives as a given and tries to affect behavior by changes in the reward structure. Stimson, by contrast, claims that if the Germans can be made to understand the evil nature of their acts, they will experience feelings of guilt that will change the motives themselves. To this end, fair trials of Nazi

57 Stimson's attitude may have been doubly shaped by his anti-Semitism (Bass 2000, p. 174; Beschloss 2002, p. 88), which made him disposed both to dismiss Morgenthau's views because he was Jewish and to place less importance on the Holocaust than on other German atrocities. In his diaries, Stimson kept referring to the death camps as "the so-called atrocities" (Beschloss 2002, p. 224).

58 Ibid., p. 521. In conversations, Morgenthau expressed the same or even harsher views (ibid., pp. 426, 488, 489, 492, 536). If the official plan of the Treasury does not explicitly refer to a reduction of the standard of living, it was probably because it was such an obvious consequence as not to be worth mentioning.

59 Ibid., p. 532.

60 August 28, 1944; cited after Bass (2000), p. 157.

criminals and humane treatment of ordinary Germans were necessary. Summary executions and starvation measures would have the opposite effect.

Stimson wanted punishment to be shaped so as to reduce the chances of future aggressive war *by Germany*. Robert Jackson, the main American organizer and prosecutor of the Nuremberg trials, wanted them to deter future wars and war crimes *by any nation*. In a report to President Truman of June 6, 1945, Jackson stated this decisive move to general deterrence as follows:

> Through these trials we should be able to establish that a process of retribution by law awaits those who in the future similarly attack civilization.... After we entered the war and as we expended our men and our wealth to stamp out these wrongs, it was the universal feeling of our people that out of this war should come unmistakable rules and workable machinery from which *any* who might contemplate another era of brigandage would know that they would be held personally responsible and would be personally punished.[61]

In theory, this aim might be incompatible with Stimson's goal. The punishment needed to reduce the likelihood of future non-German aggressions might have to be so severe as to increase that of future aggressions by Germany, since the two effects are produced by different mechanisms. Be this as it may, the Nuremberg trials did shape international law, as Jackson intended it to do.[62]

Stimson was "unalterably opposed" to the dismantling of Germany's industrial structure: "In a period when the world is suffering from destruction and from want of production the concept of the total obliteration of [the Ruhr assets] is to my mind wholly wrong."[63] In the short run, the argument made no impact on Roosevelt. After the

[61] Cited from Marrus (1997), pp. 42, 43; italics added.

[62] As noted by Kirchheimer (1961), p. 325 n. 29, the precedent might "backfire, however, if it induced the leaders of a future war to fight to the bitter end rather than surrender and face the possible future of war criminals." Similarly, Huntington (1991), p. 103, notes that "the early actions of the Alfonsín regime in prosecuting the former military rulers stimulated some Uruguayan military to back away from their commitment to relinquish power." The same argument is stated in an editorial in *The Economist* of August 31, 1996: "It is probably true that neither the generals who run Myanmar, nor President Suharto in Indonesia, nor the Communist Party in China, will be encouraged to move towards democracy by the fate of Messrs Chun and Roh. After all, Mr Roh ceded power as gracefully as any military man can. Now he has fallen victim to the process of democratisation that he helped to foster. The moral drawn by Asia's nervous dictators may well be that, when democrats are at the door, lock them up rather than usher them in." For a different view, see Orentlicher (1995), p. 382.

[63] U.S. Senate (1967), p. 613.

decision at Quebec (where Morgenthau was the only Cabinet member present), Stimson wrote a third memorandum. He first objected to both parts of Morgenthau's desire-opportunity argument, asserting that the Treasury proposals "will tend through bitterness and suffering to breed another war, not to make another war [i] undesired by the Germans nor [ii] impossible in fact."[64] He went on to claim: "Sound thinking teaches that . . . poverty in one part of the world usually induces poverty in other parts. Enforced poverty is even worse, for it destroys the spirit not only of the victim but debases the victor. It would be just such a crime as the Germans themselves hoped to perpetrate upon their victims."[65]

On another occasion, Stimson remarked that Morgenthau's plan was "just fighting brutality with brutality."[66] In his notes and conversations, Morgenthau repeatedly used this comparison with the Nazi methods as an argument *for* his proposal. I have already mentioned his idea of "taking a leaf from Hitler's book." In the same note, he cites Stimson's objection to his plan, "that you might have to take a lot of people out of Germany," and his own response, "Well, that is not nearly as bad as sending them to the gas chambers." When Harry Dexter White cited "a press man [who] got up and made a very impressive demagogic appeal against the plan on the ground it was a violation of every moral precept," Morgenthau commented that "I suppose putting a million or two million people in gas chambers is a godlike action."[67]

The coal mines were not closed. The plan for dismantling factories was maintained, but its implementation was limited.[68] Because German machinery was often damaged by the time it reached the Soviet Union, the Russians shifted to a policy of taking reparations out of current production. The aims of the Marshall Plan were hardly compatible with dismantling. German workers refused to take part in the dismantling, which they saw, correctly, as directed against German competition. Adenauer compared the dismantling program with the Versailles treaty as "the best propaganda for unbounded nationalism." A reduction in 1947 of the number of plants to be dismantled from 1,500 to 859 was followed by a further substantial reduction in 1949.

In addition to trying Nazi criminals and dismantling Germany's industrial structure, the Allies wanted (as in 1919) to reduce the risk of future

[64] Ibid., p. 621.
[65] Ibid., p. 622.
[66] Ibid., p. 526.
[67] Ibid., p. 664.
[68] The following draws on Schwartz (1991), Chap. 3.

German aggression by imposing a decentralized constitution.[69] The first step was taken at a conference in London in July 1948, with participation of the three Western Allies and the Benelux countries. The final step was the promulgation of the constitution or "Basic Law" in June 1949. In the intervening months there was a great deal of bargaining and jockeying for position between the Allies and the Germans, among the Allies, and among the German parties. By and large, the Germans seem to have been better at playing on the division of the Allies than the other way around. Although the Allies retained veto rights over the constitution, the final result was probably not very much different from what it would have been in an unconstrained process.

Initially, the Allies agreed in opposing a strong central government for Germany, fearing, in the words of the American Secretary of State, that "it could be too readily converted to the domination of a regime similar to the Nazis." The German Social Democrats claimed that Americans also opposed centralization because of their aversion to socialism. After the Prague coup of February 1948, the British and Americans changed their attitude. Their fear of a Communist takeover acted as a brake on their decentralizing tendencies: "[I]f a Western German government were so handicapped [by decentralization] that it could not deal with pressing economic and social problems effectively, a situation might develop that would be ripe for exploitation by Soviet power."[70] The French, however, used the Soviet threat to argue for the opposite conclusion: "If the Soviets had set themselves up as champions of German unity, the French said, it was only because the centralization of power in Germany would afford to the Communists the easiest means of penetrating the government and seizing control."[71] Their delegation in London proposed a loose federation of states more or less along the lines drawn up in the American Articles of Confederation. The central government was not to have the power of taxation, but would derive its revenues from customs and from allocations made by individual states. The document that was finally adopted, however, was closer to the American Constitution of 1787, with a complex balance between federal and state powers.[72]

The Allies also disagreed among themselves on the "financial constitution" of the country, that is, on the organization of the Bundesbank. In

69 The following draws on Golay (1958) and Merkl (1963).
70 Golay (1958), p. 8.
71 Ibid.
72 For a comparison of American and German federalisms, see Currie (1994), Chap. 2, notably pp. 34–35.

1946, the head of the Finance Division of the U.S. Office for Military Government, Joseph Dodge, argued for a strongly decentralized Bundesbank "to ensure that the German financial hierarchy will never play any part in disturbing the peace of the world."[73] In early 1947, the representative of the Bank of England turned the argument on its head: "If an overdecentralised system is introduced which leads to financial catastrophe such as that which occurred in Germany in 1926–32, an opportunity would have been provided for a centralising and militarising party to gain popularity, and perhaps power, as in 1933."[74] This Anglo-American controversy has obvious similarities with the French-American disagreement discussed in the previous paragraph, except that in the case of the Bundesbank, the alleged benefits and dangers from decentralization were not viewed in relation to any Soviet threat. When that threat did materialize in late 1947, however, the Americans accepted a compromise measure.

The central dilemma of transitional justice in Germany after 1945 was already captured by John Maynard Keynes in a comment on the Versailles peace treaty:

> [A] peace of magnanimity or of fair and equal treatment ... could only have the effect of shortening the interval of Germany's recovery and hastening the day when she will once again hurl at France her greater numbers and her superior resources and technical skill. Hence the necessity of "guarantees"; and each guarantee that was taken, by increasing irritation and thus the probability of a subsequent *revanche* by Germany, made necessary yet further provision to crush. Thus ... a demand for a Carthaginian peace is inevitable.[75]

If treated leniently, Germany would have the *resources* to stage a new aggressive war, and if treated harshly, a strong *motivation* to do so. In 1945, Morgenthau insisted on the first proposition while ignoring or even denying the second, while Stimson insisted on the second while ignoring the first. We cannot know whether Morgenthau's policy, as embodied in the military directive JCS 1067, which remained in force even after he left office in July 1945, would have had a greater impact had it not been for the fear of communism. As early as August of the same year, however, General Clay warned against starving the Germans: "There is no choice between becoming a Communist on 1500 calories and a believer in democracy on 1000 calories."[76]

[73] Quoted after Marsh (1992), p. 148.
[74] Ibid., p. 149.
[75] Keynes (1971), p. 22.
[76] Beschloss (2002), p. 273.

IV. ECONOMIC CONSTRAINTS ON TRANSITIONAL JUSTICE

As explained in Section II, transitional justice in South Africa has been limited by economic constraints that persist after the negotiated transition. These constraints may also affect prosecution and compensation when the transition occurs by regime defeat (as after 1815 or 1945) or regime collapse (as after 1989). If the new regime has to pay extensive reparations (as after 1815), undertake economic reconstruction (as after 1945), or embark on the transition to a market economy (as after 1989), these tasks may severely constrain transitional justice. In 1815, the constraints limited the extent of feasible reparation. In the two latter waves of transition, on which I focus here, they also limited the perceived feasibility of trials and purges.

After 1945 and after 1989, trials, purges, and compensation were subject to both hard and soft economic constraints. There was a risk or the perception of a risk that trials and purges might target individuals with economic and administrative expertise that was needed for rebuilding the economy or for carrying out the transition from central planning to a market economy. Thus after 1945, the prosecution of economic collaborators was not very vigorous in any of the countries that had collaborated with or been occupied by the Germans. In Austria, "the choice between reconstruction or denazification" was largely resolved in favor of the former goal.[77] In Holland, "the Central Purge Board [for industry] did not exclude a collaborator if his skills were vital to the Dutch reconstruction efforts."[78] In Belgium, a decree-law of May 25, 1945, which modified existing legislation so that economic collaboration with the enemy would be treated more leniently, was justified by the need for economic reconstruction and social peace.[79] In France, one aspect of a complex situation can be summarized by the construction company of Sainrapt et Brice, which, among other works for the occupant, had participated in building the Great Atlantic Wall that was supposed to protect France from invasion by the Allies.[80] After the war, the company was struck from the list of firms that were authorized to submit bids for public works, but the

[77] Stiefel (1998), pp. 409–110.

[78] Mason (1952), p. 102.

[79] Huyse and Dhondt (1993), p. 241. "This ... chirurgical operation caused in fact the decriminalization of much of the formerly punishable economic behavior: only 2% of all files resulted in a court case (against 43% for military collaborators, 33% for political collaborators and 18% for police informers)" (Huyse in press).

[80] The full story is told in Rochebrune and Hazera (1995), Chap. 3. For other discussions of economic collaboration in France, see Rochebrune and Hazera (1997); Lottman (1986), pp. 365–78; Rousso (2001), pp. 556–71; Aron (1974).

decision was reversed under the dual pressure from the Communist labor union CGT, which feared for the jobs of their members, and the Ministry of Public Works, which could not afford not to use a company that had all its equipment intact. The head of the firm, M. Brice, was excluded from the direction of the company in the summer of 1945 but reinstated five years later.

Purges in the public administration have been subject to similar constraints. After the invasion of Sicily in 1943, the Allies recognized that "since all holders of important governmental posts are members of the Fascist party they may not be removed at once without breakdown of the administrative system."[81] In France in 1944, the provisional government offered the sibylline statement that in purging the administration, "it is good to show intransigence but only to the extent that it does not interfere with the functioning of the services."[82] Because of de Gaulle's fear of a communist coup in the fall of 1944, he was willing to take on board persons whom he well knew to be collaborators, such as Maurice Papon.[83] Moreover, to prevent mass purges that would compromise the reconstruction of the country, he deliberately chose Vichy-tainted and therefore "docile" individuals as chief judge and chief prosecutor of the High Court (see Chapter 4). After the liberation, the French army abstained from purging officers who were needed for the participation in the final stages of the war that would ensure France a place among the victors.[84] In September 1944, reacting to Morgenthau's harsh draft directive on immediate denazification, General Hilldring said it amounted to "a formula for creating pandemonium behind his lines which I think is going to be a very great handicap to Eisenhower in defeating the German army."[85] Later, John McCloy managed to insert loopholes in the directive, which gave the American commanders a wide latitude of discretionary action.[86]

In the former GDR, the impact of these pragmatic considerations on the rate of decommunization is clear if one compares purges in different Länder.

> Among the state governments, a rift soon appeared between Saxony and the four other new Länder on the definition of criteria [for dismissal from public service of those who had worked for the state security]. The Saxons argued for the application of the strict criteria in use in Berlin, where intransigence was

[81] Coles and Weinberg (1992), p. 382.
[82] Cited after Rousso (2001), p. 532.
[83] Roussel (2002), p. 460.
[84] Abzac-Epezy (2003), pp. 451–52.
[85] U.S. Senate (1967), p. 560.
[86] Beschloss (2002), p. 169.

facilitated by the on-site availability of alternative (Western) officials. Officials from the four other Länder argued for more flexibility.[87]

In Poland, it has been argued that decommunization was frustrated by the fact that to implement economic reforms, the new leaders "had no choice but to rely on the experience and cooperation of many former nomenklatura members."[88] It has been objected, however, that the expertise was a fiction, or rather that the officials were experts at something else: "Communist managers do not know how to compete in a market; they know how to demand protection and subsidies from the government and how to benefit themselves by embezzling the subsidies."[89]

The purges after 1945 in the Soviet occupational sector, the later GDR, show that scarcity of competent officials is relative rather than absolute, derived from regime priorities rather than from hard necessities. The educational and judiciary sectors were more or less completely purged of members of the Nazi Party, who were replaced by *Neulehrer* (new teachers) and *Volksrichter* (people's judges) who took crash courses in their respective professions:[90] "A number of Social Democrats and Communists shared the opinion that... the retention of specialists ushered in 'the conquering of the power positions by reactionary people' in 1918 and contributed to the failure of the revolution at that time."[91] Even here, however, economic rationality set limits on what could be done. Doctors, whose training cannot be compressed into a year or less, were treated more leniently, as were managers and skilled workers.[92] It was not only that doctors and engineers were indispensable for reconstruction; unlike teachers, they were not in a position to do much ideological harm.

It goes without saying that compensation may be limited by lack of funds. In some cases, this may even provide a hard constraint, notably when the dispossessed demand compensation with payment of interest.[93]

87 Sa'adah (1998), p. 218. For the special case of dismissal vs. retention of judges, see the similar observation by Quint (1997), p. 187.
88 Walicki (1997), p. 195.
89 Tucker (in press).
90 Welsh (1991), pp. 98–99.
91 Welsh (1998), p. 327.
92 Ibid., pp. 100–101.
93 As noted by Cowen (1997), interest payment can be justified either in terms of counterfactuals or in terms of time discounting. On the first approach, the appropriate compensation is the current value of the expropriated property if an equivalent amount of money had been put in the bank. On the second, the appropriate compensation is the amount X such that at the time of confiscation, the original owners would have been indifferent between retaining their property and getting X at the date of compensation.

When some French émigrés wanted their property back with interest under the slogan "All or nothing," the answer they received was "Nothing."[94] Similarly, "according to some reports, the value of the assets confiscated from Hungary's Jews during the war, allowing for unpaid interest, was equivalent to the total national wealth of Hungary."[95] Even without interest payment, compensation to the three million Sudetengermans expelled from Czechoslovakia after World War II would have bankrupted the country. In the affluent Germany after 1990, "many asserted that any attempt to provide real compensation for [the effects of discrimination] would be quixotic and beyond the resources of the treasury of the Federal Republic."[96]

In the typical case, however, full restitution or compensation is not literally unfeasible. Rather, given the total funds available and the presence of competing aims, the authorities choose an allocation that involves less than full – sometimes, much less than full – compensation. In Chapter 6, I noted how compensation for destroyed property in France after liberation was limited to necessities. In Norway, a controversy within the administration between those who wanted owners of properties that had been confiscated and then liquidated to be repaid their full value and those who wanted to subtract the costs of administration before paying out compensation was settled in favor of the latter.[97] In a decision from 1945, for instance, the Norwegian Directorate for Compensation took account of whether a claimant could reasonably have *expected* to receive the full amount to which he would have been entitled under normal rules of inheritance.[98] Since Jews whose families had died in the extermination camps could not have expected to inherit from all their relatives, the amount they received was correspondingly curtailed, thus liberating funds for reconstruction.[99]

V. INCOMPATIBLE DEMANDS

Compared to ordinary criminal or civil process, retribution and restitution tend to be very heavily constrained by *scarcity* and by *incompatible motives*.

94 Gain (1928), vol. 1, p. 199.
95 Pogany (1997), p. 177.
96 Ibid., p. 224.
97 NOU (1997), p. 41. The final rate of compensation was 68% of the property value, but owners could apply to other institutions for supplementary compensation.
98 For a discussion of such "windfall gains," see also Quint (1997), p. 142.
99 NOU (1997), pp. 98–102.

Consider first retribution. In Belgium, the government wanted the trials to be "efficacious, quick, and equitable."[100] The Belgian Socialist Party stated that they should be "complete, quick, and without pity."[101] In Italy after World War II, the commissioner for purges wanted them to be "rapid, just, and severe."[102] In France, a statement written by jurists during the occupation stated that the repression of collaborators should be "efficacious, rapid, and equitable."[103] For the French administration after the liberation, it was important that "the will to purge swiftly not be assimilated with the will to purge less."[104] In Norway, the resistance wanted the purges to be "immediate, swift, and thorough."[105] Altogether, these statements can be summarized in terms of six desiderata:

- Trials should be *speedy,* in the sense of starting up immediately after the cessation of hostilities.
- They should be *swift,* in the sense of being concluded quickly.
- They should be *severe,* using the death penalty as well as long prison sentences.
- They should be *just,* both in the substantive sense of punishment according to desert and in the procedural sense of respecting the rule of law.
- They should be *thorough,* in the sense of convicting a large fraction of the collaborators.
- They should be *efficacious,* in the sense of using scarce resources as efficiently as possible.

The problem, of course, is that many of these desires may come into conflict with one another and with the available resources.[106] The desire for efficacy clearly reflects a concern with the scarcity of resources, but even optimally used, the resources have often been far too small.

As I argue in Chapter 8, the desire for speedy trials tends to be overwhelmingly strong, given the urgent nature of the underlying emotions. At the same time, the turbulent nature of transition often makes it difficult

[100] Huyse and Dhondt (1993), p. 113.
[101] Ibid., p. 124.
[102] Domenico (1991), p. 80.
[103] Cited after Amouroux (1999), p. 148.
[104] Rouquet (1993), p. 433.
[105] Dahl (in press).
[106] The desire for severity is the only one that does not create immediate conflicts with the other desires or with the available resources. In the long run, however, the combined desires for severity and thoroughness may come up against the limited capacity of the prison system.

to organize *anything*, and transitional justice has to compete with other equally urgent necessities. Funds, personnel, and political attention may be channeled into such forward-looking tasks as constitution making, economic reconstruction, or economic transformation, rather than into the backward tasks of trials and purges. In Belgium, for instance, transitional justice was treated as a problem of second- or even third-order magnitude.[107]

The desire for swift trials may also have emotional roots, as we shall see in the next chapter. In addition, there is often a consensus that trials and purges should be done quickly so that the country can get on with its normal life. The combined desire for thoroughness and justice (in the sense of procedural fairness) is often incompatible, however, with the desire for swiftness.[108] If all who are suspected of collaboration were to be investigated and tried within the strict procedures of the rule of law, trials might go on for decades.

The desires for thoroughness and procedural justice may themselves be mutually exclusive. As I noted in Chapter 4, transitional justice is often characterized by stark departures from the rule of law. The desire for thoroughness trumps the desire for justice. Although the actors often try to make them appear compatible with each other, they do so by transparent subterfuge (Chapter 8). And even when the rule of law does not pose a constraint (or is violated), the desires for swiftness and thoroughness may be mutually exclusive, given the limited capacity of the judicial system. In that case, the authorities may deliberately limit the number of targets, for instance by focusing on responsible politicians and high officials.

The scarcity of reliable judges is a very important constraint on transitional justice.[109] In very many cases, the judiciary have been part and parcel of the regime to be judged.[110] The German judiciary after 1945

107 Huyse and Dhondt (1993), p. 77.

108 In Norway, for instance, it was expected that the trials would be finished within one year. It turned out that several more years were needed, because the judges respected the time-consuming principle of treating cases on an individualized basis (Andenæs 1980, p. 166). This was also the case in Denmark (Tamm 1984, p. 445).

109 In Western Europe, the caseload of ordinary criminal cases often swelled after the liberation, thus adding to the strain on the system (Novick 1968, p. 86; Mason 1952, p. 131).

110 For France, see Bancaud (2002). For Italy, see Domenico (1991), p. 178, and Woller (1996), pp. 88, 222, 297. For Belgium, see Huyse and Dhondt (1993), p. 109. For Holland, see Mason (1952), p. 131. For Denmark after 1945, see Tamm (1984), pp. 569–70. For Austria and Hungary after 1945, see Deák (in press). For Greece after 1974, see Alivizatos and Diamandouros (1997), p. 32. For Argentina, see Malamud-Goti (1996), p. 185. For postcommunist societies, see Tucker (in press). Osiel (1995)

was especially notorious for its obstructionist attitude toward crimes of Nazi criminals, including (and especially) Nazi judges. The former East Germany is one of a few exceptions, reflecting its special status within the universe of cases of transitional justice. The dilemma is well stated by Peter Novick: "[T]he more rigorous the purge of the magistracy, the fewer judges would be available to aid in the work of conducting the trials of collaborators; on the other hand, an insufficient purge in that area would risk allowing collaborators to be judged by their secret sympathizers."[111] The solutions to this problem include the use of military courts, as in Belgium; of people's courts (with members appointed by the political parties), as in Austria and Hungary after 1945; of political juries (with members screened by the resistance), as in Denmark and France; and the appointment of large numbers of new (and inexperienced) judges, as in Belgium and Argentina.[112] In Germany after 1945, a proposed solution involved "closing all German courts for ten years and replacing them with a 'colonial' system, so that a new generation of judges could be educated in the meantime."[113] Needless to say, it was not implemented.

Furthermore, transitional justice may be constrained by a problem that also arises in other legal cases, namely, that the guilty have an incentive to destroy evidence of their guilt. When they are in a position of political power, they also have the opportunity to do so.[114] After Japan's defeat in World War II, "the considerable lag between cease-fire and occupation gave the government sufficient time to implement effectively its policy of systematically destroying records."[115] In France, the report of the Mattéoli Commission on the confiscation of property from Jews cites, as an obstacle to its work, the destruction of the records from the Drancy camp by the SS before they fled in August 1944.[116] In the same period, Vichy officials proceeded to the complete or selective destruction of the

argues that judges are better able to retain some autonomy under authoritarian regimes than in totalitarian systems.

111 Novick (1968), p. 86.

112 Huyse and Dhondt (1993), p. 111; Malamud-Goti (1996), p. 185.

113 Müller (1991), p. 201.

114 Exceptionally, the new leaders may also destroy evidence. Thus when Paul Milliez, the first Minister of Health after the liberation, discovered packages of letters from eminent physicians denouncing Jewish doctors, he burned them all (Bloch-Lainé and Gruson 1996, pp. 210–11). On Milliez, see also Lesourd (2003), pp. 360, 366.

115 Cohen (1999), p. 62. As he shows, the response of the prosecutors to the lack of information directly linking individuals to war crimes was to adopt a principle of strict liability that dispensed with evidence about intentions and knowledge.

116 *Mission d'étude* (2000). The report also cites a more surprising obstacle, namely, the absence of archives that "were shredded during the liberation because they bore 'racial'

documents concerning them.[117] In the last days of the war, SS personnel in the German extermination camps set inmates to the task of destroying evidence by cremating those who had died from hanging or beating, but the arrival of American troops prevented the SS from carrying out the last part of the process, which was to be the destruction of the destroyers.[118] In Argentina, "CONADEP [The National Commission on Disappeared Persons] discovered that military president Bignone had ordered the destruction of the military's program of repression."[119] Earlier, one reason behind the "disappearance" strategy in Argentina may have been to "stall investigation into the facts."[120] Hence, "evidentiary constraints could have limited the number of human rights trials even without laws limiting the scope of prosecution."[121] In Eastern Europe after 1989, some of the security files were destroyed,[122] but this does not seem to have been the most serious obstacle to transitional justice. Rather, the problem was that independent of any destruction, the files were both underinclusive (full-time agents and top party members would often not be listed)[123] and overinclusive (some alleged agents were invented by the security police to fill their quotas).[124]

observations that are incompatible with the republican culture which has prohibited any religious or ethnic remark in official documents since 1872."

117 Baruch (1997), pp. 17, 519.

118 Greene (2003), pp. 138, 141.

119 Nino (1996), p. 80.

120 Argentine Commission on the Disappeared (1995), p. 13.

121 Orentlicher (1995), p. 403 n. 263.

122 Kuk (2001), p. 205.

123 According to one estimate, in Slovakia at least 16,000 top-level agents were not listed in any register (Kritz 1995, vol. 3, p. 341 n. 11).

124 Thus in Poland, in March of each year there was an increase in the number of collaborators, because "the officials of the security police established their annual reports in March and wanted to present their activities in a favorable light" (Kuk 2001, p. 206n). In Czechoslovakia, though, the technical perfection of the system may have "made creation of false records almost impossible" (Smith 1995b, p. 93).

8

Emotions

I. INTRODUCTION

The downfall of an authoritarian or totalitarian regime can unleash very strong emotions, positive as well as negative. After the liberation in France, or after May 8, 1945, in other German-occupied countries, popular joy was everywhere. In 1989, the fall of the Berlin wall triggered similar enthusiasms. At the same time, transitions can trigger furious vindictive emotions against the leaders and agents of the former regime. In this chapter, I explore the mechanisms by which emotions may shape the legal proceedings of transitional justice. In doing so, I face a methodological difficulty. Although I have no doubt whatsoever that emotions mattered in these cases, the question is *whose emotions?* One possibility is that everybody – legislators, judges, and the population at large (except for the collaborators) – were in the grip of the same emotions. Another is that the retributive emotions, as I shall call them, were found mainly among the ordinary citizens, and that other, more cool-headed actors, concerned with preempting and preventing popular violence or motivated by electoral calculations, simply responded to them.[1] Often, the truth is likely to lie somewhere in between.[2] Because of lack of evidence

[1] In Belgium, according to Conway (2000), p. 137, "popular demands for severe action always exceeded the positions adopted by all of the major political forces," including the Communists.

[2] "In the first months after the Liberation, [Belgian] magistrates and judges acted *under the domination of passion*. ... Sometimes, the passion arose in the judges themselves, but most of the time it infiltrated the courts through the channels of the written press, through political pressures, or simply by manifestations of blackmail" (Huyse and Dhondt 1993, p. 267).

I sometimes have to elide this problem by means of suitably ambiguous formulations.

In Section II, I provide a selective overview of the emotions and those of their features that will prove most relevant for my purposes here. Section III, argues, relying on very general properties of the emotions – *urgency* and *decay* – that they do indeed have a causal role in transitional justice. In Section IV, I turn to five specific retributive emotions, and argue that there is a close link between the action tendencies they generate and the typical legal reactions in transitional justice. In Section V, I consider the relation between emotion and reason (the desire for justice) as driving forces behind these processes, arguing that there tends to be a conflict between these two motivations and that more often than not, the actors try to resolve it by subterfuge that will allow them to have it both ways. I conclude in Section VI with some brief comments on the role of guilt in motivating the behavior of perpetrators and neutrals.

II. EMOTION AND ACTION

Human emotions exhibit a great variety and complexity of properties. Here I limit myself to those that will prove relevant in later sections.[3]

I shall not attempt to say anything about what the emotions themselves *are*, but rely on commonsense, pre-analytical understandings. Instead I want to focus on their causes and their consequences. The emotions I consider are triggered by *beliefs*, notably – in the cases that concern us in this chapter – beliefs about other people's behavior and character. The emotions are also modulated by the prior *relation* in which individuals stand to wrongdoers or victims. In Eastern Europe, Bulgarians reacted relatively mildly to Soviet oppression because of the historically close ties between Bulgaria and Russia. In other countries in the region, as well as in German-occupied countries during World War II, oppression combined with foreign occupation created a breeding ground for more virulent emotions. Similarly, it was reported that the occupation of Iraq in 2003 triggered the reaction among some citizens that "Saddam Hussein may have been a dictator, but he was our dictator." Reactions to mistreatment of victims may also depend on our prior relation to them. As I discuss in more detail in Section IV, Jewish members of the Roosevelt administration reacted more strongly to the Holocaust than non-Jewish members did.

[3] For a fuller discussion, see Elster (1999).

TABLE 8.1

Emotion	Action Tendency
Anger/Indignation	Cause the object of the emotion to suffer
Hatred	Cause the object of hatred to cease to exist
Contempt	Ostracism, avoidance
Shame	"Sink through the floor"; run away; suicide
Guilt	Confess; make repairs; hurt oneself
Envy	Destroy the envied object or its possessor
Fear	Flight; fight
Love	To approach and touch the other; to help the other; to please the other
Pity	To console or alleviate the distress of the other

Emotions can short-circuit the normal machinery of prudential action by virtue of their characteristic *action tendencies*, such as those listed in Table 8.1. In Section IV, I discuss some of these tendencies in more detail. Here, I want to argue that the most important short-circuiting mechanisms are related to two specific features of the emotions: They induce *urgency* as well as *impatience*. I use these words as terms of art, defined as follows. By impatience I mean a preference for early reward over later reward, that is, a rate of time discounting less than 1, and by urgency, a preference for early action over later action. Impatience is clearly incompatible with prudence, understood as action according to long-term self-interest. Those who are unable to defer gratification may find their life to be nasty, brutish, and short. Urgency, by contrast, is often compatible with prudence, and may even be required by it. In the face of an acute danger, the opportunity costs of waiting to find out more could be prohibitive. In the cases I discuss, however, the danger had already passed, and so there would be nothing lost and possibly something to be gained from waiting. Whereas action in self-defense may brook no delay, retribution may benefit from taking one's time.

The distinction between urgency and impatience is illustrated in Table 8.2. In each case, the agent can take one and only one of two actions, A or B. In Case 1, these options are available at the same time, in Cases 2 and 3 at successive times. In Case 2, the rewards (whose magnitude is indicated by the numbers) occur at the same later time, in Cases 1 and 3 at different later times. Suppose that in an unemotional state, the agent chooses B in all cases, but that in an emotional state, he chooses A. In Case 1, the choice of A is due to emotionally induced impatience. In Case 2, it is due to emotionally induced urgency. In Case 3, it could be due

TABLE 8.2

	t1	t2	t3	t4
Case 1: *Impatience*	A	3		
	B		5	
Case 2: *Urgency*	A		3	
		B	4	
Case 3: *Impatience and/or urgency*	A		3	
		B		6

to either or to the interaction of the two. Although the idea of induced urgency is not part of the standard accounts of emotion, I believe it is a real and important phenomenon. In fact, the study of transitional justice offers some of the best evidence for its existence. This being said, it may be hard, in a given case, to determine clearly whether we are dealing with urgency or with impatience.

A third feature of the emotions that will also prove important is that they tend to have a short half-life. Paul Ekman, for instance, lists "sudden onset" and "brief duration" among the defining features of what he calls "basic emotions."[4] It is obvious from homely advice such as "count to ten" that many emotions do indeed flare up only to be quickly extinguished. A core idea in many constitutional contexts, that bicameralism is justified by its slowing-down and cooling-down effects, relies on the same mechanism. There is an intricate interplay here between the decay of emotion and the decay of memory. In general, memory fades with time. To the extent that emotions are triggered by memory, they will fade, too. At the same time, memories of emotionally charged events decay more slowly. In a statement that captures both aspects, "emotion slows, but does not eliminate forgetting."[5] What may matter more, however, is whether the memory retains the power to trigger the action tendency of the relevant emotion. When the memory of an insult fades from Technicolor to black and white, it may retain its accuracy but not its vividness and motivating force. In the next section, I consider various mechanisms that may *delay the decay* of Technicolor memory, and thus keep the associated emotions artificially alive.

A final feature is that even though emotions tend to decay with time, we usually do not anticipate that they will. When we are in the grip of a strong

[4] Ekman (1992).
[5] Heuer and Reisberg (1992), p. 167.

emotion, we tend to assume that it will last forever. George Loewenstein refers to this lack of predictive ability as a "hot-cold empathy gap."[6] Again, we shall see that transitional justice offers some counterexamples. If we can predict that our current emotion will subside, we might be induced to take immediate action – to strike while the iron is hot. In practice, this may be hard to distinguish from the urgency of emotional action. There are three different mechanisms, then, that can induce similar behavior: urgency, impatience, and the anticipation of decay of emotion. With good evidence we may be able to determine which is at work in a given situation, but often the question will remain open.

III. EMOTION AND THE DEMAND FOR RETRIBUTION

The demand for trials and purges is not a constant or invariant factor after transitions. In France in the fall of 1944, the demand was irresistible. In the Soviet Union after 1991, it was essentially absent or at least very diffuse. There are also, as we shall see, large variations over time. In this section, I discuss the role of emotions in determining the intensity of the demand for retribution. They are not the only relevant factors, however. In the only general discussion of the issue known to me, Carlos Nino lists a number of determinants of the demand for punitive measures.[7] Indicating factors that increase it by [+] and those that decrease it by [–], they are as follows:

(1) the heinousness of the crimes [+]
(2) absolute and relative quantity of the abuses [+]
(3) time span between deeds and trial [–]
(4) social identification with victims of the abuses [+]
(5) social identification with perpetrators of abuses [–]
(6) diffusion of responsibility [–].

To these I would add

(7) predemocratic regime imposed by a foreign power [+]
(8) diffusion of knowledge about the abuses [+]
(9) absolute and relative prosperity of perpetrators after the transition [+]

[6] Loewenstein (1996).

[7] Nino (1996), pp. 126–27. The factors given here are a subset of those listed by Nino, since he aims at explaining the successful *implementation* of transitional justice, rather than the demand for it.

(10) crimes committed by regime opponents as well as by regime agents [−]
(11) time span between the transition and trials [−].

In the following, I focus on factors related to (3) and (11). Specifically, I consider how transitional justice may be shaped by the immediate urgency of emotion and by the decay of emotion over time.

In many transitions, we observe an urgent demand for immediate justice. Objectively, other matters such as economic reconstruction might suffer more from delay. Subjectively, punishment of the former oppressors and collaborators becomes the more urgent task. The extralegal executions after World War II in France and Italy provide one indicator. The French practice of establishing summary martial courts to prevent people from taking justice into their own hands is another.[8] Maurice Rolland, the official in charge of the early stages of transitional justice in France, asserted that "the government should establish *justice before railroads*."[9] The widespread practice in all German-occupied countries of cutting the hair of women who had had relations with Germans is even more telling,[10] because unlike armed collaborators, these women presented no risk that could justify immediate action on prudential grounds. In the months after liberation, there was in several countries increasing popular frustration with the slowness of legal prosecutions against collaborators.

The Yokohama war trials offer another example of the impact of urgency. The trial of General Yamashita, in particular, ignored due process and mens rea requirements in favor of strict liability.[11] In his dissenting Supreme Court opinion, Justice Frank Murphy observed:

> No military necessity or other emergency demanded the suspension of the safeguards of due process. Yet [Yamashita] was rushed to trial under an improper charge, given insufficient time to prepare an adequate defense, deprived of the benefits of some of the most elementary rules of evidence and summarily sentenced to be hanged. In all this needless and unseemly haste there was no serious

[8] Novick (1968), p. 146.

[9] Lottman (1986), p. 217; italics added. The first Minister of Justice, François de Menthon, said in an interview from April 1945 that "in the aftermath of the Liberation there was no more urgent and more important task than the punishment of traitors and collaborators" (Chauvy 2003, p. 14).

[10] In France, the only country for which the phenomenon has been systematically studied, the number may be around 20,000 (Virgili 2000, pp. 74–78). For a survey of the practice in the other countries, see ibid., pp. 271–78.

[11] Cohen (1999).

attempt to charge or prove that he committed a recognized violation of the laws of war.[12]

"Needless haste" can indeed be an effect of urgency, as I have defined it. Even where there is nothing to be lost and something to be gained by waiting, the psychic momentum of emotion may prove too strong.

Toward the end of the last chapter, I indicated that transitions are often characterized by the demand for trials to be both *speedy* and *swift*, in the specific senses of these terms that I explained. Whereas the demand for speedy trials is linked to the urgency induced by emotions, the demand for a swift conclusion to the trials may be linked to the impatience they cause us to feel. Thus, the use of simplified legal procedures may be due not merely to the large number of cases but to the need for immediate gratification of the desire for revenge. This being said, let me repeat that in actual cases, the effects of urgency and impatience may be nearly impossible to tease apart from each other.

Let me now consider some consequences of the fact that emotions tend to have a short half-life. In transitional justice, this feature shows up in two ways. The desire for retribution is blunted if there is a long time interval between the wrongdoings and the transition, and also if there is a long delay between the transition and the trials. These two effects may of course be compounded, but for analytical convenience I treat them separately.[13]

In considering the effect of the time interval from wrongdoings to transition or transitional justice, let me first get one ambiguity out of the way. One of the German negotiators in the 1999 reparation settlement said that "I cannot become very emotional about insurance claims that are sixty years old."[14] Although this remark might seem to support the argument I am making here, it is actually irrelevant. We need to distinguish personal memory, based on firsthand experience, from mere abstract knowledge about the past.[15] Although such knowledge, too, can be forgotten and thus lose whatever power it might have to trigger emotional reactions, the relevant point for the present purposes is that it is *intrinsically* in what I called black and white, rather than in Technicolor. My concern here is

[12] Cited after Taylor (1981), p. 163.

[13] One might ask, if time is all that matters, whether we should not simply consider the time interval between wrongdoings and trials, and ignore the intervals between these events and the transition. It seems probable, however, that the sudden release from an oppressive regime will often cause a flare-up of emotions that had been allowed to fade.

[14] Eizenstat (2003), p. 340.

[15] McNally (2003), p. 30; see also Schachter (1996), p. 87.

with the gradual fading of the colors of an emotional experience, not with representations that lacked vividness in the first place.

Let me give some examples of how emotion decays with the time passed since the event that triggered them. In the First French Restoration, even the regicides who had voted for the execution of Louis XVI were exempt from any kind of punishment. In the Second Restoration, the *régicides relaps* who had joined Napoleon during the Hundred Days were exiled. The smaller but more recent crime outweighed the larger and more remote one.[16] In Italy, Denmark, and France, new and more oppressive occupational regimes were created after 1942–43. In Belgium and France, the Germans engaged in scorched-earth tactics as they retreated. These recent memories contributed to the intensity of demand for punishment of the collaborators. In Belgium and France, the return of detainees from the German concentration camps in the summer of 1945, when the intensity had begun to subside, brought it to a new peak.[17]

By contrast, when the East European Communist regimes fell in 1989–1990, they had been in existence for fifty years and the worst atrocities were in a relatively remote past. The Stalinist period, which by all accounts was the worst, ended in 1953. Crushed uprisings (1953 in the GDR and 1956 in Hungary), invasion (1968 in Czechoslovakia), and martial law (1981 in Poland) were also relatively distant. There was not, therefore, the same urgent demand for retribution as after 1945. Yet it is significant that in the two countries that remained harshly oppressive up to the very end, the GDR and Czechoslovakia, the demands for punishment have been the most vocal. The Spanish transition of 1978 also fits this pattern: The decision to forgo transitional justice can be explained by the long time that had passed since the worst atrocities, together with the fact that they were committed somewhat evenhandedly by both sides to the conflict.

The picture needs some nuances, however. I discuss and illustrate four mechanisms by which the decay of memory and emotion may be slowed down or even arrested altogether: communication among the victims of wrongdoing, codes of honor that keep memory alive until the desire for revenge has been satisfied, visible physical reminders of the wrongdoing, and perpetuation of the state of affairs caused by the wrongdoing.

[16] This finding, and the present analysis more generally, contrast with the claim that past emotional experiences are evaluated in the present by the "peak-end" heuristic, meaning that we pay attention only to the peak (best or worst) experiences whenever they occurred and to the most recent ones (Kahneman 1999, pp. 19–20; Kubovy 1999, p. 138).

[17] Huyse and Dhondt (1993), p. 24; Conway (2000), pp. 148–49; Lottman (1986), p. 146.

Although Louis XVIII was able to contain the demands of the émigrés for revenge in 1814, they did feel extremely strongly about what had happened to them twenty-five years earlier. A common saying about them was that *ils n'ont rien appris ni rien oublié* (they have learned nothing and forgotten nothing). Many of them wanted simply to restore the ancien régime, including feudal dues and the tithe. Others wanted to get their properties back, and not merely a monetary compensation. Still others wanted those who had purchased their properties at low prices to fund the indemnification, or perhaps even to be punished for their acts. At court the émigrés behaved with unconstrained arrogance, inducing, for instance, Maréchal Ney to join Napoleon during the Hundred Days because of the contempt they displayed for his wife. It seems reasonable to assume that their memory had been kept artificially alive by their artificial existence in exile, during which they had little to do besides thinking and talking about how they had been mistreated and hoping against hope for affairs to take a better turn.[18]

Another instance of lingering memory may be cited from the liberation of Italy. In one of the first trials after the law of July 27, 1944, that created the framework for transitional justice, a court in Grosseto condemned eleven fascists to prison for two or three years for having publicly humiliated four antifascists (by forcing them to drink castor oil) more than twenty years earlier.[19] In a society that accords great importance to honor, such humiliation would be resented deeply and remembered strongly. (Strictly speaking, of course, the sentence was a legal action and not a form of personal revenge, but the evidence indicates that in these cases, the courts acted largely to preempt and prevent more drastic acts of private reckoning.) More generally, in societies with strong codes of honor, emotions of revenge seem to form an exception to the rule of a short half-life. Revenge can go on for years and decades until each and every offender has been killed,[20] because the social norm requiring an offended person to take revenge makes it impossible for the emotion simply to fade away.

We may gain further insight into the role of memory in transitional justice by considering the process of reparation. In Chapter 2, I quoted evidence that in France, the memory of the biens nationaux extended

[18] McNally (2003), pp. 58, similarly reports that for Californians exposed to the 1989 Loma Prieta earthquake, "repeatedly discussing their earthquake stories prevented memories of the events from fading over time."

[19] Woller (1996), p. 183.

[20] Elster (1999), p. 229.

well into the twentieth century. One of the authors I cited also offered two explanations of the persistent memory:

Generations forget more quickly spilled blood than stolen goods. By their continued presence under the eyes of those who had been despoiled of them, the fortunes originating from the national estates [*les fortunes domaniales*] maintain an eternal resentment in the souls. If the nobility, over the last hundred years, had become richer, they would have been able to forget. That is not the case.... Because of their bias against commerce and industry, the nobles have been slow to understand modern obligations.[21]

The daily reminder of injustice prevents the normal decay of memory and emotion. Moreover, those who fail to improve their situation because they are stuck in the past are, as a result, constantly reminded of what they have lost.

The retributive emotions may also decay as the transition recedes into the past. In Chapter 1, I conjectured that if the Athenian oligarchs were allowed to return from exile after a few years, it was because the emotions had had time to cool down. The declining severity in the treatment of American loyalists after 1783 also fits this pattern. In Germany after World War II, "as time went on, the sentences meted out to convicted war criminals became lighter than those of the earliest trials."[22] In trials in German-occupied countries after World War II, sentencing was almost invariably more severe in the initial stages than after two or three years.[23] A dramatic example may be taken from the trials of collaborators in the French departement of Ariège after August 1944 (see Table 8.3).[24]

Although the pattern is clear, it cannot be taken as conclusive evidence for decay of the retributive emotions. It could also be due to selection

[21] Gabory (1989), p. 1063. The first comment is confirmed by an observation by Edmund Burke (cited in and translated back into English from Nettement 1860, vol. 7, p. 85) about property confiscations in Ireland: "After twenty-five years, most men passed with indifference in front of the tomb of their assassinated father; but after a hundred years the spoliated generations will still feel hatred and rage at the sight of a field of which their family had been deprived."

[22] Schwartz (1991), p. 157.

[23] For Norway, see Andenæs (1980), p. 229; for Denmark, Tamm (1984), chap. 7; for Holland, Mason (1952), p. 187 n. 36; for Italy, Domenico (1991), p. 178; for Belgium, Huyse and Dhondt (1993), p. 231ff. The only exception is France, for which Novick (1968), p. 164 n. 12, finds no evidence for the hypothesis of progressive leniency of sentencing, without, however, being able to rule it out. For some evidence in the French records against the hypothesis, see Simonin (2003), pp. 58–59. She notes, however, that the hardening of the laws against collaborators might reflect their political instrumentalization (see next chapter), rather than a genuine change of attitude.

[24] Amouroux (1999), pp. 80–81.

TABLE 8.3

Court	Period	No. Accused	No. Executions
People's court	August 19–31		55
Military tribunal	September 2–4	8	8
Special military tribunal	September 5–6	8	7
Martial court	September 13–14	2	2
Permanent military tribunal	September 19–October 25	13	4
Regular court	November and later	172	3

bias, if the most serious cases were tried first.[25] In the only study known to me that tries to eliminate this explanation, it was found that in Belgium, the same type of crime, for example, serving in the Waffen SS or being a member of a paramilitary Nazi organization, was judged much more severely in the nine months following the liberation than at later dates.[26] A striking confirmation is provided by the fact that when eight French collaborators who had been condemned in absentia in the first years after the war returned to be retried in the 1950s, they all received much more lenient sentences. The three who had received the death penalty had their sentence commuted to five years of national degradation, which was immediately lifted for two of them.[27] In this case, we are dealing with "token-identity" (the very same crime), not merely "type-identity" (the same kind of crime).

[25] In the trials after World War II, it sometimes seems that what determined the order in which collaborators were brought before the courts had more to do with how easy it was to produce evidence against them than with the severity of what they had done. Writers were tried before others because the evidence was there, in newspapers and books, for all to read (Sapiro 2003, pp. 244, 255). Economic collaborators were tried later, because they could hide behind the "complexities of industrial structures and occult accounting systems" (Huyse and Dhondt 1993, p. 240; see also Rochebrune and Hazera 1995, p. 326). In Denmark, "the organization of the office of the public prosecutor made for a natural tendency to begin with uncomplicated cases, unless a firm hand put the investigation on a different path. This firm hand was missing" (Tamm 1984, pp. 271–72; see also pp. 140–41). A further reason for trying small cases first was the need to make sure that the prison sentence, when it was finally handed down, did not exceed the length of pretrial detention (ibid., p. 272). In Germany, too, "a decision was made to proceed with the easier cases first and save the more serious for the end. Since, for reasons relating to wider political developments in Europe, the American and, consequently, German will to pursue denazification steadily ebbed, many of the most serious offenders escaped punishment, while most of those who were punished were only small fry" (Cohen in press).

[26] Huyse and Dhondt (1993), p. 232.

[27] Chauvy (2003), pp. 285–86.

Other explanations of this temporal pattern are also possible, however. The most important is the "thirst of the gods" argument, according to which the demand for retribution will persist until it has been satisfied by the punishment of some offenders, after which it will abate in intensity. This argument has a long ancestry. Aristotle observed that "men become calm when they have spent their anger on some one else. This happened in the case of Ergophilus: though the people were more irritated against him than against Callisthenes, they acquitted him because they had condemned Callisthenes to death the day before."[28] Seneca notes that "often he who has committed the smaller sin receives the greater punishment, because he was subjected to anger when it was fresh. And anger is altogether unbalanced; it now rushes farther than it should, now halts sooner than it ought."[29] Note that Seneca here identifies both the urgency of the emotions and their tendency to be extinguished quickly.[30]

We find many appeals to this mechanism in writings on transitional justice. In Chapter 2, I cited the observation that when Louis XVIII's Minister Richelieu proposed clemency after the execution of Maréchal Ney, "[h]e may have had in mind the animal tamers who go into the cage only when the ferocious animals have just had a meal." Commenting on the 1945 execution of a member of the extreme-right government of Ferenc Szálasi, László Karsai writes:

> There must have been two main reasons behind the execution of Pálffy: his trial was among the first to be held and his relationship with Szálasi was ideologically closer than that of Szakváry or Hellebronth. One might add that had he not descended from a great historic family and had he been tried in the second half of 1946, after the people's judges' thirst for blood had been quenched, he may well have received only a life sentence.[31]

In their study of transitional justice in Belgium after World War II, Luc Huyse and Steven Dhondt cite a later comment by a prominent politician, who explained the initial severity of sentencing by the fact that "the gods

[28] *Rhetoric* 1380b 11–13. See also Frijda (1994).

[29] *On Anger* I.xvii.

[30] With regard to urgency, the following passage is a locus classicus: "How else did Fabius restore the broken forces of the state but by knowing how to loiter, to put off, and to wait – things of which angry men know nothing? The state, which was standing then in the utmost extremity, had surely perished if Fabius had ventured to do all that anger prompted. But he took into consideration the well-being of the state, and, estimating its strength, of which nothing now could be lost without the loss of all, he buried all thought of resentment and revenge and was concerned only with expediency and the fitting opportunity; he conquered anger before he conquered Hannibal" (ibid., I.xi).

[31] Karsai (2000), p. 243.

were thirsty."[32] This explanation is also consistent with the fact that the demand for retribution in Chile and Argentina shows few signs of dying out. Because no trials (Chile) or few trials (Argentina) took place in the immediate aftermath of transition, there is a pent-up popular demand that has not been satisfied.

I have discussed three possible explanations for the decreasing severity in sentencing: selection bias, spontaneous decay of emotion, and abatement of the desire for retribution once it has been satisfied by the punishment of some wrongdoers. A fourth explanation relies on the common observation that war situations tend to induce a general devaluation of human life, which makes the death penalty seem less extreme than under normal circumstances.[33] After a while, other priorities and evaluations will predominate. A telling illustration is provided by the following episode. In August 1945, 5,000 captured German soldiers participated in mine-sweeping operations in Northern Norway, of whom 184 were killed during the operations. Although this practice would seem to be a violation of the Geneva convention,[34] nobody paid much attention to it at the time. Although I believe the explanation in terms of spontaneous decay is the most plausible, because best supported by what we know more generally about the emotions, each of the others may also have some explanatory power.

As noted earlier, if we could predict the decay of passion, we might be induced to take immediate action. Although strategic preemption in the heat of passion is rare, it does occur. In Belgium, on the basis of the experience from World War I, "it was believed that after a while, the popular willingness to impose severe sentences on the collaborators would give place to indifference."[35] Hence, some Belgians wanted the trials to proceed as quickly as possible, before passion was replaced by reason or interest. In France after the liberation, many felt that the purges had to be carried out immediately because "it was necessary to act before the voices of timidity reasserted themselves."[36] In a related argument, President Alfonsín decided in 1983 that the "trials should be limited to a finite period during which public enthusiasm for such a program remained

[32] Huyse and Dhondt (1993), p. 119.

[33] For a general discussion of this tendency, see Slovic (2000), Chap. 24. For examples from transitional justice, see Huyse and Dhondt (1993), p. 49, and Andenæs (1980), p. 182.

[34] But see Coles and Weinberg (1992), p. 845.

[35] Huyse and Dhondt (1993), p. 115.

[36] Novick (1968), p. 39.

high."[37] In most cases, however, I believe the demand for instant action is simply due to the urgency of emotion, rather than to anticipation of its decay.

Alternatively, when agents of transitional justice anticipate the decay of passion, they may try to capitalize on this effect, rather than preempt it. Talleyrand counted on it when he persuaded Louis XVIII to delegate retribution to parliament. In France after the liberation, firms suspected of economic collaboration had an interest in paying lawyers to drag the case out, since "it was obvious that the longer one waited, the smaller was the risk of incurring a heavy penalty."[38] In Holland, some jurists argued that the death penalty was to be avoided because "in collaboration cases the court, and the public, tended to become less severe as the memories of the occupation faded."[39] Prison sentences may be reduced when emotions fade, but the death penalty is irreversible.

IV. THE RETRIBUTIVE EMOTIONS

Let me now turn to some specific retributive emotions that shape the legal expressions of transitional justice. The argument is summarized in Figure 8.1. Whereas I believe that the causal links from belief to emotion and from emotion to action tendency are well documented, the last link in the chain is more conjectural. Here I rely on the similarity and sometimes identity of the spontaneous action tendencies and the institutionalized reactions. The inference to a causal connection seems plausible, but perhaps not compelling.

I distinguish among five retributive emotions:

- *Anger* is the "second-party" emotion that A feels toward B because he believes that B has harmed him for no good reason. The action tendency of anger is to make B suffer.
- *Cartesian indignation* is the "third-party" emotion that A feels toward B because he believes that B has harmed C for no good reason.[40] If A loves C, he will feel anger rather than indignation, that is, a second-party emotion.[41] The action tendency of Cartesian indignation is to make B suffer. Experimental evidence indicates, however, that

[37] Nino (1996), p. 67.

[38] Rochebrune and Hazera (1995), p. 333. This effect may also have been due to the inconvenience of firms remaining in a legal limbo that paralyzed their activities.

[39] Mason (1952), p. 64.

[40] Descartes (1985), Art. 195.

[41] Ibid., Art. 201.

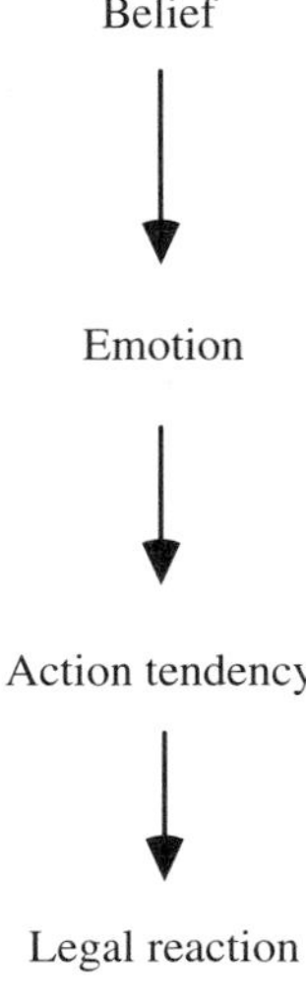

FIGURE 8.1

this third-party emotion is weaker than the second-party emotion of anger.[42]

- *Hatred* is the emotion that A feels toward B if he believes that B has an evil character. The action tendency of hatred is to cause B to cease to exist or otherwise be rendered harmless, for instance, by permanent expulsion.
- *Contempt* is the emotion that A feels toward B if he believes that B has a weak or inferior character. The action tendency of contempt is avoidance, or ostracism.
- *Aristotelian indignation* is the emotion that A feels toward B if he believes that B enjoys "undeserved good fortune."[43] The action tendency of Aristotelian indignation is to confiscate that fortune.

Whereas anger and Cartesian indignation are triggered by A's belief that B has done a bad *action,* hatred and contempt are triggered by the belief that B has a bad *character*. The antecedent of hatred is the belief that A's character is evil, that of contempt that it is inferior or base. Followers of Hitler thought Jews evil but Slavs inferior.[44] The distinction between

[42] Fehr and Fischbacher (2003), Fig. 5.

[43] *Rhetoric* 1386bff. I should note that Aristotle's account of indignation relies on a character-based, rather than (as in my discussion) an action-based, notion of desert.

[44] Goldhagen (1996), p. 469.

action and character may seem problematic, at least if one believes that a claim that someone has a bad character can be supported only by pointing to his bad actions.[45] Yet in some cases, such as sadistic torture, we tend to think that a single action provides sufficient evidence of an evil character. The same problem arises for contempt and the correlative feeling of shame. The paradox of shame is that it "involves taking a single unworthy action or characteristic to be the whole of a person's identity."[46] As for the distinction between hatred and contempt, it can perhaps be exemplified by the different emotions we feel toward someone who positively wants the destruction of other human beings and toward someone who simply doesn't care whether they are destroyed or not.[47] We may hate fanatics but feel contempt for opportunists.

To summarize, we react to the chronically bad with hatred, to the chronically weak with contempt, to the occasionally and intelligibly weak ("There but for the grace of God go I") with anger or Cartesian indignation, and to the undeservedly fortunate with Aristotelian indignation. We feel hatred for torturers and denunciators. We feel contempt for the opportunists who would enter the Nazi or Communist Party to get jobs they could not otherwise obtain. We feel anger toward the South African lawyers who failed to speak out against apartheid (the vast majority) or toward the forty out of forty-one Norwegian chiefs of police who joined the National Socialist party because they would have lost their job if they hadn't.[48] We feel Aristotelian indignation toward the beneficiaries of wrongdoing, such as economic collaborators in German-occupied countries, the white liberal elite in South Africa under apartheid, or Swiss banks that profited from the bank accounts of Jews who did not survive the Holocaust. After the French Restorations, many felt the

[45] Anti-Semitism, when it rests on the premise that the evil of Jews is intrinsic, "in their blood," does not need evidence of bad action; it also follows that Jews cannot be redeemed by good actions. In the case of a "Mischling" (half or quarter Jew), Hitler granted racial reclassification if it could be "proved [that], without awareness of his ancestry, he had fought for the party uninterruptedly and for many years prior to 1933" (Hilberg 1985, p. 79). The "Hindenburg exceptions" that protected Jews who had served in World War I did not outlast the person after whom they were named (Rigg 2002, p. 200).

[46] Lindsay-Hartz, de Rivera, and Mascolo (1995), p. 297.

[47] Thus Nino (1996), p. 141, comes close to saying that one reason we believe Nazis were evil was their (non-reason-based) belief that Jews were evil.

[48] The case of the Norwegian chiefs of police was actually more complicated, since many of them joined the Nazi Party under the threat that otherwise, the Nazi militia might take over the functions of the police (Justis-og Politidepartementet 1962, p. 432). Whereas the "lesser evil" justification was accepted for French and Danish judges, the decision that party membership would automatically imply guilt blocked this defense in Norway.

same way toward those who had purchased émigré properties at artificially low prices after they had been confiscated by the revolutionary authorities.

In transitional justice, these five emotions map into distinct legal and administrative reactions. Third-party emotions typically generate fewer and weaker measures than do second-party emotions: "Even liberal states are more likely to seek justice for war crimes committed against their own citizens, not against innocent foreigners."[49] Toward the end of World War II, the harshness of anti-Nazi measures demanded by Roosevelt's advisers depended on whether the Holocaust was seen as a third-party or a second-party crime. For Henry Morgenthau and Bernard Baruch, both Jews, it was a second-party crime.[50] Both demanded radical punitive action.[51] Felix Frankfurter, also a Jew, did not. He agreed with Stimson that the Nazi leaders must be given "the substance of a fair trial," and added that "most of these Nazi crimes have not been directed at the American government or at the American army but at the people and armies of our allies."[52] In him, these crimes triggered third-party emotions.

Among non-Jewish Americans, second-party emotions seem to have been triggered by crimes against American soldiers. Eisenhower, for instance, "wanted to reserve special treatment for the 12th SS Panzer division, which had in June 1944 killed 64 Allied prisoners of war."[53] Although the SS "had carried out countless worse atrocities against Soviet prisoners of war, . . . now the victims were Americans."[54] This set the pattern for subsequent trials. Thus,

> in the British and American programs [after 1945], because of the way in which priorities were set, very large numbers of high level German war criminals, connected to mass murder, but who had not been involved in atrocities against Allied British or American personnel, escaped prosecution while the lowliest perpetrators

[49] Bass (2001), p. 8.

[50] For Morgenthau's reactions, see Chap. 7. For Baruch, see Beschloss (2002), pp. 243, 246.

[51] Given my comments in Chap. 4 on Morgenthau's essentialist beliefs about the German national character, we should perhaps explain his reactions in terms of hatred rather than anger. It is clear, though, that he wanted the Germans to *suffer* rather than to be eliminated. His proposal to expel the Nazi elite to North Africa (Skidelsky 2000, p. 362) or to "some other part of the world" (U.S. Senate 1967, p. 448) did amount to a kind of elimination, however. The forcible removal of populations can be an alternative to physical elimination. As we know, the Nazis themselves contemplated the large-scale transportation of Jews to Madagascar before deciding on the Final Solution.

[52] Beschloss (2002), pp. 113–14; see also Bass (2000), pp. 164–66.

[53] Bass (2000), p. 154.

[54] Ibid., p. 178.

who participated in beating, mistreating, or executing even a single POW were relentlessly pursued.[55]

Aristotle singled out "sycophants," that is, professional informers, as especially deserving of hatred rather than anger.[56] In German-occupied countries after 1945, denunciators, together with torturers, were in fact especially likely to receive the death penalty, which, according to Aristotle, is what hatred desires for its object: "In Paris, of the ninety-five persons executed after sentencing, ... fifty had been torturers, ... thirty had been informers."[57] Comparable proportions apply for the forty-six executed death sentences in Denmark. One informer had his petition for clemency turned down on the grounds that "we are dealing with a person who is not merely without value for society, but of directly negative value."[58] The use of the death penalty against the major Nazi leaders and local Quislings may have been motivated by the belief that these men were intrinsically evil, although deterrence may also have been a motive. In the German "Doctors' Trial," seven doctors who had conducted medical experiments on prisoners and civilians were executed.

The legal parallel to contempt-motivated ostracism is the punishment of national degradation.[59] This sanction includes extensive loss not only of political rights but of the civil rights that are a condition for leading a normal life. In the French decrees of 1944, "[n]ational indignity was called not a crime, but a 'state' into which one entered by the performance of listed acts."[60] In the right-wing literature on transitional justice in France, the legislation against national indignity is compared to the Vichy measures against Jews and Freemasons.[61] In both cases, it is argued, people were punished for what they *were*, rather than for anything they had *done*. The argument is specious, because national indignity was the result of performing "listed *acts*," rather than merely belonging to an abstract category.[62] Yet, as I noted, the paradox is that although one

55 Cohen (in press).

56 *Rhetoric* 1382a.

57 Novick (1968), p. 163.

58 Tamm (1984), p. 373.

59 Simonin (2003), p. 43, traces the French punishment of national degradation back to a law from 1791 that required the convicted person to be set in the pillory for two hours, thus emphasizing the components of contempt and shame in this punishment.

60 Novick (1968), p. 146; see also Doublet (1945), pp. 28–29.

61 Aron (1969), p. 111; Amouroux (1999), pp. 207–8.

62 See also Simonin (2003), p. 49. The analogy between Jews and Freemasons is obviously halting, since the latter acquire their status as the result of a *choice*. Despite the common references under Vichy to the "judeo-Masonic" conspiracy, Pétain himself was fully aware of this difference (Baruch 1997, p. 119).

enters the "state" by performing certain "acts," one is punished for being in that state and not for the acts.

If we accept the Kantian view that retribution is a form of recognition of the offender as a moral agent, *nonprosecution* may also be an expression of contempt. It has been suggested, in fact, that this may be part of the explanation of the low level of prosecution of leaders and agents of the former GDR.[63] Along similar lines, one may also cite the following testimony given by a former French prisoner of war in 1947: "Once I came back to France, it would have been easy for me to lodge a complaint against M.C.; many of my comrades who felt entitled to hold him to account urged me to do so. I did not do it; the behavior of M.C. caused me to feel contempt rather than hatred or resentment; I viewed him as having a small mind and a mediocre character."[64]

The legal expression of Aristotelian indignation is clearly the confiscation and, when appropriate, the restitution of the undeserved gains. These gains are not "ill-gotten" in the sense of deriving from the agent's wrongdoings, for in that case, anger or Cartesian indignation would be the appropriate reactions. Undeserved gains in transitional justice are simply windfall gains derived from somebody else's wrongdoings. The story of the Swiss banks illustrates both kind of gains. Anger or Cartesian indignation are appropriate reactions to the profits the banks derived from acting as Hitler's foreign exchange dealer, whereas Aristotelian indignation is the normal reaction to their gains from dormant accounts of Holocaust victims. (Anger may, however, be an appropriate reaction to their evasive behavior when the latter gains were brought up as an issue.) Pure, innocent windfall gains may be rare, however. Unlike the Swiss banks that profited from Hitler's gold, women in German-occupied countries who benefited financially from intimate relations with the occupiers did not create or increase the wealth in which they shared, yet their benefits were hardly a matter of chance. In such cases, Aristotelian indignation blends with or is overshadowed by contempt.

V. TRANSMUTATION OF EMOTION

The former Czech dissident Jachym Topol recalls:

> In 1994, I came across the address of one of the communist secret police (StB) agents who tortured me at a police station during an interrogation. He allegedly killed one of my friends and raped others who were in jail. Together with two

[63] Claus Offe (personal communication).

[64] Singer (1997), p. 206. For a similar reaction, see also Kriegel (1991), p. 253.

mates with whom I was in prison, we decided to punish him. We managed to kidnap this former StB agent and to transport him to a hidden place; we were thinking of killing him. Then I stayed alone with him for a while, and he was so scared and hopeless that I could not do anything else but to release him. When my friends returned, I was afraid to say what I had done. When they found out the truth they sighed with relief. We were not able to kill him, because we are not like them. We are not animals.[65]

The phrase "We are not like them" originated with Vaclav Havel and became a mantra of the Czech dissident movement.[66] The thought behind it is a bit more complex than the cited passage would suggest. It can be amplified by citing another famous phrase, uttered by a former East German dissident, Bärbel Bohley, "We expected justice, but we got the rule of law [*Rechtsstaat*] instead."[67]

There are, in fact, three motivations that can be at work in these situations: the desire for revenge, the desire for substantive retributive justice, and the desire to follow procedurally correct principles in implementing substantive justice.[68] Topol's story illustrates the temptation of revenge. Bohley's remark expresses the frustrated desire for substantive justice. In practice, the desire for revenge and the desire for substantive justice often fuse. Although those who demand severe punishment for leaders and agents of the predemocratic regime often believe themselves to be motivated by concerns of justice, this self-image becomes less plausible when, as we have seen, the demand for justice loses its force with time. Justice presumably is timeless.

In general, adherence to due process makes it more difficult for the revenge motive to adopt the disguise of substantive justice. In transitional justice, an added reason for respecting the rule of law is that the new leaders want to demarcate themselves as much as possible from the lawless practices of their predecessors. The post-1945 trials in Western Europe were shaped by this consideration.[69] In Norway, the use of summary trials

[65] Topol (2001).

[66] Not all agreed with Havel's line: "With the call for a government of national reconciliation, the slogan 'We are not like them' (Nejsme jako oni) was coined. Skeptics responded with the words 'Yes, we are stupid.' Prominent hated potentates of normalization continue to live in their ill-gotten mansions, drawing pensions far exceeding those of their former victims. Czech ice hockey representative Jiri Kochta, upon returning from exile, is unable to return to his Prague house, occupied by the daughter of Jan Fojtik, a former politburo member in charge of ideology" (Ulc n.d.).

[67] Cited in McAdams (1997), p. 240.

[68] See, notably, Sa'adah (1998), pp. 145–50.

[69] Denmark may have been an exception. According to Tamm (1984), pp. 34–35, the use of retroactive legislation and other deviations from due process during the occupation "made it difficult for parliament and courts to create an effective barrier against the

was dismissed as an expression of an unacceptable Nazi mentality.[70] In Belgium, internment practices were severely criticized for resembling how things were done "on the other side of the Rhine."[71] In France, retroactive legislation was condemned as a Vichy practice.[72] François Mauriac saw in the willingness of Albert Camus to adopt retroactive laws "the corrosive effect of four years of fascist rule."[73] Anonymous denunciations – another Vichy custom – were not accepted.[74] In Lyon, Yves Farge admonished a crowd that "we must not get mixed up with the Nazis by engaging in blind reprisals."[75] In Italy, the same argument was made more disingenuously, when those who for political reasons wanted an end to the trials compared the special courts with those used under fascism.[76] Similar arguments were made after 1989, and not only by Havel and his followers. As noted in Chapter 5, a German court dismissed the case against Erick Honecker on the grounds that by trying a terminally ill person, "the FRG would be as guilty of violating the basic rights of its citizens as was the GDR" and would obscure the "fundamental distinction between the two political orders."

The desire for legality often goes together with a strong desire for a large proportion of the collaborators to be convicted. As Peter Novick remarks about France, "side by side with this passionate longing [for retribution] was the attachment of *résistants* to those principles of justice and equity which distinguished them from the rulers of Nazi Germany and Vichy France."[77] In post-1945 Hungary, the Minister of Justice insisted "both on the need to observe strict legal procedures and on the need to exercise revolutionary political justice."[78] In many cases, however, there is a conflict between the desire for procedural justice and the desire for

demands for adoption and implementation of exceptional measures." Rather than "since they did it, we shouldn't," the Danes seem to have thought, "since they did it, why shouldn't we?" (See also ibid., p. 43, for some concrete examples.) In France, a resistance-based group of lawyers argued that the postwar organization of the judiciary should be "modeled" *(calqué)* on that of Vichy, "so that the accused would have no reason to complain about the swiftness of the procedures: it would be the very same ones they had inflicted upon their adversaries" (Bancaud 2002, p. 108).

70 Andenæs (1980), p. 62.

71 Huyse and Dhondt (1993), p. 100.

72 Lottman (1986), p. 50.

73 Sa'adah (1998), p. 54; see also Lacouture (1980), vol. 2, pp. 183, 218.

74 Ibid., p. 186.

75 Farge (1946), p. 214.

76 Woller (1996), pp. 325, 344.

77 Novick (1968), p. 141; also Bancaud (2002), p. 108.

78 Deák (in press).

substantive justice – between the desire to demarcate oneself from the earlier regime and the desire to punish that regime as severely as it deserves to be. Bärbel Bohley's point was that by acting on the second desire, one may thwart the first. The trial of Pierre Laval shows that one may also sacrifice the second goal to achieve the first. As I now argue, new democracies can resolve this dilemma in one of three ways.

First, they can insist on respect for basic legal principles, such as a ban on retroactive legislation or on extending the statute of limitations. This has, for instance, consistently been the approach of the Hungarian Constitutional Court after 1989.[79] In the words of a former president of the court, "According to the Hungarian Constitutional Court, with the expiration of the limitation period a subjective right of the actor arises according to which he or she can no longer be prosecuted or penalized. The Constitutional Court sees in the limitations period a restriction on the power of the state to sentence, through which the State . . . *accepts the risk of an unsuccessful criminal prosecution.*"[80]

Second, the new regimes can frankly and openly accept the need to violate these principles in an unprecedented situation. After 1945, Denmark[81] and Holland[82] adopted explicit retroactive legislation, a procedure that was probably facilitated by the fact that neither country has a ban on retroactivity in the constitution. In spite of the claim to "observe strict legal procedures," the same practice was observed in Hungary after 1945: "Deliberately discarding the principles of *nullum crimen sine lege* and *nulla poena sine lege,* the Hungarian legislators stated in the first section of Law VII, 1945, that war criminals could be indicted even if at the time they committed their crime, their actions were not liable to prosecution according to the laws then in vigor."[83]

Third, and this is the most common procedure, one can use subterfuge to try and have it both ways. In Norway, the Department of Justice speciously asserted that increasing the punishment for certain offenses did not amount to retroactive legislation, since the offenders *could* have received the same penalty under the prewar legislation. The relevant criterion, however, is whether they *would* have received the same

[79] Schwartz (2000), pp. 100–102.

[80] Sólyom (2000), p. 19. Note that in the phrase that I have italicized, legal justice is explicitly identified with uncertainty (see Chap. 4).

[81] Tamm (1984), pp. 737–44.

[82] Mason (1952), pp. 128–31.

[83] Karsai (2000), p. 236.

punishment.[84] In 1948, a Belgian commentator wrote that the Dutch system of specifically permitting retroactivity "is more sincere than ours. The Belgian legislator pretended to adhere to the principle of non-retroactivity in criminal law. In reality [the Penal Code] was made increasingly severe by so-called interpretative laws."[85] In the same year, a Dutch law professor "criticized the French who – in order to avoid retroactive penalties – called the often severe sanctions of the new 'national indignity' crime 'losses of rights' instead of penalties. This seems to me a mere playing with words; a confiscation of one's entire property, or even a loss of certain rights, is as much a ... [penalty] as say a fine or the deprivation of liberty."[86] In his discussion of the French magistrates after the liberation, Alain Bancaud confirms the impression of "a certain hypocrisy" in the attempt to impose retroactivity without having the air of doing so.[87]

In Italy, the "Magna Carta" of transitional justice that was adopted on July 27, 1944, also adopted an evasive attitude on the issue of retroactivity. In principle, retroactive legislation was to be eschewed and fascist legislation to be abolished. These goals were hard to reconcile, however, with the reintroduction of the death sentence, which had been abolished in 1889. The Bonomi government's appeal to the fact that the fascist regime had used the death penalty for political crimes and thus must be judged by its own principles was not convincing, given its goal of abolishing the fascist legal system and returning to the rule of law.[88]

In spite of Bohley's complaint about only getting the Rechtsstaat, the trials of the border guards in the former GDR arguably rested on legal subterfuge. To comply with the clause in the unification treaty asserting that prosecution could only target acts that were crimes under East German as well as West German law, the Federal Supreme Court of Germany

[84] Andenæs (1980), p. 120.

[85] Mason (1952), p. 130. For arguments about the de facto retroactivity of much Belgian legislation, see also Huyse and Dhondt (1993), pp. 28–29, 64–65.

[86] Mason (1952), p. 130. For arguments about the de facto retroactivity of this French legislation, see also Novick (1968), p. 146; Lottman (1986), pp. 51–52; and, especially, Bancaud (2002), pp. 107–18.

[87] Bancaud (2002), pp. 113–16. To someone like myself who is very far from being a specialist in French criminal law, the attempt by Simonin (2003) to refute the charge that the legislation on national indignity had a retroactive character does not seem very convincing. In reviving the distinction between political and criminal justice, she ignores the fact that the national degradation was a *punishment*. Even if the retroactive law did not violate *nulla crimen sine lege*, it did offend against *nulla poene sine lege*.

[88] Woller (1996), pp. 140–41.

reconstructed an "ideal" law of the GDR from supralegal principles of natural law. Commenting on the decision, Peter Quint writes:

For all their earnestness and complexity, opinions of this sort seem to be lacking in candor. The court creates an ideal law of the GDR, through the use of techniques and principles resembling those current in the Federal Republic, solely for the purpose of saying that this hypothetical construct was "really" the law of the GDR and therefore its application today is not retroactive.... It would seem much more direct and honest to say: The law of the GDR as it actually existed was unacceptable and therefore we are applying a new law to these cases. Perhaps under prevailing interpretations of the Unification Treaty ... that acknowledgment could mean the end of these cases, but these issues nonetheless deserve a more general consideration.[89]

The rebuttal in 1995 by the Czech Constitutional Court of a petition to secure the restitution of formerly German-owned property seized after 1945 presents an especially interesting case. To grant the claim would open a floodgate of similar demands from the survivors and heirs of the almost three million Germans expelled from Czechoslovakia after World War II. To return properties in kind would have meant social turmoil. To offer more than symbolic compensation might bankrupt the country. These simple and compelling forward-looking arguments were not, however, the ones cited by the Court. Instead it made what Istvan Pogany calls a "deeply emotive judgment"[90] about historical justice:

In the 1930s, a fateful decade for the Czechoslovak Republic, each of its citizens could have realized, or rather should have realized, that right here, under the veil of propaganda and lies on the part of Nazi Germany, one of the crucial historical clashes between propaganda and totalitarianism was taking place, a clash in which *everyone bore responsibility together* for the position they adopted and the social and political role they undertook, that is, the role of a defender of democracy or an agent of its destruction.... This applies as well to the German citizens in pre-war Czechoslovakia, and to them in particular, for the conflagration which Nazism unleashed was in large part the work of their nation and its leaders. All the more so should they have manifested their fidelity to the Czechoslovak Republic whose citizens they were.[91]

89 Quint (1997), p. 203; along similar lines, also Walther (1995), p. 111.

90 Pogany (1997), p. 153.

91 Czech CC Decision (1995), pp. 747–48. The sentence I have italicized is an unusually clear statement of the principle of collective guilt. It is echoed, somewhat surprisingly, in the account by Stuart Eizenstat (2003, p. 33) about the problems he encountered in trying to get the Czech Republic to restitute communal Jewish property: "[Prime Minister] Klaus was frank enough to tell me that [in addition to his objections to doing anything that would slow down the process of privatization] he had a more fundamental concern. 'Mr.

A few years earlier, the Court had upheld similarly punitive aspects of the "lustration law" of 1991. The law blocked access to certain public offices for individuals who had been members of or served in communist organizations. When ninety-nine deputies as well as several foreign human rights groups objected to the retroactivity of the law, the Court responded along the lines of the French government in 1945, by claiming that since lustration was not a criminal punishment, the principle of retroactivity did not apply at all.[92] In these anti-Nazi and anticommunist decisions, the Court appears to have been moved both by emotion and by the desire to present itself as being moved by reason.

These transmutations[93] of emotion into the desire for justice do indeed illustrate Seneca's dictum, "anger wishes to have the decision which it has given seem the just decision." In transitional justice, the anger and the desire to appear (to oneself as much as to others) as motivated by the concern for justice have the same root cause. The wrongdoings of the enemy trigger at one and the same time a desire to punish the lawless behavior and a desire to demarcate oneself from it. When these goals clash, the outcome is uncertain. A few countries, such as Hungary after 1989, follow the adage, "Living well is the best revenge."[94] The Hungarians may have wanted to demarcate themselves not only from the communist era but also from an even older tradition. Let me recall here the 1990 meeting that I mentioned in the Preface, at which a former Hungarian Minister of Justice observed that "since the mid-nineteenth century 14 Hungarian prime ministers had been executed or forced into exile; it was time to break with this tradition of a highly politicized judiciary." I doubt, however, that the Hungarians would have displayed the same serenity had the transition taken place thirty years earlier.

Ambassador, if large amounts of Jewish property are returned I will have problems with the Sudeten Germans.'...I told the prime minister I saw no parallel between the Jewish and Sudeten German claims; the former were for communal property of the victims of Nazism, the latter for *private property of Nazi supporters*" [my italics]. These arguments ignore the fact that at the end of World War II, "the British advised the exiled Czechoslovak leader Eduard Benes to abandon any pretense that expulsions might be linked to how individual ethnic Germans had conducted themselves under the Nazi occupation, since this would limit the extent of the envisaged transfers [and] slow down what was intended as a radical solution" (Burleigh 2002, p. 799).

92 Kritz (1995), vol. 3, p. 357.

93 Elster (1999), Chap. 5.

94 This is the title of the essay on transitional justice in Hungary by Halmai and Scheppele (1997).

VI. TOO LITTLE GUILT – OR TOO MUCH?

Wrongdoers who understand that they have done wrong normally feel guilt. The normal action tendency of guilt is to atone by trying to undo the harm one has done or, if that is impossible, to impose a comparable harm on oneself, as an alternative way of restoring the moral balance of the universe.[95] In transitional justice, these reactions are absent to a remarkable degree. (I am not implying they are more frequent in ordinary criminal justice.) My impression – it is only that – is that in the immediate aftermath of transition, many wrongdoers are overwhelmed by a sense of guilt that, precisely because it is so overwhelming, is almost impossible to endure. Very soon, rationalizations, justifications, and excuses take over – not merely to provide a defense in the courts but to preserve the agent's self-image as a moral being. Like their accusers, albeit in very different ways, they engage in subterfuge. They may try to minimize the harm they did, or blame the victims ("those whom they injure they also hate").[96] By seeking out other wrongdoers, they can create a counterculture built on feelings of resentment and victimization, thus effectively blocking or slowing down the course of transitional justice. In Germany after World War II, many former Nazis tried to divert attention from their deeds by espousing a "perverse anti-Communism."[97] Other German examples were cited in Chapter 4 and are further considered in Chapter 9.

After the transition, those who remained neutral may be targeted for their passivity, and be at the receiving end of angry or contemptuous reactions. Even if they are not harassed in any way, the guilt they feel for having done nothing may strengthen their demand for retribution, as if post-transition aggression toward the wrongdoers could magically undo pre-transition passivity. The tendency for the neutrals, those in the "gray zone" between collaboration and resistance, to be especially vindictive seems to be a general phenomenon. Although I cannot cite written sources for the post-1989 East European transitions,[98] many conversations with knowledgeable individuals in the region suggest the pattern shown in Figure 8.2.

95 To illustrate: If you feel guilty about cheating on your taxes, you might send an anonymous money order to the IRS. If the IRS doesn't accept anonymous donations, you could instead burn an equivalent sum of money.

96 Seneca, *On Anger* II.xxiii.

97 Giordano (2000), pp. 199–208.

98 For a pointer in this direction, see nevertheless Kuk (2001), pp. 198–99.

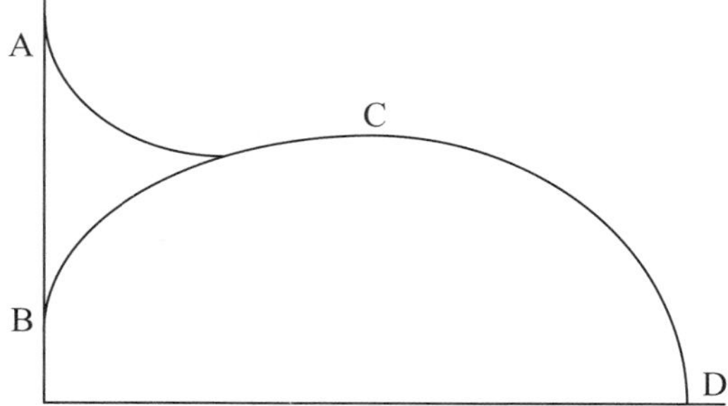

FIGURE 8.2

The ex-dissidents at one end of the horizontal axis fall into two groups. Individuals around B, such as Vaclav Havel and the left wing of Solidarity, are forgiving. Individuals around A, such as Vaclav Benda and the right wing of Solidarity, are unforgiving. Individuals around D are normally eager to be forgiven. Among the most intransigent in their demand for retribution, however, may be those in the "gray zone" around C. As we shall see in the next chapter, the fact that individuals may adopt similar policy positions for very different reasons creates possibilities both for alliance formation and mutual accusations.

In Chapter 1, I cited an early observation to this effect from Lysias's speech "Defense against a charge of subverting the democracy." Writing about Argentina after 1983, Carlos Nino comments on disgusted reactions to the hypocrisy "when those who were silent in the past suddenly become vociferous advocates of retroactive justice."[99] In Belgium, the draconian measures imposed by Antoine Delfosse, Minister of Justice in the exile government, "may have their origin in a need to stifle doubts created by his behavior during the first months of the occupation."[100] In Italy after 1944, suspect judges might lean over backward to prove their patriotism.[101] Commenting on the difference in outlook that separated de Gaulle from the resistance, A. J. Liebling wrote:

> Every Frenchman feels in some degree guilty for the debacle of 1940 – if only because he let himself be bamboozled into a sense of security before it happened. But the traitors personify the guilt of all, which makes the honest men all the

[99] Nino (1996), p. 39.
[100] Huyse and Dhondt (1993), p. 69.
[101] Domenico (1991), p. 179.

more bitter against them. In punishing the traitors, the French were punishing part of themselves. Only he who feels himself without guilt is reluctant to cast the first stone; he lacks the requisite imagination. General de Gaulle, the most self-righteous of Frenchmen, was one of the least vindictive against the erring brothers.[102]

A French defense lawyer explained the severity of the first sentences after the liberation by "the fact that many jurors were latecomers to the resistance and were eager to demonstrate a zealousness which they had not shown earlier. Later, when the deported came back from Germany, one had much more thoughtful jurors who... did not feel the need to prove themselves."[103] The *résistants de septembre,*[104] who suddenly emerged from their passivity after the liberation of the territory in August 1944, were often especially zealous in the harassment of women who had had relations with the Germans.[105] In the Algerian transition to independence, those who had joined the National Liberation Front at a very late date, even after independence, were among the most vindictive in the killing of harkis.[106] In an analogy to the French "septembrists," these were referred to as "marchians" because they joined the Front after the Evian agreements in March 1962.

In these cases, behavior that might appropriately trigger guilt fails to do so, but instead induces aggression. In other situations, guilt is induced by behavior that is essentially blameless. The reaction of American Jews to the Holocaust included two varieties of such irrational guilt. First, there is *survivor guilt* caused by the knowledge that "only the accident of geography saved them from the fate of their European brethren."[107] Second, there is *bystander guilt,* caused, in their case, not by having been *unwilling,*

102 Cited after Novick (1968), p. 157 n. 3; see also Lacouture (1985), vol. 2, p. 140. De Gaulle's lack of vindictiveness was also, and perhaps more importantly, linked to his desire to create an image of France that would justify the country having a place among the victors.

103 Lottman (1986), p. 272.

104 Referring to France, Belgium, and the Netherlands, Lagrou (2000), p. 25, writes: "The definition of what and who had been elements of the resistance, accommodation or collaboration became one of the most vehemently debated political issues of the post-war years." In France, the National Assembly adopted in March 1950 legislation saying that to obtain the coveted *carte du combattant,* one had to prove active involvement in the resistance beginning at least ninety days before the Normandy landings; to benefit from the similar Belgian act, any activity before the landings was sufficient (ibid., pp. 45, 51).

105 Virgili (2000), pp. 111–15, 208–9; Lacouture (1985), vol. 2, p. 140.

106 Hamoumou (1993), p. 250; Méliani (1993), p. 57.

107 Novick (1999), p. 75.

but by having been *unable* "to effect rescue [of the European Jews]."[108] As Peter Novick argues, the rational component of the bystander guilt was minimal. There was little the American government could have done to rescue European Jews,[109] and little American Jewish leaders could have done to influence their government.[110] Although irrational (but intelligible), these feelings of guilt are not contrived,[111] as can be seen from the fact that they induce a powerful action tendency to atone. The support of American Jews for the State of Israel depends in no little measure on the idea that "American Jews during World War II had been cravenly silent and that – like God – they were now given a second chance."[112]

[108] Ibid.

[109] Ibid., Chap. 2.

[110] Ibid., Chap. 3.

[111] By a contrived emotion, I mean one that is entertained for its consumption value, as it were – its positive effect on the self-image of the agent. Some people, for instance, feel righteous indignation when thinking about world poverty but never reach for their wallet. The grief following the death of Princess Diana was also, for the most part, contrived in this sense.

[112] Ibid., p. 165.

9

Politics

I. INTRODUCTION

Politics may impinge on transitional justice through "pure political justice" and through political interference with legal justice (Chapter 4). In such cases, the political decisions emanate from the executive. In this chapter, I focus on the role of *political parties* in shaping transitional justice, either as an end in itself or as a means to realize other goals. Although I mainly deal with assembly politics, I also consider extraparliamentary or revolutionary politics.

The influence of political parties can be decisive but may also be limited by other political actors. In some contexts, parties take second place to the executive. In France in 1815, the King controlled legislation at both ends, having both the monopoly of initiative and the right to veto amendments. In Belgium, an anomalous situation arose in March 1945 when parliament delegated the right to govern by decrees to a coalition government of national unity. The left-wing government that replaced it retained the full powers and used them to enact the decree of civil degradation that deprived tens of thousands of citizens of many basic rights. Although this bypassing of parliament was formally legal, it was widely seen as a violation of unwritten rules of the game.[1]

The political parties may also be constrained by an occupying power, as in Germany and Italy at the end of World War II. In Germany, the Allies retained formal control until 1954. In Italy, the government interpreted Harold Macmillan's aide-mémoire of February 24, 1945, as leaving it free

[1] Huyse and Dhondt (1993), pp. 149–50; see also p. 158 n. 307.

to conduct purges and trials without interference. Although the Civil Affairs administration disagreed, the Italian government was supported by the British Foreign Office and the U.S. Department of State. By the end of the year, the Allies had withdrawn from the purging process.[2] Parties may also, as we saw in Chapter 7, be constrained by the continued presence of an old regime that retains control over the military and security forces. In Argentina and Uruguay, the assemblies tried to ignore or rebel against the constraints on transitional justice that were part of the negotiated deals but retreated in the face of saber rattling by the military.

Some political parties emerge from the process of transition itself. In Eastern Europe prior to the 1989–90 transitions, the Communist parties were not political parties in the sense that concerns me here, but under the pressure of events, they reformed themselves to become competitors for electoral favor. Former resisters or dissidents may form political parties to implement the ideals they had fought for, examples including the South African National Congress, Solidarity in Poland, Civic Forum in Czechoslovakia, and the Mouvement Républicain Populaire in France. Other parties emerge from the pre-predemocratic past, in cases where the autocratic system was preceded by a democratic one. When the repressive regime has been of short duration, as in countries occupied by Germany during World War II, the traditional political parties may come back from exile or underground without missing a beat. In Uruguay, the polarization of political life in the Blanco and Colorado parties existed before the military dictatorship and persisted in attenuated form after it. In Hungary, the Smallholder Party that had preexisted the Communist regime reappeared in 1988, with a distinctive reparations policy. Often the standing of these traditional parties is enhanced or reduced by the behavior of their leaders during the autocratic interregnum. The high levels of support for the West European Communist parties after 1945, for instance, were largely due to the active communist resistance movements (and to the prestige of the USSR). Although the ultimate aims of these parties vary, their proximate aim, like that of other parties, is to win elections.

The role of electoral politics is the topic of Section II. In Section III, I discuss how ex-Nazis and post-Communists (the successor parties of the former Communist parties) have tried to shape legislation that might affect them. I conclude in Section IV by considering cases in which policies of transitional justice are motivated by a larger ideological vision, be it conservative or revolutionary.

[2] Woller (1996), pp. 354–60.

II. ELECTORAL POLITICS

To do well in elections, political parties may engage in *vote seeking,* by proposing policies which they believe will appeal to the voters. They may also engage in *vote denying,* by disenfranchising those who are likely to reject any policy package the party could credibly propose. In contemporary societies, the latter strategy is usually not an option.[3] Under unusual circumstances, such as regime transitions, it may be feasible. In Austria in 1945, the three main parties were divided on the issue of whether the five hundred thousand members of the Nazi Party should be banned from voting in the first elections. The communists were vehemently in favor of excluding them en bloc, the conservative People's Party in favor of allowing all "small" National Socialists to vote, while the socialists were somewhere in between.[4] It is hard to tell how much these differences among the parties reflected divergent views about the proper policy of denazification and how much a desire to bias the composition of the electorate in their favor, but the latter motive must surely have counted for a good deal. In the end, all members were banned.

In Belgium, the main controversy around the decree law of September 19, 1945, which deprived some sixty thousand Belgian *inciviques* of their civil and political rights, concerned the right to vote:

> It was known that legislative elections would take place in the spring of 1946 at the latest. The stakes in this first electoral confrontation were considerable. Catholic groups as well as left-wing groups assumed that the vote of the *inciviques* would almost exclusively benefit the Flemish faction of the Social-Christian party, which viewed the civic purge as an electoral maneuver intended to prevent it from obtaining a good result in the first post-war elections. Moreover, Catholic politicians had a similar interpretation of the refusal of the left-wing opposition to grant voting rights to women. They were met with the criticism that "The right want to win the election with the help of the *inciviques* or at least with the wives of the *inciviques*." ... The operation would be repeated [...] in 1946, but this time the manipulation concerned the right to stand for office.[5]

Turning now from vote denying to vote seeking, we may first consider the politics of the French Restoration. The small group of liberal deputies were opposed to property restitution and defended the rights of the purchasers of the biens nationaux. One might expect them, therefore,

[3] In earlier periods, it has been widely used; see, for instance, Keyssar (2000), Chaps. 4–5, and Guennifey (1993).

[4] Stiefel (1991), pp. 120–21.

[5] Huyse and Dhondt (1993), pp. 151–52.

to argue strongly for compensation of the original owners, so as to lift the clouds of suspicion and uncertainty that hovered over the confiscated properties. Yet success in promoting the interests of their clients would also remove any reason for these to remain clients. It was not, therefore, in the electoral interest of the deputies to promote the economic interest of their supporters. Hence, the liberals used exaggerated propaganda, spreading rumors about restitution of property and reestablishment of the tithe in order to maintain the fears of the purchasers, rather than to work for alleviating them. What looked like protection was, in fact, more akin to exploitation.[6]

For a more recent instance of vote seeking, we may again compare Austria and Belgium. In both countries, the 1949 elections, in which the voters who had been disenfranchised in 1945 were again for the most part free to vote, created similar challenges for the two major parties. In Austria,

> [w]hile the conservative Austrian People's Party took pains to gain the votes of the former Nazis by direct talks and appeals for them in Parliament, the Socialist Party supported the political ploy of establishing a fourth party [the Communists were the third]. This party was to attract the German Nationalist voters, mainly the former Nazis who in 1945 had lost their political rights, and to distract these voters from the People's Party.[7]

The socialists, one might say, succeeded only too well.[8] The new party, the League of Independent Voters – the direct ancestor of today's Freedom Party – garnered 12 percent of the vote. In Belgium, the Flemish branch of the Social-Christian party took the same line as the Austrian conservatives, through legislative initiatives to ease the sufferings caused by the severe purges, the purpose being to attract Flemish voters who might otherwise have been potential partisans of a new nationalist party. Yet the national organization hesitated to go along out of fear of losing francophone votes to the socialists.[9] In the end, the operation was unsuccessful, as a nationalist Flemish party made its appearance in 1954 (unaided, as far as I know, by the socialists).

6 Gain (1928), vol. 1, p. 420; see also ibid., pp. 326, 408.

7 Bailer-Galanda (1998), p. 421.

8 Engelmann (1982), p. 145, claimed that the Socialists' "gamble of 1949 seems to have paid off" and that "there remain no circumstances that could render Austria more susceptible to fascist infection than other liberal democracies." Had he written twenty years later, the Waldheim and Heider affairs might have made him think differently.

9 Huyse and Dhondt (1993), p. 182. The denial of the right to vote to women (they received it only in 1949) was due to the perceived sympathy of women for the collaborationist King Leopold (ibid., p. 159 n. 318).

In Denmark and France, Socialists and Communists overbid each other in taking a strong retributive stance. In France, the Communists took the moral high ground, contrasting the failure of the Socialists who had voted for the Pétain government on July 10, 1940, with the "75,000 Communists executed by the Germans."[10] The French "Socialists were competing with the Communists for the same share of the electorate; during the period when 'résistantialisme' still had some appeal, they were afraid of being outflanked on the purge issue by greater Communist implacability."[11] (Their "implacability" being purely tactical, however, the Communists were capable of going to the other extreme, as we shall see shortly when discussing Italy.) When in November 1945 the Danish Minister of Justice proposed a bill allowing for early release of some of those convicted for collaboration, the Socialists opposed it: "Transitional justice [*retsopgøret*] had become infected with party politics. The Communists had gained 18 seats in the elections, and the Socialists were losing ground. The Socialists could not, under these circumstances, afford to take a less firm attitude on transitional justice, which was one of the key planks in the Communist platform."[12] In Belgium, Holland, and Norway, too, the Communists took an especially intransigent attitude,[13] but here I have not seen it asserted that the Socialists responded by being more-retributive-than-thou.[14]

In Italy, this pattern was reversed. In his exile in Moscow, the Communist leader Togliatti initially took a hard line on the need for purges and trials. His stance softened when he returned to Italy in the spring of 1944 "with the intention of establishing the Partito Comunista Italiano as the leading force in society and with the approval of the middle classes who, because they had been the most wholehearted converts to fascism, were likely to be the hardest hit by the defascistization measures. An intensive purge could hardly be in the best interests of this policy."[15] Moreover, the demand for radical measures was also resisted by those with a fascist past who had joined the resistance movement or the Communist Party after 1943. In one Sardinian province, the prefect assessed that in both

[10] Buton (1993), pp. 202–3. The number is an exaggeration.

[11] Novick (1968), p. 179. With regard to the question of nationalization, however, one observed the opposite pattern. The Communists saw themselves forced to adopt the radical demands of the Socialists in fear of "being outflanked and of losing support at the grass roots" (Footitt and Simmonds 1988, p. 247; also Kaspi 1995, p. 372).

[12] Tamm (1984), p. 259.

[13] Huyse and Dhondt (1993), p. 124; Mason (1952), p. 138; Andenæs (1980), pp. 61–62.

[14] Brandal (2002) explicitly denies that this was the case in Norway.

[15] Woller (1998), p. 539.

the Communist Party and the Christian Democratic Party, about half the members had a fascist past, whereas the Socialists counted only 30 percent ex-fascists.[16] Later, Togliatti tried to limit the "wild purges" that took place in the North.[17] In 1946, as Minister of Justice, he proposed the amnesty bill that largely put an end to transitional justice in Italy, especially through the large discretionary powers it gave to the courts.[18] The Socialists, "who had always been more decisive in their dealings with the fascists, . . . put themselves at the head of the protest against the amnesty – not without an ulterior motive, of course, since the Socialists had to show a profile if they wanted to persist side by side with the Communists."[19] When the Communists left the coalition government the next year, however, they returned to an intransigent line and lost no occasion to decry the amnesty as the work of reactionary forces.[20]

We also find instances of electoral overbidding and underbidding in more recent transitions. In Argentina, President Alfonsín's

> government feared that if it was seen as too lenient with the military, that would impair its social ascendancy and ultimately its electoral chances. Indeed, that is what happened in 1987. Opposition parties, on the other hand, feared that if the government was too successful in its quest for retroactive justice, the Radical Party would be unbeatable. The parties were united, however, in the fear that if they gave too many concessions to the military, it would be impossible to consolidate democracy.[21]

Thus, the parties operated within a spectrum, where too few concessions to the military were as dangerous as too many concessions. Within this spectrum, Alfonsín wanted to be as severe as possible, whereas the Peronists wanted to promote leniency – not to placate the military but to reduce the popularity of their adversary with an electorate that was impatient for retribution. Hence, "in public, the Peronists took an intransigent stand in favor of retroactive justice," while "they pressed for concessions in private."[22]

In Eastern Europe, the electoral politics of transitional justice has taken two forms: *preempting*, to be discussed in the next section, and *overbidding*.

[16] Woller (1996), pp. 201–2.
[17] Ibid., p. 276.
[18] Woller notes (ibid., pp. 386–91) that the quantitative effects of the amnesty remain unknown.
[19] Ibid., p. 384.
[20] Ibid., p. 385.
[21] Nino (1996), p. 111.
[22] Ibid.

The most striking instance of the latter took place in Poland soon after transition. For reasons that I discussed in Chapter 7, the "left wing"[23] of Solidarity (Mazowiecki, Geremek, Michnik, Kuron), which negotiated the transition, were inclined to follow the "Spanish model."[24] Among the critics of this line were a group of

> ambitious and power-hungry politicians, who saw themselves as representing Solidarity's right and could draw upon at least two reasons for deep personal frustration: the first was their marginalization at the Round Table talks, and the second, the failure of Mazowiecki's government to offer them a satisfactory share of power. The leading figure in this group, Jaroslaw Kaczynski ... was not interested in historical justice. Above all, he wanted to oust Mazowiecki from power, and this, he thought, could best be done by accusing his followers of the proverbial "softness on communism."[25]

Kaczynski was, in a way, a familiar type. He was primarily a tactical anti-anti-anti-Communist who pretended to be, like some of his allies, a principled anti-Communist. Because the views of the anti-anti-Communists (Solidarity's left wing) on transitional justice naturally coincided with those of the Communists (who also embraced the Spanish model at the Round Table Talks), Kaczynski could point to the identity of their policy views to argue that there was also a suspect ideological affinity. In the presidential elections of December 1990, Lech Walesa, supported by Kaczynski (and helped by the economic downturn caused by the transition), did indeed defeat Mazowiecki. After the parliamentary elections the next year, however, Kaczynski turned against Walesa and constructed an alliance of right-wing parties that put Jan Olszewski into office as Prime Minister: "On June 4 [1992], Olszewski's Minister of Internal Affairs ... provided members of parliament with a long list of persons whose names had been found in the secret archives to be communist informers and agents.... Notably, the list included not only Walesa himself, but also the most vociferous advocates of lustration."[26] In 1995 Walesa himself deployed the strategy that had been used against him when he accused Prime Minister Oleksy of having been, and still being, a Russian spy: "From the beginning, many honest and well-informed persons suspected that the Oleksy affair was merely a brutal manipulation, designed to play

23 The phrases "left wing" and "right wing" applied to Solidarity do not apply to the economic policies of these two factions but to their moderate versus radical demands for transitional justice.

24 For the Polish tradition of comparing Spain and Poland, see Kuk (2001), p. 33.

25 Walicki (1997), pp. 191, 193; see also Kuk (2001), pp. 164–65.

26 Walicki (1997), p. 197.

upon anticommunist neuroses in the struggle for political power."[27] The escalation has been compared to the French terror; Adam Michnik spoke of "the logic of the guillotine." He might also have cited Yves Farge, Commissaire de la République in Lyon in 1944, who warned that "Un pur trouve toujours un plus pur pour l'épurer."[28] For later reference, we may note that these struggles did not lead to any legislation on lustration.

III. EX-NAZIS AND POST-COMMUNISTS

In the last section, I discussed how *incoming* leaders may use transitional justice for electoral advantage. I now consider how the *outgoing* elite may use electoral politics to shape transitional justice, notably to protect themselves against retribution. In the two cases I consider, the wrongdoers could not rely (as in Latin America) on their military power or (as in South Africa) on their economic indispensability to achieve immunity. Instead, they had to enter assembly politics and use the clout of their voters. This strategy is feasible only if the autocratic regime has been in power long enough to build an extensive clientele of party members and other collaborators and if the new regime allows them to organize themselves, either as political parties or as pressure groups that can bring influence to bear on the existing parties.

These conditions were fulfilled both in Germany after 1945 and in Eastern Europe after 1989. There are important differences, nevertheless, between these two post-totalitarian systems. The ex-Nazis included many fanatics among their leaders, whereas the post-Communist elite was mainly opportunistic. Compared to the Nazi ideology, communism was also more weakly implanted in the general population, mainly because it was imposed from outside, rather than being a homegrown product. Whereas Janos Kadar is reported to have said, "Whoever is not against me is for me," Hitler demanded and largely obtained unconditional and enthusiastic support. Except for Bulgaria, the post-Communists did poorly in the first free elections. Their surprising electoral success in subsequent elections had more to do with the poor economic performance of the new governments than with any ideological resurgence of communism. An offsetting difference, however, is that while the potential of ex-Nazi forces was sharply limited by the presence of Allied occupational forces, no similar constraint has operated on the post-Communists. Whereas

[27] Ibid., p. 203.
[28] Farge (1946), p. 224.

Allied pressure led to a ban on the neo-Nazi party in West Germany,[29] all former communist countries have legal postcommunist successor parties. Thus, in comparing the two cases, one should keep in mind both the greater strength and support of the *Ehemaligen* (former Nazis) in Germany and the strong constraints that forced them to operate by indirect lobbying, rather than by direct representation.

In my account of the claims by, or on behalf of, former Nazis, I closely follow Norbert Frei's grim study *Vergangenheitspolitik*.[30] In his account, the main issues from the late 1940s to the mid-1950s were the amnesties for certain categories of war crimes, ending the denazification proceedings, the rehabilitation of dismissed functionaries, and the release of convicted war criminals. In addition to major and minor political parties, the actors also included powerful lobby groups. The Catholic and especially the Protestant churches were vocal advocates of clemency. The self-appointed "Heidelberg circle" of lawyers, the core members of which were leading defense attorneys from the Nuremberg trials, also played an important role behind the scenes. On the side of the Allies, the main restraining forces were the American Military Governor Lucius Clay (1945–49) and his successor, the American High Commissioner John McCloy (1949–52).

Before it was banned in 1952, the neo-Nazi party (the Socialist Reich Party) had no deputies in the Bundesrat. In the first federal elections in 1949, the Socialists and the Christian Democrats each received about 30 percent of the votes, the Free Democrats (FDP) 12 percent, and the German Party (GP) 4 percent, with the rest going to various smaller groupings. If the two large parties were "soft on Nazism," it was mainly for pragmatic reasons. They both "wished to draw on the potential of the 'fellow travelers' [the most numerous and least serious category of offenders] while placing a check on any special interest parties in their vicinity."[31] When referring to the Nazi past, they tended with very few exceptions to use euphemistic or Aesopian phrases, such as "confusion" or "convulsion," because they knew that any kind of plain talk "would have been paid for by many votes."[32] Chancellor Adenauer, whose own past was

[29] Frei (2002), p. 263.

[30] I cite from the awkward English translation in Frei (2002). This work, together with the studies by Müller (1991) and Pross (1998), provides a compelling picture of the hypocritical and self-deceptive practices the Germans adopted to face or avoid facing their past.

[31] Frei (2002), p. 30.

[32] Ibid., p. 307.

impeccable, firmly believed that the reconstruction of the country would be impossible without enlisting the competent bureaucrats of the Third Reich, such as Hans Globke (who also had the advantage of knowing where all the bodies were buried, so that he could prevent Adenauer from appointing diehard Nazis).[33] He argued, moreover, that German rearmament – desired by himself as well as by the United States – required an end to the war crimes trials and commutation of the remaining death sentences. In a classic instance of a threat disguised as a warning, he told the Allied High Commissioners that if they did not show clemency, "it will be very difficult, if not impossible, to win over the minds of the German people to a voluntary cooperation in the defense of Europe."[34]

The arguments of the FDP and the GP had stronger ideological overtones. In Adenauer's first government, the Minister of Justice, Thomas Dehler, came from the FDP. Although he himself had been in opposition to Hitler's regime, he now played a very active and often demagogic role in protecting Nazi elements. He claimed, for instance, that in the French trials of German war crimes, death sentences were being passed on "the unit's translator, the clerk, the truck driver, the cook."[35] In the Oradour case, he asserted, "things [had] occurred [that] go beyond the humanly bearable," referring not to the 642 victims but to the incarcerated Germans.[36] Later, however, he struggled, with moderate success, against the infiltration in the FDP of two notorious Nazi administrators, Werner Best and Ernst Achenbach.[37] Another influential figure in the FDP, August Martin Euler, claimed that the denazification program had been undertaken "under the influence of the Morgenthau plan."[38] Commenting on the outcome of municipal elections in Hesse, he decried the pusillanimous behavior of a local chairman of the denazification tribunal who had kept a Nazi mayor off the FDP list, so that he was instead snapped up by the GP.[39]

The latter party, in fact, "systematically catered to the needs and wishes of former Nazis."[40] A GP deputy, Hans-Christoph Seebohm (later a minister under Adenauer), argued in 1948 against carrying out the death

[33] Herf (1997), p. 290.
[34] Schwartz (1991), p. 149. For other examples from the German debates, see Frei (2002), pp. 149, 152, 156, 168. For the threat-warning distinction, see Elster (2000), pp. 37–43.
[35] Frei (2002), p. 138.
[36] Ibid., p. 139.
[37] Ibid., pp. 71–75.
[38] Ibid., p. 32.
[39] Ibid., p. 39.
[40] Ibid., p. 11.

sentences imposed on war criminals on the grounds that rejecting the death penalty would "signify . . . the German people's turn away from any system based on violence and its abhorrence at the large number of death sentences carried out over the past fifteen years," thus implicitly assimilating the post-1945 executions of war criminals and the pre-1945 atrocities.[41] The tu quoque comparison between Nazi cruelties and alleged Allied atrocities was, in fact, a constant theme in the public debate. It is not surprising that at the first postwar meeting of the Waffen SS, a former parachute general could claim that the worst war crime was committed in Hiroshima, but less obvious how a leading Protestant bishop, Theophil Wurms, could assert that the actions of the American officers who investigated German war crimes did "not lag behind those of the Nazis in sadism."[42] More mawkishly, a Catholic bishop, Johann Neuhäusler, complained that the director of a prison for German war criminals had removed an advent wreath that he believed to be a fire hazard. He had "not even experienced something like that in a concentration camp. In the four Advents and Christmases that I had to spend in a concentration camp, neither Advent wreaths nor Christmas trees were kept from us."[43]

The FDP and the GP took a common stance on the issue of terminating the denazification process. Whereas the two large parties limited themselves to intervening for the two least serious categories of offenders, the FDP and the GP also wanted to terminate denazification for the two most serious categories. Given the small number of these serious offenders (twenty-five thousand out of 3.5 million denazification processes in the Western zone),

> gaining votes among these groups could have been of only limited interest. One motivating factor could have been the consideration that specially radical demands to close down the proceedings could produce more credibility among the lesser offenders than [the two large parties] had managed. But in the end, deliberations grounded in principle best explain the FDP's and the German Party's aggressive rejection of all remaining political purging.[44]

The main force behind such principled demands for an end to denazification and for liberation of the war criminals was an informal coalition of the Protestant Church, large industrialists, high state functionaries, and high officers. In 1948, in response to a petition submitted by a group of

[41] Ibid., pp. 127–28.
[42] Ibid., pp. 118–19.
[43] Ibid., p. 349 n. 77.
[44] Ibid., p. 39.

bishops headed by Bishop Wurms to Lucius Clay, another American administrator, Charles LaFollette, wrote that it was no accident that it came at a time

> when prominent industrialists such as Farben and Krupp and really big militarists such as the general staff generals and really important political figures such as Weiszäcker [a high official in the German Foreign Ministry during the war] are facing the end of their trials.... In other words, there is a possibility now of people being convicted who comprise those elements in Germany which have always made it militaristic and nationally arrogant. We cannot forget that the Protestant Church of Germany was always the State church of Prussia and certainly unless we are blind we can see a connection between this sudden rushing of the Church to the defense of those with whom it had such close ties in the past.[45]

Members of this elite were willing to consider Nazi crimes being "expiated by the violent murderers and bullies who...came from the lower societal stratum," but not by themselves.[46] The FDP, in particular, identified itself with this former and – they hoped – future elite: "[T]he individuals benefiting from [denazification and amnesty] would belong to the bureaucratic, economic, and military elite that had been corrupted in the Third Reich. In such members of the middle and upper middle class, the FDP saw something like born advocates of the great, nationally conscious, economically liberal, and anticonfessional party they hoped to be."[47] The GP, based mainly in Lower Saxony, was a more simple-minded conservative grouping. Between them, the two parties were able to exert "massive pressure" on the Chancellor, for whom "no...price demanded by right-wing coalition partners and former Wehrmacht officers was too high to pay" in exchange for Western integration and rearmament.[48]

Adenauer's government, in fact, had to pay a double price. On the domestic front, it had to pay the price of *nonretribution* to achieve internal peace. On the international front, the price for admission to the Western community was the payment of *reparations to Israel*. When offering concessions on one of these two fronts, it encountered objections on the other. Thus, in "Britain and France the Krupp pardon symbolized America's excessive haste to rehabilitate and rearm Germany."[49] In America, as noted earlier, the former Nuremberg prosecutor Telford Taylor thought that the release of Krupp would make excellent communist propaganda.

45 Ibid., p. 106.
46 Ibid., p. 187, reading between the lines of an editorial in the *Frankfurter Allgemeine*.
47 Ibid., p. 39.
48 Ibid., p. 309.
49 Schwartz (1991), p. 170.

Conversely, when Adenauer took the initiative for reparation payments to Israel, Hermann Abs, a banker with a shady past who led the German delegation to the talks,[50] first tried to delay or reduce the commitment to Israel on the grounds that Germany could not afford it. Later, he tried to use that commitment as an argument for increased American aid. McCloy, however, "immediately advised Chancellor that the object of the exercise was a gesture of fair treatment by the Federal Republic not by the United States."[51] It would indeed have been surprising to see the nation that had defeated the wrongdoer compensate the victim.[52]

In Eastern Europe after the transitions in 1989–90, members of the former elite did not have to adopt the indirect strategy of lobbying parties that did not formally represent them. As noted earlier, all countries in the region have post-Communist successor parties. Their existence is largely due to the fact of the negotiated transition. Even when the former opposition won the first free elections, outlawing its former interlocutors at the negotiation table would have been difficult for the reasons I discussed in Chapter 7. In Czechoslovakia, Vaclav Havel even went beyond allowing the Communist Party to survive when he deliberately, against the electoral interest of his own Civic Forum, adopted a system of proportional representation that would ensure a presence for the Communists in the new parliament.[53] Also, the strong constitutional courts that were established in several countries would probably have struck down legislation banning Communist parties. With the partial and limited exception of Germany,[54] membership in the post-Communist parties has not been seen as a disqualification for public office.

The main aspect of transitional justice politics has been the enactment of lustration laws.[55] In Poland, as noted earlier, there was initially a strong element of overbidding among the non-Communist parties, comparable

[50] On Abs, see Bower (1982), pp. 1–7, 13, 341–42. Although not a party member, Abs belonged to the financial elite of the Nazi regime.

[51] Cited from Schwartz (1991), p. 181.

[52] Yet this is exactly what happened fifty years later, when Stuart Eizenstat, the chief American negotiator in the compensation settlement for forced labor and slave labor, used American funds to close the gap between the German offer and the demands of the victims: "The United States was effectively paying a share of a compensation package for the wartime guilt of German companies" (Authers and Wolffe 2002, p. 245).

[53] Elster (1995), p. 113.

[54] Quint (1997), p. 394 n. 46.

[55] Nalepa (2003b), on which I draw heavily here, also discusses the question of granting access to the state security files. Her conclusions on this issue closely parallel her findings about lustration.

to the overbidding between Socialists and Communists in France and Denmark after 1945. No lustration law was passed, however. When the post-Communists took power in 1993, we would not have expected them to promote measures designed to punish their own members and supporters. Yet this is exactly what they did. Just before the elections in 1997, the post-Communist government enacted the first, relatively moderate, lustration law in Poland. A similar phenomenon was observed in Hungary. Although the first post-transition government had passed a harsh lustration law in March 1994, exposing some twelve thousand individuals to screening, it was struck down by the Constitutional Court in December of the same year.[56] After the elections in May 1994, the post-Communists came into power. Once the Court had struck down the previous law, one might think that the post-Communists would have been content to let sleeping dogs lie. Instead, they enacted a new and milder lustration law in 1996, targeting only six hundred individuals.

Monika Nalepa argues that these seemingly self-punitive measures were in fact *preemptive moves* to forestall harsher lustration laws by later governments.[57] In Poland as well as in Hungary, the post-Communist governments passed lustration laws at a time when their prospects in the next elections looked poor. If instead they had remained passive on the lustration issue, they could expect the next government to enact harsher measures, which might, however, be preempted by milder measures. For preemption to work, two conditions have to be satisfied. First, the government has to have a monopoly on introducing bills in the legislature, with no scope for amendments from the floor. Second, the post-Communists must expect that they will lose power after the next elections, but that the hard-line anti-Communist bloc will fail to get an absolute majority in parliament. To govern, the latter will have to rely on the support of a pivotal moderate party whose preferred transitional justice policy is less punitive than that of the hard-liners, while stricter than that of the post-Communists. Under these conditions, the post-Communists, while still in power, have an incentive to enact the preferred moderate legislation. Under conditions of perfect foresight, the situation can be represented as in Figure 9.1.

The preferred ("ideal") policies of post-Communists, moderates, and hard-liners are, respectively, 0, m, and 1. Any group prefers a position closer to its ideal policy to one more distant from it, regardless of whether

[56] For the Court's reasoning, see Sólyom and Brunner (2000), pp. 306–15.
[57] Nalepa (2003b).

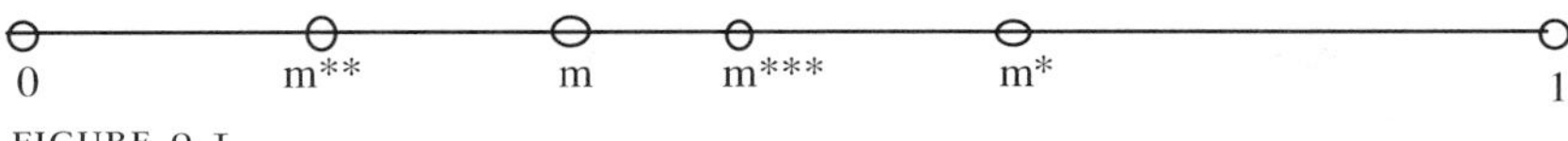

FIGURE 9.1

the deviation is in the direction of lesser severity or greater. If the post-Communists do nothing so that the status quo remains at 0, the successor government will propose a policy such as m*, which the moderates will prefer to the status quo. If the post-Communists do introduce a lustration bill while in power, they have to take into account possible responses by their successors. If they introduce a bill such as m** that undershoots m, the hard-liners can get the moderates to accept a proposal m*** that overshoots m by a marginally smaller difference. The best strategy for the anti-Communists, therefore, is to propose the ideal policy of the moderates. This reasoning unravels, however, if amendments can be made from the floor at any time. In that case, the moderates will propose their ideal policy and get it adopted so that there is no reason for post-Communist preemption.

The two conditions underlying the model did in fact obtain in Poland and Hungary. In the latter country, the predictions of the model also correspond closely to the observed events. When the hard-liners took office in 1998, they left the moderate policy in place. In Poland, the model predicts correctly that the post-Communists would enact moderate lustration, but fails in that their successors replaced it by more stringent policies. Relying on a more complex model with imperfect foresight, Nalepa suggests that the explanation may lie in unforeseeable events – among them the largest flood of the century – that threw doubts on the competence of the governing coalition and generated a composition of parliament that differed from what the post-Communists had (rationally) expected when they enacted the legislation.[58]

The measures passed by the center-right coalition in parliament went beyond simple lustration, and included the creation of a National Remembrance Institute that was authorized to investigate cases of political

[58] As Nalepa notes (personal communication), an alternative explanation of the self-punitive behavior of the post-Communists is also possible. They may have wanted to send a signal to the electorate that they had broken with their past and could be trusted to act honestly. This explanation would also fit the fact, noted in Chapter 4, that in 1990 the Bulgarian Communists extended the statute of limitations, but not by so much that crimes committed during the Stalinist period could be prosecuted. By contrast, those measures would not make sense on the preemption model. The pivotal parties are "moderate" only in the sense of not wanting to punish the *least* serious crimes, not in the sense of wanting to protect the *most* serious wrongdoers.

persecution and murder, thus bypassing the normal judiciary. The partisan nature of the legislation shows up in the designation of December 31, 1989, as the end date of the Communist regime, thus implying that the members of Mazowiecki's left-wing government were Communist functionaries.[59] Also, the president and board members of the Institute were to be elected by parliament (rather than by the ex-Communist president Kwasniewski) and have very long tenure (to prevent a later left-wing parliament, like the one elected in 2001, from replacing them). When Kwasniewski vetoed the law and the governing coalition could not muster the three-fifths majority needed to overrule him, a deal was struck with the Polish Peasant Party (a former fellow-traveler party) that reduced the power of the coalition to pursue its vindictive policies. The president of the Institute was to be elected by a three-fifths majority, and the length of tenure shortened. Recent controversies about cutting the budget of the Institute show that in Poland, the struggle over the past is far from finished.

IV. POLITICAL IDEOLOGIES AND TRANSITIONAL JUSTICE

The ex-Nazis based their struggle *against* transitional justice on an ideological vision. In this section, I want to consider some cases in which groups and parties have *embraced* transitional justice as a means to implement or consolidate a larger ideological project. I first discuss some conservative or backward-looking ideologies, and then conclude the section, the chapter, and the book by considering insurrectionary or revolutionary motives in transitional justice.

In France after 1815, a central aim of the far (ultraroyalist) right was to reconstitute the large properties that been parceled out by the Revolution. In their arguments, interest, passion, and concern for the general good blended in a manner characteristic of many political ideologies. For one ultraroyalist, Josse Beauvoir, only the great landowners deserve to be trusted, for they are more concerned "with maintaining than with acquiring." For the prominent ideological thinker Bonald, large properties were the foundation of society, "as indestructible as nature itself."[60] Landed property, therefore, was often singled out as uniquely worthy of legal protection. In Chapter 2 I cited a lawyer, writing in 1825, who expressed the

[59] Kuk (2001), p. 203.
[60] Waresquiel and Yvert (1996), p. 211.

commonly held view that "the community suffers much less from the violation of twenty pieces of movable property than from a single attack on landed property." (I also noted the anti-Semitic overtones of his rhetoric.) The leader of the ultraroyalist opposition Villèle wrote that "we must above all try to recreate the agricultural *mores* which make our nobles seek out the life of the bourgeoisie less eagerly than the bourgeoisie try to imitate the lord of the manor."[61]

One aim behind the indemnity law of 1825 was indeed to "put a halt to the parceling out" of the large estates.[62] Although the émigrés did not get their land back, it was hoped that the funds they received in compensation might enable them to buy it back, thus creating a class of large landowners who, under the strict economic requirements for voting and eligibility, would form the new political elite. In practice, however, it does not seem that many émigrés used their compensation for this purpose. The bulk of the biens nationaux seems to have remained in the hands of the purchasers.[63] Although the period between 1815 and 1848 did indeed see the reconstruction of large landed properties, many of these consolidations took place before 1825. Also, many large properties were gathered in the hands of the wealthy bourgeoisie, who always thought of land as a safe investment.[64] Once Louis XVIII had been forced to give up the idea of physical restitution of the confiscated properties, it proved impossible to reconstitute the old way of life by this indirect strategy.

A similar episode of "failed nostalgia" occurred in Hungary after the 1989 transition. The strongest demands for restitution of landed property came from the party of the Independent Smallholders. This party had dominated the government formed in November 1945, which enacted radical land reform. A few years later, it was forcibly merged with the Communist Party. It reconstituted itself at the end of 1988, and participated as a minor actor in the Round Table Talks. Its leaders

sought restitution in a very specific and limited sense – reversion to the property relations on agricultural land found in 1947. The date is crucial; it fell after the post-war land reforms which resulted in the redistribution of land from the large estates to peasants and agricultural labourers, but before the Communist-dictated

[61] Gain (1928), vol. 2, p. 419.
[62] Ibid., p. 417.
[63] Ibid., pp. 427–30.
[64] Sauvigny (1999), p. 213.

process of enforced collectivisation. The 1947 date also fell comfortably after the confiscation of Jewish-owned property (including agricultural land) and after the expulsion of much of the *Volksdeutsche* from Hungary. Thus, for the Smallholders, restitution was seen as a means of reconstituting a particular social order in Hungary, one characterised by a pronounced emphasis on the agrarian sector and by a comparatively egalitarian and homogeneous (i.e. Hungarian) peasant-oriented culture.[65]

Note that as in France after 1815, the criteria for reparation were chosen so as to exclude non-Hungarian or (as the code word goes) "cosmopolitan" Jewish elements.[66] As we also saw in Chapter 6, there is no automatic solidarity among victims. As in Restoration France, too, it would be much too simple to explain the desire for reconstitution of the former pattern of landownership in terms of simple economic interest. The Smallholders no doubt believed themselves to be motivated by the general interests of Hungarian society, rather than by the class interests of small landowners. As Marx noted, "One must not form the narrow-minded notion that the petty bourgeoisie, on principle, wishes to enforce an egoistic class interest. Rather, it believes that the *special* conditions of its emancipation are the *general* conditions within which alone modern society can be saved and the class struggle be avoided."[67] Being a junior partner in the governing coalition, however, the Smallholders could not persuade its senior partner that this coincidence of special and general interests did in fact obtain. In the end, the Hungarians chose the path of compensation rather than of restitution.

Ideologically motivated ideas of property were also important in the debates over nationalized holdings in the former GDR, where "the strong property principles of conservative ideology have played a significant part. . . . First, these principles prevailed in the basic decision to provide redress for all GDR expropriations. Second, strong property principles were important in the decision to adopt a general principle of return of expropriated property – rather than a general principle of compensation."[68] In theory, land confiscated during the Soviet occupation (1945–49) was exempt from restitution. In practice, however, the former owners of such

[65] Pogany (1997), p. 156.

[66] As noted by Shlomo Avineri (cited in Heller and Serkin 1999, p. 1406), this was a general tendency in the post-1989 transitions: "[M]ost former Socialist countries, including the Czech Republic, chose cut-off dates for restitution that coincided with the most ethnically pure moment in the country's history."

[67] Marx (1852), p. 130.

[68] Quint (1997), p. 153.

land might be able to get it back, since some of it had reverted to the state upon reunification:

The bitterly disputed question was who should have priority in purchasing this property from the federal government. This important political battle to some extent resembles an old-fashioned class struggle: in many cases it pitted the large land owners or their descendants against persons who had actually worked the land. . . . Moreover, the 1992 guidelines reflected political and ideological concerns, as they favored largely conservative private investors over the suspect successors of the former [agricultural collectives]; they also incorporated the deeply ingrained preference in Western Germany for individual rather than cooperative ownership in agriculture.[69]

Moreover, since former owners of land that had been nationalized between 1945 and 1949 and that had *not* reverted to the state were entitled to compensation, they

maintained that they should receive some of their compensation in the form of real property in eastern Germany held by the federal government. This argument drew objection on the ground that it violated the provision of the Unification Treaty stating that the [1945–49] expropriations were "not to be undone." It was also vigorously opposed by the [Social Democratic Party], and political figures from the east, on the ground that such transfers would be a "direct attack on east German interests" and "would result in" a concentration of land in the hands of the few.[70]

The issue of the large Prussian "Junker" estates thus surfaced for the third time in twentieth-century German history. In October 1918, faced with the prospect of a communist revolution in Germany, the British Undersecretary of State for Foreign Affairs, Eyre Crowe, stated that he "cared little about the danger that a collapse of the established order in Germany might pose to Great Britain. He insisted that 'we do want to weaken, if not to shatter the system of government identified with the Junker regime in Prussia.'"[71] In 1945, the fear of the Junker-capitalist-military complex was a main reason cited by the Soviets for dismantling the large estates in Eastern Prussia. Henry Morgenthau, too, wanted to break up the Junker estates.[72] After 1990, the issue still retained ideological salience.

So far I have discussed demands for transitional justice based on the desire to *restore*, more or less intact, the state that preexisted the autocratic regime. I now turn to policies that are closely linked to a will to *transform*

69 Ibid., p. 140.
70 Ibid., p. 142.
71 French (1998), p. 80. By "if not," did he mean "but not" or "perhaps even"?
72 U.S. Senate (1967), p. 465.

society – to go beyond the old order rather than restoring it. I do not have in mind the desire, which motivated the Athenians in 403 B.C. or the Allied powers in 1945, to remove the root causes of autocratic regimes. In these cases, transitional justice was linked to constitutional reform for the purpose (in Athens) of eliminating the abuses that had triggered the oligarchic regimes or (in 1945) of creating a decentralized structure that would lend itself less easily to a third German bid for power. Important as these episodes are, they were not linked to particular political ideologies. Rather, I want to discuss the situation in Italy and France at the end of World War II, when demands for punishing economic collaborators fused with demands for nationalizing the means of production, and demands for eliminating fascist and Nazi elements blurred with demands for abolishing capitalism. In Italy, the vision was mainly phantasmagorical. In France, it came closer to representing a credible alternative.

In Italy toward the end of the war, there were three radical parties: the Communists, the Socialists, and the Action Party. The last, "more a movement than a party,"[73] was numerically weak but highly active in the resistance movement. Like the Socialists, its members took a more intransigent line than the Communists on transitional justice, and like them were capable of using revolutionary rhetoric.[74] When the Communists decided to moderate their demands for transitional justice in order to remain in the second Bonomi government that was formed in December 1944, the Socialist Party and the Action Party preferred to resign and instead try to mobilize in the streets.[75] The difference in tactics reflected a strategic divergence. The orthodox communist line was that Italy first had to "complete the bourgeois revolution," remove "pre-capitalistic obstacles" to the development of agriculture, and create a "democratic republic."[76] By contrast, the leader of the Socialists, Pietro Nenni, called for a "socialist republic." When a Foreign Office observer commented that "[t]his is all very silly," one of his colleagues rejoined: "But then the Italian Socialist Party is a remarkably silly party. It is living in a world of its own making, using language coined in the '20's and doomed to be eaten up by the much more astute . . . Communist Party."[77]

Originally, the moderate line of the Communist Party was adopted independently of Moscow. After September 1943, "just as the Italian

[73] Ellwood (1985), p. 15.
[74] Kritz (1995), vol. 2, pp. 168–69.
[75] Woller (1996), p. 208; Ellwood (1985), p. 122.
[76] Ellwood (1985), pp. 77, 159; Urban (1986), p. 198.
[77] Ellwood (1985), p. 107.

Resistance gathered momentum, the PCI deviated from Moscow's policy. Rather than assuming the vanguard role in an Italian national front, it became a joint leader of the Italian Committee of National Liberation."[78] When Togliatti returned from Moscow in March 1944, however, he came with orders to pursue even softer policies. Although the party had previously refused to cooperate with the monarchy, "Togliatti, barely back from Moscow, announced in a press conference the PCI's readiness to participate in a cabinet headed by Badoglio or anyone else, even if it were invested by the king."[79] This turnabout on Stalin's part may have been a response to a speech by Churchill on February 22 to the House of Commons, in which he gave his full support to the Badoglio government:

> Churchill's speech may well have represented an implicit offer of a deal with Stalin which would circumvent the Americans: to wit, Soviet acceptance of Churchill's position regarding Italy in exchange for open British support for the Soviet Union's absorption of a two-hundred-mile-wide chunk of Polish territory. Diplomatic recognition of the royal government of Italy on March 13, 1944, together with the policy reversals of the Italian and French Communist parties, constituted Stalin's reply.[80]

Yet the imposition of a moderate policy from Moscow was not necessarily respected by the rank and file. During the liberation of Italy in late 1944 and early 1945, the Communist Party did not yet have the strict Stalinist organization it would adopt a few years later. Almost all its members were fresh and unruly recruits with only the vaguest ideas about the goals of the party.[81] In the power vacuum created by the coexistence of three authorities – the official resistance, the military government, and the Italian government – that mutually paralyzed one another, a "latent civil war" was developing.[82] In addition to the original motivation of the "wild purges" – revenge on fascists and collaborators – there now

[78] Urban (1986), p. 149.

[79] Ibid., p. 191.

[80] Ibid., p. 193.

[81] Woller (1996), p. 278. Unlike the French Communist Party, the Italian party did not have a large body of prewar cadres who were trained in democratic centralism and could serve as the transmission belt of orders from above. Whereas the French party *grew* from a membership of 340,000 in 1937 to 900,000 at the end of the war, the Italian party *jumped* from 5,000 in mid-1943 to 1,700,000 in December 1945 (Urban 1986, p. 189). Although the French party, too, had problems controlling the newly recruited militants (Footitt and Simmonds 1988, pp. 189–90), they fell quickly into line when the party leader Thorez returned from Moscow (ibid., pp. 196, 235).

[82] Woller (1996), p. 276.

emerged "an ideologically grounded intention to remove everything that stood in the way of an 'antifascist-revolutionary' reconstruction of state and society. Concretely this meant that in the summer and fall of 1945 the victims of the 'wild' purges included priests, landowners, officials in the bourgeois parties and industrialists."[83] In Turin, for instance, a Communist leader falsely told the workers in the Fiat factory that the general director of the firm had been condemned to death by the local liberation committee.[84]

As most of the wild purges were the work of partisans with links to the Communist Party, it was tempting to seek an organized intention behind the lawless behavior. A report by the Allied armed forces dated January 15, 1945, states that there was "no doubt that those who control Communist bands are preparing to seize power by force when the Germans are expelled by the Allies."[85] By other accounts, however, this was a misreading of the situation. Although strong forces within the party supported the lawless actions, Togliatti rejected them firmly. Whereas the Action Party was ready to hand over power to the local Liberation Committees, the Communist Party sent out a steady stream of directives cautioning against activism and emphasizing that the transformation of Italy "must be accomplished by means of the democratic path of the Constituent Assembly."[86]

The behavior of the purge boards in Italian firms was also used to impute social-revolutionary aims to the resistance movement.[87] A prominent industrialist in northern Italy maintained, in conversation with an Allied officer, that

> the burdening of industry with heavy financial obligations and the paralysis of the organization through purges do not only serve the aims of improving the living standard of the workers and to remove men whom they hate, in order to create a place for themselves and their friends. These measures have a much deeper significance. They are part of a vast political strategy that aims at driving industry into bankruptcy and chaos, to facilitate and accelerate its socialization and takeover by the state.[88]

[83] Ibid., p. 275.

[84] Ibid., p. 267.

[85] Cited in Coles and Weinberg (1992), p. 544. This report was not typical of Allied opinions. Ellwood (1985), p. 187, quotes a report to Washington from July 1945 to the effect that there was "no adequate evidence to substantiate such rumours which largely emanate from industrial and right-wing elements anxious to stir up anti-communist feeling."

[86] Urban (1986), p. 199; also Woller (1996), p. 277.

[87] For descriptions, see Woller (1996), pp. 285–91, and Domenico (1991), pp. 162–73.

[88] Woller (1996), p. 286.

Again, however, there is no evidence that the Communist Party had adopted this "vast political strategy." Togliatti successfully resisted the "class struggle experiments" because he knew that the Allies were ready to step in if they went too far and that foreign credit would dry up. He also knew that his aim of creating a large popular party was incompatible with a policy that would create "dread and terror" in the middle classes.[89] In the end, therefore, the link between transitional justice and social revolution in Italy existed only in the irrational hopes of some activists and the irrational fears to which they gave rise.

Many have reached a similar conclusion about France in 1944–45. A common view has been that the Communist Party "had no intention of staging a coup and of seizing power at the Liberation. Instead, the communists wanted to place themselves in as advantageous a position as possible from which to fight and win an election."[90] Although the Communists planned to use transitional justice to further these electoral prospects, purges and trials (jointly referred to as *épuration*) cannot have been elements in a revolutionary strategy since no revolution was being planned.

Many indicators support this view. Stalin's policy reversal after Churchill's speech affected the French as well as the Italian Communists. Although the ranks of the party had swelled during the occupation, the motivation of the new members tended to be patriotic rather than Marxist.[91] Some American and Allied intelligence groups thought that the Communists were going to launch a coup during the liberation,[92] but the Office of Strategic Services had a consistently skeptical attitude toward these rumors.[93] According to one Allied report, local incidents of wild purges by members of the Communist resistance, as during the "reign of terror" in Nice at the end of August 1944, were "not in line with the current Party policy and would be repudiated by its higher leadership."[94] When the Communist leader Thorez returned from Moscow on November 27, 1944, he disappointed his followers by failing to condemn de Gaulle's dismantling of the Communist-based militia.[95] In

89 Ibid., p. 289.
90 Footitt and Simmonds (1988), p. 229.
91 Kaspi (1995), p. 178; Buton (1993), p. 129.
92 Footitt and Simmonds (1988), pp. 84–85, 170–71.
93 Ibid., pp. 85, 175–73.
94 Coles and Weinberg (1992), p. 764 n. 6.
95 Kaspi (1995), p. 180; Buton (1993), p. 181. In a brilliant stroke, de Gaulle had announced the dismantling the same day he amnestied Thorez for his desertion in October 1939.

January 1945, he gave his full support to de Gaulle's policy of dismantling and disarming all resistance-based institutions.[96] In the same month, speaking before the Committee of Defense in the National Assembly, he no longer required the departure of all officers who had adopted a wait-and-see policy, but only of "active collaborators."[97] Rather than trying to foment unrest in the factories, he urged the workers to "participate with enthusiasm in the battle of production" so that the country could get back on its feet.[98]

In more recent work, Philippe Buton has challenged this interpretation:

> In light of the sources that have now become available [including documents in Russian archives], the French Communist Party appears as a party that really tried to conquer power at the Liberation, at two separate moments. During the Occupation, its aim was to achieve control based on the interior Resistance and, at the Liberation, impose its primacy on General de Gaulle. Unfortunately for the party, the failure of the national insurrection, the intelligent Gaullist policy and the international constraints prevented it from crossing the Rubicon and, after some hesitations, this aim was abandoned at the end of 1944. The party relaunched an offensive six months later, through a policy that was on all points faithful to what its homologues in the East European countries were doing.[99]

In the first of these two moments, Buton argues, the party adopted a strategy similar to that of Year II in the revolutionary calendar (1793–94), based on "linking all-out-war and mass mobilization to political radicalization. In 1944, over and above the classical tools for working the masses, the patriotic *épuration* represents the essential and novel means for this radicalization, by fusing the national enemy with the class enemy."[100] While mobilizing the masses against the class enemy, the épuration would also undermine the strength of the latter. On September 3, 1944, the main Communist newspaper endorsed a radical purge policy in the public sector that would "complete the dismantling of the state apparatus."[101] This aspect of their strategy was supported by the very general desire for a "total renewal in French public life."[102] At the same time, the policy of accusing the "trusts" (a code word for the bourgeoisie as a whole) of treason would justify massive confiscations and nationalizations of

[96] Footitt and Simmonds (1988), p. 194.
[97] Buton (1993), p. 185.
[98] Footitt and Simmonds (1988), p. 194.
[99] Buton (1993), p. 13.
[100] Ibid., p. 168.
[101] Ibid., p. 163.
[102] Footitt and Simmonds (1988), p. 242.

property.[103] This part of the strategy was supported by the widespread hostility toward the employers, caused by their perceived collaborationist attitude, that characterized the resistance in general and that led to many spontaneous actions in the fall of 1944.[104]

De Gaulle's government, and de Gaulle personally, were also to be targeted by the épuration, on the grounds that they were dismantling the very organizations that were their only source of legitimacy and legality.[105] Thus, "once it had lost legitimacy, the government could be overthrown by the Resistance, animated by the Communists, in the name of the antifascist struggle and the patriotic war, thanks to the organs of the [parallel] power and to the partially transformed or neutralized state apparatus."[106] At the same time as the Communists were using the purge apparatus to bring down their political enemies, they also manipulated it to swell their own ranks by issuing certificates of resistance in exchange for adhesion to the party.[107]

Buton notes that there is a lack of direct evidence for his position. Although he can cite a number of individual statements and acts that reflect a near-insurrectional attitude, there are virtually no contemporary and authoritative texts that affirm a revolutionary goal in the short term.[108] Instead, he attempts to reconstruct the "internal logic of Communist politics," which from 1934 onward no longer "proclaims the will to conquer power, but elaborates a strategy that will allow the party to seize it without saying so."[109] Whence the codeword of "the trusts" to mean "capitalism," and the need for Communist "submarines" or moles in the resistance movement, a "clandestinity within clandestinity."[110] It was imperative never to appear to be moved by the will to power but only by a desire to defend the achievements of the resistance.[111] In this perspective, it would actually have been surprising to find textual evidence for revolutionary intentions.

Intentions, however, presuppose an actor. Between August and November 1944, with Thorez in the Soviet Union, the leadership of the

[103] Buton (1993), pp. 152–53, 54.

[104] Kaspi (1995), pp. 363–64; Rochebrune and Hazera (1995), pp. 331–32.

[105] Buton (1993), pp. 169, 170–71.

[106] Ibid., p. 171.

[107] Abzac-Epezy (2003), p. 454. The same practice was observed in Italy (Woller 1996, p. 145).

[108] Buton (1993), p. 161.

[109] Ibid., p. 163.

[110] Ibid., p. 69.

[111] Ibid., p. 170.

French Communist Party may not have been sufficiently unified to form a coherent plan. Also, things were happening very fast. Under the turbulent conditions that obtained in France at the time, planning for revolution may have been like shooting at a moving target. As the lines of communication were poorly established, any kind of centralized orchestration would have met serious difficulties. Finally, the possibility of an Allied intervention in the case of a Communist bid for power must to some extent have acted as a deterrent.

These are arcane matters that must be left to the competence of historians. What seems uncontroversial is that many elements of a revolutionary plan were present and that the épuration had a central place among them. Whether they were actually brought together in a focused initiative remains more uncertain. If there was a plan, it did not move forward to realization. The links between the population and the resistance, between the resistance and the Communist Party, and between the population and the party were too weak to sustain a popular insurrection.[112] After the return of Thorez, whatever insurrectional plans there might have been were put to rest. Instead, Buton argues, the Communist Party now switched to its second strategy for seizing power, this time through legal and parliamentary means on the model of events in Eastern Europe, notably in Czechoslovakia. The central idea was to force the adoption of a constitution in which all powers were concentrated in a unicameral assembly that would be dominated by the Communists. To remove an alternative source of power in *les grands corps de l'Etat* (the higher echelons of the civil service), the Communist constitutional draft proposed a radical purge of the administration:

> Nobody can belong to one of *les grands corps de l'Etat* if he, his spouse, one of his ancestors, descendants, brothers and sisters, exercises or has exercised the functions of director, administrator, board member, manager or representative or had any other form of participation in the direction or in the technical

[112] For the weakness of the first link, see Buton (1993), pp. 78, 103. For the weakness of the second, see, for instance, Footitt and Simmonds (1988), pp. 119–39. For the weakness of the third, see the statement from the Civil Affairs Handbook for France that "the communist leaders, partly no doubt because of their equivocal policy in the first two years of the war, do not appear to have wielded the Paris working class into the outstandingly powerful instrument of resistance which the strength of the pre-war communist vote might have suggested" (cited in ibid., p. 166). Buton (1993), p. 165, refers to the desertion by Thorez shortly after the signature of the Hitler-Stalin pact as the "Achilles heel" of the Communist Party; that pact itself was of course a second and, one would think, a more important source of distrust.

or legal branch of firms, enterprises and establishments ... with a monopoly character.[113]

This proposed class-based purge recalls the measures taken by the Jacobins against the *ci-devants* during the French Revolution, characterized by the fact that "suspicion did not aim at those who were probably guilty of an accomplished action ... but at those who were possible authors of some potential crime."[114] Although this particular provision was not included in the document produced by the constituent assembly, the constitution did grant very extensive powers to parliament at the expense of other organs of state. Like the senators in 1814, however, the Communists overreached themselves. When the constitution was submitted for referendum on May 5, 1946, 53 percent of the electorate voted No. Buton argues that it was turned down mainly because of "opposition to Communism – a sign that the Communist victory in the Constitutional Commission harbored a perverse effect not suspected by the PCF."[115]

The attempt to harness transitional justice in the service of the revolution was taken much further in France than in Italy. In both countries, there was wide agreement in the resistance movements that purges, trials, and confiscations should produce a new set of political and economic leaders, "new men" and a "new society." Only in France, however, was there the will to use transitional justice as an instrument, perhaps a privileged instrument, for a change of the political regime. Although the details remain conjectural, it seems that the French Communist Party was close to trying but never to succeeding.

[113] Buton (1993), p. 214.
[114] Lefebvre (1989), p. 391.
[115] Buton (1993), p. 226.

References

Abzac-Epezy, C. (2003), "Epuration et rénovation de l'armée," in M. O. Baruch (ed.), *Une poignée de misérables: L'épuration de la société française après la Seconde Guerre mondiale,* Paris: Fayard, pp. 433–64.

Acuna, C. (in press), "Transitional justice in Argentina and Chile: A never ending story?" in Elster (ed.), *Retribution and Reparation.*

Adler, N. (2001), "In search of identity: The collapse of the Soviet Union and the recreation of Russia," in Brito, González-Enríquez, and Aguilar (eds.), *The Politics of Memory,* pp. 275–302.

Aguilar, P. (2001), "Justice, politics, and memory in the Spanish transition," in Brito, González-Enríquez, and Aguilar (eds.), *The Politics of Memory,* pp. 92–118.

Alivizatos, N. C., and Diamandouros, P. N. (1997), "Politics and the judiciary in the Greek transition to democracy," in McAdams (ed.), *Transitional Justice and the Rule of Law in New Democracies,* pp. 27–60.

Amouroux, H. (1999), *La grande histoire des Français après l'Occupation,* Paris: Robert Laffont.

Andenæs J. (1980), *Det Vanskelige Oppgjøret,* Oslo: Tanum-Norli.

Arendt, H. (1994), *Eichmann in Jerusalem,* New York: Penguin.

Argentine Commission on the Disappeared (1995), *Nunca Más,* New York: Farrar Straus Giroux.

Aron, R. (1969), *Histoire de l'Epuration: Des prisons clandestines aux tribunaux d'exception,* Paris: Fayard.

Aron, R. (1974), *Histoire de l'Epuration: Le monde des affaires,* Paris: Fayard.

Asmal, K., Asmal, L., and Roberts, R. (1997), *Reconciliation Through Truth,* New York: St. Martin's Press.

Authers, J., and Wolffe, R. (2002), *The Victim's Fortune,* New York: HarperCollins.

Bailer-Galanda, B. (1998), "Old or new right? Juridical denazification and right-wing extremism in Austria since 1945," in Larsen (ed.), *Modern Europe after Fascism,* pp. 413–35.

Bancaud, A. (2002), *Une exception ordinaire: La magistrature en France 1930–1950*, Paris: Gallimard.

Bancaud, A. (2003a), "La construction de l'appareil juridique," in M. O. Baruch (ed.), *Une poignée de misérables: L'épuration de la société française après la Seconde Guerre mondiale*, Paris: Fayard, pp. 61–97.

Bancaud, A. (2003b), "L'épuration des épurateurs: La magistrature," in M. O. Baruch (ed.), *Une poignée de misérables. L'épuration de la société française après la Seconde Guerre mondiale*, Paris: Fayard, pp. 172–203.

Bark, D., and Gress, D. (1993), *A History of West Germany*. Vol. 1: *From Shadow to Substance, 1945–1963*. Vol. 2: *Democracy and Its Discontents, 1963–1991*, Oxford: Blackwell.

Barros, R. (2002), *Constitutionalism and Dictatorship: Pinochet, the Junta, and the 1980 Constitution*, Cambridge: Cambridge University Press.

Baruch, M. O. (1997), *Servir l'Etat Français*, Paris: Fayard.

Baruch, M. O. (2003), "L'épuration du corps préfectoral," in M. O. Baruch (ed.), *Une poignée de misérables: L'épuration de la société française après la Seconde Guerre mondiale*, Paris: Fayard, pp. 139–71.

Bass, J. (2001), *Stay the Hand of Vengeance*, Cambridge, Mass.: Harvard University Press.

Bauer, Y. (1992), "Reflections concerning Holocaust history," in L. Greenspan and G. Nicholson (eds.), *Fackenheim: German Philosophy and Jewish Thought*, Toronto: University of Toronto Press, pp. 164–69.

Beevor, A. (2002), *The Fall of Berlin*, New York: Viking.

Benoit, W. (1995), *Accounts, Excuses, and Apologies*, Albany: State University of New York Press.

Bergère, M. (2003), "Les pouvoirs publics et la conduite des processus d'épuration," in M. O. Baruch (ed.), *Une poignée de misérables: L'épuration de la société française après la Seconde Guerre mondiale*, Paris: Fayard, pp. 116–35.

Berlière, J.-M. (2001), *Les policiers français sous l'Occupation*, Paris: Perrin.

Bernard, A. (1999), *Guerre et violence dans la Grèce antique*, Paris: Hachette.

Beschloss, M. (2002), *The Conquerors*, New York: Simon and Schuster.

Bloch-Lainé, F., and Gruson, C. (1996), *Hauts fonctionnaires sous l'Occupation*, Paris: Odile Jacob.

Boraine, A. (2000), *A Country Unmasked*, Oxford: Oxford University Press.

Bosworth, R. J. B. (2002), *Mussolini*, London: Edward Arnold.

Boughton, J. (2000), "The case against Harry Dexter White: Still not proven," International Monetary Fund Working Paper 00/149.

Bourdrel, P. (1988), *L'épuration sauvage*, Vol. 1, Paris: Perrin.

Bourdrel, P. (1991), *L'épuration sauvage*, Vol. 2, Paris: Perrin.

Bower, T. (1982), *A Pledge Betrayed*, New York: Doubleday.

Brandal, N. (2002), *Eit politisk strafferettsleg oppgjer: Det norske arbeiderpartiet og etterkrigsoppgjeret 1945–50*, Master's Thesis in History, University of Oslo.

Brito, A. B. de (1997), *Human Rights and Democratization in Latin America*, Oxford: Oxford University Press.

Brito, A. B. de (2001), "Truth, justice, memory, and democratization in the Southern Cone," in Brito, González-Enríquez, and Aguilar (eds.), *The Politics of Memory*, pp. 118–60.

Brito, A. B. de, González-Enríquez, C., and Aguilar, P., eds. (2001), *The Politics of Memory: Transitional Justice in Democratizing Societies,* Oxford: Oxford University Press.

Browning, C. (1992), *Ordinary Men,* New York: Harper.

Burrin, P. (1995), *France à l'heure allemande,* Paris: Seuil.

Burleigh, M. (2002), *The Third Reich,* London: Macmillan.

Buton, P. (1993), *Les lendemains qui déchantent: Le Parti Communiste Français à la Libération,* Paris: Presses de la Fondation Nationale des Sciences Politiques.

Calda, M. (1996), "The Roundtable talks in Czechoslovakia," in J. Elster (ed.), *The Round Table Talks and the Breakdown of Communism,* Chicago: University of Chicago Press, pp. 135–77.

Calhoon, R. M. (1991), "Loyalism and neutrality," in J. P. Greene and J. R. Pole (eds.), *The Blackwell Encyclopedia of the American Revolution,* Oxford: Blackwell, pp. 247–59.

Camerer, C. (2003), *Behavioral Game Theory,* Princeton, N.J.: Princeton University Press.

Cappelletto, F. (2003), "Public memories and personal stories: Recalling the Nazi-fascist massacres," Paper presented at the Workshop on Memory of War, Department of Political Science, MIT, January 2003.

Caro, R. (2002), *Master of the Senate: The Years of Lyndon Johnson,* New York: Vintage Books.

Carver, R. (1995), "Zimbabwe: Drawing a line through the past," in Roth-Arriaza (ed.), *Impunity and Human Rights in International Law,* pp. 252–66.

Cepl, V. (1991), "A note on the restitution of property in post-Communist Czechoslovakia," *Journal of Communist Studies* 7, 368–75.

Chateaubriand, R. (1814), "De l'état de France au mois de mars et au mois d'octobre 1814," in C. Smethurst (ed.), *Ecrits politiques [de Chateaubriand] 1814–1816,* Geneva: Droz, 2002, pp. 102–13.

Chateaubriand, R. (1816), "De la Monarchie selon la Charte," in C. Smethurst (ed.), *Ecrits politiques [de Chateaubriand] 1814–1816,* Geneva: Droz, 2002, pp. 397–537.

Chauvy, G. (2003), *Les acquittés de Vichy,* Paris: Perrin.

Cohen, A. (1993), *Persécutions et sauvetages: Juifs et Français sous l'Occupation et sous Vichy,* Paris: Editions du Cerf.

Cohen, D. (1999), "Beyond Nuremberg: Individual responsibility for war crimes," in C. Hesse and R. Post (eds.), *Human Rights in Political Transitions,* New York: Zenith Books, pp. 53–92.

Cohen, D. (2001), "The rhetoric of justice and reconciliation strategies in the restoration of Athenian democracy in 403 B.C.," *Archives Européennes de Sociologie* 42, 335–56.

Cohen, D. (in press), "Transitional Justice in Divided Germany after 1945," in Elster (ed.), *Retribution and Reparation.*

Cohen, S. (2001), *States of Denial,* London: Polity Press.

Coles, H., and Weinberg, A. (1992), *Civil Affairs: Soldiers Become Governors,* Washington D.C.: Center of Military History, U.S. Army.

Conway, M. (2000), "Justice in postwar Belgium," in Deák, Gross, and Judt (eds.), *The Politics of Retribution in Europe,* pp. 133–56.

Courtois, S., et al. (1997), *Le livre noir du Communisme,* Paris: Robert Laffont.
Cover, R. (1975), *Justice Accused,* New Haven, Conn.: Yale University Press.
Cowen, T. (1997), "Discounting and restitution," *Philosophy and Public Affairs* 26, 168–85.
Cowen, T. (in press), "How far back should we go?," in Elster (ed.), *Retribution and Reparation.*
Craig, G. (1981), *Germany 1866–1945,* Oxford: Oxford University Press.
Currie, D. (1994), *The Constitution of the Federal Republic of Germany,* Chicago: University of Chicago Press.
Czech CC Decision (1995), "Judgment of the Constitutional Court of the Czech Republic of March 8, 1995," *Parker School Journal of East European Law* 2, 725–59.
Dahl, H. F. (in press), "The Purges in Denmark and Norway after World War II," in Elster (ed.), *Retribution and Reparation.*
Davidowitz, L. (1986), *The War Against the Jews,* New York: Bantam Books.
Davis, K. (1971), *Discretionary Justice,* Urbana, Ill.: University of Illinois Press.
Deák, I. (in press), "Political justice in Austria and Hungary after World War II," in Elster (ed.), *Retribution and Reparation.*
Deák, I., Gross, J., and Judt, T., eds. (2000), *The Politics of Retribution in Europe,* Princeton, N.J.: Princeton University Press.
Delporte, C. (1999), *Les journalistes en France 1880–1950,* Paris: Seuil.
Descartes, R. (1985), "Passions of the soul," in *The Philosophical Writings of Descartes,* vol. 1, Cambridge: Cambridge University Press.
Destrem, P., and Destrem, D. (2003), *A la botte: La Bourse sous l'Occupation,* Lausanne: L'Age d'Homme.
Diesbach, G. de (1998), *Histoire de l'émigration,* Paris: Perrin.
Dietrich, J. (2002), *The Morgenthau Plan: Soviet Influence on American Postwar Policy,* New York: Algora.
Domenico, R. P. (1991), *Italian Fascists on Trial,* Chapel Hill: University of North Carolina Press.
Doublet, P. (1945), *La collaboration,* Paris: Librairie Générale de Droit et de Jurisprudence.
Dover, K. J. (1968), *Lysias and the Corpus Lysiacum,* Berkeley: University of California Press.
Dower, J. (1999), *Embracing Defeat,* New York: Norton.
Dreyfus, J-M. (2003), *Pillages sur ordonnance,* Paris: Fayard.
Dyzenhaus, D. (1998), *Judging the Judges, Judging Ourselves,* Oxford: Hart.
Eizenstat, S. (2003), *Imperfect Justice,* New York: Public Affairs.
Ekman, P. (1992), "An argument for basic emotions," *Cognition and Emotion* 6, 169–200.
Ellwood, D. (1985), *The Liberation of Italy,* New York: Holmes and Meier.
Elster, J. (1983), *Sour Grapes,* Cambridge: Cambridge University Press.
Elster, J. (1989), *The Cement of Society,* Cambridge: Cambridge University Press.
Elster, J. (1992a), *Local Justice,* New York: Russell Sage.
Elster, J. (1992b), "On doing what one can," *East European Constitutional Review* 1, no. 2, 15–17.

Elster, J. (1993a), "Rebuilding the boat in the open sea: Constitution-making in Eastern Europe," *Public Administration* 71, 169–217.

Elster, J. (1993b), *Political Psychology*, Cambridge: Cambridge University Press.

Elster, J. (1995), "Transition, constitution-making and separation in Czechoslovakia," *Archives Européennes de Sociologie* 36, 105–34.

Elster, J. (1999), *Alchemies of the Mind*, Cambridge: Cambridge University Press.

Elster, J. (2000), *Ulysses Unbound*, Cambridge: Cambridge University Press.

Elster, J., ed. (1998), *Deliberative Democracy*, Cambridge: Cambridge University Press.

Elster, J., ed. (in press), *Retribution and Reparation in the Transition to Democracy*, Cambridge: Cambridge University Press.

Engelmann, F. (1982), "How Austria has coped with two dictatorial legacies," in Herz (ed.), *From Dictatorship to Democracy*, pp. 135–60.

Eymery, A. (1815), *Dictionnaire des girouettes, ou nos contemporains peints d'après eux-mêmes*, Paris.

Farge, Y. (1946), *Rebelles, soldats et citoyens*, Paris: Grasset.

Farmer, S. (1999), *Martyred Village: Commemorating the 1944 Massacre at Oradour-sur-Glane*, Berkeley and Los Angeles: University of California Press.

Fehr, E., and Fischbacher, U. (2003), "Third Party Norm Enforcement," Working Paper No. 106, Institute for Empirical Research in Economics, University of Zürich.

Ferencz, B. (2002), *Less Than Slaves* (reprint of the original 1979 edition), Bloomington: University of Indiana Press.

Fitzpatrick, S., and Cellately, R., eds. (1997), *Accusatory Practices: Denunciation in Modern European History*, Chicago: University of Chicago Press.

Fleischer, C. A. (1972), *Makt og Rett*, Oslo: Gyldendal.

Fletcher, G. (1978), *Rethinking Criminal Law*, Boston: Little, Brown.

Footitt, H., and Simmonds, J. (1988), *France 1943–1945*, New York: Holmes and Meier.

Forster, D. (2001), '*Wiedergutmachung*' *in Österreich und der BRD im Vergleich*, Innsbruck: Studienverlag.

Franklin, J. (2001), *The Science of Conjecture: Evidence and Probability Before Pascal*, Baltimore: Johns Hopkins University Press.

Frei, N. (2002), *Adenauer's Germany and the Nazi Past*, New York: Columbia University Press.

French, D. (1998), "Great Britain and the German armistice," in M. Boemeke, G. Feldman, and E. Glaser (eds.), *The Treaty of Versailles*, Cambridge: Cambridge University Press, pp. 69–86.

Friedrich, J. (1998), *Freispruch für die Nazi-Justiz*, Berlin: Ullstein.

Frijda, N. (1994), "The Lex Talionis: On vengeance," in S. M. Goozen, N. E. van de Poll, and J. A. Sergeant (eds.), *Emotions: Essays on Emotion Theory*, Hillsdale, N.J.: Lawrence Erlbaum, pp. 263–90.

Fritze, L. (1998), *Täter mit guten Gewissen: Über menschliches Versagen im diktatorischen Sozialismus*, Cologne: Böhlau Verlag.

Gabory, A. (1989), *Les Guerres de Vendée*, Paris: Robert Laffont.

Gain, A. (1928), *La restauration et les biens des émigrés*, Nancy: Société d'Impressions Typographiques.

Gerbod, P., et al. (1977), *Les épurations administratives: XIXe et XXe Siècles*, Geneva: Droz.
Gillespie, C. (1991), *Negotiating Democracy: Politicians and Generals in Uruguay*, Cambridge: Cambridge University Press.
Ginsborg, P. (1990), *A History of Modern Italy*, Harmondsworth: Penguin.
Giordano, R. (2000), *Die zweite Schuld*, Cologne: Kiepenhauer & Witsch.
Godechot, J. (1998), *Les institutions de la France sous la Révolution et l'Empire*, Paris: Presses Universitaires de France.
Golay, J. (1958), *The Founding of the Federal Republic of Germany*, Chicago: University of Chicago Press.
Goldhagen, D. (1996), *Hitler's Willing Executioners*, New York: Knopf.
Gorce, P. de la (1926), *Louis XVIII*, Paris: Plon.
Gower, J. (1999), *Embracing Defeat: Japan in the Wake of World War II*, New York: Norton.
Goyard, C. (1977), "La notion d'épuration administrative," in Gerbod et al., *Les épurations administratives*, pp. 1–48.
Greene, J. (2003), *Justice at Dachau*, New York: Broadway Books.
Guennifey, P. (1993), *Le nombre et la raison*, Paris: Editions de l'EHESS.
Haile, B. (2000), *Accountability for Crimes of the Past and the Challenges of Criminal Prosecution: The Case of Ethiopia*, Leuven: Leuven University Press.
Halmai, G., and Scheppele, K. (1997), "Living well is the best revenge: The Hungarian approach to judging the past," in McAdams (ed.), *Transitional Justice and the Rule of Law in New Democracies*, pp. 155–84.
Hamoumou, M. (1993), *Et ils sont devenus harkis*, Paris: Fayard.
Hanich, E. (1998), "The denazification in Salzburg – a region with strong German-nationalist traditions," in Larsen (ed.), *Modern Europe after Fascism*, pp. 378–95.
Hann, C. (2004), "Property relations, historical justice and contemporary survival in the postsocialist countryside," in Max Planck Institute for Social Anthropology, *Report 2002–2003*, Halle/Saale, pp. 207–23.
Hann, C., ed. (2003), *The Postsocialist Agrarian Question*, Münster: Lit Verlag.
Hansen, M. H. (1991), *The Athenian Democracy in the Age of Demosthenes*, Oxford: Blackwell.
Harries, M., and Harries, S. (1987), *Sheathing the Sword*, New York: Macmillan.
Hayner, P. (2001), *Unspeakable Truths*, New York: Routledge.
Heller, M., and Serkin, C. (1999), "Revaluing restitution: From the Talmud to Postsocialism," *Michigan Law Review* 97, 1385–1412.
Henke, K.-D., and Woller, H., eds. (1991), *Politische Säuberung in Europa*, Munich: Deutscher Taschenbuch Verlag.
Herf, J. (1997), *Divided Memory: The Nazi Past in the Two Germanies*, Cambridge, Mass.: Harvard University Press.
Herz, J. (1982a), "Denazification and related policies," in Herz (ed.), *From Dictatorship to Democracy*, pp. 15–38.
Herz, J., ed. (1982b), *From Dictatorship to Democracy*, Westport, Conn.: Greenwood Press.
Heuer, F., and Reisberg, D. (1992), "Emotion, arousal, and memory for detail," in S.Å. Christianson (ed.), *The Handbook of Emotion and Memory*, Hillsdale, N.J.: Lawrence Erlbaum, pp. 151–180.

Hilberg, R. (1985), *The Destruction of the European Jews,* New York: Holmes and Meier.
Hilberg, R. (1992), *Perpetrators Victims Bystanders: Jewish Catastrophe, 1933–1945,* New York: HarperCollins.
Hirschfeld, G. (1988), *Nazi Rule and Dutch Collaboration,* Oxford: Berg.
Hirschman, A. O. (1972), *Exit, Voice and Loyalty,* Cambridge, Mass.: Harvard University Press.
Hjeltnes, G. (1990), *Avisoppgjøret etter 1945,* Oslo: Aschehoug.
Holmes, S. (1988), "Gag rules or the politics of omission," in J. Elster and R. Slagstad (eds.), *Constitutionalism and Democracy,* Cambridge: Cambridge University Press, pp. 19–58.
Horne, J., and Kramer, A (2001), *German Atrocities 1914,* New Haven, Conn.: Yale University Press.
Houssaye, H. (1906), *1815: La seconde abdication – la terreur blanche,* Paris: Perrin.
Human Rights Watch (1993), "The trial of responsibilities: The García Meza Tejada Trial," n.p.: Human Rights Watch.
Huntington, S. (1991), *The Third Wave,* Norman: University of Oklahoma Press.
Hurnard, N. (1969), *The king's pardon for homicide before A.D. 1307,* Oxford: Oxford University Press.
Huyse, L. (in press), "Belgian and Dutch War Trials after WW II Compared," in Elster (ed.), *Reparation and Retribution.*
Huyse, L., and Dhondt, S. (1993), *La répression des collaborations,* Brussels: CRISP.
Israël, L. (2003), "La défense accusée: L'épuration professionnelle des avocats," in M. O. Baruch (ed.), *Une poignée de misérables: L'épuration de la société française après la Seconde Guerre mondiale,* Paris: Fayard, pp. 204–28.
Justis-og Politidepartementet (1962), *Om Landssvikoppgjøret,* Gjøvik: Mariendals Boktrykkeri.
Kagan, D. (1981), *The Peace of Nicias and the Sicilian Expedition,* Ithaca, N.Y.: Cornell University Press.
Kagan, D. (1987), *The Fall of the Athenian Empire,* Ithaca, N.Y.: Cornell University Press.
Kahneman, D. (1999), "Objective happiness," in D. Kahneman, E. Diener, and N. Schwartz (eds.), *Well-Being: The Foundations of Hedonic Psychology,* New York: Russell Sage, pp. 3–25.
Kahneman, D., and Tversky, A. (1979), "Prospect theory," *Econometrica* 47, 63–91.
Karsai, L. (2000), "The People's Courts and revolutionary justice in Hungary, 1945–46," in Deák, Gross, and Judt (eds.), *The Politics of Retribution in Europe,* pp. 233–51.
Kaspi, A. (1995), *La Libération de la France,* Paris: Perrin.
Keeble, N. H. (2002), *The Restoration: England in the 1660s,* Oxford: Blackwell.
Kershaw, I. (1999), *Hitler 1889–1936,* New York: Norton.
Keynes, J. M. (1971), *The Economic Consequences of Peace,* in *The Collected Writings of John Maynard Keynes,* vol. 2, London: Macmillan.
Keyssar, A. (2000), *The Right to Vote,* New York: Basic Books.
Kirchheimer, O. (1961), *Political Justice,* Princeton, N.J.: Princeton University Press.
Knox, C., and Monaghan, R. (2002), *Informal Justice in Divided Societies,* London: Palgrave Macmillan.

Koehler, J. (1999), *Stasi: The Untold Story of the East German Secret Police,* Boulder, Colo.: Westview Press.

Kolakowski, L. (1978), *Main Currents of Marxism,* Oxford: Oxford University Press.

Kolarova, R., and Dimitrov, D. (1996), "The Round Table Talks in Bulgaria," in J. Elster (ed.), *The Round Table Talks and the Breakdown of Communism,* Chicago: University of Chicago Press, pp. 178–212.

Kozlov, V. (1997), "Denunciation and its function in Soviet governance," in S. Fitzpatrick and R. Cellately (eds.), *Accusatory Practices,* pp. 121–52.

Kriegel, A. (1991), *Ce que j'ai cru comprendre,* Paris: Laffont.

Kritz, N. J., ed. (1995), *Transitional Justice,* vols. 1–3, Washington, D.C.: United States Institute of Peace Press.

Kubovy, M. (1999), "On the pleasures of the mind," in D. Kahneman, E. Diener, and N. Schwartz (eds.), *Well-Being: The Foundations of Hedonic Psychology,* New York: Russell Sage, pp. 134–54.

Kuk, L. (2001), *La Pologne du post-communisme à l'anti-communisme,* Paris: l'Harmattan.

Lacouture, J. (1977), *Léon Blum,* Paris: Seuil.

Lacouture, J. (1980), *François Mauriac,* Paris: Seuil.

Lacouture, J. (1985), *De Gaulle,* Paris: Seuil.

Lagrou, P. (2000), *The Legacy of Nazi Occupation,* Cambridge: Cambridge University Press.

Larsen, S. U., ed. (1998), *Modern Europe after Fascism,* New York: Columbia University Press.

Lefebvre, G. (1924), *Les paysans du Nord pendant la Révolution Française,* Paris: Armand Colin.

Lefebvre, G. (1989), *La Révolution Française,* Paris: Presses Universitaires de France.

Le Grand, J. (1992), *Equity and Justice,* London: Routledge.

Le Monde (2003), "Des milliers de Roumains demandent à récupérer leurs biens confisqués par le Parti communiste," July 24, p. 4.

Le procès de Maurice Papon (1998), Compte Rendu Sténographique, Paris: Albin Michel.

Le procès Laval (1946), Paris: Albin Michel.

Lesourd, C. (2003), "L'épuration des médecins," in M. O. Baruch (ed.), *Une poignée de misérables: L'épuration de la société française après la Seconde Guerre mondiale,* Paris: Fayard, pp. 336–67.

Lewy, G. (2000), *The Nazi Persecution of the Gypsies,* Oxford: Oxford University Press.

Lindgren, A. (1985), *The Brothers Lionheart,* New York: Penguin Books.

Lindsay-Hartz, J., de Rivera, J., and Mascolo, M. F. (1995), "Differentiating guilt and shame and their effects on motivation," in J. P. Tangney and K. W. Fischer (eds.), *Self-Conscious Emotions,* New York: The Guilford Press, pp. 274–300.

Linz, J., and Stepan, A. (1996), *Problems of Democratic Transition and Consolidation,* Baltimore: Johns Hopkins University Press.

Loening, T. (1987), *The Reconciliation Agreement of 403/402 B.C. in Athens* (Hermes Einzelschriften, Heft 53), Stuttgart: Franz Steiner Verlag.

Loewenstein, G. (1996), "Out of control: Visceral influences on behavior," *Organizational Behavior and Human Decision Processes* 65, 272–92.
Loraux, N. (1997), *La cité divisée: L'oubli dans la mémoire d'Athènes,* Paris: Payot.
Lottman, H. (1986), *L'épuration,* Paris: Fayard.
Lüdtke, A. (1993), "'Coming to terms with the past': Illusions of remembering, ways of forgetting Nazism in West Germany," *Journal of Modern History* 65, 542–72.
Maas, D. (1994), "The Massachusetts Loyalists and the problem of amnesty, 1775–1790," in R. M. Calhoon, T. M. Barns, and A. Rawlyk (eds.), *Loyalists and Community in North America,* Westport, Conn.: Greenwood Press, pp. 65–74.
MacDowell, D. (1975), "Law-making at Athens in the Fourth Century B.C.," *Journal of Hellenic Studies* 95, 62–74.
MacDowell, D. (1978), *The Law in Classical Athens,* Ithaca, N.Y.: Cornell University Press.
Madelin, L. (1945), *Fouché,* Paris: Plon.
Maier, C. (1997), *Dissolution: The Crisis of Communism and the End of East Germany,* Princeton, N.J.: Princeton University Press.
Malamud-Goti, J. (1996), *Game Without End,* Norman: University of Oklahoma Press.
Mansel, P. (1999), *Louis XVIII,* Gloucestershire: Sutton.
Marrus, M. (1997), *The Nuremberg War Crimes Trial, 1945–46: A Documentary History,* Boston: Bedford.
Marsh, D. (1992), *The Bundesbank,* London: Mandarin.
Marx, K. (1852), *The Eighteenth Brumaire of Louis Napoleon,* in Karl Marx and Friedrich Engels, *Collected Works,* vol. 11, London: Lawrence and Wishart.
Marxen, K., and Werle, G. (1999), *Die strafrechtliche Aufarbeitung von DDR-Unrecht: Eine Bilanz,* Berlin: Gruyter.
Mason, H. L. (1952), *The Purge of Dutch Quislings,* The Hague: Martinus Nijhoff.
Mayorga, R. A. (1997), "Democracy dignified and an end to impunity: Bolivia's military dictatorship on trial," in McAdams (ed.), *Transitional Justice and the Rule of Law in New Democracies,* pp. 61–92.
McAdams, A. J. (2001), *Judging the Past in Unified Germany,* Cambridge: Cambridge University Press.
McAdams, A. J., ed. (1997), *Transitional Justice and the Rule of Law in New Democracies,* Notre Dame, Ind.: University of Notre Dame Press.
McDonald, F. (1982), *Alexander Hamilton,* New York: Norton.
McLemee, S. (2003), "Questioning the past," *Chronicle of Higher Education,* July 18, p. A 14.
McNally, R. (2003), *Remembering Trauma,* Cambridge, Mass.: Harvard University Press.
Méliani, A. (1993), *Le drame des harkis,* Paris: Perrin.
Merkl, P. (1963), *The Origin of the West German Republic,* Oxford: Oxford University Press.
Milgram, S. (1974), *Obedience to Authority.* New York: HarperCollins.
Mill, J. S. (1987), *Principles of Political Economy,* Fairfield, N.J.: Augustus Kelley.

Minear, R. (2001), *Victors' Justice*, Ann Arbor, Mich.: Center for Japanese Studies (reprint of 1971 edition with a new Preface).

Mission d'étude sur la spoliation des Juifs de France (2000), Paris: La Documentation Française.

Mommsen, H. (1984), *Max Weber and German Politics*, Chicago: University of Chicago Press.

Moore, C. (1984), *The Loyalists: Revolution, Exile, Settlement*, Toronto: McLelland & Stewart.

Moore, J. M. (1975), *Aristotle and Xenophon on Democracy and Oligarchy*, Berkeley and Los Angeles: University of California Press.

Müller, I. (1991), *Hitler's Justice*, Cambridge, Mass.: Harvard University Press.

Nagel, T. (1991), *Equality and Partiality*, Oxford: Oxford University Press.

Nalepa, M. (2003a), "Punish all Perpetrators or Protect the Innocent? Designing Institutions of Transitional Justice," unpublished manuscript, Department of Political Science, Columbia University.

Nalepa, M. (2003b), "Suffer a Scratch to Avoid a Blow? When Post-Communists Hurt Themselves: A Model of Transitional Justice Legislation," unpublished manuscript, Department of Political Science, Columbia University.

Nettement, A. (1860), *Histoire de la Restauration*, vols. 1–8, Paris: Jacques Lecoffre.

Nino, C. (1996), *Radical Evil on Trial*, New Haven, Conn.: Yale University Press.

Noguères, L. (1965), *La haute cour à la Libération*, Paris: Editions de Minuit.

NOU (Norges Offentlige Utredninger) (1997), *Inndragning av Jødisk Eiendom i Norge under den 2. Verdenskrig*, Oslo: NOU.

Nouhaud, M. (1982), *L'utilisation de l'histoire par les orateurs attiques*, Paris: Les Belles Lettres.

Novick, P. (1968), *The Resistance Versus Vichy*, London: Chatto and Windus.

Novick, P. (1999), *The Holocaust in American Life*, Boston: Houghton Mifflin.

Ober, J. (1989), *Mass and Elite in Democratic Athens*, Princeton, N.J.: Princeton University Press.

Offe, C. (1996), *Varieties of Transition*, Oxford: Polity Press.

Offe, C., and Poppe, U. (in press), "Transitional Justice in the German Democratic Republic and in Unified Germany," in Elster (ed.), *Retribution and Reparation*.

Orentlicher, D. (1995), "Settling accounts: The duty to prosecute human rights violations of a prior regime," in Kritz (ed.), *Transitional Justice*, vol. 1, pp. 375–416.

Orion (no first name given) (1948), *Nouveau dictionnaire des girouettes*, Paris: Editions le Régent.

Osiatynski, W. (1991), "Revolutions in Eastern Europe," *University of Chicago Law Review* 58, 823–57.

Osiatynski, W. (1996), "The Roundtable talks in Poland," in J. Elster (ed.), *The Round Table Talks and the Breakdown of Communism*, Chicago: University of Chicago Press, pp. 21–68.

Osiel, M. (1995), "Dialogue with dictators: Judicial resistance in Argentina and Brazil," *Law and Social Inquiry* 20, 481–560.

Osiel, M. (1999), *Obeying Orders: Atrocity, Military Discipline & the Law of War*, Brunswick, N.J.: Transaction Publishers.

Ostwald, M. (1986), *From Popular Sovereignty to the Sovereignty of Law,* Berkeley and Los Angeles: University of California Press.
Overy, R. (2001), *Interrogations: The Nazi Elite in Allied Hands, 1945,* New York: Viking.
Paczolay, P. (1995), "Judicial review of compensation law in Hungary," in Kritz (ed.), *Transitional Justice,* vol. 2, pp. 652–53.
Parfit, D. (1984), *Reasons and Persons,* Oxford: Oxford University Press.
Paschis, G., and Papadimitriou, Z. (1998), "Collaboration without nemesis: On the restoration of political continuity in Greece after World War II," in Larsen (ed.), *Modern Europe after Fascism,* pp. 1719–51.
Pataki, J. (1995), "Dealing with Hungarian Communists' Crimes," in Kritz (ed.), *Transitional Justice,* vol. 2, pp. 647–52.
Paxton, R. (1997), *La France de Vichy,* Paris: Seuil.
Payne, S. (1993), *Spain's First Democracy,* Madison: University of Wisconsin Press.
Pervillé, G. (2002), *Pour une histoire de la guerre d'Algérie,* Paris: Picard.
Pick, H. (2000), *Guilty Victim: Austria from the Holocaust to Haider,* London: Tauris.
Pinto, A. C. (1998), "Dealing with the legacy of authoritarianism: Political purges and radical rights movements in Portugal's transition to democracy, 1974–1980s," in Larsen (ed.), *Modern Europe after Fascism,* pp. 1679–1718.
Pinto, A. C. (2001), "Settling accounts with the past in a troubled transition to democracy: The Portuguese case," in Brito, González-Enríquez, and Aguilar (eds.), *The Politics of Memory,* pp. 65–91.
Pogany, I. (1997), *Righting Wrongs in Eastern Europe,* Manchester: University Press.
Ponteil, F. (1966), *Les institutions de la France de 1814 à 1870,* Paris: Presses Universitaires de France.
Pross, C. (1998), *Paying for the Past,* Baltimore: Johns Hopkins University Press.
Prost, A., Skoutelsky, R., and Etienne, S. (2000), *Aryanisation économique et restitution,* Paris: La Documentation Française.
Przeworski, A. (1988), "Democracy as a contingent outcome of conflict," in J. Elster and R. Slagstad (eds.), *Constitutionalism and Democracy,* Cambridge: Cambridge University Press, pp. 59–80.
Psomiades, H. (1982), "Greece: From the colonel's rule to democracy," in Herz, *From Dictatorship to Democracy,* pp. 251–73.
Quint, P. (1997), *The Imperfect Union,* Princeton, N.J.: Princeton University Press.
Raiffa, H. (1982), *The Art and Science of Negotiation,* Cambridge, Mass.: Harvard University Press.
Rees, D. (1973), *Harry Dexter White: A Study in Paradox,* New York: Coward, Mann, and Geoghegan.
Remias, P. (1999), "Crime time limit almost up," *The Prague Post,* October 27.
Resnick, D. (1966), *The White Terror and the Political Reaction after Waterloo,* Cambridge, Mass.: Harvard University Press.
Rigg, B. (2002), *Hitler's Jewish Soldiers,* Lawrence, Kans.: University of Kansas Press.
Rochebrune, R. de and Hazera, J.-C. (1995), *Les patrons sous l'Occupation,* Paris: Editions Odile Jacob.

Rochebrune, R. de and Hazera, J.-C. (1997), *Les patrons sous l'Occupation*, vol. 2, Paris: Editions Odile Jacob.

Rominj, P. (2000), "'Restoration of confidence': The purge of local governments in the Netherlands as a problem of postwar reconstruction," in Deák, Gross, and Judt (eds.), *The Politics of Retribution in Europe*, pp. 173–93.

Rominj, P., and Hirschfeld, G. (1991), "Die Ahndung der Kollaboration in den Niederlanden," in Henke and Woller (eds.), *Politische Säuberung in Europa*, pp. 281–310.

Rosanvallon, P. (1994), *La monarchie impossible: Les Chartes de 1814 et de 1830*, Paris: Fayard.

Rosenberg, T. (1996), "Recovering from Apartheid," *The New Yorker*, Nov. 18, pp. 86–95.

Roth-Arriaza, N., ed. (1995), *Impunity and Human Rights in International Law and Practice*, Oxford: Oxford University Press.

Rottleuthner, H. (1994), "Deutsche Vergangenheiten verglichen," in *Die Normalität des Verbrechen: Festschrift für Wolfgang Scheffler zum 65. Geburtstag, herausgegeben von Helge Grabitz, Klaus Bäustlein, Johannes Tuchel*. Berlin: Edition Hentrich, pp. 480–502.

Rouquet, F. (1993), *L'épuration dans l'administration française*, Paris: CNRS.

Roussel, E. (2002), *De Gaulle*, Paris: Gallimard.

Rousso, H. (1990), *Le syndrome de Vichy*, Paris: Seuil.

Rousso, H. (2001), *Vichy: L'événement, la mémoire, l'histoire*, Paris: Gallimard.

Royer, J.-P. (2001), *Histoire de la justice en France*, Paris: Presses Universitaires de France.

Ruzé, F. (1997), *Délibération et pouvoir dans la cité grecque de Nestor à Socrate*. Paris: Publications de la Sorbonne.

Sa'adah, A. (1998), *Germany's Second Chance*, Cambridge, Mass.: Harvard University Press.

Sagi, N. (1986), *German Reparations*, New York: St. Martin's Press.

Sapiro, G. (2003), "L'épuration du monde des lettres," in M. O. Baruch (ed.), *Une poignée de misérables: L'épuration de la société française après la Seconde Guerre mondiale*, Paris: Fayard, pp. 243–85.

Sauvigny, G. de (1999), *La Restauration*, Paris: Flammarion.

Schachter, D. (1996), *Searching for Memory*, New York: Basic Books.

Schelling, T. C. (1960), *The Strategy of Conflict*, Cambridge, Mass.: Harvard University Press.

Schiemann, J. (1998), "The Constitutional Court: Myopic Bargains and Democratic Institutions," unpublished manuscript, Department of Political Science, Columbia University.

Schwartz, H. (2000), *Constitutional Justice in Central and Eastern Europe*, Chicago: University of Chicago Press.

Schwartz, T. (1991), *America's Germany: John McCloy and the Federal Republic of Germany*, Cambridge, Mass.: Harvard University Press.

Sen, A. (1977), "Rational fools," *Philosophy and Public Affairs* 6, 317–44.

Sheppard, B. (2000), *A War of Nerves: Soldiers and Psychiatrists, 1914–1994*, London: Cape.

Simonin, A. (2003), "L'indignité nationale: Un châtiment républicain," in M. O. Baruch (ed.), *Une poignée de misérables: L'épuration de la société française après la Seconde Guerre mondiale,* Paris: Fayard, pp. 37–60.

Singer, C. (1997), *L'Université libérée, l'Université épurée,* Paris: Les Belles Lettres.

Skidelsky, R. (2001), *John Maynard Keynes: Fighting for Britain, 1937–1946,* London: Macmillan.

Slovic, P. (2000), *The Perception of Risk,* Sterling, Va.: Earthscan Publications.

Smith, K. (1995a), "Destalinization in the former Soviet Union," in Roth-Arriaza (ed.), *Impunity and Human Rights,* pp. 113–28.

Smith, K. (1995b), "Decommunization after the 'Velvet Revolution' in East Central Europe," in Roth-Arriaza (ed.), *Impunity and Human Rights,* pp. 82–98.

Snyder, C., Higgins, R., and Stucky, R. (1983), *Excuses,* New York: Wiley.

Søbye, E. (2003), *Kathe, Alltid Vært i Norge,* Oslo: Oktober.

Sólyom, L. (2000), "Introduction" to L. Sólyom and G. Brunner, *Constitutional Judiciary in a New Democracy,* pp. 1–64.

Sólyom, L., and Brunner, G. (2000), *Constitutional Judiciary in a New Democracy,* Ann Arbor: University of Michigan Press.

Spitz, R., and Chaskalson, M. (2000), *The Politics of Transition: A Hidden History of South Africa's Negotiated Settlement,* Oxford: Hart.

Stern, K., and Schmidt-Bleibtreu, B. (1990), *Einigungsvertrag und Wahlvertrag,* Munich: Beck.

Steytler, N. (1995), "Constitution-making: In search of a democratic South Africa," in M. Bennun and M. Newitt (eds.), *Negotiating Justice: A New Constitution for South Africa,* Exeter: University of Exeter Press, pp. 62–80.

Stiefel, D. (1991), "Der Process der Entnazifizierung in Österreich," in Henke and Woller (eds.), *Politische Säuberung in Europa,* pp. 108–47.

Stiefel, D. (1998), "Has the course of denazification been determined by 'economic necessities'?" in Larsen (ed.), *Modern Europe after Fascism,* pp. 396–412.

Sutter, D. (1995), "Settling old scores," *Journal of Conflict Resolution* 39, 110–28.

Sveri, K. (1982), "Landsviksoppgjørets merkeligste rettssak," in A. Bratholm, N. Christie, and T. Opsahl (eds.), *Lov og Frihet,* Oslo: Universitetsforlaget, pp. 345–55.

Talleyrand, C.-M. de (1967), *Mémoires,* vols. 1–5, Paris: Jean Bonnot.

Tamm, D. (1984), *Retsopgøret efter Besættelsen,* Copenhagen: Jurist-og Økonomforbundets Forlag.

Taylor, R. (1981), *A Trial of Generals,* South Bend, Ind.: Icarus Press.

Taylor, T. (1992), *The Anatomy of the Nuremberg Trials,* New York: Knopf.

Thirsk, J. (1954), "The Restoration land settlement," *Journal of Modern History* 26, 315–28.

Tiedemann, A. E. (1982), "Japan sheds dictatorship," in Herz, *From Dictatorship to Democracy,* pp. 179–212.

Tiedemann, J. S. (1994), "Patriots, Loyalists, and Conflict Resolution in New York, 1783–1787," in R. M. Calhoon, T. M. Barns, and A. Rawlyk (eds.), *Loyalists and Community in North America,* Westport, Conn.: Greenwood Press, pp. 75–88.

Timm, A. (1997), *Jewish Claims Against East Germany,* Budapest: Central European University Press.

Tocqueville, A. de (1968), *Democracy in America,* New York: Anchor Books.

Todd, E. (1996), *Albert Camus,* Paris: Gallimard.

Tökés, R. (1996), *Hungary's Negotiated Revolution,* Cambridge: Cambridge University Press.

Topol, J. (2001), "We need a beast to fight against," *Transition Online,* October 25.

TRC (1999), *Truth and Reconciliation Commission Report,* vols. 1–5, London: Macmillan.

Tucker, A. (in press), "Paranoids may be persecuted: Post-totalitarian transitional justice," in Elster (ed.), *Retribution and Reparation.*

Tulard, J. (1977), "Les épurations administratives en France de 1800 à 1830," in Gerbod et al., *Les épurations administratives,* pp. 49–62.

Tyne, C. van (2001), *The Loyalists in the American Revolution,* Safety Harbor, Fla.: Simon Publications (reprint of the original 1902 edition).

Ulc, O. (n.d.), "Dislodged Communists and dissidents in former Czechoslovakia," http://people2.clarityconnect.com/webpages6/ota/art_eng/E-72.html.

Urban, J. (1986), *Moscow and the Italian Communist Party,* London: Tauris.

U.S. Senate (1967), *The Morgenthau Diaries (Germany),* Washington, D.C.: U.S. Government Printing Office.

Vidalenc, J. (1977), "Note sur les épurations de 1814 et de 1815," in Gerbod et al., *Les épurations administratives,* pp. 64–68.

Virgili, F. (2000), *La France 'virile': Les femmes tondues à la libération,* Paris: Payot.

Vogt, T. H. (2000), *Denazification in Soviet-Occupied Germany,* Cambridge, Mass.: Harvard University Press.

Vollnhals, C. (1998), "Denazification in the Western zones: The failed experiment," in Larsen (ed.), *Modern Europe after Fascism,* pp. 149–95.

Walder, A. (1986), *Communist Neo-traditionalism,* Berkeley: University of California Press.

Walicki, A. (1997), "Transitional justice and the political struggles of post-Communist Poland," in McAdams (ed.), *Transitional Justice and the Rule of Law in New Democracies,* pp. 185–238.

Walther, S. (1995), "Problems in blaming and punishing individuals for human rights violations: The example of the Berlin Wall shootings," in Roth-Arriaza (ed.), *Impunity and Human Rights in International Law,* pp. 99–112.

Waresquiel, E., and Yvert, B. (1996), *Histoire de la Restauration,* Paris: Perrin.

Watson. G. (1999), "Disordered appetites: Addiction, compulsion and dependence," in J. Elster (ed.), *Addiction: Entries and Exits,* New York: Russell Sage, pp. 3–28.

Wechsler, H. (1998), *A Miracle, a Universe: Settling Accounts with Torturers,* Chicago: University of Chicago Press.

Welsh, H. (1991), "'Anti-faschistisch-demokratische Umwälzung' in der sowjetischen Bezatsungszone Deutschlands," in Henke and Woller (eds.), *Politische Säuberung in Europa,* pp. 84–107.

Welsh, H. (1996), "Dealing with the Communist past: Central and East European experiences after 1990," *Europe-Asia Studies* 48, 413–28.

Welsh, H. (1998), "Denazification, system transformation, and regime legitimation: The case of the German Democratic Republic," in Larsen (ed.), *Modern Europe after Fascism*, pp. 315–38.

Wieviorka, O. (2003), "L'épuration des parlementaires," in M. O. Baruch (ed.), *Une poignée de misérables: L'épuration de la société française après la Seconde Guerre mondiale*, Paris: Fayard, pp. 384–400.

Wildt, M. (2002), *Generation des Unbedingten*, Hamburg: Hamburger Edition.

Wilson, R. (2001a), "Justice and legitimacy in the South African transition," in Brito, González-Enríquez, and Aguilar (eds.), *The Politics of Memory*, pp. 190–217.

Wilson, R. (2001b), *The Politics of Truth and Reconciliation in South Africa: Legitimizing the Post-Apartheid State*, Cambridge: Cambridge University Press.

Winton, L. (1992), "Poland's government crisis," *RFE/RL Research Report* 1, no. 30, 15–25.

Witte, E., and Craeybeckx, J. (1987), *La Belgique politique de 1830 à nos jours*, Brussels: Editions Labor.

Woller, H. (1996), *Die Abrechnung mit dem Faschismus in Italien 1943 bis 1948*, Munich: Oldenburg.

Woller, H. (1998), "The political purge in Italy," in Larsen (ed.), *Modern Europe after Fascism*, pp. 526–45.

Zelikov, P., and Rice, C. (1997), *Germany Unified and Europe Transformed*, Cambridge, Mass.: Harvard University Press.

Index